Areas of
Psychology

Under the Editorship of
GARDNER MURPHY

Areas of Psychology

EDITED BY

F. L. MARCUSE

THE STATE COLLEGE OF WASHINGTON

 HARPER & BROTHERS · PUBLISHERS
NEW YORK

Library of Congress catalog card number: 53–11677

Contents

PREFACE, by F. L. Marcuse   vii

1. VOCATIONAL GUIDANCE, by A. Gordon Nelson   1

2. INDUSTRIAL PSYCHOLOGY: SELECTION AND PLACE-
MENT OF WORKERS, by Patricia Smith   36

3. INDUSTRIAL PSYCHOLOGY: EFFICIENCY IN WORK, by
Thomas A. Ryan   81

4. LEGAL PSYCHOLOGY: THE PSYCHOLOGY OF TESTI-
MONY, by Harry P. Weld   119

5. CRIMINAL AND CORRECTIONAL PSYCHOLOGY, by
Raymond Corsini   148

6. SOCIAL PSYCHOLOGY, by Robert B. MacLeod   180

7. CHILD PSYCHOLOGY, by Lois B. Murphy and Meyer
Rabban   241

8. EDUCATIONAL PSYCHOLOGY, by Frank S. Freeman   280

9. ABNORMAL PSYCHOLOGY, by Béla Mittelmann and
Laura Malkenson   333

10. CLINICAL PSYCHOLOGY, by Bernard Steinzor   372

11. PHYSIOLOGICAL PSYCHOLOGY, by Bernard F. Reiss   409

12. COMPARATIVE PSYCHOLOGY, by Herbert G. Birch   446

13. PSYCHOLOGY AND AESTHETICS, by Ralph H. Gundlach   478

INDEX   525

Preface

A goal of the American Psychological Association is to advance psychology as a science and as a means of contributing to human welfare. The present book keeps both these objectives in mind. The text also reflects the position that the distinction between pure and applied psychology is often dubious. We can obtain valuable information for many of the so-called central problems of psychology, such as learning, motivation, and perception, from the psychologist who is concerned with the problems of the mental institution, of the courtroom, and of the industrial worker.

One may ask whether a particular approach or school of thought is reflected in the pages of this book. The approach indicated may best be described as eclectic in that it draws what is valuable from many sources in a coherent and meaningful manner. Psychology is a young science and it may be questioned whether it can afford the luxury of a circumscribed approach at this time. There is little justification for acting or believing that psychology is about to end this afternoon or tomorrow morning. It is more important to ascertain what we know today, to apply this information when required as the most adequate we possess at present, and to observe in what direction psychology is going.

Areas of psychology are not always easily distinguishable. One can, however, pick out certain core problems and in addition, one can designate those problems common to two or more fields. It is the purpose of this book to give the individual an idea of the principles, problems, and procedures which are to be observed in the different areas in which psychologists are working.

A few words about the book itself. This text is designed to give an overview of psychology to the nonmajor who, having had an introduction to the area, is desirous of further general information. It is also intended to give the major who has decided to concentrate in the field of psychology some idea of problems and methods which he will meet in the different areas of psychology. There is no set sequence in which areas are to be read. The choice rests with the instructor. Names have been kept to a minimum, and only those who have made important contributions to psychology are mentioned. Suggested references, with a sentence or two descriptive of their contents, have been included for the student desirous of obtaining further information about a specific area. Finally, an outline is included at the beginning of each chapter. This is intended to indicate to the student where the author has been, where he is, and where he intends to go.

I should like to take this occasion to thank the many contributors and Gardner Murphy for their contribution and coöperation.

F. L. MARCUSE

October, 1953

Areas of
Psychology

Chapter 1

Vocational Guidance

by A. GORDON NELSON

Purpose and Scope of Vocational Guidance

Historical Background

Psychology and Vocational Guidance
 THE TESTING MOVEMENT
 OCCUPATIONAL ANALYSIS
 THE CLINICAL METHOD

The Clinical Vocational Guidance Process
 THE INITIAL INTERVIEW
 ANALYSIS OF THE INDIVIDUAL
  Types of Data Needed
  Sources of Data
  Interpretation of Data
 THE COUNSELING INTERVIEW

The Evaluation of Clinical Vocational Guidance
 SOME EVALUATION PROBLEMS
 TWO EVALUATION STUDIES
  A Questionnaire Study
  A Control-Group Experiment

Standards for Vocational Guidance Service

Suggested Readings

What is the purpose of vocational guidance? What is its history and present status? How does a professionally trained vocational counselor attempt to aid an individual who seeks his help? Is vocational guidance effectual? What criteria or standards should one apply in order to appraise a vocational counseling establishment? These questions suggest the major concerns of this chapter.

PURPOSE AND SCOPE OF VOCATIONAL GUIDANCE

At various times in his life, virtually everyone must make decisions relative to problems of vocational choice and adjustment. Vocational guidance is the process of helping an individual to make such decisions. Its purpose, in a democracy, is to further (1) the welfare of the person, and (2) the welfare of society. It is believed that the two goals are not incompatible: that the social economy is best served when the individual is engaged in useful work for which he is well suited and in which he finds satisfaction.

The masthead of *Occupations*, the journal of the National Vocational Guidance Association, includes this definition: "Vocational guidance is the process of assisting the individual to choose an occupation, prepare for, enter upon, and progress in it." This formulation implies that vocational adjustment is the result of an orderly series of events which begins with the choice of an occupation and ends with progress in "it" (the occupation originally chosen). A counselor who is acquainted with the work histories of individuals, and who has had an opportunity to observe the varied assortment of vocational adjustment problems presented by counselees, will not be satisfied with the N.V.G.A. definition. He will prefer a concept of vocational guidance which suggests that an individual, for a number of reasons, may have occasion to change his plans from time to time, and may need assistance in making the changes. Such a concept is implied in one section of a public-relations leaflet recently distributed by a counseling center. This leaflet contains the question: "Who should come to the Counseling Center?" The answer given is:

You can receive help at the Counseling Center if you:
Have not decided upon your life work.
Want to know your aptitudes, interests and abilities.
Need help in choosing a course, school or college suited to your needs.
Are thinking about changing from one type of work to another.
Are not making good progress in your present job.

A realistic definition of vocational guidance, one which shows understanding of the fact that occupational adjustment often involves the making of a number of decisions over a period of time as changes occur in the individual and in socioeconomic conditions, has been proposed by the staff of another counseling center. The workers in this agency have described vocational guidance as a process of helping a person to (1) understand his own needs, attitudes, and abilities as they have a bearing on vocational planning, and (2) relate them to the requirements of specific occupations and to labor market conditions in order that he may make an adequate personal and vocational adjustment.

Vocational guidance should not be confused with *vocational selection*. Both involve the application of psychological principles and techniques to the study of individuals and the analysis of occupations, but the two processes differ in purpose. The aim of vocational guidance is to help an individual make decisions relative to whatever problems of vocational choice he has at a given time, whereas the objective of vocational selection is to pick, from two or more applicants, the person(s) best qualified for the available position(s) in a given place of work. An applicant for a specific job is an individual who has made at least a provisional vocational choice before he has become an applicant. The process of selection is a screening process, one that is ordinarily less complex than that of guidance. There are, of course, situations in which vocational selection and guidance are interwoven. For example, a company may hire a young man on the basis of his general qualifications for a variety of positions which it wishes to fill, and then, using guidance techniques, help him to "find himself" within the organization.

HISTORICAL BACKGROUND

The "beginning" of the vocational guidance movement has been traced to the first decade of the twentieth century. Its rise and early growth were approximately concurrent with the inception and development of juvenile courts, social work, personnel services in industry, educational guidance, and the mental hygiene movement. There is reason to believe that all these "human engineering" endeavors began to take shape at about the same time for at least two reasons: (1) Toward the end of the nineteenth century, men had begun to accept the principle of societal responsibility for the welfare of individuals. (2) During the same period, psychologists were beginning to learn how to identify and appraise individual differences. Both developments were fundamental to the introduction of organized guidance services.

Brewer, author of the only comprehensive history of the vocational guidance movement, has designated Frank Parsons, a public-spirited citizen of Boston, as the "father" of vocational guidance. Under philanthropic auspices, Parsons organized the Vocation Bureau, which was formally opened in 1908. Until his death in September of the same year, he was director of the Bureau. He is believed to be the first person to employ the term "vocational guidance." His book, *Choosing a Vocation,* which was published posthumously (1909), contains a statement of basic principles with which it is difficult to quarrel today. Parsons organized a program for the training of counselors, employed the best techniques of counseling then available, refused to use phrenology and other pseudo-scientific methods which were popular at that time, and advocated that vocational guidance services be provided in the public schools. The Harvard University Bureau of Vocational Guidance grew out of the Vocation Bureau of Boston. Many colleges and universities now have similar centers.

Beginning about 1910, as the result of the work of Parsons and, of course, many others, vocational guidance programs were gradually introduced into the public schools. Boston, New York, Cincinnati, Philadelphia, and Chicago were among the first to attempt to provide organized services. In general, only large cities and relatively affluent communities have been willing, during the past fifty years, to spend the money required to found well-staffed programs. In other types of municipalities, principals, teachers, and part-time counselors ("teacher-counselors") have tried, with varying degrees of success, to provide vocational counseling. In spite of widespread recognition of the need for vocational guidance, less than 20 percent of the secondary schools in the United States now have either full-time or part-time counselors.

PSYCHOLOGY AND VOCATIONAL GUIDANCE

Psychologists have made three major contributions to the development of the theory and practice of vocational guidance. They have developed tests which make possible a relatively objective appraisal of many of the individual characteristics that have a bearing on vocational adjustment. They have analyzed the psychological requirements of a number of occupations, and have thus facilitated the process of comparing men with jobs. They have applied the principles and techniques of clinical psychology to the task of helping individuals who present problems of vocational choice.

The Testing Movement

The development of psychological tests and the determination of their usefulness have been gradual, complementary processes, both of which have been associated with the evolution of theories concerning the nature of human abilities. Early psychological testing was based upon the belief that the higher mental processes could be measured indirectly by means of tests of simple mental functions such as sensory discrimination and immediate rote memory. This belief was, at least in part, a result of the fact that the procedures employed were an outgrowth of methods used in the laboratory by men such as Helmholtz, Fechner, and Wundt. Sir Francis Galton (1822–1911) is generally considered to be the founder of individual psychology and of the mental test. He was the first psychologist to be seriously interested in individual differences and their measurement. James McKeen Cattell (1860–1944), who used the term "mental tests," and who helped to make the study of individual differences a prominent part of psychological research, believed, as did Galton, that the more complex human abilities could be appraised obliquely through the measurement of simple functions.

Alfred Binet (1857–1911) attacked the problem from another point of view, one which was to have a far-reaching effect upon the subsequent development of the testing movement. In France, between 1894 and 1898, Binet and his pupils carried on a series of investigations of the mental functions of children. Binet was the first to indicate the need for complex tests involving the use of such mental functions as memory, imagination, and comprehension. In 1905, Binet and his collaborator Simon, in response to a request from the educational authorities of Paris to devise ways of selecting mentally deficient children for special instruction, published a series of mental tests arranged in order of difficulty. This scale, which attempted to measure complex abilities by means of tests involving such tasks as the comparison of lines, the completion of sentences, and the comprehension of questions, was the forerunner of many subsequent individual test batteries, most of which were modifications of the original series.

Group tests were first developed in response to a need for screening devices which would quickly select individuals for a given purpose. Early efforts were largely confined to the adaptation and application to group needs of tests taken from individual batteries such as the Binet. The development of group testing was greatly accelerated by the work of psychologists during World War I. To aid in the classification of military personnel, they constructed the Army Alpha and Beta tests, which were administered to nearly two million men.

The above sketch indicates in a general way the genesis of psychological testing. From the early beginnings mentioned, both the construction and the use of tests have increased enormously. It has been estimated that in 1944 approximately twenty million people in the United States took a total of sixty million standardized tests, for a variety of reasons. The well-qualified vocational counselor of today would be greatly handicapped if he did not have these psychological tools available as one means of appraising the potentialities of individuals.

Occupational Analysis

A vocational counselor needs not only data about the individual whom he is trying to help but also occupational information. Such information includes facts about the duties, working conditions, personal requirements, and demand for workers in various occupations. Psychologists have made their major contribution to vocational information through their attempts to determine the personal characteristics required in a number of jobs.

In 1905, one of the earliest psychological investigations in the field of occupational analysis, a study of traits required for success in typewriting, was reported. In 1916, a German psychologist sent a list of 86 numbered traits (e.g., No. 52: "To respond rapidly with a prescribed movement to a sudden, unexpected visual stimulus") to a group of individuals who were interested in vocational selection and training. He asked these individuals to indicate which traits were indispensable in certain occupations. The numbers of the traits which the majority of the respondents stated were necessary were placed after each occupation in the following manner: "Telephone operator: 2, 29, 35, 46, 51, 61." The subjectivity and lack of precision of this approach are obvious today, but the investigation is representative of early attempts on the part of psychologists to analyze the personal requirements of occupations. Although a number of psychologists did pioneer work in the application of psychological research techniques to the study of occupations, Hugo Münsterberg (1863–1916) is considered to be the outstanding early leader in *vocational psychology,* a term which connotes both industrial psychology and vocational guidance. Münsterberg's studies revealed the value of experimental investigation as a means of determining the requirements of an occupation and the extent to which a given individual meets these requirements.

An example of an objective approach is the relatively recent work of the Occupational Analysis Division of the United States Employment Service. On the basis of painstaking investigation, the USES has constructed a General Aptitude Test battery and twenty Occupational Aptitude Patterns. Each pattern shows (with reference to tests designed to measure ten different aptitudes) the range of scores typically attained by men previously identified as successful in a specified field of work. The scores on the General Aptitude Test battery of a given applicant for employment can be compared with the twenty Occupational Aptitude Patterns, in order to determine the resemblance of the applicant's pattern of aptitudes to the pattern of any one of the twenty fields of work which have been investigated. It will become apparent in subsequent sections of this chapter that sound vocational guidance involves more than a mechanical "matching" of men and jobs, but it cannot be denied that research of the type undertaken by the USES has contributed much to the vocational counselor's knowledge of the personal requirements of a number of occupations.

The Clinical Method

Three major varieties of vocational guidance are currently offered to the public. One commonly found in secondary schools, emphasizes self-analysis by the individual, the dissemination of occupational information, and the giving of "common sense" advice. Another, most often observed in certain commercial agencies, stresses the routine use of a battery of aptitude tests and the mechanical "matching" of men and jobs. A third, usually found only in vocational guidance centers staffed by professional psychologists, employs principles and techniques of clinical psychology. What is clinical psychology? To paraphrase a definition adopted in 1935 by the Clinical Section of the American Psychological Association: *Clinical psychology* is that form of applied psychology which describes the capacities and other characteristics of an individual by means of observation, analysis, and measurement; and which, by integrating these findings with information obtained from a physical examination and a social case-study, offers suggestions and recommendations designed to facilitate the satisfactory adjustment of an individual.

The first psychological clinic was founded in 1896 at the University of Pennsylvania by Lightner Witmer. A Philadelphia elementary-school teacher, believing that psychology must have something to contribute to the solution of individual adjustment problems, brought to Witmer's laboratory a boy who appeared to be unable to learn spelling. Witmer's attempts to help this pupil may be said to mark the beginning of the Psychological Clinic at Pennsylvania. In its early years this clinic worked largely with mentally retarded and educationally retarded children, but later it began to serve a more varied clientele, and in 1920 a vocational guidance unit was added.

During the past two decades, clinical vocational guidance has developed rapidly. It should be clearly understood that the clinical method includes more than aptitude testing. It involves not only the making of a comprehensive study of the individual and of the situational factors that may have a bearing on his vocational-choice problems but also the use of a varied assortment of counseling techniques. Because it is the type of vocational guidance in which psychologists are more interested, it will be described in some detail, in the next section.

THE CLINICAL VOCATIONAL GUIDANCE PROCESS

What does a vocational counselor do when an individual comes to him for professional service? Why does he proceed as he does? In answering these questions, a modus operandi and its rationale will be described which does not differ radically from the practices and theories of the majority of clinical vocational counselors.

The Initial Interview

The first conference with the counselee is more than a registration interview. It serves several purposes. First, it provides an opportunity to decide whether clinical vocational counseling will probably be beneficial. In the second place, it enables the counselor to begin collecting data needed for the analysis of the client and his situation. Third, it is an appropriate time for the clinician to explain the nature of the service he is prepared to render. Fourth, assuming that the counselee presents a bona fide vocational problem, the initial interview helps the counselor to determine, at least provisionally, what psychological tests should be given.

A vocational counselor cannot validly assume that every person who seeks his help needs clinical vocational counseling. Sometimes, evidence obtained in the initial interview indicates clearly that the client needs only some specific educational or occupational information, and that it is not necessary to make a case-study. At other times, it will become apparent as the interview proceeds that the counselee's immediate problem is, say, primarily an emotional or a social one rather than a vocational one. Some individuals who really need psychotherapy go to vocational counselors because they incorrectly diagnose their own difficulties, or because they consider it more "respectable" to have vocational rather than emotional problems. Parenthetically, it is interesting to note that remedial reading specialists, also, report that their services are sometimes sought by individuals who do not have reading disabilities but who do have other kinds of problems. Although a competent counselor does not, of course, labor under the delusion that counseling can be neatly categorized as *purely* educational, vocational, emotional, social, etc., he should nevertheless decide, preferably in the initial interview, whether clinical vocational guidance will probably be beneficial to the individual who consults him. In order to do this, he needs a sufficiently broad background of training and experience in clinical psychology to enable him to draw valid inferences from his observations of the client's behavior and from other personal data which he obtains.

The process of making an analysis of the individual will be described in some detail in the next section. But a counselor inevitably begins during the initial interview to collect some of the data upon which such an analysis is based. He is particularly interested, at this time, in the counselee's description of the circumstances that have led him to seek vocational guidance, and in his perception of its purpose and nature. At this stage of the process, a counselor ordinarily learns more about his client by encouraging him to tell his own story freely than by asking him many direct questions.

Before the initial interview ends, the clinician "structures" the vocational guidance process, i.e., he explains to the counselee the procedures that will be followed and the reasons underlying the use of these procedures. He tries to make it clear to the client that psychological tests are but one means of obtaining information about an individual, and that they have certain limitations as well as certain values. He avoids giving the impression that he is a fortuneteller. He describes the vocational counseling process as a *joint quest*, one in which the client will have to do some thinking and make some decisions.

As stated previously, information obtained during the initial interview helps the counselor to determine, at least provisionally, what psychological tests should be given. The notion seems to be rather widespread that the use of a test or an invariable battery of tests is standard procedure in vocational guidance agencies. Actually, in working with a given individual, a competent clinician selects from a varied assortment of tests those which he believes will yield the most useful information for vocational counseling with that individual. Among the factors which have a bearing on the choice of tests are the client's age, the kind of vocational adjustment problem he presents, the amount of schooling he has had, his claimed interests, and his past vocational experiences. Sometimes the counselor does not obtain during the initial interview sufficient information to enable him to select a complete battery. In this case, he may postpone the selection of part of it until he has obtained additional data by means of a personal data sheet or questionnaire which he asks the client to answer. Frequently, an individual's performance on one test—for example an interest inventory—will suggest the desirability of including tests which were not previously assigned or of eliminating some which were previously chosen.

Analysis of the Individual

In order to make a psychological analysis of an individual and his problem(s), a counselor needs a considerable amount of data. The nature, sources, and interpretation of these data are discussed in this section.

TYPES OF DATA NEEDED

The many specific items included in the various assortment of case-study forms employed in clinics throughout the country may be conveniently subsumed under eight major rubrics. These rubrics highlight the types of information which a clinical counselor seeks in order that he may understand a client's problem(s) and vocational possibilities.

1. *Registration data.* Included are the counselee's name, address, date of registration, date of birth, and sex. The reason for the first three items is obvious. Date of birth is also a means of identification, but there are at least two additional reasons for obtaining it. First, the age factor must always be considered in assigning, administering, and interpreting the results of psychological tests. To illustrate: It has been found that many tests which emphasize speed tend to discriminate against older persons; therefore, a clinician must know the ages of such individuals in order to interpret judiciously their performances on such tests. In the second place, the age factor is related to the making of educational and vocational plans. It is known, for example, that some ocupations have a minimum and/or a maximum entrance age; that older workers tend to value job security more highly than do men in the younger age groups; and

that, according to one investigator, occupational restlessness occurs most frequently in the early twenties and forties.

At least a few women are now engaged in almost every occupation, and vocational discrimination against them is gradually decreasing, but men may still enter some fields more easily than women. (The converse is, of course, also true, but to a much lesser extent.) Another reason for recording a counselee's sex is that some psychological test manuals provide separate norms for boys and girls and for men and women. Some scholarships are awarded on a sex basis. The purpose of mentioning a few of the reasons for considering the sex factor in vocational counseling is not to suggest that it is of major importance but merely to indicate that it cannot be ignored.

2. *Physical factors.* These include items such as stature, weight, voice, personal appearance, health status, strength, and physical abilities and disabilities. A person who enjoys reasonably good health and who has no handicapping disabilities is physically qualified for a large number of occupations, and therefore does not, as a rule, need to give much consideration to physical factors in choosing a field of work. But because some occupations have rather specific physical requirements, and because some advisees display interest in vocations for which they are not physically qualified, a clinical counselor procures data about physical factors. A few illustrations will make clear the importance of getting this type of information as part of the process of analyzing the individual. A motion picture actress must be photogenic. Some occupations require an above-average amount of standing, walking, reaching, pushing, lifting, climbing, etc. Some jobs can be satisfactorily performed with below-average eyesight, but others require unusually keen visual acuity. Color blindness bars individuals from railroad employment. Mechanical dentistry is a field which should not be entered by persons who have a tendency toward bronchial or lung infections. Adequate ability to perceive depth is indispensable in commercial aviation.

All vocational counselors should be aware of the occupational implications of physical factors, but not all are qualified by training and experience to counsel with individuals who have relatively severe handicaps. This type of work, a specialty within the field of vocational guidance, is called "vocational rehabilitation." A few philanthropic and private agencies offer such service. Two publicly supported programs of national scope are currently in operation. One, under the general direction of the Office of Vocational Rehabilitation of the Federal Security Agency, includes agencies (in every state in the Union) specifically organized to provide complete vocational rehabilitation (counseling, medical service, training, placement, and follow-up) for physically and mentally handicapped persons. The other, developed by the U. S. Veterans Administration in coöperation with a large number of colleges and universities, and in accordance with certain provisions of Public Law 16 (Seventy-eighth Congress), consists of guidance centers that offer vocational rehabilitation to veterans who have service-connected disabilities. These centers also serve nondisabled veterans who seek vocational counseling.

3. *Educational factors.* Specific items such as the following may be classified under this heading: history of progress through school, present educational status, any special training received, relative achievement in various subjects taken, and any honors attained. Information of this kind has several values. The curriculum and extracurriculum of a school provide an opportunity not only to acquire certain knowledges and skills but also to "explore." Hence, an individual's academic record and his reactions to a variety of school experiences may have prognostic value, may provide clues relative to his educational and vocational aptitudes and interests. Furthermore, the subjects a counselee has taken in the past may have a bearing on his eligibility for certain types of schooling or employment in the future. A girl who has taken a straight commercial course in high school cannot enter a liberal arts college, a fact which may need to be considered in counseling with her. It is futile to discuss medicine as a possible career with a college student who has majored in hotel administration for four years, unless perchance he is eager and able to take additional work in premedical subjects before he applies for admission to a medical school.

4. *Work history*. Included are data pertaining to a counselee's experiences in and reactions to part-time and full-time jobs. A vocational counselor needs work-history information for several reasons. Skills developed in certain ocupations may influence the performances of a given individual on certain psychological tests. Such skills may also be among the chief assets of a client, and may therefore be of considerable importance in helping him to make vocational plans or adjustments. Information about a counselee's interest or lack of interest and his success or lack of success in one or more jobs may, along with other data, help the counselor and the counselee to draw inferences regarding the latter's potentialities. A work-history record which indicates that an adult client has had no work experience, or that he has changed positions inordinately, may have considerable significance.

5. *Interests*. An interest may be simply defined as a tendency to seek out or to choose an object or activity. It has already been indicated, above, that a vocational counselor seeks information about the school activities an advisee has liked or disliked, and about the work experiences that have or have not appealed to him. A careful analysis of a counselee's interests is based upon data regarding not only school and work interests but also hobbies, claimed occupational preferences, and scores on standardized vocational interest inventories. These varied types of information about interests enable a counselor to determine whether there is congruity or discrepancy between vocational and educational interests, or between claimed and inventoried interests. Does a given counselee, for instance, state in one breath that he would like to be an engineer, and in the next breath say that he has always disliked all forms of mathematics? Does he claim that he likes selling but attain a very low "persuasive" score on the Kuder Preference Record? Or, does a fairly consistent interest pattern emerge when all the evidence is carefully weighed? Research as well as clinical experience attest the importance of ascertaining interests.

6. *Aptitudes*. The meaning of the term *aptitude* tends to vary from one user to another, even among psychologists. As employed

in this chapter, it means competency to acquire the knowledge and behavior required for successful performance in a given occupation. For example, to say that an individual has aptitude for dentistry is to state that he probably has the capacity to learn to perform the duties of a dentist, if given appropriate training. A vocational aptitude is not a unitary trait, but is a particular pattern of differentiated abilities, such as scholastic ability, spatial visualization, and eye-hand coördination. Furthermore, aptitudes are not measured directly but are inferred. Psychologists do not claim that aptitude tests measure future accomplishments directly. These instruments measure only present performance, but when this performance is known to be symptomatic of future potentialities, test data are employed to estimate those potentialities. Such estimates are necessarily stated in terms of probabilities only.

In order to appraise a client's aptitudes, a counselor needs various types of data. These include information not only about psychological test performances but also about behavior in other situations which "test" the functioning of abilities. To illustrate: a clinician who is attempting to estimate a high-school boy's aptitude for farming finds it very helpful to have evidence regarding the boy's ability to complete successfully courses in vocational agriculture and related subjects, to operate and repair farm machinery, to recognize problems which exist on his father's farm, to secure a satisfactory monetary return from a supervised farming project while still in school, etc.

7. *Personality factors.* Although many formal definitions of the term *personality* have been proposed, the word is generally used loosely by laymen, and with many different connotations by psychologists. In this chapter, "personality" refers to an individual's affective qualities, particularly as they influence his own behavior and that of others in work situations. Included are such traits as persistence, coöperativeness, sociability, dependability, and aggressiveness. Several studies have shown that discharges from employment are much more frequently associated with personality difficulties or deficiencies than with inability to do the work required.

On the other hand, there is a dearth of data regarding relationships between specific personality characteristics and success in specific occupations.

Although the scant evidence available does not indicate that certain personality traits are closely related to success in this or that vocation, information about personality factors may, nevertheless, be of considerable value in vocational counseling. Such information may, for example, enable a clinician to assist an individual to become better adjusted in his present position. It may prompt a counselor to recommend psychotherapy. It may lead him to help some of his clients to select types of work in which they are not likely to be handicapped by their severe personality disabilities.

8. *Socioeconomic factors.* Vocational counseling would be a far less complex process than it is if it did not involve consideration of a group of factors which are often labeled "socioeconomic." A few illustrations will make clear the nature of such factors: A. cannot afford the costly training required for entrance into the occupation which interests him most; B. cannot practice the vocation for which he is qualified because his family situation makes it imperative that he remain in a community which has no need for the services represented by this vocation; C.'s wife is insistent that he enter a field of work which will yield a higher income than the one in which he is now happily engaged. The extent to which socioeconomic circumstances have a bearing on vocational planning varies from one client to another, but the systematic collection and careful interpretation of information about such factors is an essential part of the counseling process.

SOURCES OF DATA

Information about an individual may be collected in numerous ways. It is the aim of this section to consider briefly some of the general sources of counselee data most frequently "tapped" by clinical vocational counselors.

1. *The initial interview.* In an earlier part of this chapter, mention was made of the fact that a clinician begins to obtain informa-

tion about his client during the initial interview. At the close of this interview, the counselee may be asked to fill out a questionnaire that is designed to elicit at least a modicum of information about each one of the areas of data required (described in the previous section). The use of a questionnaire saves time. Furthermore, a counselor who knows that by means of a questionnaire he will later obtain many of the facts he wishes to have, is less likely to feel that he must "cross-examine" a client during the initial interview. Thus, he can conduct the latter in a more informal way; can direct his attention more fully to the observation of counselee behavior; can, in short, use the interview more profitably. Questionnaires are most useful for the collection of factual material about an individual's background. They are much less useful than an interview for gaining insight into counselee attitudes and feelings.

2. *Personnel records*. Records are another source of information. If they have been kept over a period of years and are fairly complete, they provide data about the developmental history of an individual as well as about his present status. Counselors who work in schools or colleges are more likely to have access to personnel records than are those who are employed in guidance centers or psychological clinics. Cumulative record folders kept by educational institutions vary greatly in respect to the quantity and quality of information they contain. At their best, they afford very useful data about physical factors, educational status, work history, interests, abilities, personality factors, and socioeconomic circumstances. Unfortunately, in few schools or colleges are such records satisfactory.

3. *Reports from other people*. Another source of information is reports. Such reports may be oral or written. They may come from parents, friends, teachers, ministers, social workers, psychiatrists, physicians, or employers. Their usefulness is a function of their reliability and validity, which may be difficult to ascertain. One finds it easier to evaluate reports when he knows the individuals from whom they have been obtained. Reports which include factual information are ordinarily of greater value than those which consist only of expressions of opinion, but there are instances in which opinion

data alone are very helpful. For example, most vocational counselors are probably not competent to appraise aptitude for professional art work; they may employ art aptitude tests as one source of information, but they must also rely heavily on the judgments of individuals who are qualified to estimate potential ability for performance in this field. Similarly, vocational counselors rely on the trained opinions of physicians when counseling with individuals who have handicapping physical disabilities.

4. *Psychological tests.* Tests have been widely publicized, and are popularly associated with vocational guidance much more frequently than are other sources of information about individuals. Testing enables a counselor to obtain relatively objective information about the general intelligence, interests, aptitudes, achievements, and personality traits of his clients. The fact that tests have been standardized upon representative groups of people makes it possible for a clinician to compare, quantitatively, an individual's performance on a given test with the performances of others with whom he may legitimately be compared. Furthermore, many tests, particularly when they are administered individually, afford an opportunity to observe the behavior of clients and to appraise the quality of their performances.

Like all techniques for studying individuals, psychological tests have weaknesses as well as strengths. The vocational validities of many tests have not been established. Most personality tests are still in the experimental stage of development. Little progress has been made in measuring persistence, creative imagination, and certain other traits which experience indicates are related to adjustment in the world of work. No one is more aware of the shortcomings of psychological tests than the competent clinician who employs them in his daily practice.

In spite of their limitations and deficiencies, psychological tests are useful. A number of studies have shown that vocational counseling which utilizes test data plus other types of information is more effectual than counseling which involves the use of other types of information alone.

Brief comments have been made, above, concerning the sources of personal and situational data most commonly used. There are, of course, other sources such as work-samples, themes and autobiographies submitted by counselees. A competent counselor makes use of all pertinent information available to him. He does not place inordinate confidence in any one source. Rather, he compares information obtained from one source with information obtained from other sources. In general, the greater the agreement he finds, the more confident he can be that he has reliable and valid data upon which to base an analysis of the individual. On the other hand, discrepancies in the data suggest the need for further study of the individual.

INTERPRETATION OF DATA

Information is of little value until it is interpreted. Valid interpretation of personal and situational data in their relation to a given counselee's problem(s) makes heavy demands on the training, experience, and judgment of a counselor. He must estimate the individual's personal and socioeconomic assets and liabilities and their probable implications for occupational choice and adjustment, in order that he may be prepared to discuss with his client possible solutions to the problem(s) presented.

Appraisal of vocational potentialities involves more than a psychological analysis of the individual: it also requires an understanding of the duties and requirements of occupations, as well as information regarding vocational trends. A clinical psychologist who is proficient in analytical and adjustment techniques but who has had little contact with, and who has little knowledge of, the occupational world is not well qualified to do vocational counseling. Although much research still needs to be done, occupational literature has grown in quantity and in quality during the past twenty years. Here are two examples of very useful vocational studies that have been published recently: The *Occupational Outlook Handbook* (Bureau of Labor Statistics), published in 1951, contains authentic information on more than four hundred major occupations. This volume includes not only vocational supply-and-demand summaries, based on careful research, but also information regarding duties, training requirements, and earnings in the fields of work covered. *Predicting Success in Professional Schools* (Stuit *et al.*), reviews the results of many studies of relationships between predictive indexes and success in college in the fields of engineering, law, medicine, dentistry, music, agriculture, teaching, and nursing. The committee that prepared the book has summarized in tabular form the conclusions it reached regarding each vocation. Table 1.1 illustrates the method of presentation.

A clinician's initial or precounseling "diagnosis" is tentative; it may be modified when an opportunity is provided to note client reactions to suggestions, and to discuss courses of action proposed by the counselee. To illustrate briefly: Interpretation of the information gathered regarding a veteran indicated that he was probably most interested in and best qualified for semiskilled mechanical work which did not require contact with oil or grease (to which he was allergic). The counselor was able to suggest several occupations of this type, but, for one reason or another, none of these appealed strongly to the veteran, and the objective he finally selected was one that he mentioned himself during a counseling interview—machine cutter in a corset factory. This vocation, for which he could obtain on-the-job training in his home town, was of the same general nature as those suggested by the counselor but it appealed to the veteran more than any that the counselor had originally listed.

The Counseling Interview

After a counselor has collected, and has made a provisional interpretation of, all the data he believes he needs, he holds one or more interviews, the purpose of which is to help the counselee understand his vocational potentialities and decide upon a course of action that will probably lead to a satisfying solution to his problem(s). The clinician's function is not to prescribe answers, but to conduct a two-

TABLE 1.1. Essential Qualifications, and Recommended Predictive Tests and Standards, for Success in Training for Medicine

Essential Qualifications	Recommended Tests and Standards	
	High-School Graduates	College Students
Superior aptitude for college and medical school work	Graduation in top quarter of high-school class American Council on Education Psychological Examination for College Freshmen (Thurstone & Thurstone)	Undergraduate standing in upper third of class with minimum average of B Miller Analogies Test Scholastic Aptitude Test for Medical Schools, Form 1 (Moss, Hunter, & Hubbard), available in Veterans Administration guidance centers)
High achievement in the natural sciences	Average of B in high-school science courses Coöperative General Achievement Tests, Revised Series	Average of B in college courses in biology, chemistry, and physics Coöperative College Biology Test ACS Coöperative General Chemistry Test for College Students Coöperative Physics Test for College Students Graduate Record Examination
Interests typical of successful physicians	Vocational Interest Blank for Men, Form M (Strong), (score of B-plus or A on Physician key)	Vocational Interest Blank for Men, Form M (Strong), (score of B-plus or A on Physician key)

Essential Qualifications	Recommended Tests and Standards	
	High-School Graduates	College Students
	Vocational Interest Blank for Women, Form W (Strong), (score of B-plus or A on Physician key) Kuder Preference Record (high Scientific and Social Service scores)	Vocational Interest Blank for Women, Form W (Strong), (score of B-plus or A on Physician key) Kuder Preference Record (high Scientific and Social Service scores)
Well-integrated personality	Observation of counselee's behavior during interviewing and testing Case history An Inventory of Factors STDCR (Social introversion, Thinking introversion, Depression, Cycloid tendencies, Rhathymia) (Guilford) The Adjustment Inventory, Adult Form (Bell) California Test of Personality, Form A: Adult (Thorpe, Clark, & Tiegs)	Observation of counselee's behavior during interviewing and testing Case history An inventory of factors STDRC (Guilford) The Adjustment Inventory Adult Form (Bell) California Test of Personality Form A: Adult (Thorpe, Clark, & Tiegs)

Source: Dewey B. Stuit, et al., *Predicting Success in Professional Schools*, The American Council on Education, 1949, p. 79.

23

way discussion. The course this discussion will take cannot be predicted; it depends upon such factors as the nature of the problem(s) originally presented, the counselee's prior knowledge of himself and of the world of work, his feelings about the counselor's interpretations and suggestions, and his ability to propose solutions himself. A clinician must decide "as he goes along" what his own responsibility is; his responsibility changes from time to time within a given interview.

The eclecticism implied in the last paragraph is at variance with the point of view of "nondirective" counselors. The latter hypothesize that each individual possesses a "capacity for growth" which enables him, under appropriate conditions, to arrive at solutions to his problems. The sole responsibility of the counselor is to provide the appropriate conditions, which nondirective counselors describe as a "permissive atmosphere." The counselor creates such an atmosphere by listening and by accepting, reflecting, and clarifying the feelings of the client. It is not difficult to accept the capacity-for-growth hypothesis, but it *is* difficult to believe that this capacity functions only, or always, under 100 percent nondirective conditions.

Techniques frequently employed by an eclectic counselor include the following: creating a permissive atmosphere, explaining test results and other data, asking the client questions designed to clarify his thinking in respect to issues connected with his problem(s), furnishing educational and occupational information or referring the counselee to sources of such information, suggesting alternative courses of action and their probable outcomes, and considering with the client solutions which he (the client) proposes.

Most counselors hold that the ultimate aim of all guidance is increased capacity for self-guidance on the part of the counselee. Therefore, they try to assist a client, with whatever problem(s) he presents at a given time, in a way that will develop his problem-solving ability. It is believed that a counselee benefits in a more general and in a more permanent way by being helped to think through a problem than by being told precisely what to do about it.

THE EVALUATION OF CLINICAL
VOCATIONAL GUIDANCE

How can the effectiveness of clinical vocational guidance be appraised? Does this professional service really help individuals to make better occupational decisions than they would make if they did not receive it? These are questions which every thoughtful reader will have raised by this time.

Some Evaluation Problems

One problem connected with evaluation is that of deciding what criterion of vocational adjustment to employ. Should it be production on the job? If so, how should production be assessed or measured—by noting earnings, by recording quantity of output, by rating employees? Or should the criterion be job satisfaction? If so, how can this be determined? A third criterion sometimes suggested is the extent to which a client has carried out the educational and vocational plans made at the time he received counseling. Is this necessarily a valid criterion, or could a change in a given advisee's plans be an indication that he has been confronted with new conditions and has made judicious use of principles and techniques for solving vocational choice problems which his counselor has previously taught him?

Another problem in evaluation is that of ascertaining whether an individual's adjustment (however defined) should be attributed to the counseling which he has received or to other factors. Human behavior is continuously affected by so many influences that it is very difficult to trace the effect of any one.

The timing of evaluation research also presents a problem. How long an interval should there be between a final interview and a follow-up study designed to evaluate the effectiveness of the guidance process? If such a study is made too soon, the hoped-for effects of counseling may not have had time to become manifest; or, if observable, may be only temporary.

The relationship of the kinds of problems presented by clients to the effectiveness of the counseling received is a subject that has received little attention in the literature of vocational guidance. However, it appears to be reasonable to assume that a counselor would tend to have greater "success" in helping individuals who have relatively simple problems than in aiding those whose problems are complicated. Clinical counselors have found that there are various "types" of vocational counseling problems. One investigator, for example, made an analysis of the case records of 200 disabled veterans who were required to undergo counseling at a Veterans Administration guidance center before they could receive a Government subsidy for vocational training. It was found that the vocational choice problems presented by these men fell in one of the following descriptive categories:

1. Prior to receiving counseling the veteran had made clear-cut, appropriate educational and vocational plans, which were merely confirmed by the counselor.
2. Client's precounseling vocational goal was confirmed, but he needed assistance in educational planning.
3. The counselee needed assistance in the selection of one of two or more stated vocational objectives, and in educational planning.
4. No clear-cut claimed vocational goal. Interests were vague and/or mixed. Needed assistance in selection of an objective and appropriate training.
5. Veteran presented complex and difficult counseling problem for one or two of the following reasons:
    a. Apparently had no vocational interests. Wanted "tests" or the counselor to *tell* him what to "be."
    b. Had formulated definite vocational and educational plans, but these were considered by the counselor to be inappropriate.
    c. Immediate need appeared to be therapy (physical and/or psychological) rather than educational-vocational counseling.

Another investigation yielded evidence which seems to support the assumption that the effectiveness of counseling is related to the types of problems which advisees have. A study was made of the stability of the vocational objectives of some 200 veterans by means of a follow-up of the men six months or more after they had been counseled at a guidance center. It was found that 68 percent of the men whose preadvisement vocational goals were merely *confirmed* by advisement were continuing to work toward those same objectives, whereas only 37 percent of the veterans whose original objectives were significantly *changed* during advisement were continuing with the plans decided upon at the guidance center. This study suggests that a comparative evaluation of two or more counseling centers, or of two or more counselors, should take into consideration, among other factors, the types of vocational counseling problems presented by the individuals who received guidance, and the frequencies of the various types encountered in the centers being compared or by the counselors being compared.

What proportion of individuals really need vocational guidance? The answer to this question has a bearing on the evaluation of the advisement process, for if a certain percentage of individuals who have received counseling would probably have "got along" well without it, one may legitimately ask how much real benefit they received from it. One writer, in commenting on the value of the guidance centers established for veterans, has stated that even if advisement were successful in only 25 percent of the cases counseled the gain would be appreciable. It is pertinent to inquire whether this percentage would, *per se,* be a valid indication of the value of counseling. Perhaps a large proportion of the successful cases would have made a satisfactory vocational adjustment without advisement. Very little is known about the incidence of the need for vocational guidance among various groups of individuals, but two studies may be mentioned which shed some light on the problem. One investigator, in a study previously referred to found that in a group of two hundred disabled veterans, approximately 20 percent had made what appeared to be excellent vocational and educational plans *before* they came to the guidance center. An additional 25 percent had, *before* advisement, chosen vocational objectives which counselors at the center approved; this group needed assistance only in planning

educational programs which would help them to attain their occupational goals. In another study, one in which the subjects were 115
adult paraplegics, it was found that about 43 percent of the men
had made sound vocational plans *before* they received counseling.
Although the comparable percentages in these two independent
studies are substantially the same, one can not, of course, conclude
that similar results would have been obtained if the subjects had
been high-school juniors, college sophomores, or some other group.
Furthermore, to say that evaluation studies should take into account
percentages such as those reported above does not necessarily mean
that a vocational counselor should receive no "credit" at all when
he merely confirms the preadvisement objectives of counselees.
Intensive research involving the use of follow-up interviews and
other techniques may reveal that confirmation of plans by a trained
counselor reassures some clients, keeps them from abandoning good
ideas, and stimulates them to work toward their chosen goals.

Two Evaluation Studies

The bothersome problems associated with attempts to evaluate
vocational counseling have not kept investigators from trying to
appraise its effectiveness. Summaries of two investigations designed
to estimate the worth of clinical vocational guidance are presented
below. They illustrate some of the difficulties and shortcomings of
evaluation research.

A QUESTIONNAIRE STUDY

In 1940, a follow-up questionnaire was sent to 125 clients who
had received vocational counseling at a guidance center between
1934 and 1937. Returns were obtained from 81 individuals. One
naturally wonders about the 44 counselees who did not reply. Furthermore, in interpreting the results it is necessary to bear in mind
the fact that the replies of respondents who reported that they had
had no work or formal education subsequent to the time they received guidance were discarded. Fifty-five returns were analyzed.
Of the 81 individuals who returned questionnaires, 65 were between

16 and 20 years of age. The group, as a whole, was superior in aptitude test performance to a random sampling of the population.

In respect to their vocational adjustment, respondents were rated as "satisfactorily placed," "unsatisfactorily placed," or "undetermined"—on the basis of their replies to the questionnaire, and statements made by them in supplementary letters and/or oral communications. Comparisons were then made between the ratings and the suggestions previously offered by the counselors at the center. Table 1.2 summarizes the findings of this part of the study.

TABLE 1.2. Accuracy of Vocational Predictions

Accuracy	Number of Cases	Percent
Recommendation acted upon and found satisfactory	28	51.0
Failure to succeed when acting in opposition to recommendations	8	14.5
Recommendations acted upon and found unsatisfactory	1	1.8
Success when acting in opposition to recommendations	8	14.5
Impossible to judge whether prediction is correct	10	18.2

SOURCE: E. C. Webster, A Follow-up on Vocational Guidance, *Journal of Applied Psychology,* 1942, 26:289.

The accuracy of educational predictions was also investigated. The criteria employed were these: If a counselee had succeeded in a course recommended or had failed in a course taken in opposition to the recommendations made, the guidance center was given credit for having made a successful prediction. If, on the other hand, the counselee had failed in a course of study recommended or had succeeded in one opposed by the counselor, the prediction was regarded as incorrect. Table 1.3 constitutes a summary of this part of the study.

An attempt was also made to obtain the opinions of respondents regarding the general value of the guidance they had received. The

Table 1.3.   Accuracy of Educational Predictions

Accuracy	Number of Cases	Percent
Academic success in particular courses accurately predicted	37	60.6
Academic failure in particular courses accurately predicted	14	23.0
Academic prediction proved incorrect	4	6.6
Impossible to judge accuracy of prediction	6	9.8

Source: E. C. Webster, A Follow-up on Vocational Guidance, *Journal of Applied Psychology*, 1942, 26:290.

following question was asked: "In view of all events which have occurred since the examination, do you believe that vocational guidance was (or would have been had recommendations been followed): (check appropriate answer) extremely valuable ( ), of definite value ( ), of some slight value ( ), of dubious value ( ), a waste of time ( ), definitely harmful ( )." A summary of the answers to this question is given in Table 1.4.

Table 1.4.   Subjective Evaluation of
Guidance Examination [a]

Opinion	Number of Cases	Percent
Extremely valuable	5	8.6
Of definite value	28	48.3
Of some slight value	15	25.8
Of dubious value	6	10.3
A waste of time	3	5.2
Definitely harmful	1	1.7

[a] "Guidance Examination" is the English phrase which connotes the clinical approach in guidance—i.e., it means not only psychological testing but also the making of a case-study, and counseling interviews.

Source: E. C. Webster, A Follow-up on Vocational Guidance, *Journal of Applied Psychology*, 1942, 26:292.

The reader should not find it difficult to criticize unfavorably the methodology of the study described above. Unfortunately, investigations with similar weaknesses are rather frequently found in the literature.

A CONTROL-GROUP EXPERIMENT

Results have been reported of an investigation designed to test the following hypothesis: If a group of college students were left to their own devices, they would not show as satisfactory an adjustment as they would if they received formal counseling at a college guidance bureau. The experimental method employed consisted of a comparison of the adjustment of 384 counseled students with the adjustment of an equal number of individually paired and selected noncounseled students. The experimental group was carefully matched with the control group on the basis of age, sex, college class, size and type of high school, high-school rank, aptitude test scores, and performance on the Coöperative English Test.

The adjustment of the counseled students was determined by having trained judges classify them on the basis of counseling data, and information collected in follow-up interviews. The adjustment of noncounseled students was appraised on the basis of data obtained in follow-up interviews, and in terms of the extent to which these individuals had maintained the educational and vocational plans which they had claimed at the time of their admission to the college.

It was found that 68 percent of the noncounseled group had achieved what was considered by themselves and the evaluating judges to be satisfactory educational and vocational adjustment, whereas 81 percent of the counseled students had achieved what was judged to be correspondingly satisfactory adjustment. The difference between these two percentages was found to be statistically significant.

It is pointed out in the report of this investigation that the control group was composed largely of students who had remained in the college for three quarter-terms, and thus does not constitute a representative sampling of all noncounseled students. Therefore, according to the report, one can not conclude from this study that 68 percent of *all* noncounseled students in this college achieve satisfactory adjustment. This conclusion, it is pointed out, could have been drawn only if the controls had been selected at random from the total freshman population at the time of their matriculation in the college.

Although it has weaknesses, the investigation briefly described above is one of the most carefully conducted guidance-evaluation studies reported in the literature. The findings suggest that vocational counseling can be worthwhile. One should not assume, of course, that similar results would necessarily be found if the work of other counseling bureaus were similarly investigated; better, equivalent, or poorer results might be found, depending in part on the competency of the individuals who did the counseling.

STANDARDS FOR VOCATIONAL GUIDANCE SERVICE

Vocational guidance services available to the public vary greatly in quality; anyone can call himself a vocational counselor. An individual who wishes to receive competent vocational counseling should take the trouble to investigate the qualifications of the individual, organization, or agency he intends to consult.

The National Vocational Guidance Association has published a directory which contains a list of, and useful information about, agencies that have been investigated and subsequently approved by the Ethical Practices Committee of the N.V.G.A. The Committee has authorized and encouraged the reproduction of the following statement of general *minimum* standards employed in appraising agencies that requested evaluation.

Minimum Standards for Vocational Guidance Service [1]

An agency, organization, or individual that provides vocational guidance service should meet the following requirements:

[1] Reprinted from National Vocational Guidance Association, *1951 Directory of Vocational Counseling Agencies,* St. Louis, Ethical Practices Committee, Washington University, 1951.

1. *Recognition.* The agency (organization or individual) should be recognized by suitable educational institutions such as approved colleges and universities or by state or local supervisors of guidance, and be endorsed by professional organizations such as the National Vocational Guidance Association and the American Psychological Association.

2. *Personnel.* The staff should consist of competent and properly qualified people. Supervisors and those who work without close and direct supervision should possess the qualifications of Professional Members of the National Vocational Guidance Association.

3. *Procedures.* The agency should adhere to the standards set forth in the statement, "Principles and Practices of Vocational and Educational Guidance," obtainable from the national headquarters of the National Vocational Guidance Association. Among the methods which are specifically disapproved as vocational guidance procedures are: astrology, handwriting analysis, numerology, palmistry, phrenology and physiognomy, the practice of vocational guidance entirely or mainly by correspondence, the routine practice of counseling in one interview, and the giving of vocational advice entirely on the basis of tests.

4. *Advertising.* The agency should limit its publicity to dignified announcements and descriptions of its services, adhering to professional rather than to commercial standards. It should not indulge in self-praise or promise good results, either directly or by implication. It should not advertise in newspapers, magazines, or on the radio, and should not put more than a plain listing in telephone directories. The offer of free or low-cost aptitude tests as a method of sales promotion is disapproved.

5. *Fees.* Fees, if any are charged, should be reasonable in relation to service rendered. An approved agency does not pay fees to others for recommending clients to it, does not accept fees for recommending clients to a school or other agency, and does not require a client to pay a fee for guidance in order to qualify for ostensibly free job-placement service.

SUGGESTED READINGS

1. Brewer, J. M., *History of Vocational Guidance.* New York: Harper, 1942. Deals with the rise and early development of the guidance movement.

2. Bureau of Labor Statistics, U. S. Department of Labor, *Occupational Outlook Handbook* (Bulletin No. 998). Washington, D.C.: U. S. Government Printing Office, 1951. Contains a discussion of methods employed in estimating vocational trends as well as data on the outlook in 400 occupations.

3. Froehlish, C. P., *Evaluating Guidance Procedures* (Bulletin Misc. No. 3310). Washington, D.C.: U. S. Office of Education, January, 1949. Reviews the literature on evaluation and contains a bibliography of 177 items.

4. Grumer, M., Aims and scope of vocational counseling, *J. Social Casework,* 1949, 30:330–335. A discussion of vocational guidance from a social worker's point of view.

5. Kaplan, Oscar J. (ed.), *Encyclopedia of Vocational Guidance.* New York: Philosophical Library, 1948. A useful two-volume reference which includes articles on various aspects of vocational guidance written by over 280 contributors.

6. Mathewson, R. H., *Guidance Policy and Practice.* New York: Harper, 1949. A thought-provoking book which deals chiefly with the philosophical, psychological, and sociological concepts and assumptions underlying guidance programs and practices.

7. Nelson, A. G., Types of vocational counseling problems: a study of two hundred disabled male veterans, *J. Clin. Psychol.,* 1947, 3:252–256. Report of an investigation designed to determine the kinds of vocational counseling problems presented by a group of disabled veterans, and the incidence of these types of problems.

8. Nelson, A. G., VA counseling and high-school counseling, *School and Society,* 1949, 70:357–358. A discussion of the question: To what extent should VA vocational-counseling procedures be applied to the counseling of high-school students?

9. Reed, A. Y., *Guidance and Personnel Services in Education.* Ithaca, N.Y.: Cornell, 1944. A comprehensive and judicious treatment of nonclinical student personnel work in schools and colleges.

10. Stuit, D. B., *et al., Predicting Success in Professional Schools.* Washington, D.C.: American Council on Education, 1949. An excellent summary of the research on the prediction of success in certain types of professional schools.

11. Super, D. E., *Appraising Vocational Fitness.* New York: Harper, 1949. Generally acclaimed in reviews as the best book published to

date on the use of psychological tests in vocational selection and guidance.

12. Williamson, E. G., and Bordin, E. S., Evaluating counseling by means of a control-group experiment, *School and Society*, 1940, 52:434–440. Describes an investigation designed to determine the effectiveness of the vocational-counseling service of a college guidance bureau.

Chapter 2

Industrial Psychology:
Selection and Placement
of Workers

by PATRICIA SMITH

Introduction

Selection Versus Placement

Techniques of Effective Evaluation
  VALIDITY
  RELIABILITY
  STANDARDIZATION
  SUITABILITY

Establishment of Selection Procedures
  CRITERION
  JOB ANALYSIS
  CHOICE OF ITEMS IN SELECTION PROCEDURE
    Personal History
    Interviews
    References
    Tests
  VALIDATION OF ITEMS IN SELECTION PROCEDURE
    Personal History
    Interviews
    References
    Tests

Combination of Selection Devices
Results
Summary of Steps in Devising a Selection
Procedure

Selection, Placement, and Guidance

Summary

Suggested Readings

INTRODUCTION

Although a great variety of psychological problems has existed in industry as long as industry itself, it is only within the past two or three decades that a profession of industrial psychology has been developing. The existence of such a professional group has been known to the general public for even a shorter time. The aims, functions, and special techniques of the industrial psychologist are still but little understood by the general public, or even by many in industrial management.

It is first necessary to distinguish psychology from those methods which are based primarily upon experience and are used by anyone who meets a psychological problem and deals with it himself. There is the same distinction in psychology which exists between professional medical care and home remedies. It should also be noted that we have psychological quacks, using methods similar to those of the medical quack. Professional psychologists have been engaged in a campaign to educate the public and otherwise control the activities of these charlatans.

With regard to the home remedies which are used in solving practical problems, the main difficulty is that no one really knows whether or not they are successful in solving the problem. There is usually no check upon the results of the method, or when there is we usually do not know whether the results were caused by what we did or by other factors over which we had no control and which were not even noticed at the time. It is such difficulties which the industrial psychologist tries to overcome.

The aims of the psychologist in industry might be outlined as follows:

1. To investigate critically and in an unbiased manner the ways in which psychological problems are handled at present.
2. When solutions are found to be inadequate, to develop new methods which are then tried out and evaluated in critical fashion.
3. To formulate general principles which will aid in the solution of new problems as they arise.

In other words, the main task of the industrial psychologist is *research* rather than *administration*. His job is to be considered as distinct from that of the personnel manager, who handles such problems as training workers, working out methods of promotion, trying to reduce the turnover of workers in a certain department, hiring workers when vacancies arise, and smoothing over the complaints of a worker who complains of unfair treatment by his supervisor and wants to quit. These are all obviously problems which involve human behavior and to this extent are psychological. In addition the personnel manager has problems of office procedure—how to keep records in an efficient manner—and other matters such as studying the labor market, and knowing where to look for workers of a certain kind. Many of the psychological problems he solves by "home remedy" methods, using his experience and his "knack" for dealing with people to work out a rule-of-thumb answer. Often he is dissatisfied with the results and suspects that something better could have been worked out if he had more information available to him.

It is at this point that the psychologist enters the picture. He is called in by the personnel manager or higher management to develop the knowledge that is needed. At first, management usually expects the psychologist to know all that is necessary from his previous studies and research. They soon find, however, that the psychologist makes his real contribution by doing research on the spot, investigating the conditions as they are actually present in that particular plant at that specific time, making his recommendations, and checking these recommendations again by research methods. It is true that he brings with him specialized knowledge gained from the research of others and from his own previous investigations. He cannot be sure, however, that what is true in Company A under certain conditions will also be true in Company B, even when the conditions are apparently similar. In addition, it is seldom that the conditions are more than superficially similar to those studied before.

It is true that we have listed a third aim—to develop general principles which will help in solving new problems as they arise. This is still largely a goal rather than an accomplished fact. The principles which the industrial psychologist has to work with are principles of investigation—ways of ensuring that we secure accurate and useful information. In the main, they are principles which apply in any research in psychology whether in industry or elsewhere, but there are some special developments which aid the work in industry. Our psychological principles as contrasted with our methodological principles are still so broad, however, that they only suggest solutions to particular problems. We cannot predict specific answers on the basis of our principles without checking the prediction in the particular situation.

This chapter and the one which follows will be devoted to examples of the research which psychologists have done on various problems which arise in industry. We begin with the selection or placement of workers as they enter a particular organization. Later we shall consider the factors which determine the efficiency of the worker on the job.

SELECTION VERSUS PLACEMENT

When the average manager of a manufacturing concern thinks of an industrial psychologist, he usually thinks in terms of a man who specializes in the selection of employees, and especially in their selection by means of psychological tests. There is good reason for the concentration of the industrialist upon the selection and testing phases of the work of the psychologist in industry as in these areas the effects of his efforts are largest and most readily observable in the profit and loss statement of the firm. Even a slight improvement in the dependability and productivity of new employees will be reflected in decreased training costs, increased production and profits, and lowered overhead. Management's interest in the economic implications is matched by the interest of the applicants in securing jobs which they can perform successfully and which will furnish them opportunities for good wages and personal satisfaction.

The obvious importance of proper selection both to management and to the worker tends to obscure the other equally important but less readily evident aspects of the psychologist's work in industry. It is only in recent years that the industrialist has come to realize the importance of many other psychological functions. Especially, when the supply of applicants became very small during the war years, it became increasingly clear that proper placement was certainly as important as, if not more important than, selection. That is, with a scarcity of people from whom to choose, the employer was obliged to hire almost everyone who applied, and could no longer really screen, or *select*. It became essential, therefore, that he place on the difficult jobs those few applicants who were able to do them, and that he reserve for the less capable those jobs that were within their capacities. Moreover, he had greater need than ever for using any special skills or aptitudes of his new employees. The emphasis shifted, then, from selection to placement, and the task of the employment office resembled that of the vocational guidance bureau much more closely.

TECHNIQUES OF EFFECTIVE EVALUATION

What are the techniques which are used to evaluate applicants? The kind of procedures which the modern employer may use are not really very different from the kinds which were available for use when the first farmer surveyed the supply of eligible young women in order to take himself a wife. The farmer undoubtedly used the *interview*—except in rare cases he certainly talked with those in whom he was interested in order to ascertain which one most nearly suited his needs and requirements. He could have obtained a complete personal history on each, but probably he preferred to do this in conversation even though he could have asked each to write a summary for him—a sort of *application blank*. Also, he probably talked to others about each girl and in doing so heard various opinions of her. This is similar to the investigation of *references*. He unquestionably investigated other qualifications by *testing* the achievement of each girl in such things as cooking and sewing. And lastly, he couldn't avoid making inferential judgments of other aptitudes for behavior which could only be predicted by indirect techniques. All of the procedures which were used by our farmer friend are used today; some have been modernized and systematized rather thoroughly, and some are used with the same somewhat intuitive philosophy that characterized the farmer's investigations. The effectiveness of any of these techniques for the purpose of predicting the future performance of persons, however, depends upon the degree to which the procedure satisfies the following characteristics of a good evaluative device: *validity, reliability, standardization,* and *practicality.*

Validity

The first and primary consideration in deciding whether a given method of evaluation is satisfactory is that of validity. A decision after an *interview,* a judgment from *personal history data,* a *reference,* or a *test* is valid if it predicts what it is supposed to predict—if it measures what it is supposed to measure. If a clothing manufacturer, for example, wanted to be able to predict from some sort of preëmployment test how well a girl would be able to sew after experience and training on the job, he would want to have a valid test of sewing ability. He would want those girls who had good scores on the test before they were employed to be the ones who later did best on the job, and those who performed poorly on the test to be those who failed on the job.

Validity is always stated in relation to some particular job; a test may be valid for certain sewing jobs and not for others, and be of no use whatsoever in predicting success in bookkeeping. Therefore, in each case the psychologist must establish what is meant by success —whether, for example, the most successful sewing machine operator is the one who sews most rapidly, or the one who sews most accurately, or the one who can sew the greatest variety of garments, or the one who can always be depended upon for regular attendance. He must establish his *criterion,* or standard for judging. Then he must find out whether his test will predict his criterion. He must determine whether differences in scores on the test given before employment will show a reasonably close relationship to the differences in later success on that particular job. After the proof of the relationship between test and criterion is established, the psychologist could say that the test was valid for that job.

Reliability

Of course the most important characteristic of any predictive device is its validity. But, in addition the psychologist seeks certain other features in his measuring technique. In addition to being valid, it should be reliable. A measure is reliable if it is consistent; if we repeat a measurement, we want to draw the same conclusions from the second administration as from the first. A person doing well on one trial should retain his relative position and continue to do well on the second trial, while, conversely, the person who does not perform satisfactorily on the first trial should continue to be below average on the next attempt. In other words, the measurement should be accurate; we should be able to depend upon the results of whatever predictive device is being used.

As one can readily see, in most situations a valid measure must be reliable, since an inconsistent and variable measurement could not show any systematic relationship to later performance on any job except by chance. But because a test is reliable, we cannot assume that it is therefore valid. For example, we can measure height rather reliably, but this dependability of measurement would not insure that height would be a valid predictor of success in sewing, book-keeping, or garbage collecting. Its validity would depend upon a proven relationship between height and success on a particular job.

When a measurement is shown not to be very reliable, the psychologist, by changing the length, method of administration, or construction of the test or tests, is often able to improve the situation. After suitable reliability has been obtained, the test has a better possibility of serving effectively as a predictor of some criterion. It is important, therefore, that the psychologist know the reliability of the measures he uses, and also of the criterion he is trying to predict.

Standardization

As another important aid to the success of an evaluative technique, we make sure that our methods are standardized. The methods of administration and scoring should be uniform, so that every individual has an equal opportunity to do his best; moreover, the evaluator should be able to refer to norms or representative scores so that he can compare the individual's performance with that of others of the same age, sex and training. Without adequate norms, the examiner has no basis for judging whether a given performance is good, bad, or indifferent. Obviously, standardization is necessary, but not sufficient, for both reliability and validity.

Suitability

Practical considerations also must be taken into account in evaluating a proposed method. Applicants must not be offended, frightened, or otherwise driven away by the nature of the procedure. The time taken for each applicant cannot be so long that the applicants object or that the procedure requires a large staff for administration. The procedure should be suitable in difficulty and general nature for the group on whom it is to be used. It is preferable, also, for the employment technique to seem reasonable to the applicant; it is better for there to be some obvious relationship between the job and the technique since the applicant is then more likely to take the test seriously and try to succeed. This plausibility is called "face validity." Of course, it is not nearly so important as true validity. As a last but important requirement, a procedure should certainly cost less than the expense of training a person for the job; otherwise, it would be cheaper simply to hire all the applicants and to keep only those who do well.

The work of the industrial psychologist in setting up selection and placement methods involves the consideration of all the above-mentioned factors and the integration of satisfactory techniques into a smooth, unified procedure by which an applicant may be evaluated through a number of methods and either rejected or chosen for a particular job for which he seems best suited. All of this is rather a highly technical process, involving a great deal of statistical analysis and requiring specialized training. It is just in the use of these laborious methods of validating that we find the differences between the psychologist and the would-be psychologist, or in some cases, the charlatan. There is no mystery concerning the procedures involved, however, and we may perhaps gain some insight into them if we follow a psychologist as he introduces a new selection procedure into a factory. For the sake of simplicity, we will confine our illustration to the process of selection, and postpone our discussion of the procedures used for placement.

ESTABLISHMENT OF SELECTION PROCEDURES

Let us examine a typical relatively uncomplicated problem which confronts an industrial psychologist, and follow his steps as he finds a solution. The story begins, with the psychologist, who has worked in this company only a short time, examining the report of discharges and "quits" which he receives from the personnel department. He notices that in most departments about the same percentage of persons leave the company, but in the shipping department, the turnover rate is much higher. Further examination shows that almost all of these terminations of employment have occurred among people on one particular job, the packing of small units into boxes for shipment, and that at present almost all are new employees.

There are over 200 persons in the packing department, and the turnover rate is so high that 75 or 80 are being trained every year. Since it costs the company at least $100 to train a new packer, the cost involved in this turnover is amounting to $7,500 or $8,000 a year. Obviously, some expenditure on the part of the company is warranted, if it will decrease this cost. Moreover, these workers who have left the company have also made investments in time and effort which have been wasted when they quit their jobs. An investigation of the causes of this waste is clearly justified.

The psychologist immediately considers the possibilities that (1) a supervisor who is responsible for the work of people on that particular job is less kind and understanding than other supervisors, or (2) the training of new people on that job has not been satisfactory, or (3) working conditions are not equal to those in the rest of the plant, or (4) pay is not in keeping with other wages in the factory and in the community, or (5) the people on that job happen neither to like one another nor to enjoy working together, or (6) a less stable and dependable kind of person has for some reason been hired for that job. He checks all these possibilities with the available evidence and concludes that the probable source of the difficulty lies not in any of these factors, but in the fact that the persons being hired for the job simply have not been able to learn the packing work to the satisfaction of the company. The difficulty seems to be one of selection.

The steps through which the psychologist must go before he can evolve a new and improved method of choosing trainees for the packing department are all, of course, designed to satisfy the requirements of a satisfactory method of evaluation. First he must establish his criterion, then analyze the requirements of the job, make a tentative choice of evaluative devices, check the validity of his techniques, combine them into an integrated program, and then follow the later results of the procedure and continue improvements and revisions. Let us examine these steps in more detail.

Criterion

The most critical step, perhaps, in the entire process, is the first one of deciding upon the criterion of success on the job. In this situation, the psychologist is helped by the fact that a large number of persons have failed, so that the trainers, the supervisors, and even the other workers on the job have worried about the turnover and have tried to decide why so many have failed. Here the problem of the criterion is relatively simple. The number of boxes which each packer completes are counted by a mechanical counter, and the packers are paid a bonus for each box completed in excess of one hundred per day. In previous years, most employees were able to earn a reasonable amount of bonus money, but those packers who have recently failed on the job have failed to produce even the minimum hundred. Since all have been carefully trained in the same method, the differences in the performance of the packers seemed to be almost entirely a matter of speed. The psychologist ascertains that, in the past, the average worker has taken eight weeks to learn to work rapidly enough to complete a hundred boxes a day. Therefore, he feels that he can use as his criterion the number of boxes per day completed after eight weeks of training, thus equalizing to a large extent the effects of experience on the job. He checks with the supervisor and with top management, and finds that this criterion is satisfactory with them. Comparison of the average daily production for the eighth and ninth weeks with the average for the tenth and eleventh weeks shows the criterion to be consistent and reliable. After certain allowances are made for extraneous factors, such as delays in the supply of work, production at the end of the learning period is established as the criterion against which various selection devices will be compared. In this case, the production criterion reflects adequately differences both in ability and in perseverance, and covers the factors involved in success on the job.

Job Analysis

The next step has been started before the first is finished. The psychologist must analyze the job so that he knows it thoroughly. First of all, he wants to make a complete job description. He obtains a thorough knowledge of the job by the use of every possible source of information—observation of the workers, questioning of workers, trainees, and supervisors, reference to training and time-study records, examination of slow-motion films of the job, and finally, if possible, actual performance of the work himself. He is then able to describe the job accurately, and to understand the requirements of the work. The description of the job is quite detailed, but to summarize it, he finds that the packers are required to fill standard-sized boxes with small, irregularly shaped packages, following written lists of items which vary from order to order. The packers must assemble the items to fill the order, estimate the most effective positions for the items within the box, and pack the items rapidly and safely into the carton. When items arrive broken, or when the order is inaccurately filled, the packer loses credit for packing the entire box, so that it is important to him that the items arrive undamaged and that the correct number and kind be included. The items are arranged before the packers in bins, so that it is possible to pick up a number of each kind from a sitting position at the packing bench.

The psychologist now estimates the abilities, aptitudes, and personal characteristics which are required by the job. The effectiveness of this step depends upon the experience and the judgment of the psychologist, as well as his ability to observe the job accurately. He decides on the basis of the job analysis that the packing requires considerable dexterity in the use of the two hands together (which seems to be important in picking up the objects rapidly and in placing them in the box), perceptual speed or rapidity in observing and grasping details (such as, for example, whether the label on the object matches that on the order), ability to grasp spatial relations (to tell quickly whether a small object will fit into the remaining area in the box), adequate hand span (to enable the packer to pick up a number of objects at once), and, lastly, persistence in sticking to a repetitive task. He sees no reason to expect that other physical and mental characteristics will make much difference in the success of the employees. Having listed these job requirements, he now considers various methods of discovering these characteristics among the applicants for the job.

Choice of Items in Selection Procedure

The third step is to make at this point a tentative list of techniques to be tried in an attempt to predict before employment the productivity of new employees on the packing job. All of the techniques available are evaluated for indications of validity, reliability, proper standardization, and suitability, as well as for the way in which various techniques will fit together.

PERSONAL HISTORY

First the information which can be gained from personal history data is considered. It is possible that some of the items in the personal history of the individual will be related to how well he works out on the job, especially since the job analysis has indicated that persistence may be one of the factors making for success on the job. Personal history data are most easily and rapidly gathered by having the applicant fill out an application form. Probably there is no employment technique which has been used more widely than the application blank, in its innumerable variations. Almost all employers place great reliance upon the past history of the applicant, although very few have made a check to see whether those portions of the applicants' background upon which decisions are made are actually valid predictors of later success. The first studies which were done to determine the usefulness of the items included on the application blank were made shortly after the turn of the century, and repeated attempts since that time have confirmed the results of the early work. Only a few items have consistently proved to be of any value, and the items which do predict vary greatly from situation to situation.

The psychologist knows that whatever judgments have been made in the past for the packing job have not been successful in picking good prospects, but he is hopeful that a more careful check will show that there are some items that might prove useful.

All the old application blanks in his company include age at employment, sex, marital status, number of children, miles lived from the factory, education, weight and height at time of employment, number, duration, and kinds of jobs previously held, and some indication of the reason for leaving previous employers. Also the blanks indicate father's occupation, age of husband or wife, previous criminal convictions if any, foreign languages spoken, subjects liked best and least in school, hair color, eye color, name of family physician, and a number of similar items. Previous investigators have sometimes found the first group of items to show some relationship to job success, and the last group to be largely irrelevant. All the information will be analyzed to see if any of it is predictive of success on this job.

If the personal history data prove valid, it will make the selection task much easier, because the histories are certainly inexpensive, plausible, and otherwise very *suitable* and practical. The methods of obtaining the data in the past have been remarkably uniform in this plant, since the same clerk has apparently asked the same questions in exactly the same way for fifteen years; files are available for a number of years for all the applicants for that particular job, so it is possible to obtain norms for comparison of any given person with all the persons who applied. Therefore, it seems that the personal history data may well qualify as being adequately *standardized*. There is at first no indication of the *reliability* of the information. The psychologist arranges to have each of the packers fill in a new application blank, so that the statements made on the two occasions may be compared. He finds the agreement very high, so that he can consider these data reasonably reliable. On the basis of his preliminary analysis, he feels that he is justified in including personal history data in his tentative program, since previous investigators have sometimes found some such items to be valid for similar jobs, and since the personal history data satisfy the requirements of reliability, standardization, and suitability.

INTERVIEWS

Next, our psychologist turns his attention to the possibility of including in his tentative selection system judgments based on interviews of applicants. The interview, like the application blank, is very frequently used and heavily weighted in the decisions of most employment managers. Unfortunately, objective studies of the results of interviews show that the performance of most interviewers is characterized much more by self-confidence and enthusiasm than by accuracy. Many otherwise objective employment managers insist that they are able to tell "the moment they see a person" whether he will be able to succeed in a given job. It is a matter of great pride for many people that they make their judgments of men in an intuitive and impulsive manner, while they would be grossly insulted were anyone to accuse them of such subjectivity in the much simpler operations of balancing a bank account or of deciding whether it was time to change the oil in their automobiles. Moreover, a person who would agree heartily if one accused him of being poor in arithmetic, lacking mechanical ability, or being incapable of legible penmanship or accurate spelling, would be both hurt and antagonized if one suggested that he had no knack in judging people. Every man considers himself a psychologist, and most men consider themselves also born interviewers. The psychologist knows that many such judgments are based upon such factors as resemblance to previous acquaintances (admired, ignored, or hated), clothing, height, weight, hair, eye and skin color, and other such superficialities. Unfortunately for the accuracy of such decisions, no objective study has shown any relationship between anv of these and later job success.

Interviewers who utilize these techniques do not trouble to check their own accuracy, and yet have great confidence in their performance.

The wide use of the interview is probably due to this confidence in personal judgments of men, and also to the obvious face validity and suitability of the interview. Reliability, true validity, and standardization are much less readily demonstrated for this technique, and this is particularly true of the intuitive form which is most commonly used by the industrialist. First of all, the attempts which have been made to determine the reliability of the interview have been rather discouraging. A number of studies were made shortly after the turn of the century, almost all showing low agreement among interviewers who had no special training in interviewing but relied on wide experience in human contacts for their decisions. Many of these investigations dealt with the interviewing by sales managers of applicants for sales positions.

One early study of the reliability of the interview, for example, investigated the agreement among three executives in their estimates of 34 new salesmen. This company marketed a product which was rather difficult to sell, and therefore suffered from very high turnover among its salesmen. The company had adopted a policy of paying salesmen strictly on commission without advance payments to the men. Their problems of selection were further complicated by the fact that new salesmen had to be put through a two-week training period at their own expense. Before the company could even consider a change in salary policy, they had to establish some effective method of selecting salesmen. Therefore, they wished to check the consistency and accuracy of evaluation by their executives. One executive (Executive A) had some contact with the salesmen during their training period and interviewed each for a half hour before the course started. Executives B and C saw each of the trainees for an average of an hour a day, during which time they explained the product and company to the trainee, listened to sample sales talks, and raised objections to them and criticized them.

All three executives coöperated in deciding what characteristics were required by good salesmen and in the relative importance of each. They worked out a rather careful plan for rating each sales- man on each of these characteristics and for combining these ratings into an overall evaluation. Executive A rated the salesmen after his interview with the privilege of revising his estimates after the train- ing period was completed. Executives B and C rated after the train- ing period. The ratings by each rater were translated into ranks, the salesman receiving the best rating by rater A being given rank 1 for that rater, and the poorest, rank 34. The ratings of the men were similarly translated into ranks for Executives B and C.

One might expect that there would be reasonably close agreement, at least between B and C—but the correspondence was no better than one could expect if the ratings had all been done by tossing cards down a flight of stairs. Executives A and C actually tended to rate opposite to one another, one tending to rate high the men that the other rated low. Obviously, there is no evidence to warrant the assumption that raters will agree with each other in their estimates, even after rather good opportunity to observe the persons whom they are to rate. This particular kind of interview is not consistently *re- liable*. The *validity* of the estimates of these same three executives was also investigated. The rankings by the executives were com- pared with rankings on a criterion—actual sales figures after two months in the field. The correlations were again no better than we might expect from chance, so that even after rather careful analysis of the job and ten hours of observation, these ratings were neither reliable nor valid.

Several more attempts to show reliability and validity of the inter- view were made during the last war. For example, the Aviation Psychology Program of the Army Air Forces conducted an extensive investigation of the effectiveness of the interview in predicting suc- cess in elementary pilot training. These interviewers were presum- ably skilled, and their judgments were supplemented with a wealth of data on each pilot. They were guided in their interviews by a list of the areas to be covered and by a list of questions, but the manner of putting the questions was left to the examiner. A number of interviewers participated. The interview was planned to reveal as much as possible about the relationship between the background of the subject and his present personality, and between both of these and probable success in pilot training. The results showed that the interviews would not differentiate the successes from the failures in this situation. Results of Navy investigations were similar.

The psychologist consequently is not particularly hopeful about the free and unobstructed interview as a predictive device. He recognizes, however, that the interviews which have proved so unreliable and invalid are also unstandardized. Since lack of uniformity of procedure, method of interpretation, or standards of comparison usually mean unreliability and invalidity, he feels that the interview in a standardized form might be more reliable. An investigator, for example, who has recently given considerable attention to the improvement of interview methods, criticized the early interview studies because the interviewers were untrained sales managers, without adequate job specifications and without interview plans, who could not be presumed to have the knowledge of human behavior, the intelligence, the interest, and the attitudes necessary for good interviewing. Most of the criticisms do not apply to the military investigations, the results of which are so discouraging to the use of the interview. However, a closer look at the evidence suggests one source of difficulty which should have been obvious at a much earlier date: the interviews so far mentioned were conducted at the discretion of the interviewer, so that in each interview questions were asked in a different manner, in a different sequence, with different phrasing and emphasis. The interviews varied from interviewer to interviewer and even from one time to another with the same interviewer. They were not *standardized,* even though each interview attempted to cover the same content. In an attempt to avoid this variability, "patterned" interviews have been developed and some investigators have produced carefully standardized procedures, in which a trained interviewer conducts a planned interview designed to discover whether the applicant has the characteristics required for the particular job under consideration. Questions are carefully phrased, and the interpretations of the responses are based on careful analysis. It is even possible to secure a rough norm for comparison. This sort of interview is directed in large part to prediction of job stability—will the applicant stay on the job and exert reasonable effort if hired?

Several studies show that such interviews have good validity, for example, in comparing the ratings made on the "patterned" interview with the subsequent performance of a group of over 400 new employees of a metal-trades firm. The applicants were interviewed by trained interviewers, who used the patterned interview technique and rated each applicant 1 ("outstanding"), 2 ("good"), 3 ("fair or marginal"), or 4 ("unsatisfactory—normally unemployable"). All the applicants were hired without regard for their ratings. After a year and a half, the foremen (who were unaware of the interview ratings) were asked to divide the employees into those who were above average, and those who were below average, in productivity, attitude toward supervision, and general overall desirability. Results are shown in Figure 2.1. Of those rated "outstanding" by the interviewers, all were included in the above average group by the foremen, and the percentage of successes declined with succeedingly poorer interview ratings until only 3 percent of those rated unsatisfactory turned out to be above average as employees. The validity of this type of interview, by these interviewers, for these jobs was satisfactory.

Our psychologist examines the varying results of the studies which have been reported on interviewing, and decides that when interviews have been successful, they have (1) been standardized, (2) been conducted by trained and qualified persons, (3) been designed to select persons for rather routine and unskilled jobs such as easily learned machine operations, truck driving, and the like, where persistence and dependability are important factors in job success. Remembering that the last item on his list of requirements for the packing job was *persistence,* he decides that the interview might be useful after all, if properly handled. He knows that the process of selecting and training interviewers and standardizing the

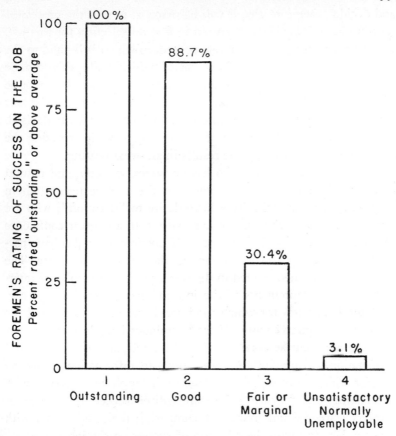

INTERVIEWERS' RATING OF SUCCESS ON THE JOB

FIGURE 2.1.   Relation Between Interviewer's Ratings and Later Success on the job. (Modified from R. N. McMurry, Validating the patterned interview, *Personnel*, 1947, 23:2–11. Courtesy of *Personnel* and the American Management Association.)

interview procedures is very time-consuming and expensive. The decision to attempt to use these techniques is influenced, however, both by the high cost of present turnover and by the fact that he knows he will soon have to improve selection procedures for several other jobs. He will wish to use the interview for these jobs, as well, and decides, therefore, that it will be practical to start the process of training interviewers by concentrating first on selecting for this job. He decides to set up an interview procedure which is limited to the features of the applicant's background which reasonably can be expected to be related to persistence on the job, and which cannot be discovered from the application blank. He tries to combine the best features of the standardized interviews which have been devised, and sets up standard methods of asking questions, interpreting the answers, and summarizing the results in an overall rating.

Interviewers are chosen who have a warm, friendly, and natural manner; who are more intelligent than the average person whom they will interview; who have little desire to "show off"; who are not talkative; and who are not burdened with any great confidence in their own ability to judge people. If possible, they also have psychological training and experience in the particular industry. The interviewers are then trained in the purposes and principles of interviewing, the requirements of the job under consideration, the psychological processes for which the interviewer must watch, and the techniques of interviewing. These techniques include ways of putting the applicant at ease, securing the applicant's confidence and coöperation, giving the applicant adequate information about the job for which he is applying, allowing the applicant to do most of the talking, and following the standardized procedure. The interviewers learn the importance of comparing their judgments with one another, and with the criterion of success on the job.

In order to check the reliability of the interview process, each of the interviewers makes a judgment on the same series of applicants, and the ratings of each interviewer is compared with that of every other interviewer and with the average of all interviewers. It is then clear whether any interviewer is in disagreement with the others, and whether their judgments are reasonably consistent. After discrepancies are ironed out, the *interview* is in shape to be considered part of the tentative selection program. It now qualifies on the grounds that there is reasonable possibility of its proving valid, that it is suitable, that it has been standardized, and that it is reliable.

REFERENCES

The psychologist then turns his attention briefly to the use of references, and letters of recommendation. Even a cursory glance at the literature on references is discouraging, however; few people are willing to say a kind word for this form of evaluation. For one thing, the persons who write letters of recommendation seldom know anything about the job for which the applicant is now being considered; moreover, there is no guarantee that they remember the applicant, that they have records against which to check, that they are capable of forming good judgments about people, that they have the time and the desire to be accurate, or even that they are not lying to get rid of an undesirable employee. Such references are usually presented in an unstandardized manner, so that the phrasing may mean all things to all people. They are inconvenient, take a great deal of time both for the former employer and for the prospective one, and are otherwise not particularly suitable. The few studies that have been done on reliability indicate that agreement among references is often very low. For example, one study involved contacting eight former employers of an applicant to obtain opinions of his character. Two employers did not answer, four gave him very high recommendations, including specific mention of dependability and honesty, while two accused him of immorality, laziness, incompetence, and financial irresponsibility. Such discrepancies certainly discourage the use of references as a major basis for making a decision about applicants.

The psychologist feels, nevertheless, that it is worth while to check the dates, places of employment, and reasons for leaving employment indicated on the application blank. A standard form is devised to be mailed to former employers, enabling them to check very quickly the accuracy of the applicant's statements. If the work history items in the application blank turn out to be valid, this checking procedure will improve their reliability, and not prove too impractical.

TESTS

So far our psychologist has found means that may help him decide whether applicants are sufficiently persistent for the packing job, but he has done nothing to help him decide about their hand dexterity, perceptual speed, spatial relations, or hand span. To predict these factors, he turns to the last of his kinds of evaluative devices and begins to consider the possible kinds of psychological tests which might help him in his task.

Industrial tests are used for a wide variety of purposes, and are constructed in an equally wide variety of ways. There are almost as many tests as there are psychologists—many of the tests having been designed for highly specialized situations. Psychological tests may be classified in a number of ways. First of all, they may be separated according to the different purposes for which they are designed. Thus there are *general intelligence* tests, intended to predict how well a child will do in school or an adult will perform at primarily verbal and numerical tasks such as clerical work and various other occupations for which they have been shown to have predictive value. There are also specialized *aptitude* tests, designed to measure the probable ability of the individual to learn, after suitable training, specific tasks such as piloting a plane, repairing an automobile, driving a truck, supervising a group of factory workers, or selling life insurance. There are *personality* tests, designed to estimate an individual's relative position in such characteristics as sociability, introversion-extraversion, masculinity-femininity, and the like. *Interest* tests are designed to secure a similar estimate of the relative strength of the individual's preferences and aversions for various occupations and activities. There are *attitude* tests which in industrial situations are sometimes practical for evaluating workers' satisfaction with various aspects of their jobs or with the company, and also sometimes used to determine their reactions to fellow-workers with the view to finding persons who will do well as supervisors or as personnel workers. *Achievement* or *trade* tests are set up to determine how much an individual knows about a certain area or how well he has learned a certain task. Typing tests, for example, give an estimate of the rapidity with which an individual can type at the time of the test; similarly, driving tests ascertain how skillfully a driver can operate an automobile or truck. Such tests attempt to estimate the present state of an individual's skill, as contrasted with aptitude tests, which attempt to measure potential for learning a skill.

Tests may also be categorized in other ways. For example, we may contrast *group* tests, which may be administered to a number of persons at the same time, with *individual* tests which must be given singly. We can also compare *verbal* tests, in which words and mathematical symbols are featured in both the questions and the responses, with *performance* tests, which call for manipulation rather than verbal response. Again, we may classify tests according to their method of presentation—whether the test is presented and performed by the use of *paper and pencil* or whether it involves the use of a gadget or *instrument* of some sort. Some tests are *power* tests, with items of increasing difficulty so that a score reflects how far the individual is able to proceed without finding the material too difficult for him; other tests are *speed* tests, in which there is a time limit, or the score is the actual time taken to complete the task, so that speed seriously affects or completely determines the score on the test. Some tests, of course, are a mixture of both of these; the items become increasingly more difficult; while a time limit is also imposed.

We may classify tests in yet another way—according to whether they are *structured* or *unstructured*. Most industrial tests belong to the first classification; the testee is presented with a series of definite questions, problems or tasks, with the purpose of obtaining a quantitative score to indicate the extent to which his behavior differs from that of other testees. There are, however, several tests of an entirely different character; the material is purposely designed to be ambiguous and unstructured, and is designed to enable the tester to understand qualitative aspects of the testee's behavior. Evaluation of this type is thought to be more desirable in higher-level jobs. We find unstructured tests primarily among the personality, interest, and attitude tests—various projective techniques (for example, the Rorschach, the Thematic Apperception Test) belong to this classification. Since these tests are too long and difficult to administer and score, and their validity is still in the process of being established, they are not widely used.

Perhaps the most important distinction between tests is that between tests called *pure* and those called *complex*. Many psychologists believe that there is compelling evidence that intelligence is not one ability, but a large number of abilities. For example, we would include in intelligence tests verbal ability (or ability to handle word meanings and ideas conveyed by words), numerical ability (or the ability to manipulate numbers and similar symbols), spatial relations abilities (the abilities involved in grasping the arrangement of elements within a spatial pattern and manipulating visual images in space), perceptual speed (facility in perceiving the relevant detail among irrelevant material, or the speed of grasping visually presented material), word fluency, and a number of others. A pure test on the other hand measures primarily one of these abilities or factors, and has little relationship to other abilities. Thus, a pure spatial relations test gives scores which reflect almost exclusively the spatial relations factors, and are hardly affected at all by differences in verbal, or numerical, or perceptual abilities.

Some tests of "mechanical ability" show relationships to a number of these factors. They are, then, complex tests. When a complex test is used for selection purposes, it is hoped that the test will reflect just the same abilities, in just the proper proportions, that are required for success on the particular job. When the industrial psychologist uses pure tests, he uses several at once. He picks the tests to match the abilities indicated by his job analysis, checks the validity of each, and combines the scores in such a manner as to give proper weight to the different abilities required by the job. Complex tests are apt to be tailored to one particular job, and of little use for predicting success in other kinds of work. A number of pure tests can be combined in various ways so that the same tests are useful for a wide variety of jobs. This versatility is very useful when the same applicants may be considered for a number of jobs; if the employment office used complex tests, it would have to try one test for each job, to see which type of work suited the applicant best—a very time-consuming procedure. With pure tests, a series of short tests may give information about the ability to learn a number of jobs. Complex tests are quicker, however, if only one job has to be considered. Confronted with the literally thousands of tests which have been constructed, and with the possibility of having to construct an effective new one, the psychologist begins to consider the pros and cons of these various kinds for his own particular situation. In order to get an idea of what we must face in making even a tentative choice, let us examine a few sample tests—good, bad, and indifferent.

The Army Alpha Intelligence Test was devised when World War I made sudden demands upon the Army to expand its force. Psychologists were asked for a group test of intelligence to help select possible officer material and to eliminate the intellectually unfit. Psychologist A. S. Otis had assembled test material with the view to constructing a group intelligence test of his own. This material he contributed to the Army psychologists, who assembled it into the first group intelligence scale. It was so useful to the Army that it stimulated a testing boom after the war, when a wide variety of industries tried the Alpha type of intelligence scale in an attempt to predict success on a great and varied number of jobs. For certain kinds of work, chiefly clerical and administrative, tests of this sort proved effective; in other situations, where general intelligence was not a major factor in job success, the tests were disappointing. Many of our present group intelligence tests are patterned after the Alpha. They are well standardized, satisfactorily reliable, easy to administer and score, and adaptable to many purposes. The Alpha is an intelligence test which tests the sort of ability that is related to school success. It is a group test; it does not require individual administration, and can be given to relatively large numbers of persons at one time. It is a verbal, rather than a performance test; the respondent must answer questions that deal with symbols, rather than manipulate concrete material. It is a paper-and-pencil test; no apparatus is required besides the test form, a pencil, and a watch. It is a timed test, with items that become increasingly more difficult, and hence is a mixed speed and power test. The Alpha is also a structured test. It is highly complex, involving numerical, perceptual, reasoning, and other factors in rather unspecified amounts. It is unlikely that it will be useful in predicting success on the packing job, since it samples a wide number of abilities which the job analysis does not indicate to be involved in packing. Previous investigators have not found tests of this general nature to be useful for manual tasks of this kind. General intelligence tests are, then, excluded from the tentative list of tests to be tried in this case.

Figures 2.2–2.5 show various kinds of aptitude tests, differing in several important respects. The first test (see Fig. 2.2) is a modified Koerth pursuit test. The examinee tries to keep the stylus in contact with a metal spot which rotates on a disk at the rate of one revolution per second. By now the student should be able to classify this test as (1) an aptitude test, (2) a test individual in administration, (3) a performance rather than a verbal test, (4) an instrumental test rather than a paper-and-pencil test, (5) a speed test rather than a power test, and (6) a structured test. During World War II, this test was included among the large numbers of tests investigated by the psychologists in the Army Air Forces Aviation Psychology Program. In these studies, the rotary pursuit was found to be not a pure but a relatively complex test, involving not only coördination but also a rather ill-defined spatial aptitude which has not been well investigated. Its reliability and standardization are satisfactory.

The psychologist suspects that the kind of coördination tested by this test is different from the finer work required by the packing job. Moreover, the pursuit test is a one-handed test while the packing job is two-handed, so that the test does not fit in too well with his job analysis. In addition to these considerations, he would prefer a test

FIGURE 2.2. Sam Rotary Pursuit Test. In the rotary pursuit test, the examinee endeavored to keep the stylus on a small brass rotating target with one hand. At the same time, he depressed one of two keys with the other hand, corresponding to light signals which alternated in an irregular order. The examinee's score was the amount of time on the target during the period the key corresponding to the light signal was depressed. Time on the target when the incorrect key was depressed was not recorded by the automatic clocks. The test thus involved a coördination test with divided attention. The examiner's control panel is shown in the left foreground. (Courtesy of U.S.A.F.)

FIGURE 2.3. Minnesota Rate of Manipulation Test. (From G. Murphy, *An Introduction to Psychology*, Harper, 1950.)

in which the apparatus is not so likely to get out of order (a consideration of suitability), and he is wary of the test on the grounds that it is not only complex, but its complexity is not even well understood. He eliminates such complex coordination tests from his tentative list of tests to be tried out.

Figure 2.3 shows the Minnesota Rate of Manipulation Test. This test may be given in a number of ways: (1) placing the blocks into the holes with one hand; (2) turning over the blocks with both hands; (3) moving each block from one hole to the next hole above; (4) picking up the blocks, turning them and placing them, using just one hand; and (5) the same as (4) with both hands. It is the two-handed sections which interest our psychologist, since the job requires simultaneous use of both hands. This test is again an individual, performance, instrument, speed, structured aptitude test. There has been little analysis of the factors involved (as is true of most tests) but an intelligent guess would suggest that it would be less complex than the rotary pursuit. It is simply constructed and would not be likely to get out of order very easily. Moreover, he finds a number of previous studies in which it has been reasonably successful in predicting speed of packing on similar jobs. With the previous success of the test in mind, plus indications of good reliability and standardization, the psychologist places this test as number one on his tentative list with the hope that it will predict the hand dexterity requirements of the job.

A test may prove useful for purposes other than those for which it has been designed. A good example of this fact is the Minnesota Vocational Test for Clerical Workers, sample items of which are shown in Figure 2.4. Originally designed, as its title indicates, for the selection of routine clerical workers, it nevertheless has proved to be equally useful for certain factory jobs. The reason for this success has been suggested by the results of test analysis, which show that this test is almost a pure test of perceptual factors. It is a group test, verbal, paper-and-pencil, speed, and structured. It is really suitable only for persons with good reading facility. It is quite re-

TEST 1. NUMBER COMPARISON

SAMPLES   79542 – 79524
                              5794367 – 5794367
                             66273894 – 66273984
                            527384578 – 527384578
ITEM 131   82637281028 – 82637281028
ITEM 191   3212 – 3212

TEST 2. NAME COMPARISON

SAMPLES   John C. Linder – John C. Lender
              Investors Syndicate – Investors Syndicate
                 New York World – New York World
                 Cargill Grain Co. – Cargil Grain Co.
ITEM 131   Villaume Lbr. Co. – Villaum Lbr. Co.
ITEM 191   A. S. Hinds Co. – A. S. Hinds Co.

FIGURE 2.4. Items from Minnesota Clerical Test. In these items, the subjects are to check those which are exactly the same. (Arranged by Dorothy M. Andrew, under the direction of Donald G. Patterson and Howard P. Longstaff. Courtesy of the Psychological Corporation.)

liable, and easily administered and scored. Since the psychologist decided in his job analysis that he would like to make an estimate of perceptual speed, he adds this test to his tentative list.

A test which resembles certain aspects of the job to a much greater extent than do the above tests is the Brown Spool-Packer Test. Both hands are used in removing spools from a tray in front of the subject and packing them in a small box. The score for the test is the number packed in a given time. It is an individual, instrumental, performance, structured speed test. A similar test using blocks rather than spools proved to be almost a pure dexterity test. Spool-packing is not likely to cause maintenance difficulties. There is no evidence, however, that it has been used successfully in the prediction of success in packing operations, although it seems likely that it should. Tentatively, then, this is listed among the possible tests to be used.

Another relatively pure test, shown in Figure 2.5, is the Minnesota Paper Form Board. It was devised to substitute a paper-and-

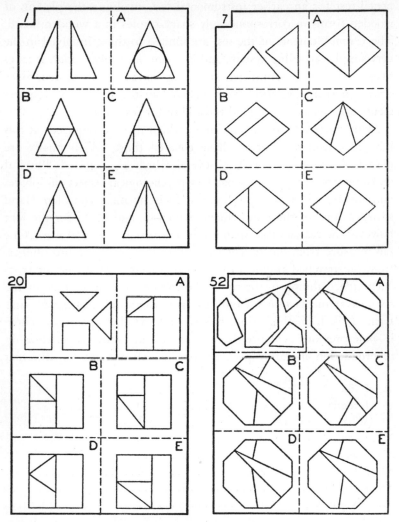

FIGURE 2.5. Items from Revised Minnesota Paper Form Board Test. The test is to pick a figure (from *A* to *E*) which shows how the parts can fit together. (From the *Revised Minnesota Paper Form Board Test*, prepared by R. Likert and W. Quasha. Courtesy of the University of Minnesota Press.)

pencil test for an earlier instrumental test involving the placing of wooden forms in correspondingly shaped holes in a wooden board. The verbal elements of the test are limited to those involved in the very simple recording system, and it is almost purely spatial. It takes twenty minutes to administer, and is rapidly and easily scored. Since ability in spatial relations was included in the list of job requirements, this looks like a good possibility for testing it.

Many more tests of the aptitudes which may be required on this job are considered but we have covered those which finally are placed on the list, as well as several which are rejected. Physical measurements are a somewhat less psychological aspect of job requirements, which our psychologist feels he must consider. Hand span was one of the requirements which he had listed for the job; however, he realizes that span can be measured in several ways. One can measure from outstretched thumb to the tip of the little finger, from outstretched thumb to the tip of the middle finger, or from outstretched thumb to the tip of the forefinger. The average of the six measurements (three from each hand as an index of hand span) seems a likely method, since this is a two-handed operation. There is some previous evidence that such a measure shows a relationship to production in candy packing jobs, which are not too different

  1. I like ....
  5. I regret ....
  9. What annoys me ....
 15. I can't ....
 25. I need ....
 30. I hate ....
 36. I secretly ....
 39. My greatest worry is ....

FIGURE 2.6. Items from the Rotter Incomplete Sentence Blank. "Complete these items to express your real feeling. Try to do every one. Be sure to make a complete sentence." (From J. B. Rotter *et al.*, Validation of the Rotter Incomplete Sentences Blank for college screening, *J. consult. Psychol.*, 1949, 13:348–356. Courtesy of the American Psychological Association and the *Journal of Consulting Psychology*.)

from the job he is considering. Measurements are reliable, easily and quickly taken, and the procedure is well standardized. This test qualifies for the tentative list.

1.	Most workers are less efficient than workers ten years ago.	A	B	C	D	E
2.	A person is likely to rise to the top in his kind of work so long as he is ambitious, even if he is not suited to the kind of work.	A	B	C	D	E
3.	Almost any kind of person can succeed in almost any kind of job if he tries hard enough.	A	B	C	D	E
4.	Human being hardly ever learn to avoid making the same mistake twice.	A	B	C	D	E
5.	Most people lack patience with a "shrinking violet" type of man.	A	B	C	D	E
6.	Most people spend too much time thinking about themselves.	A	B	C	D	E
7.	Most employees are disgusted with employees who "get by" rather than do their full share.	A	B	C	D	E
8.	Most people think that someone is reading their thoughts.	A	B	C	D	E
9.	Most people have fears about other people that are later found to be incorrect.	A	B	C	D	E
10.	Most people feel that they do not get the credit they deserve for things they have accomplished.	A	B	C	D	E
11.	Most people try to determine the real reasons why others are nice to them.	A	B	C	D	E

FIGURE 2.7. A Supervisory Attitude Test. "Each of these statements relates to problems that supervisors have in evaluating their employees and conditions relating to employment. You are to decide for each statement whether you (A) strongly agree, (B) agree, (C) are undecided or uncertain, (D) disagree, or (E) strongly disagree." (From M. M. Mandell, Supervisors' attitudes and job performance, *Personnel*, 1949, **26**: 182–183. Courtesy of *Personnel* and the American Management Association.)

Figure 2.6 is the only unstructured test that has been illustrated here; it is a sentence completion test, designed to find out about the motives, fears, and hopes of the subject, i.e., his personality. The psychologist feels that many personality, as well as attitude, tests (Fig. 2.7) are easily "faked" by an applicant who wants to make a good impression. These tests, as well as the interest and trade tests, are not suited to the unskilled job which he is considering and consequently he does not use them. Trade tests (Fig. 2.8) are used

1. Q. What are the timbers called on which the flooring rests in a frame building?
   A. Joists (beam).
3. Q. Which edge should be used for the top in setting floor joists?
   A. Crown (chamfered edge).
7. Q. What does the number of a saw near the handle mean?
   A. Number of teeth (points) to the inch.
12. Q. What are two ways of joining baseboards in the corner of a room?
    A. Miter, cope, butt, dado (square).
15. Q. What do you call the end post used to support stair rails?
    A. Newel.

Figure 2.8.   Items from Trade Test for General Carpenter. These questions are intended to be administered orally to determine whether an applicant has the necessary knowledge of the skilled trade for which he is applying. (From L. A. Thompson *et al.*, *Interview Aids and Trade Test Questions for Employment Offices*, 1946.)

when it is desirable to find out how much skill or knowledge an individual has. In this case, he does not expect, or even especially want, his applicants to be skilled packers when they are hired. He simply wants them to be able to learn the job after training. For that reason, he prefers an aptitude rather than a trade test for the job.

All the tests which the psychologist has placed on his tentative list are reasonably reliable, suitable, and are either well standardized or can be easily standardized. These considerations plus indications from previous validation studies or from test analyses show that there is a reasonable chance that the tests will be valid for this job.

A requirement of a good industrial selection program is that it should cover adequately the requirements of the job. The requirement in this job of persistence has been covered by the interview, supplemented by the personal history data given by the application blank and checked by the use of references. Hand span is covered by the measurement of those physical properties of the applicant. Spatial relations ability is involved in the Minnesota Paper Form Board. Perceptual speed, similarly, is the major factor in the Minnesota Vocational Test for Clerical Workers. On the tentative list are two tests for dexterity in the use of the hands together—the Minnesota Rate of Manipulation Test and the Brown Spool-Packer Test.

Both dexterity tests look as if they'd have a reasonable chance of working out. However, the testing time should be as short as possible, and it would obviously be wasteful to include two tests designed to measure the same ability. In other words, regardless of how promising the tests are individually, if they are likely to be too closely related to one another, it is wasteful to include both of them and only the better should be retained.

The Brown Spool-Packer Test has the advantage of "face validity." It is reasonably short, and otherwise quite practical, except for the requirement that it must be administered individually. It has not, however, been shown to be predictive of success on packing jobs, so that it is only a good guess that it may be useful. The psychologist fears that it so closely resembles packing work that previous experience in other packing jobs might give some applicants an unfair advantage and improve their scores. This would make the test a mixed aptitude and trade test. Some people would do well because of experience and some because of aptitude. If this should happen, scores would be impossible to interpret. On the other hand, the Minnesota Rate of Manipulation Test is less appealing to the subjects, and looks less as if it is related to the job. It takes a little longer (even when use of the test is limited to the two subsections of the test involving use of both hands) and must also be administered individually. In its defense are some very strong arguments. In the first place, it is somewhat more reliable than the Brown Test.

It is much less likely to be subject to distortion of scores by practice on the job. Previous studies have shown that it is quite successful in predicting skill in several different kinds of packing jobs. It is a more widely used test, so that he may have the use of information from a variety of testing situations to aid him in the administration of the test.

With these factors in mind, our psychologist decides to start with this test and to eliminate the Brown Test from his tentative list. His selection of tests has been made on the basis of a careful evaluation of all the information available both on tests and on the job. The care with which the tentative list is selected determines the eventual success of the whole selection procedure.

Validation of Items in Selection Procedure

Up to this point the psychologist has been choosing tests by intelligent guesswork. However carefully he has evaluated the tests, the process is still just a very highly trained kind of guessing. He must follow his preliminary selection by proof or disproof of his guesses. He must check his tests and other selection techniques to see if they will be of any value in this situation, i.e., he must validate them. He must find out which, if any, are successful and how he may best combine effective devices for an integrated selection system. Amateurs in the use of tests, as well as quacks, have frequently felt that their judgment is so infallible that they need not bother with the tedious validation procedure. It is only when management and employees demand proof of the effectiveness of the procedures, both in dollars-and-cents savings for management and employees and in increased satisfaction for both, that the absolute necessity for proper validation becomes apparent. All the procedures including the interview must equally be subjected to critical analysis, as no one procedure may be assumed to be useful just because someone in authority likes the idea. Without validation *no one* can know whether or not any procedure actually helps to select successful employees.

The validation procedure, of course, consists of comparing results of the various selection devices with the criterion which has been established for success on the job. In order to have a clear-cut validation of a selection procedure, it is necessary that the applicants be tested and interviewed *before* they are hired, that they be hired without regard to the results of the testing and interview procedures, and that their success *after* the completion of the training period be compared with the pre-employment results. This use of applicants for test validation unfortunately involves a time delay while a sufficient number of applicants are hired, trained, and brought to the point of proficiency so that a criterion score can be obtained from them. On a job such as the packing job, this delay involves only a few months, and is not seriously inconveniencing, especially since the company has managed to survive under its present hiring policy for a good many years and will probably not collapse in the short intervening time.

In some very complex jobs, involving long learning periods, this delay becomes truly serious. In these cases, it is sometimes useful to get an advance idea about how well the proposed selection devices will work by checking them with workers who are already employed. This procedure sometimes enables the psychologist to eliminate certain tests which show no relationship whatsoever to the criterion for this group of experienced workers, and thus to cut down on his testing and interviewing time for the applicant group. Validation on experienced operators, however, is severely limited in its usefulness. In the first place, if the good experienced workers tend to score high on a test while the poor workers score low, there is no guarantee that the difference is not due to differences in the way they have learned this particular job. This is particularly true of tests which closely resemble the job. Because training on the job may have seriously affected scores on the tests, the psychologist cannot assume that the results which he has obtained in testing experienced workers will be obtained when he tests people without experience. What he wants his testing to do is to predict *before* employment how well an individual will do *after* training on the job.

The second reason why experienced workers do not make a satisfactory group upon whom to validate a test is that some experienced employees are not as well motivated to succeed in the tests as are applicants. Their jobs do not depend upon success and they do not all exert maximum effort. An even more serious difficulty, however, is that experienced employees are a selected group, not representative of the kind of people who apply for the work. Many of the applicants have tried the job, have failed or have not liked the work, and have left the company. The group of experienced workers, then, represents those who were good enough at the work to stay on the job. It is asking a good deal of a test to require it to separate the best workers in the experienced group from those who are only fairly good—but good enough to be there to be tested.

The psychologist feels that it is not necessary to bother the present employees for a preliminary validation of test results and proceeds directly to check his judgments with applicants. He uses his tests, plus the interview procedure and the application blank he has set up on a group of applicants for the packing job. The employment policy remains unchanged from the policy in effect before testing was started. Applicants are hired without regard to test scores, and all are given an equal chance to succeed. After the learning period is completed, criterion figures are gathered for each of the new employees. The psychologist relates these figures to the predictions which were made on the basis of the various selection devices.

On the basis of this study, he picks out the valid techniques. For the sake of the illustration, let us assume that he obtains results closely in line with those obtained in other similar investigations (although over and over again psychologists have learned that each situation is different and what may work in one situation may be of no use in another). If everything comes out according to expectations, then, the results will be somewhat like this . . .

PERSONAL HISTORY

This is one area where the psychologist does use the information from experienced employees, since he can check the responses on the application blanks filled out before employment with the later success on the job both for those who stayed with the company and for those who left. He separates all the old application blanks into two groups—those who were hired and who produced at least as much as the average of the group, and those who were hired and failed. He then examines the application blank responses for each of the groups, and picks out questions that separate the successful from the unsuccessful. He finds only a few. First of all, more married applicants succeeded than unmarried ones. Secondly, applicants who had worked in industries in another, larger town within the preceding two years did not work out as well as those who had remained at home. Lastly, female employees stayed somewhat longer than male employees, if they were 30 years of age or older. No other items seem to have been useful. To be sure that these items will be predictive with the kind of applicant the firm is now getting, the psychologist checks the results for the new group which has just completed training, and finds that the same factors seem to be operating. These checks are technical and statistical in nature; their net result is to discover how much better than chance the prediction by the device will be—what its batting average is. A score set up by weighting the application blank items can be used just as if it were a score from a test.

INTERVIEWS

In this case, the psychologist checks the ratings by his interviewers against the criterion by making a statistical analysis. He finds that these results are satisfactory, and that an applicant rated "outstanding" had at least five times as good a chance of succeeding as did one who was rated as "unsatisfactory, normally unemployable." This is another successful device.

REFERENCES

Since these were to be used only to make the application blank items more reliable, and furthermore, it is found that applicants have not previously falsified the four items from the application blank that proved to be useful for selection (marital status, previous experience in city industries, age, and sex), there is no need to use references.

TESTS

The Minnesota Rate of Manipulation, Turning Test (Two-Handed) predicts success on the job moderately well. If the applicants had been picked on the basis of these test scores, more of them would certainly have succeeded than without selection. The prediction of this test is not nearly as good as that of the interview, however. The Minnesota Rate of Manipulation, Two-Handed Placing and Turning, is a test involving picking up blocks, turning them over, and placing them in holes with both hands. It does better than the other part of the Minnesota Rate of Manipulation Test. Looking at these results, the psychologist immediately checks to see how closely the scores on the two parts of the test agree. He finds that persons who do well on one part of the test tend to do well on the other part, and that both portions are quite reliable, so that he may as well use only the more predictive portion of the test. In the Minnesota Clerical Test both portions prove to be successful, to a much larger extent than the previously investigated tests. They are quite reliable, and not too closely overlapping, so that both halves are worth while. In the Minnesota Paper Form Board, the relation between test scores and the criterion is fairly good, so that it seems warranted to retain the test, although it is the longest in time of the tests being used. Hand span measurements prove to have almost no relationship with success on the job, so they are eliminated from consideration. The psychologist's original analysis of job requirements was apparently wrong in this respect, and hand span, at least as he was measuring it, was useless for predicting job success. He checks to make sure, now, that his selection devices do not overlap one another too greatly, and finds that there is a reasonably low relationship among them. He knows, then, that they are not predicting the same aspects of job success.

Combination of Selection Devices

Obviously, the psychologist cannot now set up a procedure by which he eliminates applicants who are included in the bottom half of *each* of these test, application, and interview scores. If he did so, practically everyone would be eliminated and, although he would hire no failures, he also would hire no successes! By the use of statistical devices, however, he can set up the tests so that they can be combined with the interview and application blank for most effective screening. The total time for the whole process of screening is less than one hour.

He makes sure that the testing and interviewing are standardized and the process runs smoothly. He also establishes local norms or standards for comparison of applicants. Since management must foot the bill for the services of the psychologist, it is natural that the results of psychological methods be evaluated not only in terms of the intangible benefits they will produce, but also in dollars-and-cents return on the investment. With these factors in mind, the psychologist prepares a report to management, outlining the advantages and disadvantages of the proposed procedure. When he receives the approval of management, he makes sure that current employees and supervisors understand the new employment method. Since they have coöperated in many of the preliminary stages of the preparation of the program, their continued support is easily obtained and the selection procedure is ready to go into effect. Applicants for the job are given a full explanation of the reasons for the employment procedures, and of the value to them of better prediction of job success.

Much misunderstanding surrounds the use of psychological selection procedures, most of it based on early abuses and failure to apply sound psychological principles and to convince workers, unions, and management of the legitimate functions of these methods. In recent years it has become more evident to both workers and management that it is to their mutual advantage for persons not to be placed on jobs for which they are ill suited and at which they will be both unproductive and dissatisfied. Proper evaluation in the employment office can result in higher earnings by employees, which are of value both to them and to the community; higher production of the product, benefiting the economy in general and the manufacturer in particular; fewer dissatisfied employees and fewer who have wasted their time and effort on a job which they cannot do. The proper person in the proper job can also result in better community relations, lowered overhead and training costs, increased profits, improved quality, and a lower selling price for the product. The general decrease in human and material waste which results is desirable for all components of any economic system.

The procedure has gone very smoothly in our example. If we were to chronicle an actual case instead of a hypothetical one, we would find the procedure beset by difficulties, interruptions, and frustrations for the psychologist. Employees being used in the study would ask for leaves of absence; some would quit and return to work after a few weeks in the middle of the study; some would want to transfer to another department where a friend was working; and a wide variety of personal, factory, local, state, national, and international crises and acts of God would interfere. It is part of the training of the psychologist to be able to guard against the distortion of his data by such factors. We have not meant to imply that our psychologist's activities should serve as a step-by-step guide to successful selection of employees. It is the principles upon which he relies in making his decision which will remain the same from situation to situation and constitute his professional stock in trade.

The task is almost completed—except that later checks must be made to see that the procedure is working and to evaluate its weaknesses and possible areas of improvement. Periodically, norms must be revised and a new check must be made to make sure that conditions in the job or in the employment situation have not changed, altering the relationships between the selection procedures and later success on the job.

Results

After the new procedure has gone into effect and the results have been evaluated, the psychologist is able to present his report. Most of the employees hired under the new procedure are earning enough to make bonus money, so that their average earnings have gone up sharply, as has the production of the department. The turnover rate in the department has been reduced by half, and is declining as the employees hired under the old system gradually leave. The reduction in turnover alone is sufficient to pay the costs of the program, and to finance its maintenance. Morale in the department is reported to be much higher, and the supervisors are now able to give their attention to other aspects of their job of facilitating satisfaction and productivity in the department.

Summary of Steps In Devising a Selection Procedure

The psychologist in our example has established a procedure for the selection of packers in this factory, under the conditions now operating. He has done his best to pick his evaluative devices intelligently, and has checked each of them against a reliable and representative criterion of success on the job. He has compared them with each other, and combined them into an integrated program. He is prepared to continue improvements and modification of the methods he has devised. In establishing this integrated plan he has made use of many kinds of training and experience—psychological, statistical, and industrial. The results of his work, if properly applied, work to the common benefit of management, workers, and the community.

SELECTION, PLACEMENT, AND GUIDANCE

In the actual situation, it is not usually necessary to send away from the factory door many applicants just because they fail to pass the screening process for a particular job. Most of those who fail for one job will nevertheless be perfectly satisfactory employees in other jobs requiring different abilities. Here the concentration will be upon placement rather than upon selection. The manner in which a variety of tests are combined to predict success on a number of jobs is too complex for discussion here. Before such a program can be developed, howver, it is necessary that the effectiveness of selection devices be established for each job in just such a detailed manner as was followed for the packers.

It is in the placement and guidance aspects of the use of psychological methods of evaluation that the limitations of these methods become most evident. When we are dealing with groups of people, as for example when we are picking from 100 persons those 50 most likely to succeed in a given job, our selection devices are useful if they enable us merely to do better than other nonpsychological methods. But when we concentrate upon the individual, advising him what to do with his life (guidance) we need greater accuracy from our predictive devices. Most of the tests used for the selection of packers are not accurate enough, for example, to form an adequate basis for advising a specific individual to train for that occupation as contrasted with all other occupations. In the selection situation—or in the situation where tests are used for placement within a given factory—the applicant has already made up his mind what he wants to do, and the tests merely give us a means of telling him the probability that he will succeed in one of several available jobs. In the guidance situation, on the other hand, tests must be very good to assume the responsibility of deciding the future course of action of the individual.

Careful and intelligent validation of selection devices will, in the future, give the guidance counselor a much better basis for his work, so that he may devise more reliable and more valid tests suitable for individual prediction. Until the day when industrial psychologists greatly improve the tests for industrial occupations no one can honestly say that he can "infallibly place the square pegs in the square holes and the round ones in the round holes," but satisfactory use of tests and interviews can immensely decrease monetary costs and increase human satisfaction with work.

SUMMARY

One aspect of the psychologist's work in industry is the construction of satisfactory techniques for the selection and placement of new employees. The techniques which are available are interviews, personal history data, references, and tests of various kinds. Any one of these devices is satisfactory if it is valid for the particular job, reliable, standardized, and suitable to the specific situation. The particular techniques which are chosen depend upon the judgment of the psychologist who tries to match the selection devices to the requirements of the job, and upon the relation which they show to success on the job and to each other. The effectiveness of the devices depends in large part upon the manner in which they are *combined*, since a *single* selection device seldom covers all the important aspects of a job. Where traditional selection and placement procedures have proved inadequate, properly constructed evaluative procedures have been shown to be successful not only in saving money for management but in increasing the wages and satisfaction of employees. Psychological techniques in this area are not by any means a panacea for industrial ills, and their construction requires training, experience, and hard work. When properly used, however, they should form an integrated part of a progressive program for the utilization of manpower.

SUGGESTED READINGS

1. Dorcus, R. M., and Jones, M. L., *A Handbook of Employee Selection*. New York: McGraw-Hill, 1950. A summary of the published literature on the selection of employees. It contains abstracts of studies which are invaluable to anyone attempting to evaluate a test. The interested student will find that a scanning of this literature will give him an estimate of the kind of work that has been done in the area.

2. Fear, R. A., and Jordan, B., *Employee Evaluation Manual for Interviewers*. New York: Psychological Corporation, 1943. The authors present an outline of their procedure for interviewing and for evaluating the results of interviews.

3. Ghiselli, E. E., and Brown, C. W., *Personnel and Industrial Psychology*. New York: McGraw-Hill, 1948. A thorough, elementary presentation of selection and placement techniques. Very little discussion is given to specific tests and their applications.
4. Gulliksen, H., *Theory of Mental Tests*. New York: Wiley, 1950. An advanced text in the construction and analysis of tests giving the basic techniques of test construction.
5. Harrell, T., *Industrial Psychology*. New York: Rinehart, 1949. Includes discussion of military applications of industrial selection procedures, as well as other recent studies.
6. Maier, N. R. F., *Psychology in Industry*. New York: Houghton-Mifflin, 1946. A systematic, well-written summary of techniques and theory in the field, at an elementary level.
7. Thorndike, R. L., *Personnel Selection: Test and Measurement Techniques*. New York: Wiley, 1949. Specifically designed to cover the testing aspects of industrial selection and placement, this is a very good and recent summary of recommended procedures. Discussions of administration of a testing program are especially good. This text assumes a knowledge of basic statistical methods.
8. Tiffin, J., *Industrial Psychology*. New York: Prentice-Hall, 2d ed., 1947. Discussion of many specific applications of psychological tests, with special emphasis on measurement of visual performance.

Chapter 3

Industrial Psychology: Efficiency in Work

by THOMAS A. RYAN

Introduction

Efficiency

EFFORT AND ITS MEASUREMENT
Muscle Tension
Pulse-Product
Electrical Resistance of Skin
ENERGY CONSUMPTION AND ITS MEASUREMENT
FATIGUE AND ITS MEASUREMENT
Rate of Performance
Physiological Changes
Fatigue Tests
Qualitative Changes
INDIRECT MEASURES OF EFFICIENCY
Long-Term Production Trends
Turnover Rates
Absenteeism

Efficiency and Motivation
MONOTONY OR BOREDOM

Efficient Methods of Work
MOTION STUDY

Some Specific Factors in Efficiency
NOISE
TEMPERATURE
LIGHTING

Accident Control

Training Methods

Summary

Suggested Readings

INTRODUCTION

Once a worker is employed in a particular job, both management and the worker are interested in his effective training in the work, in the proper evaluation of his performance so that he will be paid a fair wage and promoted when he deserves it, in maintaining the physical conditions of work so that he can work most efficiently, in finding the best and most economical methods of doing the work, and in maintaining his interest and motivation to perform the task.

Some of these problems are almost entirely psychological problems; that is, they have to do with factors in human behavior. Others are a mixture of psychological and nonpsychological. For example, the search for the most adequate method of doing a job is partly a problem in engineering—of deciding on the most satisfactory tools and materials to be used in the work. But so long as someone is using the tools or machines, it is necessary to consider the adaptation of these tools to the characteristics of the operator. It does no good, for example, to design an airplane which outclasses all other planes in its aerodynamic qualities, if only one person in a million can operate it without crashing.

Before we can discuss the contributions which the psychologist can make to the solutions of these problems it is necessary to decide more exactly upon what is meant by some of the terms and problems we have mentioned. We want to achieve *effective* training methods, we want to work *efficiently,* we want to find *economical* methods of doing the work. These are terms which many of us use frequently, but how often do we stop to consider exactly what they mean? Do we measure the effectiveness of a training method in terms of how many dollars it costs to train a new worker, in terms of how fast the worker learns, or in terms of how much effort is required to learn? If it is measured in terms of monetary cost, do we include the cost of attempting to train those who fall by the wayside, or do we consider only the cost of training those who ultimately make satisfactory progress? One method may cost more than another but the average level of performance achieved may be greater. How do we allow for both the cost of training and the level of performance achieved?

With this example and many others like it we become aware that all three of the terms *effective, efficient,* and *economical* imply an evaluation of a method, a situation, or a person, but they do not clearly indicate the basis upon which the evaluation is to be made. Before we can talk about an efficient method of work, therefore, we must decide upon what is meant by an efficient method, then we must find ways of evaluating the method from the point of view that we have decided upon. The point of view which we choose should not be arbitrary, or chosen only because it is an easy way out, but should be chosen as representing the most widely useful and meaningful approach to the problem.

EFFICIENCY

We shall consider the term (total) efficiency to mean the ratio between what the worker accomplishes and what he puts into the work (his input or cost of work). The input should include the energy used in doing the work, the effort which the individual puts forth, the time which he devotes to the task, the fatigue resulting from the work, any adverse effects upon his health or general adjustment, and any risks of accident entailed in the work. We shall also have to reckon the satisfaction which the individual gets from his accomplishment as a part of the output, or else consider lack of satisfaction or dissatisfaction as a part of the cost of the work. The terms *effective* and *economical* will be used here as synonyms for total efficiency.

This point of view on efficiency entails difficulties, as we shall see in considering the various problems in this field. By arbitrarily refusing to consider some aspects of the cost of work we could make our task much easier, but we cannot eliminate these costs to the individual by ignoring them. They exist and must be taken into account somehow.

An extreme short cut which is often used is to ignore all factors in the cost of work altogether, except for the time element, and to equate efficiency with rate of work. This is the equivalent of saying that the most efficient method of walking to work is to race at top speed even though we arrive in a state of collapse. In the long run, this short-cut technique of using rate of work as a measure of efficiency would become equivalent to our more complex measure. Deterioration of health would eventually slow the worker down. Excessive fatigue might eventually affect his rate of work. Even dissatisfaction with working conditions may have its effects upon rate of work which are not offset by the pay incentives. The difficulty with this approach in terms of speed is not that it is completely incompatible with the more complex approach we have suggested, but that it is even less practical. To evaluate a method we would have to have average rates of work over periods of years. Temporary increases would not indicate what would happen in the long run, and it would be dangerous to assume that they would.

The result has been that those who have looked upon efficiency from the point of view of speed have, in practice, considered only short-term rates, usually without clearly analyzing the consequences of such a method. One of the criticisms which has been raised against self-styled "efficiency experts" has been that they have too often taken this shortsighted point of view.

In the physical and biological sciences, efficiency has referred to a ratio between useful output (measured in terms of *physical* work in units of foot-pounds or the equivalent) and input in terms of the energy (calories or British Thermal Units) used in doing the work. This also is a more limited approach to efficiency than the one we are proposing. In some situations, the energy cost is correlated with the other factors which we have mentioned, such as effort and fatigue. This is especially true in heavy muscular work. In lighter skilled tasks and mental work, however, the energy consumption is low in comparison to the effort and fatigue and is not closely correlated with them. We must therefore maintain a distinction between mechanical efficiency which takes only energy cost into account, and the broader notion of total efficiency.

One of the basic contributions which psychologists and physiologists can make to industrial problems is the development of measures of effort, fatigue, dissatisfaction, and other aspects of the cost of work to the individual (i.e., all aspects of input, which is the denominator in our definition of total efficiency as output over input). Once these measures are available, many different problems can be solved by the use of the same methods. Until these methods are developed and validated some of the key problems in the field of industrial psychology can be solved only by guess work and hunches.

The problems involved in this kind of research are complex and technical. We can only sketch some of the main techniques which are now in use. We shall attempt now to indicate how certain of the variables that enter into the denominator in our definition of total efficiency are measured.

Effort and Its Measurement

The most obvious method of evaluating effort (one of the factors in our denominator) would be to ask the worker to estimate how hard he is working. This is the direct approach, since by effort we mean the individual's feeling of "working hard," "experiencing difficulty," and so on. Since this is the direct method, it must ultimately furnish us with the criterion which is used in validating other methods. Nevertheless, it is not a satisfactory method for practical use. In the first place, the worker must depend upon memory for comparing his present effort with that which he experienced last week or two months ago when he was using a different method or working under different conditions. There is no absolute scale of effort to which he can refer. Secondly, in some conditions he may not want to report truthfully.

For these reasons it is desirable to find other indicators of an individual's effort. Obviously, effort must be related to some internal physiological changes, certainly changes in the nervous system, and probably also changes in other bodily systems. The intact nervous system not being very accessible for study by present methods, the first search has been in other parts of the body.

This field of research is still in its exploratory stages, so we shall indicate here only some of the main directions in which this search is progressing. It will be noticed that there is a great similarity between the bodily changes studied in evaluating effort and those involved in emotion. This is not surprising if we compare feelings of effort and of emotion. Both can be considered as being a form of moblization of the various bodily resources. The main difference is probably in the kind of motivation involved, and in the kind of resistances to be overcome. Even in these respects, the distinction between work and emotion is not sharp, work often being carried on in situations which involve fear, insecurity, dislike for the work or fellow workers, and so on. Three typical indices of effort which are being extensively studied are the following:

MUSCLE TENSION

It is possible to amplify the electrical activity of muscles so that even the slightest contraction is detectable. It is found that this electrical activity is increased as a task becomes more difficult, or if the task is carried out under disturbing conditions such as loud noise. This is true even when the task does not require the use of the muscles whose activity is recorded. An individual's reaction time is speeded up as the level of muscular activity increases from a low level of relaxation to a higher level. (See Fig. 3.1.)

The main problem in the use of muscular action potentials consists in finding a method of measurement which can be applied to normal working situations and tasks. Most of the studies so far have been carried out in the laboratory with subjects who are relaxed before the work begins, and conditions are carefully controlled so as to eliminate extraneous disturbances. The older amplifiers were also very sensitive to electrical interference from other equipment unless the experiments were carried out in an electrically shielded room. Many of these difficulties are now being overcome, so that the tension index will be tested under more normal working conditions.

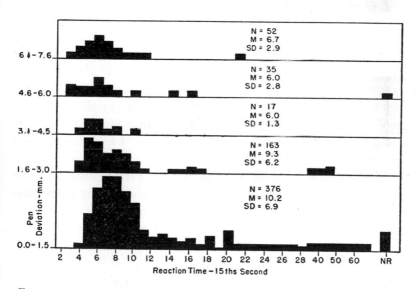

FIGURE 3.1. Frequency Distributions of Pen Deviations (Muscle Potential) in Relation to Reaction Time for 14 College Students. (From R. C. Travis and J. L. Kennedy, Prediction and control of alertness, *J. comp. physiol. Psychol.*, 1949, *42*:45–57. Courtesy of the American Psychological Association and the *Journal of Comparative and Physiological Psychology*.)

PULSE-PRODUCT

The pulse rate alone is not found to be very sensitive to changes in effort. The rate does increase during work, even in mental work with a minimum of muscular activity. To be useful, however, it should also be possible to correlate the pulse rate with changes in the working conditions. This has not been possible. There is some indication, however, that if we take both the rate and the pressure of the pulse into account, we can find a more sensitive relationship to effort. The *pulse-product* (the product of the rate and the pressure) is an indication of the total amount of working being done by the heart at a given time. There are some preliminary results indicating that this product is related to effort in mental work as well as more active muscular tasks.

ELECTRICAL RESISTANCE OF THE SKIN

It has long been known that the electrical resistance of the skin (usually measured on the palms) drops suddenly during startle or other sudden emotional episodes. This change reflects the activity of the sweat glands which are controlled by the autonomic nervous system. A measure of skin resistance is often a part of the device known as the lie detector (p. 138), a lie being reflected in a sharp drop in resistance level.

More recently it has been found that the average level of resistance over a period of time (as distinguished from momentary fluctuations) reflects the degree of alertness or effort of the subject, and is closely related to the overall level of muscular tension in the body. For example, the resistance is high during sleep, falls upon awakening, falls further when the individual arises, and so on. Of special interest here is the fact that the resistance falls when an individual is given a problem to solve and that it rises again on solution (Fig. 3.2). There is experimental evidence that the average level during work upon a task is related to how hard the individual is working.

Apart from the technical difficulties in using these indicators for

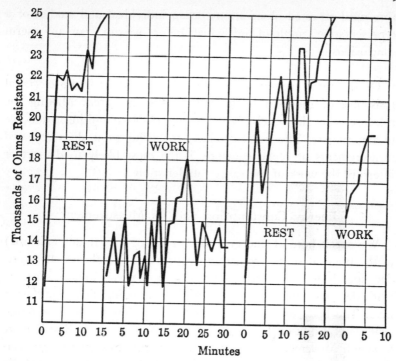

FIGURE 3.2. Skin Resistance Changes Before and During Mental Work, and During the Recovery Period Following Mental Work; Record of One Subject. (From an unpublished thesis by T. K. Kirby, 1942, in the University of Cincinnati Library. Courtesy of T. K. Kirby.)

practical studies in the field, there is one additional precaution in their use which must be stressed. All of these indicators reflect a general physiological state of the organism, and are subject to a great many influences. If we wish to use them to study some particular problem, for example finding the best and least effortful method of doing a job, we must realize that many other influences are operating at any given time. The results we obtain on a particular individual at a given time may be the result of what someone else said to the individual before he started work, the anticipation of a party that night, or his health at the time. We will therefore need repeated observations on an individual and studies of a representative sample of individuals before we can draw any useful conclusions.

Of the three measures which we have described, the electrical resistance of the skin is the most easily measured. Making the measurements also involves the least interruption and inconvenience to the subject. The pulse-product, requiring as it does repeated measurements of blood pressure, is the most likely to distract or interrupt the work of the subject under study

Energy Consumption and Its Measurement

We speak here of energy (another factor in our denominator) in the physical sense—something expressible in calories. In everyday speech we often use the word in a psychological sense as equivalent to effort. For clarity we are avoiding this latter usage here. The body uses energy continuously, even in its most quiescent state. Additional energy is required to sit up, and still more to stand. Movement increases the consumption of energy still further. When we measure the mechanical efficiency of the body in performing a task, we are concerned primarily with muscular activities and with work whose outcome can be expressed in physical units such as the foot-pound (the work done in raising a pound of weight one foot). Efficiency is then proportional to the ratio of the work accomplished in a given time to the energy used in doing the work. Usually we count into the energy consumption only the additional amounts needed for the work beyond the energy which would be consumed whether the individual were working or not. In other words, we take some period of rest as a point of comparison, subtracting the energy used during rest from the total energy used during work.

The most practical way of measuring the energy used by an individual is by determining the amount of oxygen he has taken into the body during a period of time. His oxygen intake must keep pace with the bodily requirements, and very little is stored in the body. The oxygen, in turn, is closely proportional to the amount of energy released in the body. We shall not go into the various methods of measuring oxygen consumption except to say that the subject wears a mask which permits him to breathe air from one source and exhale though another channel. The mask may be attached to a tank which has a device for direct reading of the amount of oxygen used, or it may be attached to a bag which the subject carries on his back if the task requires locomotion.

Work, as defined by the physicist, implies movement, and is measured by the distance traveled, multiplied by the force required to move. There are many tasks, however, where the outcome is not meaningfully expressed in foot-pounds. In most cases, the output is expressed in terms of the natural units of the task—square feet of wall painted, miles walked, number of bricks laid, and so on. (See Table 3.1.) If we could dispense with a strictly physical notion of work in muscular tasks such as walking or bricklaying, why could we not extend this to mental work? (By mental work it should be reëmphasized we mean only that the muscular activities

TABLE 3.1. Cost of Work in Lifting Loads by Crank
(Calories per Meter-Kilogram)

Height of Crank Axis (in cm)	Load (Meter-Kilograms per Turn)				
	6.5	13.0	19.5	26.0	32.5
55.3	27.8	16.5	13.8	14.4	16.5
82.7	26.1	15.5	13.9	13.5	14.6
114.3	17.0	13.5	12.4	12.1	14.2
162.2	22.2	18.4	18.5	20.5	22.2

SOURCE: E. Atzler, Probleme und Aufgaben der Arbeitsphysiologie, *Ergebnisse der Physiologie*, 1928, 27:720.

are not central to the task. As we have seen, the muscles are active even in solving arithmetic problems "in the head," but in this they are used as auxiliary equipment, and the movements or forces exerted by the muscles are not the goal of the activity.) It is true that we could express output in terms of problems solved, letters dictated, words spoken, and so on. We could also measure the energy per problem or per letter. The difficulty is not in principle but in fact. Various experimenters have attempted to find the energy consumed in solving mental arithmetic problems and the like. The amounts of energy required are very small in comparison to the energy required in even a moderate amount of muscular work.

As a result, is is very difficult to measure the energy required for mental tasks, and it is also doubtful whether the amount of energy used reflects any important aspects of the cost of work to the individual. It is obvious that the amount of effort involved in solving complex multiplication problems without pencil and paper is intense. Yet, if the individual remains relatively motionless while he is working, the energy consumption will be only a few percent greater than the amount used in the resting state. It is for this reason that we must be careful to distinguish effort from energy in the physical sense.

The principal use of energy measurements is therefore for muscular activities in which the exertion of force is focal in the task and it is not applicable to mental work where the muscular activity is incidental. There has been relatively little study of the energy requirements of muscular tasks in which there is much skill in timing and coördination and where the exertion of force is secondary. The operation of many machines would fit in this classification. The use of energy as a measure of cost of work in this kind of activity still remains to be validated.

Fatigue and Its Measurement

Fatigue, like effort, is in the denominator in our definition of total efficiency and obviously must be reckoned in the cost of work. Like effort, the term fatigue originally referred to feelings or experiences of the individual, feelings of weariness, tiredness, or exhaustion. Feelings of tiredness, however, are very difficult to quantify or compare accurately. Thus, if a worker has used two different methods of doing a job it is difficult for him to make an accurate comparison of the degrees of tiredness resulting from the two different methods. As an illustration, suppose you try to compare your condition after doing a certain kind of work on days when the weather is cool with your feelings on days when the weather is warm. Even if we could be sure that all factors other than the weather were the same on the two days, the comparison would still be very difficult to make, unless the effects were extremely different in the two cases.

Aside from the difficulties of quantifying feelings of tiredness, there is also a real possibility that these feelings do not tell the whole story of the cumulative effects of work. Often in children and sometimes in adults we observe someone who insists that he does not feel tired, but who staggers when he walks, makes foolish mistakes in his work, gets angry over trivialities, or becomes silly or euphoric. We may be inclined to say that he is "really fatigued, but doesn't know it." We tend to speak as though fatigue were a general condition of the body which may be reflected in feelings of tiredness, but also in other ways such as loss of the ability to work, emotional sensitivity, inability to carry on other activities, and so on.

It is quite legitimate to use the term *fatigue* as a collective name for all of these varied effects of work. It is an error, however, to assume that because we use a single term we must be referring to a unitary phenomenon. These various effects of work do not necessarily have their basis in the same internal bodily changes, but may instead depend upon quite independent physiological processes and changes. The only things which these physiological changes may have in common is that they all build up during the course of work in differing proportions depending upon the conditions and the nature of the work. If there is a common core of physiological change which always results from work it remains to be discovered. The unitary nature of fatigue is something to be proved by careful research, not something to be assumed simply because we have a word, *fatigue,* which has such broad application. The following methods, while inadequate for industrial purposes, attempt to measure fatigue and will be briefly described.

RATE OF PERFORMANCE

Physiologists, who were first to study fatigue experimentally, singled out changes in capacity to perform the work as the central feature of fatigue. In working with a single muscle in isolation, this is the most obvious change which could be observed. Under carefully controlled laboratory conditions it was also possible to get the subject to work nearly at his limit of capacity on simple muscular tasks. It was thought at first that this kind of experiment would lead to the discovery of the basic nature of all fatigue. This hope was never fulfilled, although the experiments did throw much light on fatigue resulting from heavy muscular work.

A modification of the above approach to fatigue through change in capacity to perform is often made in industry. The argument which is used or implied runs somewhat as follows: "If fatigue reduces capacity to perform we should expect performance rate to decline toward the end of the day." Some go further than this and decide: "Since we cannot measure capacity directly, but only in terms of performance, why not define fatigue as a decline in performance rate as a result of previous work?" Under this definition, if a worker maintains his pace throughout the working day he has shown no fatigue.

There would be no objection to any arbitrary limited definition of fatigue if other effects of work were taken into account under some other term. What has happened, however, is that a limited definition of fatigue in terms of reduced production has been adopted, and then all other effects which come under the broader meaning of fatigue are forgotten or ignored. In fact, there is a question whether actual performance in the factory situation actually reflects changes in capacity, to say nothing of other effects.

In the normal situation, we do not work anywhere near our limit of performance. If we did we should not be able to continue very long. Instead we allow a substantial safety factor. Under the influence of a daily quota, the fact that we know when the work is to end, and a variety of other factors, we may allow a greater safety margin in the morning than we do toward the end of the day. As a result our performance may remain level or even increase with time, even while capacity is declining.

We should expect that the nearer our actual rate of performance approaches our capacity the greater would be the *effort* required to maintain the pace. Thus fatigue would be reflected in greater effort for any given rate of performance. If, therefore, we were able to secure accurate measures of effort, we could also apply these measures to a study of fatigue. It certainly would be a more sensible approach than that which considers only the output rate by itself.

PHYSIOLOGICAL CHANGES

This involves the measurement of various physiological changes resulting from work, e.g., the numbers of white blood cells, amounts of various chemicals in the blood, analysis of urine for products of certain glands. Urinalysis as indicated is one example of the use of physiological measures for the study of fatigue. Chemicals, which have their origin in the cortex of the adrenal gland, appear in the urine in varying amounts depending upon the activities of the subject. When laboratory subjects performed a task much like operating airplane controls, requiring constant attention for periods of several hours, it was found that their steroid output at the end was higher than was normal for that time of day. It was also found that pilots showed increased steroid output which was correlated with the number of hours they had flown during the day. At present it appears that the steroid output index is a promising measure of the amount of stress involved in a task. How useful it will be for the analysis of factory work, in which the stress is of a different kind, still remains to be seen.

FATIGUE TESTS

These are methods of studying the effect of the work upon ability to perform other tasks with varying degrees of resemblance to the original work. For example, measuring the individual's ability to perform a test of muscular coördination after a day's work as compared with his performance before work and as compared with his performance on days when he does not work. Another example of a fatigue test is a test developed to investigate the effects of visual work (reading, fine inspection, etc.) under various conditions of illumination. The ordinary oculists' tests of visual acuity fail to show any effects of fatigue, probably because they do not require continuous adjustment. The subject can get a good score by pulling himself together for short intervals and resting between these intervals. For this reason, Ferree and Rand developed a test which measures ability to *maintain* visual adjustment. It is known as the *"l-i"* test because these two letters were used in the test. The subject had to look at these two letters under standard conditions and try to see them clearly and continuously. Whenever his visual adjustment slipped so that the letters blurred (for example, when the *l* and the *i* no longer looked different from one another) the subject pressed a key and held it down until his vision cleared up.

This test has been useful for studying the effects of amount, color, and distribution of illumination. The principal objection that has been raised against it is that the subjects have to be carefully trained and practiced in distinguishing between clear and blurred vision. Most of the studies have therefore used only a small number of subjects.

Dozens of different tasks have been tried out as fatigue tests at one time or another in studying the fatigue resulting from many different kinds of work. Only a small number have shown consistent effects of work, either consistent from time to time for the same individual or consistent from individual to individual.

The main difficulty with fatigue tests, however, is that even if we find a test which shows the effects of work in a consistent manner, it is difficult to tell how important these effects are. For example, suppose we find the *"l-i"* test is 10 percent better under one illumination than it is under another. This shows that the first illumination is better, but whether the difference is enough to justify a large expenditure to change the illumination it is not possible to say. Questions of this kind cannot be answered until we have much more fundamental knowledge of the nature of the effects of work, in other words, until we know what changes in the bodily system are reflected in the fatigue test, and how important these changes are in the general economy of the individual.

QUALITATIVE CHANGES

The third approach to fatigue is by analyzing the internal coördination timing and qualitative aspects of the performance. This procedure was used by the British during World War II in a study of the fatigue of pilots. A training device which simulated flight conditions was arranged so that details of the performance could be recorded. After several hours of continuous operation there were subtle changes in the timing of movements and their interrelationships to one another. It was also evident that the standards of performance had deteriorated. For example, a certain meter which had to be centered would be allowed to deviate farther from its correct position before any corrective movement would be made. At the same time, the pilots were convinced that their performance was no poorer at the end than it had been at the beginning of work.

This method of study holds much promise in the analysis of fatigue. The main reason why it has not been explored more systematically at present is the difficulty of arranging recording devices which will show these qualitative changes. It is so much easier to record *how much* is accomplished rather than *how* it is accomplished, that the stress up to the present has been upon gross output at different times of the day. As we have seen, the approach through output alone has not been very fruitful, so that we should see more of the qualitative analysis in the future.

Indirect Measures of Efficiency

It is evident that developing direct methods of measuring efficiency is a complex field of research in itself. The farther this field progresses, the more satisfactory will be our methods of solving practical problems in industry. Many of these problems must now be solved by opinion and guesswork, with many disputes as a result. The fact that we have recognized the incompleteness of our methods of measuring efficiency does not mean that we believe it necessary to await further fundamental research before attacking practical problems. Important information can be gathered about these practical problems even by methods which are incomplete. Also it is often possible to obtain indirect indicators of efficiency where direct study is not feasible. Some examples of these indirect methods follow:

LONG-TERM PRODUCTION TRENDS

This method has been widely used to investigate the effects of such factors as rest periods, hours of work, changes in personnel policies, and so forth. In any single study this method is open to question because economic conditions and many other factors may be varying, in addition to the particular variable under study. If a given factor has a consistent effect in repeated studies under different conditions and in different plants, we can be more certain of a bona fide causal relationship. We are able to get something like experimental control of other variables by canceling out their effects.

Our earlier objections against production rates as indicators of efficiency are less powerful in relation to long-term trends. If a new policy or procedure increases output at the expense of increased cost to the individual, he is less likely to maintain the increased rate of work over periods of months or years. Studies of production trends under varying conditions suggest that a worker adjusts his rate in the long run so that he expends on the average a certain quota of "energy" (*effort,* in our terms). If the hours of work are shortened, for a time the worker keeps on at about the same pace. Gradually, however, his hourly rate increases and then levels off at a new value which eventually may more than compensate for the lost time if the original hours were too long. As a result, total production is actually increased, in many instances, by shortening the hours of work, if the original hours are above the optimal number.

TURNOVER RATES

A job which has inefficient conditions of work is likely to produce a greater incidence of dissatisfaction among the workers. In periods when other jobs are available we may expect this dissatisfaction to be reflected in increased turnover. This indicator is, of course, a function of economic conditions, but may be useful for comparing different plants or departments during the same period. Its usefulness is also limited to comparing broad policies which affect large numbers of workers, and it would tell little about the conditions in a small group of jobs.

ABSENTEEISM

Like turnover rates, absentee rates may reflect dissatisfaction and poor motivation, or the effects of the work upon the health of the worker. The same limitations apply to both indexes.

EFFICIENCY AND MOTIVATION

Motivation and *effort* are closely related terms. Effort, as we have said, refers to how hard the individual feels that he is working. Motivation refers to the factors which determine how hard the individual will work, including those which determine whether he chooses to work at all in a particular job. The relations between motivation and effort are more complicated however, than that of simple cause and effect, because the feeling of effort is not exactly correlated with how hard the individual is actually working, that is, how much he actually produces. For example, if one is really interested in a problem, he feels little effort in working at it; in fact it may be an effort to stop work. Yet in this case we would say that the motivation is high.

For these reasons it is profitable to differentiate *intrinsic* and *extrinsic* motivation. By intrinsic motivation we mean those factors which make the task itself interesting and appealing. Such factors produce a high level of activity without a corresponding increase in effort. Extrinsic motives would be those factors which induce an individual to work without making the task itself more interesting. Thus the promise of additional pay may produce an increase in output, but the individual also feels that he is working harder to gain this goal.

We should expect that intrinsic motives would be more efficient than extrinsic motives, since the former require a lower level of effort. This is not necessarily so, however, since other factors in cost must also be considered. We hear stories of artists who "burn themselves out" because of their intense desire to create. In other cases a milder form of intrinsic motivation may also produce excessive cumulative fatigue, increased risk of accident, or later satiation and dissatisfaction with the task.

The fact is that almost no research has been directed toward the problems of intrinsic motivation except in a negative way. Monotony or boredom is a state of negative motivation which is obviously inefficient because of the dissatisfaction which it creates. This problem has received some attention, and we shall mention some of the research more specifically later. Apart from this problem, the primary concern in industrial motivation has been with the effect of extrinsic factors such as pay, the nature of the supervision, company policies, and the like. Even here, the interest has been in the effects of these factors upon production or upon the opinions and attitudes of the workers, rather than their effect upon efficiency proper. In some cases the problem of efficiency is simply ignored, in others it is assumed that increases in production mean increases in efficiency.

Through lack of factual knowledge, therefore, we are limited in this discussion of motivation to its effect upon productivity and can say little about the relationship of these results to efficiency.

The trend of recent results has led to an increased emphasis upon the social factors in the working situation, and a deëmphasis of economic incentives like pay, bonuses, and profit-sharing. The most influential studies have been those carried on by the Western Electric Company. In experiments upon such specific factors as the effect of lighting and rest periods upon production, the investigators found production increasing without apparent relation to these experimental variables. Rest periods, for example, seemed to increase production, but when they were removed, production failed to return to its original level. It was finally concluded that the most influential factors in the situation were that the experimental subjects had been isolated in a special experimental room, had been consulted about the course of the experiment, had not been strictly supervised, and had been taking part in an activity which was regarded as important by management. In addition, the group of subjects developed a closely knit social group with one worker serving as an informal leader.

After concluding that these social motives and attitudes were so important in the experimental studies of production, the Western Electric investigators began an extensive program of interviewing in the plant. The purpose of this interviewing was partly to gather additional research data, and partly to contribute to supervisory training and generally improve worker morale. They found that the workers, when assured that what they said was in confidence, would talk at length about their relations with supervisors, other workers, and company policies. Often, the mere opportunity to talk in this manner seemed to have a beneficial effect upon the workers' attitudes and feelings toward the working situation. In addition, they found that the general understanding of worker reactions to various techniques and policies was extremely valuable to management and useful in the training of supervisors.

One general conclusion from these researches of the Western Electric Company is that large organizations have inadequate communication between the various levels of the organization. Workers are given inadequate understanding of the reasons back of various company policies and of the problems of management. Conversely, management has inadequate information upon the attitudes and feelings of the workers toward these policies.

Conclusions like these have reinforced a parallel development in the study of industrial motivation. Researchers in the field of social psychology have been developing methods of evaluating or measuring attitudes by means of questionnaires and controlled interviews. Some of the simpler methods which are used for this purpose are extremely superficial, but can still yield information of practical value. For example, management may have introduced a policy which it believes will increase morale, that is, make the workers more favorably inclined toward management. A questionnaire which the workers can answer anonymously, and which is analyzed by an independent consultant, might turn up the fact that the workers regard this move with indifference or with actual dislike. The questionnaire might also reveal misunderstandings or misinterpretations of the policy which contribute to this attitude.

We have said that such a questionnaire would be a superficial approach to the problem. By this we meant that it probably would not succeed in explaining fully the reasons why the workers feel as they do. Nevertheless, it is still valuable to get even a crude indication of these attitudes. Management then has an opportunity to correct its mistakes of policy or to try to make a better explanation to the workers for the need of the policy. Too often in the past, management has depended upon its general impressions, which can be completely false when workers are unwilling to express their real reactions to the situation.

It must be stressed that the construction of attitude questionnaires is a task for a trained specialist. Inadequately worded questions and faulty methods of sampling can produce a completely distorted picture. The layman, hearing of these methods, is likely to feel that they are so simple he can use them himself without expert advice. The simplicity is deceptive, however, and the beginner cannot estimate the effects of wording, question order, or other factors upon the validity of the replies. Even the expert must use pretests and revise his questionnaire several times before it can be used.

At its present stage, the study of motivation in industry has brought us some very broad points of view which are not yet sufficiently specific to allow us to control motivation in concrete situations simply by deductions from principles. Practical problems of motivation must still be met from experience, "hunches," and guessing. In addition to the extremely general findings, recent research has also developed specific tools for evaluating the results of policies based upon experience and intelligent guessing. This means a definite advance, in that we can maintain a closer check upon the actual results of various methods or policies which affect worker motivation.

Monotony or Boredom

Modern industrial methods have been criticized frequently because they make the work so much more uniform and repetitive. The worker makes the same ten motions over and over again with almost no variation. For this reason, it is assumed, work in a modern factory must be much more monotonous than work in less standardized activities.

There are two lines of argument which have been advanced against these criticisms. The first is a matter of values which we cannot settle at this time, and which is broader than the field of psychology alone. This is the argument that industry has provided other advantages which offset the increased monotony of the work—better sanitation, health services, shorter working hours, and increased productivity which raises the standard of living.

The other argument is one which is capable of psychological investigation. It can be pointed out that no one has ever proved that increased repetitiveness increases boredom. Two sorts of observation may be cited to indicate that repetitiveness itself does not cause monotony. One observation is that frequently workers do not dislike repetitive operations because they become automatic, requiring no attention, and leaving the worker free for conversation, daydreaming, or other activity. Another observation is that workers vary considerably in their tendencies toward boredom. Under the same conditions some workers are reasonably content; others suffer so much from boredom that they cannot remain on the job.

The problem of individual differences in boredom is the one which has been investigated most. It turns out to be very complex, in that the susceptibility of the individual depends upon his total personality structure. No one simple and measurable trait can be used to predict which workers will fail to adjust to a repetitive job. Instead, susceptibility to monotony seems to depend upon the total adjustment of the individual to his family and general living conditions. Further research is still needed to develop methods of diagnosing the relevant factors.

One popular belief about this problem has been contradicted. This is the belief that one must be unintelligent to be adaptable to repetitious work. No direct investigation of this problem has ever shown that the relationship is close. There are always numerous exceptions, with intelligent individuals adjusting satisfactorily and unintelligent individuals failing to get along in the repetitive task.

EFFICIENT METHODS OF WORK

Some ways of doing a task are clearly less efficient than others—they require more effort, more fatigue or dissatisfaction or they are more dangerous, for the same amount of work accomplished. In other cases, there are several ways in which a job may be done, but it is not so obvious which methods are the more efficient. In

FIGURE 3.3a. Layout of Work Place for Packaging Wood Screws—Old Method. (A) Envelopes with gummed flap; (B) ½-inch No. 5 wood screws; (C) ¾-inch No. 5 wood screws; (D) 1-inch No. 7 wood screws; (E) 1-inch No. 9 wood screws; (F) moistener; (G) filled envelopes.

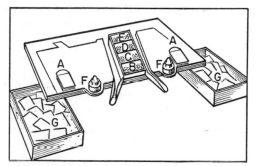

FIGURE 3.3b. Layout of Work Place for Packaging Wood Screws—First Improvement.

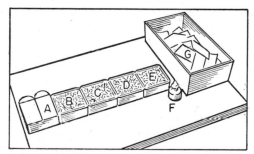

FIGURE 3.3c. Layout of Work Place for Packaging Wood Screws—Second Improvement. (Reprinted with permission from R. M. Barnes, *Motion and Time Study,* 3d ed., Wiley, 1950, Figs. 126–128.)

such cases, a final solution awaits the application of measures of effort, fatigue, energy requirements, accident rates, boredom, and any other costs to the individual. Pending full solution of these problems of measurement, several stop-gap procedures for evaluating methods of work have been devised. (See Fig. 3.3.)

Motion Study

In designing methods of work for manual tasks, especially the more repetitive kinds of work, industrial engineers make frequent use of motion study which is a part of a general body of techniques known as methods engineering. Much of what is now called motion study was originated by Frank and Lillian Gilbreth, who have recently become known to the general public through the book (and movie), *Cheaper by the Dozen*. Their contribution (in addition to the dozen) consists of a procedure for evaluating the effectiveness of a method of work, and also a set of empirical rules for improving the effectiveness of the method.

The aim of motion study is to make the work easier, to increase production without increased cost to the worker. The thinking in back of the procedures is therefore clearly in terms of *efficiency* as we have used the term in this chapter. In practice, however, the industrial engineers have had to rely upon output alone and on opinion about the cost of work. They are not to be blamed for this because, as we have already seen, much remains to be done before we have fully validated measures of the cost of work. Meanwhile the engineers have had to work with whatever was available.

The way in which these engineers have evaluated methods of work is known as *time study,* and for this reason we frequently hear the term "time and motion study." Time study alone is used for other purposes such as setting wages, however, so that we should not think of the two as inseparable. Time study, as its name implies, is a careful measurement of the time required to do the task, and also to do each part of the task. The time required by a particular worker at a particular time is, however, meaningless by itself. We do not know whether he is a skillful worker or how hard he is working. The engineers have tried to get around this difficulty by estimating the skill and effort of the worker and using a system of corrective factors for interpreting the actual time taken by the worker to do the job. The reliability and validity of these corrections are still highly doubtful. Consequently, the use of time study to evaluate the efficiency of the work is, in practice, of doubtful value, even though it is based upon a correct conception of efficiency.

The rules for improving methods of work devised by the Gilbreths and extended by later workers are still highly valuable, in spite of the difficulties in measuring efficiency of a method of work. The reason is that many of the rules are of such obvious effect in reducing the difficulty of the task that they scarcely need validation. Yet they are things which need to be pointed out because they are frequently overlooked. For example, one of the rules stresses the pre-positioning of tools and parts. It seems obvious that if a screwdriver must be picked up every few seconds in the course of the work, it would save time and effort to have the screwdriver in a fixed position so that the worker would not have to search for it each time. Yet a job might be done for years without this obvious improvement unless someone calls attention to it. Perhaps the greatest contribution of motion study has been the emphasis upon critical evaluation of each phase of the method and the breakdown of traditional or habitual ways of doing things.

Other examples of rules which do not seem to need validation may be mentioned briefly:

1. Avoid using the hand for holding; a simple fixture can often perform this function, freeing the hand for other activity.
2. Use momentum to assist in movements, and arrange movements so that they do not have to overcome momentum.
3. Arrange gravity feed for materials and parts so that they are delivered near the working area.
4. Arrange the working place so that finished work can be dropped into a hole or chute for disposal.

Opponents of the method have contended that the worker really has to work harder after the method has been "improved." At the same time that the method is improved new standards are set in keeping with the increase in speed which the engineer expects to occur. If the engineer is wrong in thinking that he has made the work that much easier, the worker still has to meet the new standard if he is to receive the same pay as before. Debate over this point will be endless until we have our valid measures of the cost of work, and are able to use them after the worker has become fully accustomed to the revised methods of work. Often, of course, reports that the new method is harder may be based upon early experience, before the new method has been fully learned. Another approach to the problem would be to make long-term studies of production under different methods with the workers paid an hourly rate rather than a piece rate.

Another objection which has been raised by many psychologists is that motion study has been based upon the notion of one standard way of doing a given task. Gilbreth spoke of the "one best way." While the engineers would admit that they have not necessarily found the *best* way of doing the job, they do often think in terms of the "one best way so far discovered." The objection to this is that methods of work need to be adapted to the individual worker. What is best for one is not necessarily the best for another. There have been some experiments in which it was shown that some workers were well adapted to working with two hands simultaneously, while others were not.

Gilbreth took at least partial account of this fact of individual differences. His approach was to select workers who could perform well under the revised methods. So far, however, selective methods have not developed to the point where they can make selections upon such a detailed basis. (See the preceding chapter.) It must also be stressed that some of the rules of motion study probably hold for everyone, while others are based upon a certain kind of manual dexterity. The ideal would therefore be to design new methods which would take account of universal factors in efficiency while allowing enough flexibility to allow for individual differences. Research upon individual differences in reaction to methods is still in its infancy, however.

The main limitation which must be kept in mind about motion study is that, by its very nature, it is concerned only with methods of performing certain simple muscular tasks. It can be applied to many factory tasks and to the simpler kinds of clerical work, but since it is concerned with economy of motion it has little bearing upon methods of doing more complex "mental" tasks—executive tasks, the various professions, selling, teaching, and the like. In these other areas, no systematic general procedure has been developed. There are, instead, handbooks of procedure, written out of experience within a given job or profession, but having little bearing upon other activities. Perhaps such restrictions in scope will always be necessary. In addition, however, these handbooks have never been empirically tested or validated, even to the extent that motion study procedures have been validated.

SOME SPECIFIC FACTORS IN EFFICIENCY

So far the factors we have considered have been exceedingly broad and complex—motivation and interest, and methods of work. It might be expected that we should find more clear-cut results when we turn to some of the specific physical factors in the environment. The effects of temperature, lighting, and noise would seem to be much simpler than those of motivation. Fundamentally they are simpler, but if we are to measure their effects upon efficiency, measures of the cost of work are just as essential here as they are in the more complicated areas. In order to avoid undue harping upon this point, we shall give brief résumés of the known effects of each of these factors without pointing out in each case that the effect upon efficiency is only partly known.

Noise

More is known about the effects of meaningless sounds (clatters, buzzes, etc.) than of the meaningful sounds such as conversations, radio announcements, etc. The former kinds of noise often have little effect upon output in the experimental situation. In fact, sometimes, output is increased by the noise. Muscular tension also increases, however, so that the increases in output are not increases in efficiency.

Temperature

In experimental situations, high temperature and humidity produce deterioration of heavy muscular work, but have little effect upon performance in mental tasks such as addition, taking an intelligence test, or the like. Whether performance in these latter tasks requires more effort is only indirectly known. For example, both high and low temperatures increase errors in clerical work, and increase accident rates in some occupations such as mining. This might indicate that the subjects of experiments upon temperature compensate for the unfavorable conditions by working harder.

Lighting

This problem is complicated by the fact that poor lighting conditions may have effects upon the visual mechanism as well as the same general effects upon effort and cost of work which are produced by other factors. There is general agreement that poor distribution of light and glare are handicaps to efficient work. There is less agreement upon the optimal amounts of light for various kinds of work.

As far as performance is concerned, output in normal visual tasks such as reading does not increase with illumination beyond certain low minimal levels. For example, in reading 10-point type (a system of sizes), nearly maximum speed is reached when the illumination is only 3 foot-candles (see Table 3.2). This low level seems inadequate to most persons, however, and may lead to additional fatigue even though output does not suffer. It is therefore agreed that some additional safety factor should be added, but the investigators in this field cannot agree on how much to add. Some contend that we never can have too much light if it is properly distributed, and that we gain by large increases over the minimum level. Others are doubtful whether anything over 40–50 foot-candles will add anything except expense. According to the latter group, therefore, most factories, offices, and schools now have sufficient light. According to others, we could gain in efficiency by still further increases, if the increases are produced by properly designed lighting systems.

TABLE 3.2. Critical Levels of Illumination Beyond
Which There Is Little Change in Output

Task	Critical Level (Foot-Candles) [a]
Reading 10-point type (speed)	3
Reading 10-point type (fatigue, blurring)	3
Reading 12-point type (speed)	Between 1 and 10
Reading performance (school)	4–6
Educational achievement in school	4–6
Computing arithmetic problems	Less than 9.6
Sorting mail	8–10
Setting 6-point type by hand	13–25
Time to thread a needle	30

[a] To present a concrete idea of the meaning of the foot-candle unit of illumination, a 100-watt bulb in a bridge-lamp shade will give 10 foot-candles at a distance of 52 inches, and 25 foot-candles at 34 inches. There is, however, variation with the size and color of shade, brightness of walls and the like.

SOURCE: M. A. Tinker, Illumination standards for effective and comfortable vision, *J. consult. Psychol.*, 1939, 3:11–20. (Courtesy of the American Psychological Association and the *Journal of Consulting Psychology*.)

ACCIDENT CONTROL

Accidents are clearly a cost of work to everyone concerned, and in some occupations a very heavy element in the total cost to be considered. The problem of controlling accidents is so complex, however, that we can touch but briefly on only a few important points here. Some of the factors to be controlled lie in the working situation—such things as temperature (Table 3.3), lighting, hours of work, policies in "housekeeping," and even general features of motivation and morale resulting from company policies and management procedures. In other words, these factors are the same ones which affect efficiency in general. Other factors are within the individual worker. Some persons tend to have consistently higher accident rates than others—a consistency which is greater than can be accounted for on the basis of chance alone, and which does not depend upon the kinds of work or the inherent danger of the job. Even when individuals are matched in terms of the kind of work and general risks, some have greater accident tendencies than others.

There is probably no single feature which is characteristic of the high-accident or "accident-prone" individual. Some may be prone to accidents because of peculiarities of eyesight, muscular coördination, or other deficiencies of specific aptitudes. Others may be accident-prone because of motivational factors—their interest in safety precautions cannot be sufficiently aroused. Other characteristics are more subtle, and we do not know exactly why they are related to accident tendencies. For example, it was found that accident-prone taxi drivers had a statistically higher incidence of dealings with juvenile courts. In another case it was found that there was greater incidence of divorce among accident repeaters.

For occupations like bus and truck operation, it has been possible to weed out potentially accident-prone applicants by means of a battery of aptitude tests. In other cases accident tendencies are not related to the aptitudes involved in the job itself, so that it

TABLE 3.3.   Accident Frequency in Relation to
External Temperature

Factory	Sex of Worker	External Temperature					
		32° or Less	33°– 37°	38°– 42°	43°– 47°	48° or More	Extreme Variation
6-inch shell factory	Female	2.84	2.12	1.96	1.55	1.17	1 to 2.43
9.2-inch shell factory	Female	1.72	1.53	1.38	1.28	1.16	1 to 1.48
6-inch shell factory	Male	3.77	2.88	2.64	2.44	1.76	1 to 2.14
9.2-inch shell factory	Male	4.16	3.64	3.00	3.33	2.99	1 to 1.39

. SOURCE: Reprinted, with permission, from H. M. Vernon, *Industrial Fatigue and Efficiency,* Dutton, 1921, p. 209.

is more difficult to select for accident liability in this manner. In any case, tests are only a partial solution to the problem at the present time, because they cannot cover all of the possible factors involved.

There have been several trials of a clinical procedure for treating those who have already shown a tendency to repeat accidents. Coupling a testing program with a general appraisal of the individual has reduced accident rates in a group of automobile accident repeaters as compared with a control group of similar drivers who were not treated by the clinic (Table 3.4). It still remains to be known what features of the clinic produced this improvement.

TRAINING METHODS

Training of new workers is a problem which many industrial managers consider to be one of their most serious and difficult. In recent years there has been a trend toward developing special training departments and special instructors instead of the older and more haphazard methods of teaching by supervisors and fellow workers. The cost of training is high in either case, involving as

TABLE 3.4.   Reëducational Effect of Driver Test Clinics [a]

Number of Accidents Accruing to Groups of Repeaters
Accidents per 100 Drivers

	Untested (N = 79)	Tested (N = 101)
Before summons to clinic (15 months)	195	221
After summons to clinic (9 months)	38	18
Accidents after as per cent of accidents before (9 months in each case)	32.5 percent	13.7 percent
Advantage of reëducation by driver test clinic (compared to police attention, safety campaigns, etc., alone)		57.5 percent

[a] Comparison of accident record before and after clinic operation, tested and untested repeaters. Nine months follow-up, Manchester, N. H., January, 1937.
SOURCE: H. R. DeSilva, The "why" of accidents, *Traffic Safety*, July, 1938.

it does the time of the instructor, the wages paid the trainee before he is productive, and the cost of materials wasted.

One method of reducing the costs of training is to reduce turnover, thus reducing the number who have to be trained. This is an approach through *selection* which has already been discussed. Another approach to the reduction of cost is through speeding up the learning process itself. This is an area in which research can pay large dividends.

As any who have read an elementary textbook of general or experimental psychology will know, there has already been a large amount of research upon the factors which affect speed of learning. Much of this work is difficult to apply to the factory situation, however, because it has been directed toward theoretical problems of the nature and basis of learning. It has studied kinds of learning material and learning situations which are very remote from the material to be learned in the training period for an occupation.

We can secure certain rough guides for setting up training programs from the general research upon learning, but we cannot assume that recommendations based upon these results will necessarily work out in practice. Just as selection procedures must be worked out by direct validation in the field, so training methods remain only suggestions, guesses, or hunches, until they have been tried out under controlled conditions and demonstrated to be effective.

During World War II, much was written about training. Most of these writings consisted of descriptions of methods without any real evidence about their effectiveness. In the haste of an emergency it is, of course, often out of the question to set up adequately controlled validations of the training procedures. Consequently, the best time for making such studies is before the emergency arises, if we wish to gather basic knowledge about how to improve the training process.

The studies which did attack the validation of training procedures during the war were usually of a highly specific kind—seeking better methods of teaching radio code, training aerial gunners, and the like. In such cases there are usually many specific details and features of the job which require special training methods. Information upon these factors is of little value in setting up training methods for a different task. What is needed, therefore, is a coördinated research program aimed at finding general features of effective training methods for whole classes of occupations. For example, there may be important facts about learning mechanical jobs in general which would be of much wider value than the special factors in training an automatic screw machine operator.

We are therefore faced with a situation where the information available is either too general or too specific in character. On the one hand we have general facts about learning derived from the laboratory, and, on the other, special methods of code learning. What industry needs is something in between these extremes. Meanwhile the person interested in industrial training should become familiar with the general results of research upon learning in the laboratory. He will find many hints there even though he does not find concrete rules and procedures.

This is not the place to review these factors in learning. They can be found in many elementary and advanced texts on psychology. As one example of the kind of information and of the way in which it may be applied, we shall mention just the factor of distribution of practice. In general it is found that learning is more rapid and retention better if practice sessions are short and spaced apart than it is if the practice is massed together. This rule has been found to hold in general for memorizing of verbal materials, for muscular skills and for a few factory operations where it has been tested. We can therefore expect that for any kind of task there is an optimum spacing of practice which will vary from task to task. The optimum will also vary depending upon whether the criterion of efficiency is in terms of the amount of time actually spent in practicing, or the total time elapsing before the task is mastered.

These results call attention to a factor which must be considered in setting up a training program. They do not tell us what the optimum arrangement is for a particular job or occupation. In setting up a training method for a particular job, therefore, the designer must estimate the possible range of distributions which can be used, and try out various combinations in order to discover the best arrangement for this job. The principal gain resulting from the laboratory studies of this factor is that we can now be alert to the possible effect of distribution of practice.

SUMMARY

In introducing these chapters on the field of industrial psychology, we stressed the professional and technical nature of the work which psychologists do in the area, contrasting these activities with those of the administrator or executive. The brief surveys of special problems which comprise industrial psychology—such problems as selection and placement of workers, controlling efficiency of performance, and training—have indicated some of the progress which research has made, and also where there are gaps which still remain to be filled by further research.

The important general principles which are stressed throughout are those of scientific method. There is the need for establishing the reliability of any measures which are used. Still more crucial is the importance of checking the validity of any method, whether it be a method of selecting workers, of reducing accidents, of training new workers, or of designing a better method of doing the work. The important contributions which the psychologist makes are to be found in his design of research to ascertain these facts. He must know how to control extraneous factors experimentally and to analyze his results statistically to rule out the effects of change. In connection with many of the problems, particularly those involving efficiency of work, the factors to be controlled and manipulated are not only psychological but physiological and social as well.

In addition to the general principles of scientific method which the psychologist uses, there is also available to him a growing literature of research already carried out. While he usually finds this body of experience insufficient for solving the specific problem with which he is faced, he uses it in formulating his provisional approach to the problem. Thus it is no longer necessary to approach each problem completely afresh.

SUGGESTED READINGS

1. Barnes, Ralph M., *Motion and Time Study*. New York: Wiley, 3d ed., 1949. A textbook presenting modern motion study procedures with many concrete illustrations of the application of these techniques.
2. Bartley, S. H., and Chute, E., *Fatigue and Impairment in Man*. New York: McGraw-Hill, 1947. An extensive survey of the research upon the effects of work upon the human organism.
3. DeSilva, H. R., *Why We Have Automobile Accidents*. New York: Wiley, 1942. Research into the causes of automobile accidents and into methods of reducing accident rates.

4. Poffenberger, A. T., *Principles of Applied Psychology*. New York: Appleton-Century-Crofts, 1942. This general textbook of applied psychology includes valuable chapters on fatigue and efficiency of work, and is written by a psychologist who has done much research in this field.

5. Roethlisberger, F. J., and Dickson, W. J., *Management and the Worker*. Cambridge, Mass.: Harvard, 1939. An extensive account of the Western Electric Company researches on worker motivation and social interactions.

6. Ryan, T. A., *Work and Effort*. New York: Ronald, 1947. An analysis of the problems of efficiency in work and a summary of research in this field.

7. Vernon, H. M., *Industrial Fatigue and Efficiency*. New York: Dutton, 1921. Embodies many of the results obtained by the British Industrial Health Research Board upon such problems as the effects of hours of work, rest pauses, and the like.

8. Vernon, H. M., *Accidents and Their Prevention*. New York: Cambridge University Press and Macmillan, 1936. A survey of factors in industrial and highway accidents, including general factors like lighting, temperature, and fatigue, as well as individual differences in accident tendencies.

9. Viteles, M. S., *Industrial Psychology*. New York: Norton, 1932. A general survey of the field of industrial psychology, containing chapters on each of the topics discussed in the present summary.

Chapter 4

Legal Psychology:
The Psychology
of Testimony

by HARRY P. WELD

Introduction

Immediate Report
> PERCEPTION
> CONDITIONS OF PERCEPTION
> EXPERIMENTAL STUDIES

Subsequent Report
> THE AUSSAGE EXPERIMENTS
>> Method of Report
>> Fidelity of Report

Identification
> DIRECT IDENTIFICATION
> INDIRECT IDENTIFICATION
>> Questioned Documents
>> Deception Tests

The Effects of Testimony
> EXPERIMENTAL METHODS
> RESULTS—GROUP JUDGMENTS
> RESULTS—INDIVIDUAL JUDGMENTS

Suggested Readings

INTRODUCTION

The importance of the psychology of testimony was first advanced by Hans Gross, the celebrated criminologist, in the 1890's. In a book the fourth edition of which was translated into English under the title of *Criminal Psychology,* he, among other things, attempted a psychological analysis of many aspects of the problem of testimony. In a narrow sense testimony means a report about something that has been observed; but the psychology of testimony is concerned not only with all the conditions which contribute to the report, but also with the effect of the testimony in determining the verdict of judge or jury.

Chief of the conditions which contribute to the report is observation, but as we shall see, observation itself involves a number of factors. Experimental studies which deal with some of these factors were begun by Binet in 1896. The method which he employed is now called description. This procedure was concerned with *immediate* description and observation.

The classical experiments in the study of testimony in the narrow sense, i.e., the report of the observed facts, are known as the Aussage Experiments. They were initiated by William Stern in Germany about the beginning of this century, and they quickly spread to France, Switzerland, and later to America. The aim of these experiments was the determination of the reliability of the report *subsequent* to the observation. Thus the experiments approximated the study of testimony as it is given on the witness stand. The reliability of report was found to depend upon a number of conditions. The most important of these is the kind of report, whether, that is to say, the witness is allowed to tell in his own way what he observed (the narrative form) or whether his report is in answer to questions (depositional, questionary, or interrogatory form). Other factors are the relative suggestibility of questions, the age, sex, and intelligence of the witness, etc. Most of the later experimental work has been devoted to the study of the one or the other of these factors.

A special kind of testimony which is based either upon direct observation or upon inferences drawn from observed facts is *identification*. Such observed facts are obtained by many different techniques, two of which are of special psychological interest. The one, the examination of questioned documents, is based in considerable part upon the writing habits of the individual who wrote, or attached his signature to, the document in question. Its techniques have been devised by experts outside of psychology in relatively recent years. The other, deception tests, originated in psychology and psychologists have contributed to its development. One of these deception tests is the association reaction test, first proposed in 1904 by Wertheimer and Klein, and a year later independently by Jung, the psychiatrist. Many studies looking to the improvement of the test have since come out of Germany and America. The other deception test is known as the lie detector. It was in principle first suggested by Benussi in Austria, and its development both as regards apparatus and experimental procedure has been largely in America.

In a court trial a number of witnesses present their testimony in serial order—the one following the other. One witness is for the state or the plaintiff, another for the defendant; one testifies to some peculiar circumstance, another merely strengthens or, it may be, weakens, testimony already produced. The result is a mixed mass of evidence which in some way must be sifted, weighed, evaluated as for or against the defendant. How the juryman, judge, or advocate accomplishes this and eventually reaches a judgment is a problem which a dozen years ago was first attacked by the author and his students. The methods employed and the important results will later be discussed as *the effects of testimony*.

IMMEDIATE REPORT

Gross thought that the problem of observation (description) could be reduced to that of perception. But, although perception is fundamental, observation, as we now know, is much more than mere perception. In the first place, observation, as the term is employed in the study of testimony, usually implies a number of perceptions. For example the policeman in observing the scene of an automobile collision will note the position of the cars themselves, any skid marks that are visible, etc. Every one of these is a separate perception, and taken together they constitute an observation. It is true that under special circumstances an observation may consist of a single perception, as for instance the sound of a gunshot, a flash of lightning, a whiff of sewer gas. Reports of such observations in the courtroom are generally not regarded as reliable testimony unless substantiated by other observers. In the second place an observation is usually made with an intent to take note of what is happening, to remember what is observed, and perhaps to report it as testimony. This intention may be weak or strong, and as a consequence the observation, and the report as well, may be bad or good, may be inadequately or adequately made.

Perception

Nevertheless, as has been said, perception is essential to observation. Any sense modality may be involved and sometimes more than one in a single perception. In the courts, however, most of the reported observations are visual. Auditory perceptions are less, smell, taste, and touch least, frequently reported. Testimony about colors and much of the testimony based upon auditory, olfactory, and gustatory perceptions are by the courts often regarded as "expert" (or "nonexpert") testimony. For example, if a witness testifies that he heard men talking in an adjoining room, the court would probably accept the testimony as nonexpert; but if the witness declared that he heard John Doe's voice, the court would regard the statement as expert and require the witness to give evidence of his familiarity with John Doe's voice, and the way in which it was distinguished from other voices. The reasons given by the courts for this distinction are various and are usually based on an old psychology which regarded the object perceived as an inference. The real reason is that the courts are not interested in the psychology of observation as such, but rather in whether the observation is reliable.

Conditions of Perception

It is common knowledge that one may perceive objects or events more distinctly in a good light, clear atmosphere, and at an optimal distance. Consequently, if a witness testifies to an observation made under such conditions the court will, other things equal, accept the observation as possible. On the other hand, if the conditions for perceiving are regarded as unfavorable, the testimony may be questioned. Sometimes the courts are in doubt about the conditions of an alleged observation. Could, for instance, the driver of a truck have perceived a pedestrian in time to avoid hitting him on a drizzly day in December at 5 P.M. in New York City? The problem becomes more difficult when two or more witnesses disagree as to the visibility at that time and place. If the conditions are not familiar to the court, it may accept testimony that is based upon perceptions that could not have occurred. It may, for example, accept the statement of a witness that she recognized the faces of two persons whom she had previously seen only once, at a distance of two hundred feet in bright moonlight. It is not generally known that the perception would have been questionable at a distance of fifty feet. Similarly, a witness standing on a city street in bright sunlight and looking through a basement window into an unlighted room, could not have seen what he testified to have seen in the interior of the room. Simultaneous contrast, a condition of visual perception not generally known, would have made the alleged observation impossible.

Another condition of perception which the courts recognize is the disposition or priming of the observer to see or not to see certain objects or events which are in the field. We shall discuss this condition of perception later in connection with some of the experimental results of observation and report.

Experimental Studies

The only way to study observation in its own right is to give the subject something to observe which he must describe as he observes. It is for this reason that the method for the study of observation is called description. It consists in laying before the subject a simple object like a postage stamp or a cigarette, or it may be a number of small objects, or again it may be a picture of some sort, and in asking him to describe what he observes. The duration of the observation may vary from a fraction of a second to several minutes, and the description may be oral or written. It is obvious that if even a few minutes elapse between the observation and the report the observer might forget to record some things that he had in fact observed.

The results are not easy to generalize because they do not readily lend themselves to quantitative treatment, because they vary according to the relative complexity and meaning of the thing observed, and because of individual differences among observers. The most general result, however, is that all descriptions are incomplete. Many features, sometimes important ones, are not mentioned. On the other hand there is a pronounced tendency for certain features to be observed. In descriptions of the postage stamp, for example, the word inscriptions, the color of the stamp, and the number inscriptions were mentioned most frequently. In descriptions of pictures all observers tend to see objects in the foreground and to fail to see objects in the background; all tend to describe animate objects, particularly human beings, and to fail to see inanimate objects. Sometimes these tendencies may conflict with each other; a human individual, for instance, may not be seen because he is in the background.

Another attitude common to all observers is to seek for the meaning of the object or picture. Objects that are familiar in our culture like postage stamps and cigarettes are always named in the descriptions, and those features which are most essential

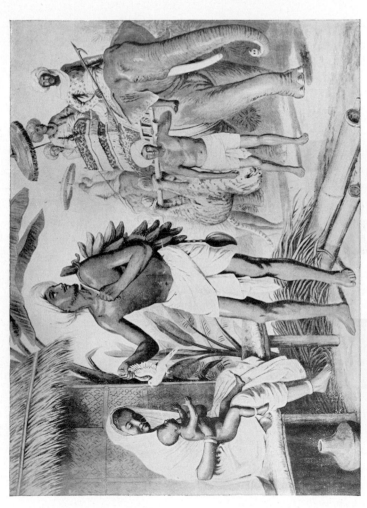

FIGURE 4.1. Individual Differences in Report. (From Leutemann, *Types of Nations*, 1915. Reprinted by courtesy of C. H. Stoelting Company.)

to the meaning of the object are the ones that are observed. The first thing an observer wants to know when he is shown a picture is, "What is it?" "What is it a picture of?" When he finds a meaning those objects that contribute to it get described, and all other objects if described at all are reported vaguely as if they merely constituted a part of the background. It may happen that a part of the total configuration has a meaning of its own in which case it may get described at the expense of the whole. A single illustration may help to show the significance of these attitudes. In an experiment using the description technique and based on a colored picture of a scene in India, only two of a possible fifty objects were mentioned by every one of one hundred observers (Fig. 4.1). On the average about one-half of the objects in the picture are not mentioned at all many of which are clearly visible; the ankus in the hand of the mahout who walks beside the first elephant and the harness of the elephants are distinct enough but no one noticed them. It is obvious that there is something selective about the descriptions. The observer sees what is meaningful to him or, it may be, what is puzzling to him. Had he been an Indian ethnologist he would have seen the ankus, the way in which the elephants were caparisoned, and other details of Hindu material culture. The observers in this experiment were disposed to see in other ways. Only 28 percent localized the picture in India; 12 percent in a tropical country; 3 percent thought it was Africa. When asked to give a title to the picture 54 percent entitled it a hunting scene, 14 percent a geographical scene, 18 percent a domestic or village scene. When the descriptions are studied with reference to the titles the selectiveness is apparent: if the title is a hunting scene, the elephants, tiger, and men in the howdahs are described in some detail; if on the other hand the title is a village or domestic scene the characters in the little drama on the left side of the picture take precedence in the description.

When we consider the conditions of perception, the various sets or tendencies of the observer which lead to the selectiveness of observation and which dispose him to see certain things and not to see other things which are before his eyes, we can readily understand why no two descriptions are ever alike. There are, however, still other reasons for these individual differences. There are language difficulties; some observers cannot find the right words to describe their observations. Another and more important reason is that the average person does not know how to observe. He does not distinguish between what he sees and what he infers, he does not know what to look for and consequently may miss seeing the important facts, he does not conceive that he may have a bias which blinds him to facts that do not fit in with his preconceived notions, he may not realize the difference between a fact and its use, e.g., instead of describing a postage stamp he writes about its history and its usefulness for human communication.

The courts have long recognised that no two witnesses may be expected to agree in every detail; if they ever do, collusion is suspected. But it is frequently assumed that the failure to agree is the result of a failure in memory. As we shall see, forgetfulness may play a part, but the fundamental reasons for disagreement are the various factors which, as we have seen, underlie individual differences in observation.

SUBSEQUENT REPORT

We now turn to the study of reports of observations which are made not at the time of the observations, but at a later time.

The Aussage Experiments

Most of the investigations have been made by presenting a picture, or a short moving picture, or a short dramatic action which has been carefully prepared and rehearsed. In the case of the pictures the observers are usually told to observe the picture carefully, and that after an interval (which may be varied from five minutes to several days) they will be asked to report what they observed. It may be, however, that the observation is made without any hint that a subsequent report will be required. For the dramatic action the observers may be similarly instructed or, as most frequently happens, the request to report comes as a surprise. For instance, a teacher while lecturing to a class may suddenly be interrupted by the entrance of a stranger who addressing the teacher makes two or three remarks of a threatening or insulting character with appropriate gestures. He then leaves the room either of his own accord or he is ejected by the teacher or someone whom he calls to his aid. After a predetermined interval of time the observers are asked to report what happened.

METHOD OF REPORT

The report, as we have seen, may be either in a narrative or interrogatory form. Both are written. In both forms we may count the number of items reported, or of answers made, by an individual; the result is a measure of the absolute *range* of a report. The relative range would be this result divided by the actual number of items in the picture or the number of questions asked. Similarly, we may count the items or answers that are correct and obtain coefficients for the absolute and relative *accuracy* of the report. Still other useful values may be obtained from the questionary. After the answers are written, the subject may be asked to mark with the letter c the answers which he is reasonably sure are correct; the result in relation to the total number of answers given is a measure of the *assurance* of the witness. There are, however, degrees of assurance which range from complete uncertainty ("I don't know" or "I cannot recall") through doubt ("I think so but am not sure") to the highest degree of assurance which theoretically at least, may be measured by asking the subject to mark with the letter a (attestation) those answers to the correctness of which he would be willing to take oath. The number of answers thus marked taken in relation to the total number of answers gives a coefficient for the *tendency to oath*. Neither assurance nor tendency to oath is, however, always warranted, i.e., a witness may be quite certain or willing to take oath that he is right and yet be wrong. *Warranted assurance* is measured by the ratio of the number of answers marked *c* that are in fact right to the total number of answers and *warranted tendency* to oath by the ratio of the number of attested answers (*a*) that are right to the total number of answers made. Furthermore, such answers as "I am not sure," "I think so," may be regarded as showing a tendency on the part of the witness to be cautious. Consequently, a measure of caution may be determined by counting the number of times such answers appear together with those answers that were not marked with assurance. Still other measures have been worked out in the experiments, but these are the important ones.

FIDELITY OF REPORT

The fidelity of a report depends upon a number of factors. Chief of these is good observation, which, as we have seen, depends upon the conditions of perception and the attitudes of the observer. An errorless report is exceedingly rare, but it occurs more frequently in the narrative than in the questionary. One investigator, for example, found no errors in 2 percent of the former and in only 0.5 percent of the latter. The reason for this difference is that in the narrative only those items which impressed the observer get reported, and as a result the range is narrower and accuracy greater. If an interrogatory is given after the narrative has been completed, the subject often recalls with accuracy and assurance items that did not appear in the narrative. The form of the report is then an important condition for the reliability of report.

Another condition is whether or not the observation is made with the intention to report. If the observation is made with the intention to report it later (intentional memory), the range of the report is about twice as great as it is when the observation is made without the intention to report (incidental memory). This is partly due to the fact that if we know we will be asked to report or to testify, we will observe more carefully. But the difference between the two results is probably related to a similar finding in learning experiments. If, for example, we learn a series of words with the expectation that we shall be asked to recite in 24 hours, we will do better than we would if unexpectedly asked to recite.

The interval of time which occurs between the observation and the report also has an influence upon both the accuracy and range of the report whether in the narrative or deposition. In general the loss in accuracy has been found to be approximately 0.3 percent per day during a period of twenty-one days. For longer periods the loss per day decreases somewhat. It should be noticed that the rate of forgetting does not correspond to that of learning experiments, such, for example, as the Ebbinghaus Law of Forgetting. The result is not surprising because the conditions are different. What psychology needs to know and does not know is what kind of thing is remembered and what kind is forgotten. There is some evidence to show that it is the meaning of the picture of the event that is remembered and the details that were not essential to that meaning are forgotten. The fact that there is a loss in accuracy without a loss in assurance means that inaccurate details are unconsciously substituted for forgotten ones in order to fill out the memory picture. The experiments also show that after an interval assurance remains approximately constant. Since there is a loss in accuracy with time, warranted assurance and warranted tendency to oath also decline in time.

The effect of attestation, as this term is employed in the experiments, is to increase accuracy and caution. The number of errors is nearly twice as great in unattested as in attested reports, but attestation does not guarantee accuracy. In unpublished experiments made by the author with a total of one hundred subjects the percentage of correct answers was 67.6; the percentage of all answers attested was 36, and of those attested that were correct 85. Thus the observers were willing to take oath to the correctness of 15 percent of their answers that were in fact incorrect.

Another factor that has a bearing upon accuracy of testimony is the age of the witness. In a very general sense it seems safe to conclude that the testimony of children is smaller in range and is less accurate than that of adults. Furthermore their warranted assurance is much lower than that of adults because their assurance is too great.

Children are also as a rule more suggestible than adults. There is, moreover, a qualitative difference that is significant. The young child usually merely names the objects or persons which he observes. At about the eighth year he begins to report actions and to find meaning in the picture. At a still later age he reports spatial and temporal aspects and mentions the significant features of the objects or persons observed. In the courtroom judges have pointed out that children do not understand the obligation of the oath, that they are peculiarly susceptible to the influence of others, that their testimony may naturally be self-contradictory, and that the testimony of the children of parties in divorce, or about criminal conduct of a sexual character, has little weight.

The question of the effect of the sex of the witness upon the accuracy of report is not easy to answer. Some experimenters have concluded that the accuracy of men is greater although their range is less than that of women. But the differences in these respects are small and in some cases not significant. There is no question but that in general the testimony of women concerning the color of objects, household furnishings, clothing of other women, etc., is superior to that of men. On the other hand, men are more accurate concerning distances and temporal duration, actions which as a result of their experience they are better primed to observe and report.

There seems to be no question but that men are on the whole less susceptible to suggestion than women and exceed them in warranted assurance and in warranted tendency to oath. It is the opinion of the courts that women are less accustomed to the witness stand, that they are more extravagant in their statements, and that they are likely to confuse what actually happened with their interpretation of what happened.

Both the experimenters and the courts recognize differences in the personality of witnesses. As has been said, the experimenters have to some extent measured the difference between the cautious and the bold witness. In addition to these, forensic writers distinguish the rambling witness, the dull and stupid witness, and the flippant witness. Evidence of the traits which would characterize these latter types would hardly be found in experiments even though they are well known to the courts.

Of greater importance to the courts is the question of the moral character of the witness because they are always on guard against a deliberate attempt on the part of the witness to mislead. In the psychological experiments it is always assumed, probably with justification, that the observer is highly motivated to report as well as he can what he observes. In the courtroom it is for the judge or the jury to decide from the testimony and from the behavior of the witness whether he is telling the truth. But, in general witnesses of known immoral character such as gamblers, drug addicts, prostitutes, servants in brothels, bootleggers, and private detectives in general and particularly in divorce cases are suspect. As a rule the courts do not like expert witnesses such as alienists, specialists who deal with questioned documents or ballistics, and professional men in general. This is principally because they so frequently disagree and also because expertness is not easy to define. Conversely the testimony of witnesses of high moral character such as clergymen, police officers in general, lawyers of high standing, etc., has great weight.

IDENTIFICATION

Frequently testimony may merely take the form of an answer to a question of identity. The question may be, "Is this the person you saw?" "Is this the body of John Doe?" "Is this John Doe's hat, shoe, automobile?" "Is this document genuine?" "Is this the guilty person?" The answer may be an affirmative, a negative, or an expression of doubt. Some identifications are direct, others are indirect.

Direct Identification

Direct identification is a recognition. The recognition may occur either in an original observation, i.e., a person is seen committing a crime and is at that time recognized; or the recognition may occur subsequent to the original observation, i.e., although not originally recognized, a person may later be identified as the person seen committing the crime. Since we normally recognize persons or things familiar to us, direct identification would present no special problems were it not that our identification is sometimes mistaken. We accost a person as an acquaintance and perhaps discover that he is a stranger; a man was mistakenly identified by a woman as the person she had married three and a half years previously, and also by a judge as the man for whom he had performed the wedding ceremony. What then are the conditions for mistaken recognition?

The most general condition for mistaken identification is inadequate observation. Normally a person is perceived as a whole, as a living unity, as a configuration, and the parts that make up the whole are usually only vaguely perceived. If, however, there is some exceptional feature such as unusual size, or some blemish or deformity, or if the observer happens to have a tendency to note some special characteristic such as the color of the eyes, the shape of the face, the quality of the speaking voice, or the carriage of the body, then this characteristic has a special significance in the configuration. When, for example, we speak to a stranger mistaking him for an acquaintance, it is either because their configurations are so similar as to mislead us, or because the recognition is based upon the similarity of a characteristic that the two persons have in common. In such cases a closer scrutiny often reveals the mistake. There are, however, well-attested cases in which two persons were not only similar in appearance but possessed in common two or even three similar characteristics such as similarities in speech, in quality of voice—and even similar scars. In cases like these identification is highly uncertain. But even so, it is probable that a more adequate observation of details would have resulted in the discovery of differences which would have made a correct recognition possible.

Sometimes the cause of inadequate observation lies in the conditions of perception. If the illumination is poor, the distance too great, the observation time too short, if the culprit is masked or otherwise disguised, then naturally the perception will be unclear and subsequent identification difficult. When in such a case the witness is faced with a suspected person and asked to identify him the witness is an easy prey to suggestion. (The fidelity of his report is increased if all forms of suggestions are studiously avoided.) If there are several witnesses to the crime they should not be allowed to discuss among themselves the appearance of the culprit; if there is a preliminary examination in which the witness is asked to describe the crime no suggestive questions about the identity of the culprit should be asked; the identification itself should not take place within prison walls or while the suspect is in the custody of a police officer or even when the suspected person is alone. Suggestion may largely be eliminated by presenting the suspect among a number of other persons of similar size and similarly dressed. When this procedure is followed direct identification at a period subsequent to the original observation rests upon the quality of the observation. In an experiment in which a mask was worn in a disguise and later presented for identification among nine other masks, only five of twenty-three subjects recognized it; six of the nine masks were falsely recognized by one or more subjects.

Indirect Identification

Indirect identification derives from inferences based upon perceptions of similarity, of difference, or of the behavior (physiological or psychological) of the individual. Two bullets, one taken from a man who has been killed and the other fired from a particular rifle, have marks so similar that it is inferred that both were fired from the same rifle; the rifle used in the murder is thus identified. Two samples of handwriting while showing similarities nevertheless reveal differences which lead to the conclusion that the two samples were not written by the same person as was claimed. In some instances the discovery of the facts from which the inferences are drawn requires special techniques which have been developed outside of psychology either in crime detection laboratories or by experts who work alone. Certain of these techniques, as, for example, those employed in fingerprinting, ballistics, blood typing, and questioned documents, utilize the microscope, the photographic camera, chemical reagents, a vast amount of special knowledge, and in some instances psychology. In discussing this topic of identification by the indirect method we limit ourselves to two techniques which are of psychological interest.

QUESTIONED DOCUMENTS

A question frequently asked of an expert is whether a certain document is real or a forgery. The document may have been written by hand or on a typewriter, and the study of each has its particular techniques. If the document was supposed to have been written by a particular individual, the expert first studies samples of the handwriting of that individual to learn his writing habits. From the samples it may be determined whether the writer prefers a particular kind of pen point—whether stiff or flexible, whether a sharp, medium, or stub point; whether he habitually holds the pen loosely or tightly, between the thumb and index finger, or between the index and second fingers; whether he writes with his right or his left hand; whether his writing movements are with the fingers alone or with the fingers and forearm; whether his writing movements are cramped or free; whether he writes at a characteristic rate or with a characteristic pressure; whether the letters are formed and connected in habitually characteristic ways; and, to make an end, whether the general style of his handwriting conforms to the fashion of the period or of the country in which he learned to write. For example, a person who learned to write from the old Spencerian copy books of the last century would probably continue to write in the Spencerian style for the remainder of his life, and a person who learned to write and spell in Germany and later migrated to another country might continue to make certain letters and to spell cognate words as he had earlier been taught (Fig. 4.2a, Fig. 4.2b). There are also habitual ways of punctuation—a person may use commas sparingly and semicolons not at all, or he may freely use both; he may have his own preferences in the use of hyphens, in the construction of

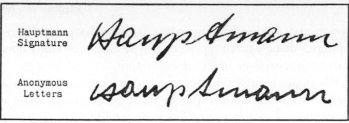

| Hauptmann Signature | |
| Anonymous Letters | |

FIGURE 4.2a. Comparison of Handwriting Samples from Automobile License Application of Hauptmann and Selected Letters Taken from the Ransom Notes of the Kidnaper. (Courtesy of C. Sellers, California Examiner of Questioned Documents.)

Comparison of Spelling	Ransom Notes	Defendent's Writing (Dictated Specimens)
where		
our		
house		
later		
not		
anything		
money		
be		
the		

One of Eight Exhibits of A. V. Osborn

FIGURE 4.2b. Comparison of Spelling in Dictated Material (subsequent to arrest) and in Ransom Notes. (Courtesy of A. D. Osborn, New York Examiner of Questioned Documents.)

sentences and the use of connectives, he may have favorite words and phrases that are often repeated, and he almost certainly develops a characteristic style or mode of expression.

Furthermore because the individual is an organism and not a machine, variations in his own writing are to be expected. These variations are not solely a matter of hasty, or careless writing, because as we all know if we should carefully write our own name a number of times, no two signatures would be alike. The variations are however in superficial parts of the letters and in their size and relative proportions; and it is important to realize that the variations are themselves habitual. From careful observation of all these things the expert learns to know the characteristic writing habits of the individual and he may at once detect the unusual variations if they occur in a questioned document. Sometimes the question is whether a signature is genuine or a forgery. A signature is usually forged either by imitating or by tracing a genuine signature. The former may often be detected from a knowledge of the writing habits of the person whose signature is questioned. The latter may be more difficult. A tracing must be made slowly and not with the speed and freedom of handwriting. Consequently slight tremors of the hand usually occur although they may not be evident to the naked eye; the expert, however, may readily discover them by magnification either with a microscope or by photographic enlargement.

Contrary to what one might expect it is often easier to date a document, to discover a forgery, to trace the writer of an anonymous letter, if it is written by typewriter than by hand. Just as a person develops habits of handwriting so also he develops habits in typewriting. Naturally, some of the former, such as punctuation, spelling, and construction of sentences, will be carried over into the latter. In addition there are in typewriting habitual differences in touch, in spacing after commas and periods, in spacing between lines and paragraphs, in the width of margins, in the length of lines, in the frequency with which signs such as those for "and" and "percent" are used, in the way in which numbers and especially fractions are typed, and the like. If the expert has a sufficient number of samples of typing of an operator, he can by skilled observation and deduction say whether or not that operator typed the document in question or whether different parts of the document were typed by different operators.

Furthermore, the expert is often asked to identify the particular machine upon which a document was written, or to say whether all parts of the document were written on the same machine, or again to determine the approximate date or the genuineness of a document. An account of the techniques and skills which are employed in solving such problems as these are beyond the scope of this chapter. It should be said, however, that the testimony which the expert gives on the witness-stand is an opinion, and however competent an expert he may be, his opinion will have greater weight if he can show the jury samples of the facts upon which his opinion is based.

DECEPTION TESTS

A person who has committed a crime may be expected to react emotionally to any word or question that is relevant to his crime simply because he fears detection. Two techniques have been developed to obtain evidence of this emotional response if it occurs.

In the one, the association reaction method, a series of words is given to every one of which the testee is asked to respond with the first word that comes to mind. The nature of the reaction word and the reaction time—the time it takes the testee to respond—are employed to indicate the presence of emotion. The technique, therefore, is as follows: Some of the words in the series are insignificant, i.e., they have no relation whatever to the crime; others are "critical," i.e., they are in some way associated with the crime. If, for example, a pocketbook has been stolen from a locker, then the words *locker* or *pocketbook,* or the name of some other object known to be in the pocketbook, would be critical. If the testee is innocent and therefore ignorant of the details of the crime, all the words of the series would tend to be insignificant for him, his word reaction times would be similar; if, on the other hand, the testee should be guilty, the critical words may be expected to remind him of his crime, excite his fear of detection, and to result in responses with words not normally associated to the stimulus word, and with reaction times that are greater than the average of the nonsignificant reactions. Although the method as here outlined has in many instances been successful in eliciting a confession of guilt, and at the same time cleared other suspects from suspicion, the inferences drawn from the data lack certainty—they are probabilities of a low degree of reliability. Attempts have been made to increase the reliability of the results by giving the test to a number of persons some of whom are known to be innocent and then treating all of the data statistically. The reliability of the results are undoubtably increased, but they still do no more than make plausible an inference of guilt, and it is questionable whether the inference would satisfy the demands of testimony in a court of law.

A more promising method is the lie detector, which is both an instrument and a technique. The instrument gives a continuous record of any changes that may occur in blood pressure, heart rate, respiration, and skin resistance (to electric currents), resulting from the emotional state of the individual who is under examination. The technique consists first in obtaining a record of the normal action of the physiological processes, and then in asking a series of carefully prepared questions to one or more of which the subject may tell a lie in order to avoid detection, it being assumed that the lie will be accompanied by an emotion. There are two procedures: In the one, the relevant-irrelevant test, obvious questions are asked some of which pertain to the crime and some do not. Skilled operators are necessary to eliminate the possibility that a nervous but innocent person is involved. In the other, and perhaps more desirable procedure, the peak of tension test, questions are asked the significance of which are not known to an innocent person. In such a case specific physiological responses to the critical question would occur only in the guilty person because only the operator and the guilty person would know what question was critical.

A reliable interpretation of the results requires caution and knowledge of all the factors involved. If the subject has an abnormally high or low blood pressure, or some heart disease, a change in blood pressure may be hard to detect. It sometimes happens that the clue to emotional response is a fall instead of a rise in blood pressure, or is a decrease in heart rate after the critical question is answered. Or, again, the clue may be restricted to an irregularity in breathing. Some persons are emotionaly abnormal: the feeble-minded, the psychotic, and the psychopathic individual may be either so apathetic or so emotional that their records are meaningless. Finally there are psychological factors to be considered. A normal and innocent person may be highly nervous from the mere fact that he is being tested or that he is suspected of guilt, and the record may show guilt instead of innocence. In a study of eighty-one innocent persons with the revelant-irrelevant technique 8.6 percent showed more pronounced reaction to relevant than to irrelevant questions. Subsequent testing revealed that this was due to nervousness in the first testing. It has also been suggested that in the peak of tension procedure the experimenter may unconsciously give clues to the subject either by vocal inflection or by other behavior, which may result in a differential response. A guilty person, on the other hand, may show no physiological response because a lie is nothing for him to get emotional about, or because he has no fear of detection.

The courts have properly been cautious about accepting as evidence the results of the lie detector. The test is relatively new, and the courts question whether it is sufficiently developed to justify them in accepting the results as expert testimony. The most that can be said in answer to this question is that with optimal conditions— the best instrument, techniques, and operators—there is still an estimated probable error of about 10 percent and that about 20 percent of the records give results too indefinite to make possible an accurate diagnosis of guilt or innocence. With so large a margin of error the courts can hardly know how to evaluate the results as testimony. Nevertheless the lie detector is still a useful method. It is of value to the police in sifting suspects, it frequently elicits a confession, it in a measure protects the innocent, and in special circumstances may be helpful to the courts.

THE EFFECTS OF TESTIMONY

No account of the psychology of testimony would be complete without a discussion of the question, How, psychologically, does the jury reach a decision from the testimony presented to it? The question is not directed to the reliability of the testimony as in the experiments we have been discussing, but rather to the way in which a juryman evaluates the relative correctness of testimony, and how he may be influenced by the assurance or caution or even the personality and character of the witness.

Experimental Methods

The problem has been attacked experimentally in two ways. In the first, a report of the testimony in a criminal trial was divided into installments and read to the subjects. The first installment however was merely the indictment, the last was the decision of the jury in the actual trial. Neither of course, was testimony, but they were included to see what if any effect they might have on the judgments. At the end of every installment the subjects were asked to make a judgment of the relative guilt or innocence of the defendant in terms of the following nine-point scale: 1. certainty of innocence; 2. strong belief in innocence; 3. fair belief in innocence; 4. slight belief in innocence; 5. doubtful; 6. slight belief in guilt; 7. fair belief in guilt; 8. strong belief in guilt; 9. certainty of guilt.

This method obviously does not take into account factors that would occur in an actual trial such as the opening and closing statements of counsel, the personalities of the witnesses, the cross-examinations and the charge of the judge, any one of which might influence the judgment of the juror. Consequently a second method was devised to investigate these factors in addition to the testimony. In this method an actual trial in a moot court was utilized. This trial was of a civil case—a suit for damages—fabricated by a professor of evidence in a law school, and the counsel were law-school students. There were three juries, one of twelve men, another of twelve women, and a third of ten men and seven women. Every member of these juries made his judgment in terms of the above nine-point scale after the opening statement of counsel, after every direct examination, after every cross-examination, and after each of the summing-up statements of counsel and the charge of the judge. In addition, after the trial was over, each jury in charge of a foreman went to a separate jury room where for thirty minutes the evidence was discussed and polls were taken.

Results—Group Judgments

Many of the results obtained under both methods described above were similar and may be treated together. First to be considered are the group judgments of all the subjects or jurors. These were obtained by taking the median judgment of every installment to represent the central tendency and the quartile deviation on each side of the median to represent the variation (Fig. 4.3). In the figure, taken from the criminal case, the median of the first installment was 5.8, which means that there was a slight tendency for the subjects to believe the defendant guilty merely upon hearing the indictment. In the civil case a similar result occurred after the opening statement of the counsel for the plaintiff. It will also be noticed from the figure that thereafter the median rose with the evidence for the prosecution and fell with that of the defense. Similarly the median rose with the evidence of the plaintiff and fell with that of the defendant in the civil case. We may say therefore, that the direction of the group tendency as represented by the median is in general a function of the testimony. In the criminal case there is evidence that as a particular kind of testimony accumulates the central tendency continues to move in one direction, but by relatively smaller steps. In other words there is here something like a law of diminishing returns which, however, may be cut across by a particularly strong bit of testimony. This means that the first witness for a side is usually the most effective and that subsequent witnesses for the same side were progressively less effective. This result, except in so far as the influence of the first witness for a side is concerned, did

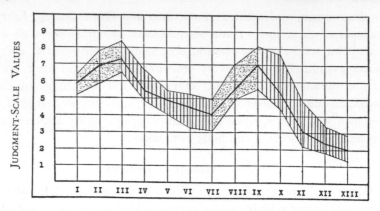

INSTALLMENTS OF EVIDENCE

FIGURE 4.3.   Relation Between Judgments of Innocence or Guilt and Installments of Testimony. The central black line represents the median value of all the judgments of innocence or guilt for each installment: (1) represents certainty of innocence; (9) represents certainty of guilt. The width of the figure on either side of the black line represents 25 percent of the judgments above and 25 percent below the median figure. The barred portion shows the effect of the evidence for the defendant, the stippled portion that for the prosecution. (From H. P. Weld and M. Roff, A study in the formation of opinion based upon legal evidence, *Amer. J. Psychol.*, 1938, *51*:609–629. Courtesy of the *American Journal of Psychology.*)

not appear in the civil case; it is probable that the number of witnesses was too small to show the diminishing returns, and it is possible that the cross-examination interfered with the trend. In other experiments the order in which the testimony of the prosecution and defense was presented was varied. The result showed that the effectiveness of a bit of testimony depends in part on the time at which it is introduced, e.g., a certain bit of evidence was more effective at the end than in the middle of the testimony. A result that came out of the civil trial was that the opening and summing-up statement of counsel, the cross-examinations, and the charge of the judge had the same effect upon the judgment of the jurors as did the testimony itself.

In making a judgment there is a tendency for an immediately preceding judgment to influence the next one. That is to say, no single installment except the first is judged in an absolute sense, as if it stood alone. Instead, the judgment expressed as a degree on the scale is made relative to the preceding judgment. A crude analogy may serve to make this statement clearer. Let us think of the nine-point scale as a stairway of nine steps. If it is a criminal case, the ninth step is guilt, the first step is innocence. At the beginning—before any evidence is presented—the juryman, assuming that he comes to the trial with no prejudice, stands on the fifth step, i.e., the neutral, indifferent position; if forced to a judgment it would be "doubtful." (It might be argued that in our culture where a man is innocent until proved guilty a juryman should start on step one.) After hearing the first installment of the evidence he may go up or he may go down one or more steps, but in either case *he starts from five*. Suppose further that after the trial has progressed for some time, the last judgment made by some juryman was three. In making the next judgment, he goes on from that three; he does not go back to five and judge the next installment from there. The significance of this fact is important. Let us again suppose a second juryman whose last judgment was eight instead of three, and suppose further that the evidential value of the next installment supported the innocence of the defendant, and both jurymen moved down one step. The one who stood on three has his belief in innocence strengthened, whereas the one who stood on eight has his strong belief in guilt merely weakened.

A corollary of the above statement is that the series of judgments is cumulative. This means that at any point in the proceedings the last judgment made is a final judgment that includes all of the testimony present up to that point. The evidence for this appeared in the moot trial (civil case) in which after the members of the jury had completed their judgments on the nine-point scale they were taken into a jury room for a discussion and a poll concerning the liability of the defendant. In the jury room 37 of the 41 votes were forecast by the final judgments in the courtroom. Of the exceptions, three had expressed "doubt" as their final judgments but on every poll in the jury room voted for the plaintiff. These three explained later that despite their expression of doubt they had a slight leaning toward the plaintiff, and since they were required to vote for or against the defendant they voted against him. The other exception was the only one of forty-one jurors who changed his vote as a result of the discussion. He explained that in so doing he accepted the contention of the other jurors that the testimony of the plaintiff was unsubstantiated by other proof. The fact that only one juror was influenced by the discussion is contrary to the results of many psychological studies of the effect of discussion on opinion, namely that discussion frequently leads to change in opinion. The reason for this exception to the rule is that every juror came into the discussion with his final judgment already made; he had listened to all the evidence and the cumulative results of that evidence was his final judgment. It will be recalled that the first poll was taken as soon as the members of the jury had retired. None of the juries reached a unanimous decision on the first vote so that, with discussion interpolated, three more polls were taken and as we have said only one changed his vote on subsequent polls. The final vote at the end of the thirty-minute period was as follows: jury A (men), 10 to 2 in favor of the defendant; jury B (women) 8 to 4 in favor of the defendant; jury C (mixed), 11 to 6 in favor of the defendant. No outstanding differences were found between the men and women jurors. When the medians of the men's judgments were plotted on the same graph with the medians of the women's judgments the curves were found to coincide in most cases and to be quite similar throughout. In the jury room, 13 out of 19 women and 16 out of 22 men voted for the defendant; the ratio is almost exactly the same.

Results—Individual Judgments

This study of the group judgments tells us nothing about individual differences. Before discussing this topic, however, two things should be said. First, as the juror listens to the testimony he weighs or evaluates both the witness and what the witness reports. This process of evaluating may be unconscious, and it depends upon certain attitudes or dispositions which the juror may not know he has; but it is as if he asked himself some such questions as, "Is the witness trustworthy?" "Is what he says probable?" "Can what he says be true?" He may discredit a witness because he seems flippant in manner, or is loudly dressed, or is overly cautions, or is dogmatic, and as a consequence he tends to discredit what the witness says. On the other hand, he may find the witness trustworthy and tend to accept his report without question. This does not mean, however, that irrespective of the witness, a report may not be judged in its own right; the statement of an untrustworthy witness may be accepted because it seems plausible, or is supported by other testimony. Similarly, the report of a credible witness may seem improbable because it does not fit in with the juror's own experience. In some such way, then, every juror weighs or evaluates the testimony. Secondly, the juror must now evaluate the testimony in another way. The question he might now ask is, "What is the significance of this testimony for or against the plea of the defendant?" In the experiment, the answer of each juror to this hypothetical question is indicated by the judgment he recorded at the end of an installment of the testimony.

We may now turn to the individual differences. If we take the series of judgments as made by each individual and compare them with each other, we shall find that although no two were alike some of them showed certain similarities. There are a few persons who from the beginning to almost the end of the series recorded no judgment except "doubt." Upon inquiry it was found that these jurors came to the experiment with the idea that a judgment should not be reached until all the evidence was presented. It is significant, however, that no one of them was able to maintain that attitude until the end; in every case a conclusion was reached before all the evidence was in. There were other jurors who early in the experiment reached a conclusion concerning the guilt or liability of the defendant, and except for variations in certainty their judgments remained the same throughout the series. These individuals gave little if any weight to any testimony that was opposed to their belief. There is another group of jurors who were easily influenced by every statement of every witness. So long as the testimony was for the prosecution they considered the defendant guilty, and when the testimony was for the defense they judged the defendant innocent. These individuals were credulous, tending to accept all testimony at its face value. By far the largest number of individuals were those who moved more or less gradually up and down the scale of judgments exactly as the median moved in the group judgments. These were the jurors who listened critically to the testimony, evaluated both the witness and the report, and based their judgments primarily upon the weights they assigned to the testimony as it unfolded. The differences within the group derive from the differences in the weights which they assigned to each evidentiary fact. The same bit of testimony might be regarded as highly significant to one, and of little importance to another juror.

All this is much less complex and much more immediate than it sounds. Under the general determination to solve the problem, the juror first weighs the testimony, and then makes a judgment relative to the plea of the defendant. The judgment is generally based in part upon the immediately preceding judgment, and in part upon the weight he has assigned to the evidentiary fact. But the juror himself may be quite unaware of these steps in the process. As he listens the testimony seems to him to be in some degree probable or improbable, strong or weak, and further proof or disproof of the accusation at issue.

SUGGESTED READINGS

1. Crosland, H. R., *The Psychological Methods of Word-Association and Reaction-Time as Tests of Deception.* Eugene, Ore.: University of Oregon, 1929. Probably the most thoroughgoing account and critique of the word-association method.
2. Gross, H., *Criminal Psychology.* Translated by H. M. Kallen. Boston: Little, Brown, 1911. The book that brought the problem of testi-

mony into psychology. It contains many interesting observations, but the psychology is outmoded.

3. Inbau, F. E., *Lie Detection and Criminal Interrogation.* Baltimore: Williams and Wilkins, 2d ed., 1948. The best and most recent study of all phases of the lie-detection test.

4. Moore, C. C., *A Treatise on Facts or the Weight and Value of Evidence.* Northport, N.Y.: Edward Thompson, 1908, 2 vols. A rich mine of judicial opinions on the factors involved in fidelity of observation and report.

5. Osborn, A. S., *Questioned Documents.* Albany: Boyd Printing, 2d ed., 1929, pp. xxiv–1042. An account of the problems and techniques employed in the investigation of questioned documents with over 300 half-tone illustrations. By one of the greatest experts of his time in this field.

6. Weld, H. P., and Danzig, E. R., A study of the way in which a verdict is reached by a jury, *Amer. J. Psychol.,* 1940, 53:518–536.

7. Weld, H. P., and Roff, M., A study on the formation of opinion based upon legal evidence, *Amer. J. Psychol.,* 1938, 51:600–629. Some parts of this chapter are, with the consent of the *Journal,* taken from this article.

8. Whipple, G. M., *Manual of Mental and Physical Tests.* Baltimore: Warwick and York, 1915, tests 31, 32. The best secondary source of the methods and principal results, with an excellent bibliography, of the early experiments.

9. Wigmore, J. H., *The Science of Judicial Proof.* Boston: Little, Brown, 3d ed., 1937, especially chaps. 17, 19–20, 25, 27. An invaluable secondary source of the psychology of testimony, with excellent bibliographies up to 1937.

Chapter 5

Criminal and
Correctional Psychology

by RAYMOND CORSINI

Introduction
TOWARD A NEW PENOLOGY
DEFINITIONS
STATISTICS OF CRIME

The Psychological View of Crime
THE CLASSIFICATION OF CRIMINALS

Theories of Criminal Behavior
PSYCHOLOGICAL THEORIES
SOCIOLOGICAL THEORIES
THE CONCEPT OF FREE WILL
EVALUATION OF THEORIES

The Functions of Correctional Psychologists
EVALUATION
THERAPY
Individual Therapy
Group Therapy
Case Histories
GENERAL DUTIES

Research in Criminology
PERSONALITY AND CRIME
SOCIAL FACTORS AND CRIME
SEX AND CRIME

ALCOHOL, NARCOTICS, AND CRIME
EXPERIMENTAL PRISONS
POSTPENAL ADJUSTMENT PREDICTION
FUTURE RESEARCH

Conclusion

Suggested Readings

INTRODUCTION

The criminal problem has plagued every society. In defense, through the centuries, various societies have developed methods for coping with those who break laws. Preventive, judicial, and punitive measures have been established but still crime continues and even increases despite all efforts taken. Thinking men have speculated endlessly about crime, but many questions remain unanswered. Where, in the last analysis, lies the cause of criminal behavior? Why do some people persistently break the law? Are laws but social artifacts? Are some people constitutionally more inclined to crime than others? What is the best way to deal with the criminal problem: should we attempt to improve social standards, should we concentrate on moral instruction, or must we be primarily concerned with personality development? How should we regard the criminal: as an individual who must be punished ruthlessly, or as a sick person who needs to be treated? Is the criminal a foul animal that preys on the good people of society, or is he the inevitable product of a competitive society? Should we punish or treat the criminal? If either or both, why and how?

These are pertinent questions with which we as citizens of society, as well as students of human behavior, must concern ourselves in view of the enormous material and psychological cost of crime. It is the proper function of social scientists, be they lawyers, psychiatrists, sociologists, psychologists, or anthropologists, to study the vexing problems of crime so that the above questions, among others, can be answered.

Toward a New Penology

Psychological practices in criminal work cannot be fully appreciated without knowledge of the development of the new penology. The old classical penology was firm, stern, and implacable. Whoever committed a crime must be punished, be it man, woman, child, or animal. The change from this mechanically strict concept of punishment to our emerging concept of treating the criminal as the product of a social environment and one who must be dealt with in a reasonable and humane manner can be dated from the fermenting period of the mid-eighteenth century, during the struggle of rationalism against superstition. The same philosophers who gave impetus to the French and American revolutions effected changes in the official concepts of criminal action.

Among the important men of this period, John Locke and David Hume should be mentioned. Together, in spirit, they preached the doctrine of humanism, and the worth-whileness of man on earth. The most important individual of this period in penology, however, was Beccaria, who was profoundly influenced by Montesquieu and Voltaire, both of whom satirized the criminal justice of their times. Beccaria's *Essay on Crime and Punishment,* published in 1764, helped establish the new penology. His thesis was that the greatest happiness of the greatest number should be the basis for all social action. He argued that while crime was wrong, the reason for punishment should be prevention of future crime rather than revenge on the particular individual. Such seemingly reasonable and innocuous statements were, in his day, a revolutionary credo.

An important figure in early scientific criminology was Sir Francis Galton. He originated the modern method of fingerprint recording and he attempted to isolate pure criminal types by means of superimposed photographs. Galton was an hereditarian and he believed that the most effective manner to deal with the problem of crime was to prevent criminals from reproducing themselves. He was thus an early proponent of eugenic sterilization which has been adopted and advocated in some states in this country. In America, Hugo

Munsterberg entered the courts and pointed out the gross unreliability of witnesses. Two of his students distinguished themselves in criminology, William Moulton Marston, who later developed the lie detector, and Norman Fenton, who established the first prison guidance center. Other present-day psychologists of note in this area are J. L. Moreno, who has studied the nature of institutional interpersonal relations, G. I. Giardini, who has pioneered in penal classification, and Augusta Bronner, who has played an important part in the establishment of court clinics for delinquents.

Definitions

One of the complications of studying crime is that a large number of emotional values are attached to criminal behavior. Crime is *malum in res,* evil in the law, and not necessarily *malum in se,* evil in itself, i.e., a particular crime is not necessarily a crime everywhere. To take the proper scientific attitude toward crime we should proceed as in any science to classify in an objective manner. One important aspect of classification is definition.

Laws are rules which govern the actions of people as members of particular groups. They are commandments or proscriptions which apply to certain competent people in that society. Methods of enforcing laws and for punishing offenders are usually stated in conjunction with laws. *Criminology* is the study of crime in all its branches, detection, parole, etc. *Crime* is the violation of law. It is a crime only when it is done by a competent person under volitional circumstances and usually when malice, fraud, or negligence is present. *Criminal* is a term with many meanings. If we apply this term to all who have committed crimes, large or small, it would include almost everybody. It could refer to anyone ever convicted of committing a crime, or only to one currently in the act of committing a crime. Often this term is made synonymous with a repeater or recidivist or with a professional criminal. *Criminal psychology* is best regarded as a grouping of selected portions of the more basic divisions of psychology, which relate to nonconforming behavior.

Statistics of Crime

In order to obtain some idea of the extent of criminal behavior the following statistics are presented. It is obvious, since stealth is the essence of crime, that accurate data cannot be readily obtained. The most successful crimes are not those which are not solved by the police, but those which do not even reach official attention. It is entirely probable that there are a thousand violations of the law for each one that comes to official attention. The national cost of crime is incalculable, for the reasons stated above, and also because authorities have difficulty in agreeing how to estimate this cost. Figures from one to twenty billion dollars a year have been quoted, and the sum most often given is ten billion dollars. This is a toll of $66 per year for each man, woman, and child in the United States. Arrests annually number some 23,000,000. Of these, 600,000 are for serious violations. Sixty thousand institutionalizations occur annually and at the beginning of the second half of the twentieth century we find over 200,000 people in jails, penitentiaries, and prisons. According to the Federal Bureau of Investigation, during 1948 a serious crime was committed every 18.7 seconds, on the average, and by the year's end the total had reached an estimated 1,686,670 offenses. Each day 36 persons were feloniously slain, 255 were victims of agravated assaults or rape; there were 1,032 burglaries and 150 robberies, 462 automobiles stolen, and in addition, 2,672 miscellaneous larcenies.

It may be helpful in comprehending the above data to consider the typical crime picture in a city of 100,000 such as Lowell, Massachusetts; Tacoma, Washington; Knoxville, Tennessee; or Reading, Pennsylvania. We would expect the police of these cities to receive information, in any year, of the following crimes: 6 murders, 4 manslaughters, 12 rapes, 56 robberies, 76 aggravated assaults, 392 burglaries, 975 thefts, and 165 stolen autos. Over a long period of time approximately 87 percent of murders, 83 percent of manslaughters, 74 percent of rapes, 36 percent of robberies, 31 percent of burglaries, 22 percent of larcenies, and 27 percent of auto thefts would be cleared on the books. At any time 130 of the city's population would be in a penal institution and each year about 40 would be entering, and 40 leaving penal institutions.

The inadequacy of criminal statistics and the fallaciousness of "facts" is shown by the statistics of crime in relation to sex. The ratio of men to women arrested is approximately twenty-five to one. In addition it was shown in one study that 57 out of every 100 men brought to trial were convicted, while only 43 out of every 100 women brought to trial were convicted. Typical women's crimes such as prostitution and abortion tend to be prosecuted with less than equal vigor than typical male crimes such as rape and auto theft. While statistics would indicate women are less criminalistic than men, such statistics must be interpreted cautiously. It would not be safe to assume, in spite of available data, that women are less criminally inclined than men.

THE PSYCHOLOGICAL VIEW OF CRIME

Modern psychology views man as a sentient, self-aware, goal-striving organism with remarkable properties for adjustment and endowed with powers of communication and coöperation. Individuals are continually compelled to maintain interindividual and intra-individual balances which involve the resolution of impulses and desires. These impulses are directed to a variety of interlocking long- and short-term goals. Satisfaction in the achievement of a goal usually causes lessened activity, but never ends activity for long. Man is continually readjusting himself to new inner and outer drives. The attitudes of an individual to other people, objects, and events is a direct function of the perceived effect of these on the goals of the individual. Whatever threatens the satisfaction of drives is undesirable—it becomes "bad." If the disturbing action is controllable and punishable by law, then the action which transgresses the law becomes a crime. Crime is then, essentially, an illegal way of satisfying human goals.

Laws can be explained by this theory as arising out of the desires of individuals not to have their various goals threatened. There is then but slight difference psychologically between actions commanded or proscribed by law or by custom, etiquette, game rules, and club bylaws. Laws are codified rules of action which restrict individuals for the benefit of the group and which can be enforced by the police powers of the state.

The Classification of Criminals

The social sciences deal with elements that differ in degree rather than in kind and the resulting classifications tend to be less satisfactory than those in the natural sciences. We recognize that each person who commits a crime is unique and that a multiplicity of factors is involved in the act. Nevertheless, we must attempt some meaningful organization in our classification. We can emphasize the crime, or as in the present chapter, the kind of individual involved.

The *accidental criminal* breaks the law through inadvertence, with lack of intent. For example, a drunken driver involved in a fatal accident might be found guilty of criminal negligence and homicide. The *situational criminal* finds himself in the position wherein he will feel that he must commit a crime as the lesser of two evils, contrary to his usual law-abiding manner, e.g., an individual who steals because some one he loves is starving. The *irresponsible criminal* is a dement or an ament and cannot be considered as capable of full judgment, e.g., the neighborhood idiot who steals because of the overpowering effects of the taunts of other children. He may steal something that is useless to him merely to satisfy his friends. The *neurotic criminal* has a personality maladjustment and obtains a measure of relief through his criminal action, e.g., an individual who writes bad checks using his own name and makes no efforts at concealment. Later analysis showed, among other problems, strong guilt over sexual activities and covert hatred for his father, a minister. By committing this crime he received punishment which he wanted unconsciously for his sexual misconduct, and by his own punishment he punished his father. The *psychoid criminal* is the peculiar individual who is often called "psycho-pathic." He operates in an unfathomable manner, and is generally unpredictable, e.g., an individual with a long history of behavior deviations. He steals articles of little or no personal worth; he is a habitual liar. He may be in prison for putting rocks on a railroad bed—"to see some excitement." In contrast to the other types of criminals the background motivations of the psychoid are difficult to understand. His intelligence is normal. The *professional criminal,* contrary to general opinion, is a rather rare individual. He accepts crime as the normal manner of living; e.g., there was a certain individual who worked as a racing bet collector. He would frequently be arrested for bookmaking, would pay a fine and be released. He did not view his illegal actions as reprehensible, since respectable people placed their bets with him and since he paid for police protection. Arrests and fines were part of his business and were duly accepted.

THEORIES OF CRIMINAL BEHAVIOR

The psychologist is interested in understanding phenomena so that they can be controlled. The psychologist's concern with understanding criminal causation contrasts with the police policy of fighting crime at its terminal end. Our interest in theories stems out of a basic belief that the most logical way to control or manipulate conditions is at the beginning, not at the end.

Psychological Theories

System constructors in psychology have been, in general, too busy with the broad framework of their fabrications to devote much specific attention to crime. However, there is no reason to believe that psychologists feel that criminal behavior is essentially different from other types of behavior. By inference, if we accept the theoretical outlines of any particular psychological school, we can easily interpret their approach to criminal behavior.

The early schools of modern psychology, which evolved in the seventeenth century, the empiricists and associationists, argued that the contents of the human mind came from sense-experience and that thinking was a process of associations of ideas. The importance of these concepts lay in the denial of extramaterial or superhuman influences in human thought and action. The psychophysicists who succeeded these "armchair" schools of psychology, while not concerned with man as a total functioning being, gave impressive and detailed evidence of the natural laws of thought. At the turn of the twentieth century there occurred a revolution in psychological thinking; the "constructive crisis" and the dynamic, the behavioral, and the Gestalt schools came into being.

Sigmund Freud, the founder of the *dynamic* school, and his followers, argued that the cognitive elements in a person's consciousness were less important in causation and motivation than unknown or unconscious motivations. One's behavior, they said, was determined to a large extent by forces of which one is ordinarily unaware, and which are often suppressed by feelings of guilt. As an example, a person may unconsciously desire self-destruction, but he is unaware of this drive because it is repressed. He may kill himself in an accident which will seem truly accidental when viewed by a casual observer, or he may commit a murder for which he will permit himself to be captured by leaving obvious clues, and in this way obtain death. Dynamic thinking explains many puzzling crimes, which seemed on the surface to have no motivations.

John Watson, the founder of *behaviorism,* felt that the basis of human action was conditioning, and he attempted to deny the man within, the phenomenal awareness that people have. Watson believed that by proper environmental manipulation the behavior of any person would be determined in every respect. In short, he said if we can control the environment we can control the nature of the individual. In a famous passage Watson asserted that given a dozen healthy well-formed babies he could make anything he would of them . . . "even a thief." The person who is brought up in a criminal environment accepts these values.

The point of view held by the *Gestalt* school was that the individual could be considered as a type of tension system, with drives emanating from within in terms of desired goals. When the goals were in sight the behavior of the individual differed from when they were not, and fundamental aspects of behavior, such as perception, were affected by the dynamics of tension. Lewin schematized the Gestalt system by a topological vector system which placed the individual in a field of attraction and repulsion. His behavior was determined by the strengths of the various forces. As an example, if a person desired a car and if he feared arrest, what he did in relation to a particular car at a particular moment depended on the strength of all the attracting drives and the strength of all the repressing forces.

A large number of theoretical viewpoints exists which cannot be dignified as schools. Some of the theories which attempt to explain criminal behavior will be briefly cited. *Frustration-aggression;* here crime is considered as an aggressive reaction which follows a disturbance of the personality which in turn is based on frustration. The frustrated individual becomes angry and even becomes aggressive. The nature of the aggression may be diverse and the object of the aggression may be the individual himself. Moreover, the aggression may be overt, such as suicide or robbing, or it may be covert, such as a psychosomatic reaction. The simultaneous existence of aggression against an object and the subject is the Samson complex in which the criminal is the victim as well as the aggressor. In this theory summation may occur, i.e., many small frustrations may combine their effects to create a state of readiness of tension which will find expression in a manner not related to the strength of the precipitating factors. In studying crime one is often impressed by the fact that prior to the criminal act the individual was affected by a relatively minor disturbing event which can hardly explain the magnitude of the resulting behavior. The precipitating event acts as a trigger and allows the accumulated tension to find release—in this case in criminal action. *Constitutional theories* assert that there is a direct relationship between the body type of an individual and his personality. The most famous constitutional theory in criminology was held by Lombroso, who felt that the criminal was an atavistic throwback to primitive man and was to be identified by physical peculiarities. Implicit in such theories is the contention that criminal classes are genetically inferior and that eugenic methods of control are necessary. It may be pointed out that the frequent addition of some physical abnormality to the description of fictional or comic strip criminals may indicate that the public leans toward this theory. Data supporting Lombroso's contention have not been found.

Sociological Theories

Sociologists view crime as a function of the nature of the society, and insist that crime can be predicted by knowledge of climatic, cultural, architectural, economic, and political factors. According to the sociologists' frame of reference, the individual is an unpredictable unit, but the behavior of groups can be predicted. Investigation in this area is frequently concerned with the impoverished type of environment that a criminal or juvenile delinquent may come from. These studies are concerned with the degree of social disorganization that may characterize a community as a result of economic unrest due to unemployment or a change in the economic means of production. This social disorganization in turn is believed to lead to personality disorganization, which may manifest itself in the form of criminal behavior.

The Concept of Free Will

Explicit in the law and implicit in the thinking of most people is the free-will theory. It holds that criminal action follows independent personal decision, and that individuals must be held personally accountable for their actions. The free-will theory embodies an hedonistic concept of the individual weighing the pleasurable effects of antisocial behavior against the unpleasant prospects of punishment. This theory which gives the individual responsibility, contrasts with both the behavioral theory which gives him no responsibility, and the social theory which is not concerned with individual responsibility, believing it to be a fiction. The law, though it holds to a free-will theory, nevertheless accepts the possibility of individuals being unable to make a free decision. The acceptance of incompetence to decide, the so-called insanity plea, is a recent acquisition of the law, dating from 1843.

Evaluation of Theories

The importance of theories in criminology may not seem obvious, but if we do not possess explicit theories we operate on the basis of implicit theories. While most policemen, wardens, and judges might deny acceptance of any of these theories, close analysis of various opinions reveal that they are actually held and frequently acted upon. For example: "The criminal is a no-good rat and he should be destroyed" (free-will); "He never had a chance the way he was brought up" (behavorial); "He is not really bad. What he actually needs is understanding" (dynamic); "He was tempted by the things he wanted and couldn't get" (Gestalt—free-will).

As we have seen, there are many theories to explain criminal behavior. One set of theories focuses on the environmental field, another on the individual. It is obvious that these are interconnected, that the field must affect the people just as people determine the field. The problem whether slums create criminals or vice versa is a chicken-egg problem. What is important is to learn what the nature of causal interactions are and to what degree a change in one affects the other. Both phases are of equal importance since crime is necessarily an individual-social reaction. Even the most enthusiastic followers of special schools borrow from other schools in criminology. This is probably fortunate because no one as yet has managed to explain completely why people commit crimes. The eclectic approach which attempts to take the best from the various schools of thought is the common-sense way of handling this problem. Often it is possible to explain particular criminal occurrences in several ways, depending on the premises and biases of the student.

THE FUNCTIONS OF CORRECTIONAL PSYCHOLOGISTS

Clinical psychology is still in its adolescence and like adolescents is growing at a rapid rate and is confused by its maturation which brings increasing responsibility. As a result of this state of affairs, correctional psychologists tend to have a wide divergence of duties and psychologists in one correctional system may operate quite differently from those in others. For the purpose of systematic exploration of the function of correctional psychologists we will divide the field into three broad areas: evaluation, therapy, and general duties.

Evaluation

The psychological evaluation of the prisoner in court, on probation or parole, or in an institution varies enormously from a simple statement of his level of intelligence to a complete psychological report. In some situations only intellectual evaluations are required, while in other cases detailed analysis of causative factors, personality structure, dynamics, individual abilities, suggestions for treatment, and prognosis are wanted. Very often, in various agencies, overlapping evaluations are made by parole and probation officers, social workers, and psychiatrists. The correctional psychologist's unique contribution lies in his use of testing techniques of an objective nature. He must present and interpret data on intelligence, achievement, aptitude, personality, and interests.

The most common element of evaluation is intelligence. Through the use of various tests the psychologist is able to present an overall intellectual evaluation and to point up strong and weak areas. Tests such as the Stanford Binet, the Wechsler Bellevue, and the Pintner Paterson are commonly used for this purpose in individual measurements. In some agencies, with a heavy case load, a combined short individual test and verbal group test, such as the Otis or Terman-McNemar are used. Intellectual evaluations in a correctional setup are complicated by the various negative attitudes prisoners may have toward the tests plus the diversity of cultural backgrounds they represent. For this reason it is well to point out that it is not the test only that yields an I.Q. Responsibility for the intellectual estimate falls on the psychologist, who uses tests for supporting evidence, but does not restrict himself to a mechanical interpretation of any test.

Depending on the policy of the organization or on the needs of the individuals, the psychologist may measure academic achievement, vocational abilities and aptitudes, interests, and attitudes. In large organizations these tests tend to be done by vocational and educational specialists, while clinical psychologists stress intellectual and personality factors. Intelligent and effective guidance depends a good deal on accurate information concerning the individual's interests and aptitudes which can most efficiently be obtained through the use of standard tests interpreted by individuals trained in the field of guidance.

Evaluation of personality calls for the greatest amount of clinical skill and has greatest importance in criminological work. The psychologist uses standardized tests, such as the Minnesota Multiphasic Personality Inventory; projective techniques, such as the Rorschach; and the interview. In using standardized tests the examiner compares responses to questions made by the subject with various clearly defined groups. Projective techniques consist of ambiguous situations to which the subject reacts naïvely. Interpretation of the meaning of these reactions is very difficult to do and calls for a high order of interpretative skill. Some psychologists lean most heavily on the interview, and indeed some refuse to use tests at all. The most common method, however, is for the psychologist to use a judiciously selected combination of the three.

Therapy

The method for the correction of criminals can be outlined on the basis of our knowledge of the way human beings react and on the basis of specialized experience in the treatment of prisoners. We must take the attitude that it is not a criminal we are dealing with, but a person accused or convicted of a crime. We must make him understand that we believe he is worth while, but that his action was bad. As Clarence Darrow said, we must love the criminal but hate the crime. We punish the action, not the person. A common fundamental error in penology today is in not making this distinction. By taking the attitude that the individual who commits an evil deed is himself evil, we attack the individual's sense of his personal worth, weaken his basic defense, alienate him from society, and consequently lessen the possibility of successful resocialization. In education and in counseling the appeal is to reason and logic. The student as counselee listens to the instructor or counselor and sometimes acts in conformance to the information he has absorbed. But the essence of therapy is quite a different thing. The tools are not only facts and logic, but feelings and emotions as well. The individual *knows* his actions were wrong, he rarely defends them as being right, but often does not know himself why he commited the crime. In a study in which the experimenter attempted to find the prisoner's own reason for his criminal action, two-thirds of the responses indicated lack of good reason, even from the prisoner's point of view.

Psychologists have become more and more therapy-conscious. They realize that evaluation not followed by treatment is sterile. Although there are segments within the profession as well as outside who feel that psychologists should not do therapy, nevertheless the amount of therapy performed by psychologists has increased. It is rather difficult to attempt deep therapy in a prison because practical considerations preclude spending many hours with one patient. It is also difficult to obtain the entire confidence of prisoners who are suspicious and resentful of personnel who represent the police powers of the state. Regardless of these difficulties, some real advances have been made in the adjustment and resocialization of those prisoners whose crimes had emotional maladjustment as the driving principle.

The employment of therapeutic measures is one that requires the finest discrimination and judgment in terms of to whom to offer it, how deep to go, and where to stop. It is clearly indicated in those cases where there is a direct relationship between personal maladjustment and the crime, especially in those crimes involving sex and murder. The use of therapy is a cheap means of assisting men to better adjustment.

Therapy has two main heads: individual therapy and group therapy. Under the first head, hypnoanalysis and nondirective therapy have been used as well as variants of orthodox psychoanalysis. Under the category of group therapy a large number of techniques has been used, the best-known being psychodrama. While it is the fashion to describe therapy as surface or depth therapy, such a dichotomy tends to hide the fact that the depth of therapy varies in intensity on an imperceptible scale. We will describe in some detail nondirective counseling (individual therapy) and psychodrama (group therapy) as examples of therapies which have been used by psychologists in prison work.

INDIVIDUAL THERAPY

The essential idea of the nondirective approach as formulated by Carl Rogers is to allow the individual to cure himself. This is done by permitting the subject to talk about whatever is on his mind. Through discussion in a warm and accepting situation, and by the specific techniques of the nondirective method, the subject obtains a new understanding of himself, which very often is of considerable value in better social adjustment. If an angry inmate enters the psychologist's office and berates the institution or some individual, he often feels better after he has had his say. This is therapy of an immediate or surface type because it helps to adjust him. The therapist might have said nothing, indeed he could have been asleep, but as long as the subject believed he was pouring his troubles into a sympathetic ear it helped him to compose himself, if only temporarily.

Why therapy works is often mysterious. Sometimes something fairly evident to all and told to the subject many times by many people is suddenly rediscovered by him. The ultimate factors in individual therapy of this and other kinds appear to be (1) remembering forgotten traumatizing events and (2) integrating and assembling material already known to the subject. The result is insight, or new understanding, which usually occurs in a most remarkably sudden fashion.

GROUP THERAPY

Much that is called group therapy is not that at all. Lectures on mental hygiene, debates on morality, exhortations about efficient behavior, inspiring talks, and illustrative case histories may be of value but they are not necessarily therapy. The essence of therapy is the involvement of the emotions of the subject in relation to his own problems. The chief value of group therapy is stated to be its relative economy. But group therapy need not be considered to be merely a cheaper form of individual treatment. It has values of its own, not found in individual treatment. Even more than in the case of individual therapy do group therapists have their different approaches. But the essential is the creation of a real group in the sense that the individuals are united in a common aim with a real interest in each member and a real transference toward the therapist. The method of psychodrama is the contribution of J. L. Moreno and is based on the spontaneity principle. The description of the method below is a variation on the form of psychodrama.

Once the group has obtained coherence, i.e., becomes a "true" group, one of the subjects volunteers to "act" in the following session. This gives him several days to prepare, and serves to heighten his tension. The day of the session arrives and he either explains to the group what his problem is or does so in an open interview with the therapist, perhaps with some questions from the floor. Next the subject is asked to pick a situation, either a real one in the past or perhaps an imaginary one which he thinks will illustrate his problem, or if he cannot do so, or if the therapist thinks it is better, he is sent out of the room and a situation is prepared for him. He is called in and the situation is outlined. If the subjects who will be portrayed in the drama are known to the subject he is asked to pick out members of the group to act various parts. Such persons are known as auxiliary egos. The subject then again leaves the room, the therapist outlines the scene to the rest of the group, being especially careful to instruct the auxiliary egos how to act, and the subject is asked to come in and the drama starts. The auxiliary egos do whatever they can to get the subject to speak freely and follow all leads that promise emotional outburst. The therapist stands behind the subject and by gestures advises the auxiliary egos how to act. The drama which usually starts slowly gathers momentum and suddenly—in most cases—the subject is no longer acting. He is really and truly involved, and the drama approaches a climax. At the moment of greatest emotionalism, the therapist slaps his hands, the drama ends, and the main actor is immediately sent out of the room, not to reappear until the next session. At the following session he is permitted to indicate his feelings and a general discussion follows.

The essentially novel element in this method is the sudden disruption of a session at its climax and the interval of days or a week between the session and the discussion. It has been found that this is the most effective method. The reason may be that we allow a disturbed individual to reorganize his thoughts and that in solitude he can more clearly understand the reasons for his emotionalism. In any event, be it individual or group therapy, insight is preceded by discomfort and emotional disturbance.

CASE HISTORIES

No matter how honestly presented, case histories create a false impression since they are usually of successful cases—which are generally in a minority. While failures are confusing to patient and therapist alike it is just as important to analyze them, since in an instructional situation they can be of benefit. For this reason we shall present two cases that are considered to be successful and two that are unsuccessful.

Case 1. A. was a male 37 years old. He was born in Boston of a middle-class family. His father was a telephone engineer. His first arrest occurred in 1931 at the age of 19. A. impersonated a famous athlete at a summer resort. He was arrested on a charge of attempting to defraud an innkeeper, but because there was no clear evidence that he actually intended to defraud, the charge was dropped. His next arrest occurred in 1937 for fraud and embezzlement, but again he was not convicted. His third arrest, which resulted in a conviction and a one-year term, was in 1945 for forgery, and his fourth arrest occurred in 1948, again for forgery. He was married in 1933, divorced in 1938; remarried in 1938, divorced in 1946 and again remarried in 1947.

A. asked to see the therapist and made a strong plea for personal attention. "Something has to be done for me. I know my actions are not normal. I have got to be cured." Three one-hour therapy sessions were held in which the subject talked continuously almost without participation on the part of the therapist. At the end of the third session, the subject announced that he completely and entirely understood the reasons for his previous inexplicable behavior and that he would have no trouble in the future.

A. was seen several times after, and stated that he was getting along excellently. He began and continued for two years a college course in accountancy while in prison. A.'s wife wrote to the therapist several times, mentioning the great improvement that had occurred. Other individuals who knew A. over a three-year period commented on A.'s enormously improved behavior.

A. throughout his life had a great desire to appear important. He traced this to his mother's extreme desire to make a social impression and her great drive for social acceptance. He related his impersonation of the athlete to his desire to receive approval, and stated that whenever he obtained a job he worked long hours in order to receive many promotions. A. had stated to employers that he was a college graduate and the college he claimed to have gone to, by error, substantiated his claim. His second arrest was for juggling funds. He had tried to create a good impression on his employer by crediting paying customers' money to non-paying customers but took nothing for himself. His third and fourth arrests and conviction were overdrafts of his own checks. In each case the checks had been made out in saloons. It was his custom of many years standing to enter bars, spend whatever money he had on him in buying drinks for the house, and then to cash a check or two in order to continue buying drinks for the strangers at the bar. Despite his knowledge of the stupidity of his actions and the agonized protests of his wife, he would repeat this strange series of actions periodically. In the two cases where he was arrested, there was no money in the bank when the checks went through. He had actually passed hundreds of bad checks but had made them all good, and he would have made these checks good too if he had been permitted.

In the course of relating the above, the subject suddenly received "insight"—an immediate understanding of the causes of his peculiar behavior. His explanation, to which he held from then on, was that he had impersonated individuals and forged checks in an attempt to be a conspicuous success because of his mother, and that he was trying to purchase respect and approbation from the barroom acquaintances and those whom he hoped to impress by his impersonations.

Case 2. B., a male, was 47 years old. This was his first arrest and conviction, on a morals charge of lewd conduct with a child. He admitted his guilt, and prior to therapy stated he did not know why he had acted in a manner so foreign to his usual behavior.

In therapeutic sessions the subject gave his biography and went over the details of his crime. He produced a great deal of material in five consecutive one-hour sessions. His sixth sesion produced less than one-tenth the quantity of the fifth session, and the seventh session was totally unproductive. Following a mutual agreement between subject and therapist, the subject enrolled in group therapy for a year. His own evaluation as well as that of the therapist about the value of group therapy for his specific crime and its motivations was that it had been to no avail. Another unsuccesful course in individual treatment ensued. The contact was finally terminated.

The subject's criminal action was not explicable to the subject either before or after therapy. Either the reasons were based on deep, sensitive areas that could not be reached by that therapist at that time, or else it is possible that actually no deep, unconscious desires were in existence. This subject was very coöperative and felt that he needed some assistance because of his fear of future recurrence of the crime, but therapy failed.

Case 3. C. was a male, 27 years old. He had an extensive history of maladjustment, with three convictions for robbery, forgery, and car theft. He received a dishonorable military discharge. He was suggested for group therapy by his cell partner who was enrolled in the group. His first reaction to psychodrama was one of deep suspicion, but later he became active as an auxiliary ego. He finally volunteered to bring up a problem.

In the psychodramatic session he announced in a tone of finality that he was a real criminal, and that he had always been bad. He had always been a thief, never liked to work, no one loved him, even his parents hated him and he hated them in return. He said that he was known as the Robin Hood of Texas because he liked to distribute his ill-gotten gains to the poor. He believed he would spend most of his life in prisons.

When asked to suggest a scene, he stated he would like to act out a persistent daydream. In this fantasy he shows up at his home. He is well dressed, has a lot of money and a new sporty car. He is a success. Three of the inmates volunteered to act the parts of members of his family. While the subject was out of the room, the therapist reinterpreted to the auxiliary egos the subject's dynamics and needs and suggested the course of action they should take during the forthcoming session. We shall summarize the actual scene in order to give the reader the "feel" of a psychodramatic session.

C.: (*Knocks on a door. His "mother" and "father" are sitting and talking.*)

FATHER: Come in. Say, Ma, look who it is. It's Elton!

MOTHER: Elton—when did you come out! (*Rushes to him.*)

C.: (*Repulsing mother.*) I am going soon. I just stopped for a minute.

FATHER: What's your rush, Son? Sit down—let Ma and me take a look at you. Say, you look prosperous!

C.: Yeah, I got a pile.

MOTHER: Where did you steal it!

C.: Who said I stole it? You're always accusing me. The last time I came out of the reformatory and the Army I said I would go straight, but what did you do? Jim's check didn't come in and you blamed me for stealing it. That's what you did. (Jim is Elton's brother.)

FATHER: Well, didn't you?

C.: You know Goddamn well I didn't! I ran away because you accused me—always insinuating—and that's why I got caught on this last one. And the check showed up the day after I left. You always thought I was no good. You always favored Jim. I wore his cast-off clothes, I wasn't any good compared to him.

FATHER: Aw, Son, let bygones be bygone. Look, you got some money and a nice car. Let's start a little machine shop, you and me. Won't that be nice?

C.: In the pig's eye! You rum-soaked moron, if you think I'll give you a penny of my dough, you're crazy!

MOTHER: Don't talk to your father like that.

C.: Aw, shut your face. You're just a slut, you are. A fine mother. Jim is nothing but a bastard. You didn't think I knew that did you? Well, you don't mean nothing to me, I hate you all. (*Enter Jim.*) And you, you cockeyed pussyfooting little bastard, what the hell do you want?

JIM: Listen, jailbird, what the hell you doing here? Who do you think you are?

C.: This is my house as well as yours, what are you going to do about it?

JIM: Beat it. You can't get away with that stuff here. I'll call the cops.

C.: You sneak. Calling the cops all the time. I've got a mind to beat the shit out of you.

MOTHER: Get out of here. Go away. You are no good. (*Starts crying.*) My baby. My baby. I love him so much.

FATHER: Now you got your mother crying. Aren't you sorry?

C.: No, I hate her. I hope she dies. She never did anything for me.

JIM: Get out. No one wants you.

C.: Shut up. *Shut up!* Shut up, all of you. I'll go. I'll get the hell out, but before I go I want to tell you just what I think of the lot of you.

JIM: Who wants to hear what a thief—an ex-convict has to say. I got an honorable discharge from the Navy. What did you get? Dishonorable!

C.: Keep your mouth shut or I'll kill you. I'll burn the whole house down. I'll kill you all. Goddamn you all, damn you.

THERAPIST: (*Slaps hands twice.*) That's all. You can go out now.

The following week Elton explained to the therapist and the group that he had not been able to eat, sleep, or work for two days. He could think of nothing else but his family. He now saw his father and mother and brother in a different light, as wronged by him and his foolish actions and he felt so moved that he had cried. He had written to his family for the first time since he had left home several years before, begging for forgiveness. This subject has been followed for several years and has shown a consistently good prison record in contrast to his previous performance. Contact with his family has been maintained. Every indication of improvement is present but it remains to be seen what his postprison record will be.

Case 4. D. entered group therapy, stayed for two sessions, and left, saying that the whole business was "a lot of bunk," that he was no actor, and that he wanted no part of this nonsense. The therapist agreed that he should leave if he wanted to. The rest of the group attempted to argue with him to remain but without success. He left the group.

General Duties

In many agencies the psychologist is a jack of all trades, and is given a wide variety of tasks for which he is considered to have special personal qualities. While his education and training may assist his capacity to do this job, the nature of some of these tasks does not necesarily exclude others from doing them. Such tasks include membership on clinical or administrative boards, lecturing to groups on general psychological topics, writing of case reports, research work, remedial teaching, and administrative work. The amount of such duties varies with the institution or agency. In some cases, the psychologist will do relatively little psychology and will be increasingly drawn into administrative, nonpsychological areas.

RESEARCH IN CRIMINOLOGY

There is little significant research about crime and criminals in terms of dynamic causation. Descriptions of crimes, autobiographical accounts of criminals, psychoanalytic investigation of individuals, sociological studies of delinquency areas, and fractional studies of criminal groups exist, but the sum total of these tends to contribute relatively little to a worth-while understanding of the dynamics of criminal behavior. We are much richer in theory than we are in facts. The reasons for this lack of knowledge lie in the complexity as well as the expense of such research. Also, there is often a lack of coöperation on the part of social agencies as well as legal complications in such research.

Personality and Crime

The first quarter of the twentieth century saw a number of investigations of criminal intelligence. By and large the results indicated a large percentage of mentally subnormal individuals in penal institutions. Further, large-scale and better controlled investigations have, however, deëmphasized the significance of mental deficiency as a cause of crime. It can now be stated with some assurance that the distribution of intelligence of convicted criminals is not much different from the population in general, and probably equal to that of the social classes from which these people come. Low intelligence as a causative factor in crime has not been shown. We find, however, that people who commit certain types of crimes tend to be more homogeneous with respect to intelligence than prisoners in general. The hierarchy of intelligence goes from embezzlers, forgers, and other white-collar criminals down to rapists, murderers, and assaultists.

The personality of criminals is thought by some to be abnormal by definition. It is the actual practice of some agencies if a convicted person does not appear to fall into any other nosological group, such as feeble-minded or psychotic, that he be classified as psychopathic. Some agencies however, report normal personality in over 50 percent of cases. The problem here is not so much the personality of accused or convicted men but the reliable standardization of personality evaluations, a problem which has not as yet been met. However, most authorities agree that the percentage of personality abnormalities is probably greater among convicts than among free people. A survey of 113 studies using objective personality tests on criminal groups showed that 42 percent of the comparisons between criminal and noncriminal groups favored the noncriminal as having less problems, while the remaining 58 percent of the tests showed no significant difference. From such psychometric data it is impossible to come to any reliable conclusion about the relationship between personality disorganization and criminality.

The relationship between physiological elements and criminality has long interested research workers. In the early part of the nineteenth century there was considerable interest in phrenology and numerous heads of criminals were examined for bumps of criminality. This passed as a fancy. Cesare Lombroso, in the middle of the nineteenth century, announced with energy and conviction that criminals were throwbacks, biological atavisms. He bolstered his detailed observations with specific cases. Charles Goring, an English physician, studied three thousand convicts and announced that a detailed examination showed that there was no difference in terms of anthropometrics, except that the convicts were of slighter stature than nonconvicts. But Ernest Hooton, an American anthropologist, examined another sample, and in the main supported Lombroso. Recently, it was found that an equated sample of delinquents were stronger and huskier than nondelinquents. The proposition that the criminal is a biologically different person and that his criminality is due to this difference has not been proved. Differences that do exist may be explained by other reasons, such as cultural selection, feeding habits, and so forth.

It seems certain that the broad statement that all people convicted of crime are abnormal is not true.

Social Factors and Crime

A number of studies has been made in an attempt to find the relationship between ecological conditions and crime. It is the general conclusion that a crude positive correlation exists between the social disorganization of an area and the amount of delinquency. This knowledge is interpreted by some as indicating causal relationship between poor environment and crime, but such studies can tell us nothing about the nature of causation. That a depressed tenement area produces more delinquents than a high-income area is worth knowing, but more important is to know why certain individuals in either of these areas become criminals and why others in the same environment do not.

A major research study which attacked this very problem was conducted by Sheldon and Eleanor Glueck. The Gluecks, together with a team of specialists, compared two groups of boys, one delinquent and one not. Each delinquent boy was paired with a nondelinquent on the basis of ethnic origin, age, intelligence, and nature of residence. Four hundred and two factors which might possibly be of causal value were evaluated. The results of this inquiry showed that delinquents in comparison to equated non-delinquents tended to be physically mesomorphic (solid, muscular); temperamentally restless, impulsive, extraverted; attitudinally hostile, stubborn; psychologically direct, concrete, and socioculturally reared in homes of poor understanding and affection. While there seems to be a reasonable degree of assurance in the differentiating capacity of the above points, these findings are best considered suggestive until further work is done on another group. Furthermore, it should be noted, as the Gluecks point out, that these differences between delinquent and nondelinquent might not have been found prior to institutionalization. Some or all of the differences might be due to institutionalization and might not have been found in the preinstitutional period.

Sex and Crime

The curve of distribution of the ages of sex criminals is bimodal, i.e., falls into two groups. The younger group tends to be convicted of forceful rape and is intellectually below average. The older group is convicted of lewd crimes against children, tends to have high ethical and moral ideals, and is of above average mental ability. A study of older sex offenders made in New Jersey in 1949 showed this group to have a low rate of recidivism, and showed that progression from the less serious to the more serious sex crimes was infrequent. Most of these offenders were found to be undersexed and violence occurred in only 5 percent of cases. Another recent study found that all of the sex criminals studied were suffering from emotional disorders. The most clear-cut factor in this sex criminality was stated to be emotional deprivation that was present during childhood. About one-half of these individuals were considered to be untreatable by available methods. It is believed, although it is uncertain, that individuals practicing homosexuality in prison return to heterosexual behavior on release. As indicated the amount of homosexuality that occurs in prison is unknown and widely discrepant estimates have been published.

Alcohol, Narcotics, and Crime

It is generally agreed that there is a substantial relation between crime, alcohol, and narcotics. It is estimated that while 2 percent of the general adult population are excessive drinkers, there are fifteen times as many intemperate drinkers in a criminal population. The role of alcohol and narcotics seems to be similar. Each is resorted to for purposes of stimulation, although both are physiologically depressants and their optimal effect is to induce a stupor. The relationship between addiction and crime is rarely unequivocal, since the great majority of alcoholics and 75 percent of drug addicts do not have criminal records. It is quite possible that drug addicts and alcoholics will commit crimes in order to obtain their sources of pleasure. It is, however, the more maladjusted person who uses drugs and alcohol most frequently; and rather than blame either drugs or alcohol for crime, it would be more important to find out what caused the maladjustment in the first place.

Experimental Prisons

A number of prisons experimental in design and treatment have been proposed, and in some cases, built and operated. Jeremy Bentham in 1797 proposed the Panopticon, built in the shape of a hollow cylinder to permit constant observation of prisoners by a guard in a central tower. Although this monstrosity was never built, its principles were partially utilized in some European and American prisons. One of the most radical experiments in modern penology in convict self-government was attempted by Thomas Osborne at the Auburn prison in New York. His success was tremendous at first, but when he later attempted a similar setup at Sing Sing, he was subjected to abuse and persecution, was forced to resign, and his idea was crushed. Howard B. Gill in 1927, at

Norfolk, Masachusetts, designed, built, and ran a community prison on the philosophy that life within the walls was to be as normal as possible, and that self-improvement and rehabilitation could best be secured by a positive program of rewards rather than by a negative program of rules and punishment. As in the case of Osborne, Gill found himself in the midst of a fierce political battle, and after seven years of experimentation, he resigned. However, the principal of the community within prison walls has gained some momentum, and persists in various diluted forms in some of our prisons.

Postpenal Adjustment Prediction

The sad fact that from one-half to two-thirds of people released from penal institutions return eventually has spurred the study of the prediction of postpenal adjustment. Over fifty studies have been made which compared people who succeeded on parole with those who failed, and a number of criteria for parole success have been published. Nevertheless, with some few exceptions, parole boards have disregarded these "tests" of parole success and depend on their subjective judgments. The reasons are sometimes stated to be the conservatism of parole boards and lack of confidence in these methods of predicting postpenal adjustments. From the point of view of statistical theory, any scheme for the evaluation of the success of parole may be of value over pure chance, but does not succeed in every case. Parole boards are interested in judgments about individuals and tend to remember the exception more than the rule, i.e., that some people succeed when all criteria point the other way. It is because of these cases that they feel their judgment superior to mathematical schemes.

Future Research

The world of criminology is an untapped source for basic research which besides the exciting prospect of uncovering valuable theoretical discoveries also has immediate practical values. We know very little about the effects of imprisonment on individuals. Some authorities have suggested a greater extension of probation and parole, especially for juveniles because of their feeling that people become worse in prisons. We also have little real knowledge of the differential values of different types of institutions. Effective research in this matter has been suggested, but little has been done. Two studies throw some light on this problem: two matched groups were followed through two different kinds of institutions, one progressive in its orientation, the other traditionally custodial. Recidivism from the progressive institution was less. Another study compared the attitudes of men in two such institutions. Those in the progressive institution felt that they had benefited more by their stay than did the people in the less progressive institution.

We need to know more about the effect of imprisonment on people. It is conceivable that even the most progressive and advanced penal systems make their charges worse or little better than when they entered. The sexual problem within institutions is important and little is known about the effects of prison on sexual patterns of behavior. The comparative abilities of parole boards and parole adjustment tests to make effective decisions is not known. No one knows which types of penal treatment are most effective. We do not even know the actual value of such progressive measures as vocational education or psychotherapy on the future behavior of offenders. Knowledge of these and similar matters can lead us to changes and improvements in our vast and expensive penal systems.

CONCLUSION

Crime is wasteful social friction. It is a threat to the very existence of the society in which it occurs as well as being a distressingly painful matter for both victim and criminal. It is the evident duty of social scientists to regard the solution of the problems of crime as worthy of their attention. For certain reasons, however, crime does not appear to have received the proper amount of careful scientific attention that it deserves. The sun and the moon have been studied more intensively than the penal institutions at Alcatraz or Elmira.

In this chapter we have brought attention to some fundamental questions about crime and have indicated that the approach of scientific methodology may assist in the control of crime. We have reviewed some theories of criminal behavior and have indicated that an eclectic approach is most proper at this time. We have also pointed out some facts about crime and criminals which may conflict with fictions entertained by the public in general.

The functions of psychologists in correctional work have been described and a summary of some research findings has been made. While we may have been critical of the overall value of psychological work and of research findings to date, nevertheless in strict justice it must be stated that workers in this area are pioneers in an important social field.

Progress in criminology is dependent in part on a change of attitude by the community. This is the lesson we have learned from progress in such areas as mental diseases, alcoholism, syphilis, and drug addiction. To hate the criminal and to want revenge is an expensive satisfaction. Criminals are people in trouble. The study of these people, how they got into trouble, how to help them, and how to change them, contributes not only to their specific problem but has value for society at large.

SUGGESTED READINGS

1. Beccaria, Cesare, *An Essay on Crime and Punishment*. Albany: W. C. Little, 1872. This book is a classic in penal literature. It contains the first statement of the new penology.
2. Bromberg, W., *Crime and the Mind*. Philadelphia: Lippincott, 1948. A persuasive presentation of the Freudian viewpoint of crime. The dynamics of criminal behavior are fully described.
3. Conwell, Chick, *The Professional Thief*. Chicago: University of Chicago, 1937. (Annotated by E. H. Sutherland.) The authentic story of a professional criminal.
4. Fallada, Hans, *The World Outside*. New York: Simon & Schuster,

1934. Although this is a novel, no other book so strikingly presents the prisoner's point of view. In addition the reader obtains knowledge of German penology before Hitler.

5. Glueck, S., and Glueck, E., *Unraveling Juvenile Delinquency*. New York: Commonwealth Fund, 1950. The culmination of ten years of the most precise study of the causative factors in juvenile delinquency.

6. *Journal of Criminal Law & Criminology*, Northwestern University. R. H. Gault, ed. A journal devoted to the study of the many aspects of crime.

7. Lindner, R. M., *Stone Walls and Men*. New York: Odyssey, 1946. This book contains a description and criticism of modern penology.

8. Stanley, L. L., *Men at Their Worst*. New York: Appleton-Century-Crofts, 1941. The portrayal of an institution, prisoners and a prison physician who served in San Quentin for thirty years.

9. Sutherland, E. H., *Principles of Criminology*. Philadelphia: Lippincott, 1947. A standard well-balanced textbook, describing crime in all its phases.

10. Taft, D. R., *Criminology*. New York: Macmillan, 1950. A standard textbook with a strong sociological viewpoint.

11. Wines, F. H., *Punishment and Reformation*. New York: Crowell, 1895. A classic in penological literature containing a moving and revolting account of man's brutality to man.

Chapter 6

Social Psychology

by ROBERT B. MACLEOD

The Place of Psychology in the Social Sciences
SOCIAL PSYCHOLOGY DEFINED
THE ENVIRONMENTS OF THE INDIVIDUAL
GENERAL PSYCHOLOGY, SOCIAL PSYCHOLOGY, AND
   SOCIOLOGY
THE METHODS OF SOCIAL PSYCHOLOGY

Four Types of Social Psychology
THE GROUP MIND
MOTIVATION-ORIENTED THEORIES
LEARNING-ORIENTED THEORIES
SOCIAL DYNAMICS

The Motivation of Social Behavior
NEEDS
GOALS
REGULATORS
       Functional Autonomy
       Systematic Self-Regulation

Development of Socialization
SOCIAL BEHAVIOR IN ANIMALS
THE WORLD OF THE INFANT
THE DIFFERENTIATION OF THE SELF
ROLES, ATTITUDES, AND BELIEFS

Psychological Groups
      Psychological and Sociological Group
        Membership
      Multiple Group Membership
      Some Typical Psychological Groups
          National Group Membership
          Racial Group Membership

Social Interaction
      Communication
      Persuasion
      Leadership

Applications of Social Psychology

Suggested Readings

THE PLACE OF PSYCHOLOGY IN THE SOCIAL SCIENCES

What can we learn about people from the study of their interactions with one another? This, broadly stated, is the problem of social psychology. As practical citizens we are interested in building a society in which people can live together peacefully and happily. As scientists we are interested in discovering and formulating the laws that govern social relations. At no time in history has there ever been a greater need for the application of the scientific method to the study of man in his relations with other men. Wars, as the UNESCO manifesto puts it, begin in the minds of men. It is human purposes, human fears, human misunderstandings, that lie behind the conflicts that threaten our continued existence. It is human reason, leadership, sympathy, and understanding that will save us from catastrophe. The task of the social psychologist is through the scientific study of man in his social relations to provide the facts and principles that must be known and understood if we are to build a satisfactory society.

Psychology is only one of the sciences that contribute to the solution of social problems. If, for instance, we try to understand the origin of war, we may gain insight from many different disciplines, each of which reveals specific and important causes of war. The economist may point to the need for new markets and for new territory to absorb surplus population. The political scientist may demonstrate how for an authoritarian regime a war is a way of securing stability. The sociologist or anthropologist may show how warlike behavior serves as a support for traditional social values. Still other ideas will be suggested by the historian or the geographer. Each of these interpretations may be true; but none is complete. If we are to understand a social phenomenon like war, or racial prejudice, or the disintegration of moral values, we have to bring together the insights of all the social sciences. Psychology's contribution is simply this, that any social force, whether it be defined in terms of economics, politics, geography, or history, operates through the medium of human beings. When Hitler convinced the German people that they had been cheated in the Versailles Treaty, that they needed more territory, that the Jews were threatening their national life, what was psychologically important was not the formal truth or falsity of these propositions but the fact that the people believed them. The psychologist's task is to understand social forces as they are apprehended by people and as they operate to motivate the behavior of people.

Social Psychology Defined

Social psychology may be defined as the scientific study of those aspects of human behavior and experience that pertain to other people. In a very broad sense, of course, all psychology is social, since there is no item of behavior or experience that is not directly or indirectly related to other people. We must distinguish, however, between behavior that is incidentally conditioned or determined by other people and behavior that bears direct reference to other people as people. When I limp because of a faultily constructed shoe, my behavior is partly determined by the incompetent shoemaker, but we do not call it social behavior. If, however, the shoemaker becomes the object of my resentment, my behavior is now directed toward another person as a person. He may be a purely fictitious person, and my resentment may be utterly unjustified, but my behavior is none the less social. The most obvious examples of social behavior are, of course, to be found in the interactions of people with one another in simple face-to-face situations—on the playround, in the classroom, and so forth. But a person may behave nonsocially even when he is surrounded by other people; and he may behave socially even when he is physically isolated. The hermit praying for the welfare of mankind, the politician preparing his speech for tomorrow's meeting, and the student grumbling about the unfairness of his instructor are all behaving with reference to objects, real or fictitious, that have the characteristics of people. They are behaving in a social world. If we are to understand them, we must know something about the structure and properties of that world, how they apprehend it, and how they feel themselves related to it.

The Environments of the Individual

We cannot conceive of the individual except in relation to his environment. In biology we recognize that the organism is both a product of its environment, in the sense that it has evolved in an adaptive way, and a determiner of its environment, in the sense that its structures select those variables in the physical world to which it will respond. In psychology it is equally important that we understand what we mean by "environment." Let us begin by distinguishing two kinds of environment, the *geographical* and the *psychological*.

The geographical environment is that which surrounds the individual but is regarded as independent of the individual. The psychological environment is that which surrounds the individual as it is apprehended and reacted to by the individual. The geographical environment may be again subdivided into *physical* and *cultural* environments. The physical environment is described in the language of the natural sciences, i.e., in terms of light waves, sound waves, molecular motions, and so forth. The cultural environment consists of the products of human activity that are already present when the individual is born, and to which he accommodates himself as he grows up. The infant does not know how to speak; yet he is surrounded by a language which he partially, but only partially, learns. The language is part of his culture. That culture also contains habitual ways of doing things (customs), preformed judgments of right and wrong (mores), standards according to which different kinds of activity can be assessed (values), enduring forms of human organization (social institutions), and so forth. For the American child there is awaiting him a culture in which a home is a rectangular structure of stone, brick, or wood, rather than a round mud-and-wattle hut, in which children are expected to go to school, in which the taking of things that "belong to" other people is considered wrong, in which it is obviously desirable to be stronger than or better than or wealthier than other people. The geographical environment is thus prior to the individual, and can be studied as something independent of any given individual. Yet if we are to understand the individual we must know something about both his physical and his cultural environment.

The psychologcal environment is the world as the individual apprehends it and reacts to it. It is much more variable than the geographical environment, and much richer in its dimensions. Colors, sounds, smells, and other sensory qualities have no existence as such in the physical world; they are peculiar to experience. Psychological space and time are not identical with physical space and time; and the objects and events of perception are not mere copies or representations of physical objects and events. The world as the individual perceives it is not identical with the world as it is measured and described by physical science. Its properties and organization are codetermined by physical stimuli, by traces of past experience and by existing motivation.

But the psychological environment contains much more than the objects, events, and relationships of perception. Man is unique among the animals in that his behavior is ordered within a framework that extends far beyond the limits of present perception. Through memory and imagination he ranges backward and forward in time and outward in space, and through language this non-perceptual world becomes stabilized. Each person has notions of geography and history, which may or may not be correct, but which regulate a good deal of his thinking. He has ideas about other races and other nations, about institutions like the Church, Big Business, and the Republican Party, about other people whom he may never have seen. These are all nonperceptual cognitive structures. Just as the perceptual object may bear little resemblance to the physical object, these structures may be wild distortions of the facts established independently by the geographers, historians, anthropologists, and sociologists. Nevertheless they constitute a part of the psychological environment of the individual, which must be understood if we are to explain his social behavior. To say, for instance, that a person is prejudiced against a particular "race" or religion, or believes strongly in the democratic ideal, is meaningless until we find out what in his psychological environment correspond to "race," religion, and democracy.

The perceptual environment is roughly analogous to, but as indicated not identical with, the physical environment. In the same way the nonperceptual psychological environment is roughly analogous to, but seldom identical with, the cultural environment. As we shall see later, the process of socialization is in part the process of assimilating the culture into which the individual is born. But this assimilation is never complete. The customs, mores, and values of a culture are only partially represented in the psychological world of any given individual. This is why the subject matter of social psychology can never be identical with that of the social sciences that deal independently with the structure and organization of culture.

General Psychology, Social Psychology, and Sociology

Social psychology as a subject is intermediate between general psychology and sociology; in many universities it is taught in both departments. In psychology we begin with the individual. We study such basic functions as perception, memory, imagination, thinking, and motivation; we try to relate these to the facts of the physical and biological sciences; we watch their development, and we observe their variation from individual to individual and from situation to situation. When we try to understand the person as a whole, however, we find that we cannot consider him in isolation from his society and his culture. In sociology, on the other hand, we begin with society. We study its structure, organization, and development, and the ways in which its various groups and sub-groups interact with one another. It is possible to observe societies, to make generalizations, and to derive principles that have no direct relationship to the individual. In other words, it is theoretically possible to have a sociology that is relatively independent of psychology. Nevertheless, we find in practice that we have a better understanding of the behavior of groups if we keep in mind the facts and principles of individual behavior.

Psychology and sociology thus have a common field of interest in the study of the individual in society. Social psychology also draws heavily on cultural anthropology, the comparative study of cultures, especially of those that are widely different from our own; on economics and political science, which are concerned with specific aspects of social organization; and on history, which places the relation between the individual and society in temporal perspective.

The Methods of Social Psychology

The methodology of a science is the way in which it collects, treats and interprets its facts. There is no unique social psychological methodology. The standard methods of psychology and the other social sciences have, however, been adapted to the study of social behavior and experience. The most important of these may be classified under six heads: (1) *The phenomenological method* is the systematic, unbiased description and analysis of direct experience. In general psychology, the ordering of colors in terms of hue, brightness, and saturation is a product of phenomenological analysis. In social psychology, as we shall see later, we must apply the same sort of descriptive analysis to such phenomena as selfhood, the expressive characteristics of other people, the value characteristics of objects, and so forth. (2) *The experimental method* always involves a controlled situation in which the various elements can be deliberately manipulated in such a way as to permit the testing of a hypothesis. We usually think of the experimental method as restricted to the laboratory, but this is not necessarily the case. A deliberately planted rumor, for instance, can be part of a legitimate experiment if the social psychologist has sufficient knowledge of the situation to interpret the results in terms of clearly formulated hypotheses. (3) *The clinical-biographical method* is designed to provide an analysis of the individual as he is and as he has developed. Through direct observation, interviews, tests and other devices the life history of the individual is reconstructed and thereby rendered more intelligible. Although this method seldom includes the possibility of experimental control, it frequently provides insights and hypotheses that can later be tested experimentally. For a study of leadership, for instance, we find some of our most useful information in the life histories of people who have become leaders. (4) Included under *sociometric methods* we have a number of devices for the representation of group structure, of the relations of group members to one another, and of changes in the group that occur through time. Sociometric methods may be used in purely descriptive studies, or in studies in which experimental variations are introduced and the results measured. (5) *Survey methods* have been steadily gaining wider acceptance in the social sciences. In a survey we try to find out something about a population rather than about an individual. Essential to the method is the statistically designed sample. Where it would not be feasible to interrogate each member of a particular population, we select a representative sample for observation or questioning. The most familiar form of survey is the public opinion poll, where the members of a sample group are interviewed and questioned about some particular issue. For some types of survey, e.g., an election poll, the respondent may be presented with a written question and a set of alternative answers, e.g., "agree, disagree, undecided," one of which he must check. In other surveys, designed to elicit the deeper feelings of people, the interviewer may use "open-ended" questions, i.e., questions which merely open up a topic but do not indicate any particular kind of answer. The answers of all the respondents are then coded and analyzed after the survey has been completed. Although the limitations of the survey method have occasionally been dramatically exposed, as in the 1948 presidential election, improvements in the techniques of sampling, interviewing, and analysis are steadily reducing the margin of error. (6) *The method of cultural analysis* has until recently been more popular with historians, sociologists, and anthropologists than with social psychologists, but it holds considerable promise for the psychological study of social groups. In wartime the analysis of enemy propaganda may reveal important things about the state of mind of the enemy. Through the analysis of moving pictures, comic strips, newspaper reports, popular novels, and so forth, we may learn more about what appeals to people than by interviews; and considerable attention is now being paid to the historical study of such cultural products as literature, music, and painting as a way of identifying the psychological characteristics of different national, racial, and linguistic groups.

FOUR TYPES OF SOCIAL PSYCHOLOGY

Psychological interest in social behavior is as old as the history of psychology. Plato and Aristotle applied their theories of man to the problems of social organization and political behavior. Hobbes and Rousseau presented contrasting psychological explanations of the way in which individuals come together into groups, Hobbes arguing that the basis is fear, Rousseau contending that man is essentially good and sociable. The doctrine of the greatest good to the greatest number, that played such an important part in the reformist movement of the early nineteenth century in England, is based on a set of psychological assumptions about man. At every point in history we find that the current theory of society contains implicitly a psychological doctrine of man.

The Group Mind

It was not until the late nineteenth century, however, that anything like a science of social psychology began to appear. Whereas classical psychology was concerned almost exclusively with individual mental processes, notably the process of cognition, certain pioneers of the nineteenth century began to look at social phenomena as such to see if there could be such a thing as a science of society. This was one of the manifestations of the increasing emphasis in the nineteenth century on the doctrine of evolution, of which Darwin's theory is the most dramatic expression. If we conceive of all nature as evolving according to law into more and more complex forms, with new properties emerging at each stage of the development, one naturally wonders whether the phenomena of human interaction do not represent a new emergent in the evolutionary process. This, in fact, was the argument of many of the late nineteenth-century thinkers. It was argued at this time that, analogous to the individual mind, there must be a group mind, and that this group mind manifests itself in ways that cannot be reduced to terms of the functions of individual minds. Exponents of this view argued that different groups could accordingly have different types of mentality, and that the comparative study of language, art, and morals, for example, might reveal laws of group mentality. The concept of "group mind" has tended to fall into disrepute, just as the term *mind* as a basic concept in individual psychology has tended to disappear. The term *mind* suggests a special kind of immaterial substance or entity which could have no place in the material world; and to talk of a group mind suggests a mysticism that could not readily be incorporated into science. While we may reject the notion of a group mind, we cannot evade the problems that gave rise to it. We must still raise the question as to whether or not there are phenomena of group behavior, modes of group interaction, and forms of group organization that cannot readily be reduced to terms of individual psychology. It may be, for instance, that the problems of national difference may be stated better in terms of national attitudes or national traditions than in terms of the psychological make-up of individuals.

Motivation-Oriented Theories

Quite apart from the doctrine of the group mind, the evolutionary movement contributed another concept to developing social psychology, the concept of instinct. It was argued by McDougall, for instance, that all human behavior is to be understood in terms of certain inherited purposive dispositions, deeply rooted in biological organization, that initiate, direct, and regulate all that we do. We have an instinct to fight, he claimed, an instinct to escape from danger, instincts to mate, to hoard, to seek shelter, and so on. Many writers argued that among man's instinctive dispositions is gregariousness, and that consequently the fact of social life is to be explained ultimately in terms of an inherited gregarious disposition. Although the theory of instincts lent support to the argument that wars are inevitable because of our inherent pugnacity, that capitalism is natural because of our inherent acquisitiveness, that the brute facts of human nature will always place restrictions on human progress, it was also argued that instinctive drive can be redirected to good ends, that man can find a "moral equivalent" for war that will give expresion to his pugnacious tendencies without doing anybody any damage. Basic to the instinctivist position is the argument that man's social behavior is to be understood in terms of his fundamental motivation. Freud's doctrine was essentially this, and many subsequent writers, who have rejected the concept of instinct, still explain social behavior in terms of fundamental human drives, needs, desires, or wishes.

Learning-Oriented Theories

The doctrine of instinct was attacked on many grounds, but the two most common arguments were as follows. First, instincts are claimed to be purposive dispositions, but the concept of purpose does not belong in natural science. Purposes do not exist in nature; they are interpretations of nature. Secondly, human nature is highly variable and it differs so much from culture to culture that, even if there are instincts, they play no significant role in determining why people do what they do. Even if there are some broad dependable motives underlying social behavior, we must seek an explanation of concrete social acts not in inherited dispositions but in environmental influences. This latter point represents an environmentalist, as opposed to an hereditarian, point of view. This kind of social psychology, which has drawn considerable support from sociology and anthropology, lays its major emphasis on the problems and the laws of learning. From this point of view the major problem of social psychology is to explain how the individual, born into a particular society with a particular culture, learns to be a member of that society.

Social Dynamics

Both the motivation-oriented and the learning-oriented social psychologists have stressed the distinction between heredity and environment. In recent years, however, many psychologists have questioned the usefulness of such a dichotomy. All behavior and experience, they argue, are determined by both heredity and environment; and to ask which is the more important is like asking which is the most important leg of a three-legged stool. From the point of view of social dynamics, or field theory, the essential questions are rather: What forces in the contemporary situation determine the behavior of the individual? How do individuals as they are at present constituted interact with each other as members of groups? How do differently structured groups come into being, maintain themselves, and interact with other groups? The emphasis in social dynamics is less on the origins of social behavior than on the forces that direct and regulate behavior as it is actually observed in a concrete social setting. In recent years this type of emphasis has led to such interesting studies as that of the relative efficiency of democratic and authoritarian leadership in small groups, the conditions that facilitate and inhibit communication between people of different cultural backgrounds, and the factors that affect the morale of industrial workers.

The four types of social psychology we have described are not mutually exclusive. They represent rather an interest in different kinds of social, problems, each of which belongs legitimately in a general social psychology. We may ask: What are the psychological characteristics of social groups that differentiate them from other social groups? What is the fundamental motivation of social behavior? How do social attitudes develop in a particular social context? What are the forces that operate in and among social groups? Each of these problems deserves more detailed consideration.

THE MOTIVATION OF SOCIAL BEHAVIOR

The problem of motivation is to understand and explain why people do what they do. The study of social behavior reveals no unique principles of motivation, but it focuses attention on some aspects of motivation that are frequently underemphasized in general psychology. Social behavior cannot be explained as merely the expression of a gregarious instinct. Most of us are, of course, gregarious; but to call this an instinct adds little to our understanding. Nor is it sufficient to say that social behavior has been learned. Everything we do is in part a product of learning, in the sense that it is affected by the residues of previous experience; but the concept "learning," like "instinct," has little explanatory value.

In motivated behavior we have, typically, an individual in a state of tension, in which a need is directed toward a goal-object or goal-state. If we are to progress toward an understanding of motivation, we must find answers to several basic questions. (1) How is behavior initiated? What conditions, internal and external to the individual, determine the emergence of needs? (2) How is behavior directed? How are goals established, and how are they related to one another? (3) How is behavior regulated? How do nonmotivational factors affect our needs and goals? (4) How are tension systems related to one another within the framework of the total person? Initiation (needs), direction (goals), and regulation (regulators) are not separate and distinct processes, since each is involved in every motivated act. We may clarify the problem, however, by considering each in turn.

Needs

A need is a state of disequilibrium in which something essential is lacking. Sometimes it is felt merely as a general or local state of unrest, accompanied by the feeling that "something must be done about it." Often we do not know what it is we need. At other times it is a clearly articulated experience, including full awareness of what is wanted. The most familiar examples are possibly the so-called primary physiological needs, related to the organism's homeostatic system. The organism tends to maintain itself in an optimum state by means of a complicated self-regulating system which operates more or less automatically. If the organism is to continue to function satisfactorily its water content must be regularly replenished, certain essential nutrients must be ingested, the body temperature must be maintained, and so forth. Much of this self-regulation is strictly a matter of physiology. The secretion of sweat serves automatically to reduce body temperature if too much heat has been generated; and the clotting of blood in a wound is an automatic safeguard against too much loss of blood. In some cases, however, the behavior of the whole organism becomes involved; and at this point homeostasis becomes interesting to the psychologist as an example of the way in which some of our simpler needs are initiated. If the organism becomes dehydrated, this fact is signaled through the mechanism of thirst. The individual feels the need as a warm dryness at the back of the throat, and his behavior becomes accordingly directed toward water. Similarly, when further food is required, a general hunger-need may be felt; and in cases of special food deficiency, e.g., salt, calcium, or phosphorus, this state of affairs may lead rapidly to the development of special cravings for food containing these substances. In each of these cases the need is the initial stage of behavior directed toward the appropriate goal object.

There is thus a meaningful relation between organismic deficiency and psychological need. But this is far from being the whole story. Needs are not necessarily accurate indicators of states of organismic deficiency. There is no evidence, for instance, that the lack of certain essential vitamins, whether it results in clinical symptoms or is subclinical, leads spontaneously to the generation of appropriate cravings, and there is no assurance that behavior initiated by physiological need will always be directed toward the appropriate object. Furthermore, only a small proportion of the goals of behavior are related in any direct way to physiologically generated needs. Most of our food-directed behavior bears little relation to hunger. We usually eat whether or not we are hungry, and even if we are hungry the hunger pangs are assuaged early in the meal. We continue to eat, not because we are hungry, but because the food tastes good, or because we want to keep up our strength, or because we do not wish to insult our hostess. Similarly, the needs that initiate most of our sexual behavior have little to do directly with physiology. In other words, although physiological needs have been called primary, they are not necessarily basic. They account for only a small and relatively unimportant segment of motivated behavior.

For the motivation of most of our behavior, and particularly of social behavior, we must look for needs of a different order. The so-called secondary or derived needs bear no necessary relation to

existing tissue-states of the organism; yet these are the real initia-
tors of most of our behavior. When Jean Valjean stole the loaf
of bread, it was not his own hunger but the thought of his starving
children at home that impelled him to break the law. The student
who needs a particular book for the essay he is writing has a
genuine feeling of need that may for a time dominate his behavior. For the tennis player who needs a new racquet, or the
schoolboy who needs a new bicycle, the need is a real and substantial fact. The day-to-day motivation of people is more intelligible in terms of needs such as these than in terms of instincts,
primary drives, or physiological homeostasis.

Three points about the secondary needs deserve emphasis. In
the first place, they are generated within a situation. The need for
the library book arises in the context of a broader and more enduring system of goal-directedness, the essay-writing situation.
The mathematician's need for a new symbol is dictated by the problem he is attempting to solve. Such needs emerge in response to
the objective requirements of the situation. In the second place,
many such needs can be fully understood only in terms of the more
inclusive needs of the self. The self is a psychological fact. As we
shall see later, it comes into existence during the course of individual development, and it grows into different patterns. Just as,
on the level of physiological homeostatis, needs for water, salt, and
calcium may be generated, so there may emerge needs of the self,
appropriate to the structure of the self and to the structure of
the situation in which the self is behaving. Thus we frequently
recognize in the self a need for security, a need for attention, or
a need for the release of aggression. And, finally, a fixed list of
basic needs would be meaningless. An organism with a constant
and automatic supply of water will never become thirsty; a person brought up in a culture that places no value on individual
superiority will not develop a need for prestige. For particular
specifiable situations there may be a list of predictable needs; but,
in theory at least, the number of possible needs could be extended
indefinitely.

Goals

Any concrete example of motivation involves not only a need but also a goal. The goal is that toward which behavior is directed, the attainment of which brings about a release of tension. Goals are definable cognitive structures. They may range in concreteness and specificity from clearly perceived objects, like the glass of water we desire when we are thirsty, to a dimly imagined future state of affairs, like the ambitious boy's picture of himself as President of the country. What is important is that the goal is always apprehended as having demand character, or valence. It looks good, or right, or desirable; it is as though it exerted an attractive force.

Needs and goals should be considered, not as separate components of motivation, but rather as opposite poles of a single motivational continuum. Both are always present, but they are not always equally important to our understanding of motivation. On the simpler and more primitive levels of behavior we find "need" the more useful concept. A water-deprived organism needs water; the need dictates and defines the acceptable goal object. The behavior of the simpler animals is directed primarily by need; and the same is probably true in the newborn. As we progress to more complex forms of behavior, however, we find needs becoming less and less directive. There are presumably needs underlying the boy's ambition to become President; but these are vague and diffuse, capable of being satisfied in many different ways. It is the goal that defines the direction of his behavior. If we are to understand his motivation, we must be clear about his goals. When we speak of a "need for security" or a "need for social approval," our language is imposing a false specificity. Such terms are convenient labels, but they do not represent concrete motivational systems. The self has needs; but, although these may delimit, they do not define the goals of the self. When we consider motivation on the level of the self, it would be more nearly correct to say that goals determine needs than to say that needs determine goals.

To plot the goal structure of an individual is not easy. We are prone to confuse logically implied goals with concrete, psychologically present goals. Many writers have argued, for instance, that there is only one goal to life, namely the attainment of happiness or the maintenance of a state of physiological equilibrium. Such, however, would be a serious oversimplification. Happiness is not a goal of motivation. It may be a by-product of motivated behavior, or it may be a value consideration that enters into a judgment. Nor is physiological equilibrium or the reduction of tension a goal. It may be a predictable outcome of behavior, and it may bring its incidental rewards, but in the strictly psychological sense we are not directed toward equilibrium. It is sometimes said that the goal of evolution is the survival of the species, and the large part played by reproduction in animal behavior makes such a statement appealing. Although the preservation of the species may be an *outcome* of reproduction, it is not the concrete goal toward which the animal is directed in his behavior.

Goals are psychological facts, just as truly as are colors, sounds, needs, and emotions; but psychologists have not yet discovered a way of describing them adequately. Much of behavior is, of course, simply and clearly directed. When I wish to post a letter it is the letter box I seek, and not the garbage can. Such a goal can be directly reported, and we have no reason to challenge the correctness of the report. There are other kinds of directedness in life, however, that are far less easy to specify. I have written a letter to apply for a job. But, in this case, is the goal the job, the salary I hope to receive from it, or the home I plan to establish after I have saved up some money? It may be that all these goals are real for me, the attainment of one being instrumental to the attainment of another. It may be, however, that I really do not want this job at all, that I would prefer a different job, but am applying for this one because of parental pressure. A person may find it difficult in a case like this to report correctly on his "real" motivation. Much of the directedness of motivation can be so ill defined as to be capable of many expressions. Analysts are fond of pointing out, for instance, that a hatred of one's father developed during childhood may later express itself in various alternative forms of resistance to authority or in physical symptoms. This has sometimes been interpreted as an argument for the hypothesis of unconscious motivation. Within limits, this argument is justified. There are undoubtedly many tensions in the individual which do not come to consciousness, yet which affect the direction of behavior. Whether these may be regarded as unconscious goals, however, is still a debatable question. It may be that the psychoanalyst in uncovering what appear to be unconscious goals is actually by his procedure creating a spurious specificity of directedness.

Regulators

We come now to a third set of variables in motivation. These are the relatively stable regulating factors. Need-goal systems do not operate in a vacuum. They operate within the context of the capacities and abilities of the person and of the world as he apprehends it. The motion of a billiard ball is determined not merely by the impact of the cue but also by its own weight, its roundness, the resistance of the air, the smoothness of the table, and so forth. Similarly, the directedness of behavior is dependent on a number of silent organizers.

First we have the structure of the person himself, his capacities, abilities, habits, and temperamental characteristics. Intellectual capacity, for instance, sets limits to the complexity and remoteness of one's goals, to one's ability to plan for the future, to recognize the incompatibility of one goal with another, to see alternative ways of attaining the same objective; and temperamental characteristics will affect one's persistence in the pursuit of an objective and one's ability to withstand frustration. Secondly, we have the way in which the person apprehends himself. Each of us has usually a picture of himself lurking in the background of his motivation. This is sometimes referred to as the social role. A person may think of himself as the assiduous scholar, the happy-go-lucky adventurer, the self-effacing drudge, the rugged individualist. He may accept this role with full or partial awareness that it is a role, or he may believe that this is what he really is. In every case, however, the role helps to select and define the goals toward which he directs himself. Those goals are accepted which are compatible with the dominant role. Thirdly, we have attitudes and beliefs. These are concrete ways in which the individual apprehends the world in which he lives. An attitude is usually either pro or con, although it may vary in strength. A person may approve or disapprove of Communism, he may like or dislike people of another nation, he may welcome or resist ideas that seem to be new. Beliefs are more stable structures. A belief is that which is accepted as true, or at least as sufficiently probable to warrant one's depending on it. We believe that the earth is round and that a heavy object when released will fall. We may believe something even when we have a negative attitude toward it. We may believe that spinach is good for us even though we resist eating it. More frequently, however, we find that attitudes and beliefs support each other. The wish may actually be father to the thought, i.e., the attitude may generate the belief. We may without adequate grounds dislike a particular individual or group, and for this reason find it easier to believe unfavorable things about the object of our dislike. Fourthly, the culture in which we live may be so patterned as to eliminate many decisions for us. The way in which we dress, eat, and speak to one another, the simple rules of right and wrong behavior, and the functions of the various implements we use may all have been learned through experience, but once learned they constitute a fixed framework which contributes to the regulation of behavior. We may conform to a pattern of culture without ever realizing that we are conforming; and we may first become aware of this only when we discover that other cultures have quite different patterns. And, finally, there are values. We have mentioned that happiness is not a goal, but that it may be a value. By value we mean that which is apprehended as intrinsically good. One frequently quoted list includes six basic types of value, the theoretic, the economic, the aesthetic, the social, the political, and the religious. Values may be represented in the individual as attitudes or interests, but basically they are different ways of looking at life. Different cultures and different individuals may reveal different scales of value, which serve as silent regulators of conduct.

FUNCTIONAL AUTONOMY

The principle of functional autonomy asserts that, however a need-goal relationship may have developed, it may become established in the psychological field as an identifiable, relatively autonomous system. This is a rejection of the theory that would explain away the contemporary motivation of the individual by reducing it to terms of original instinct, primary drive, or early childhood experience. As we shall see, the developmental problem is an important one, but it represents only one of several possible approaches to the understanding of human behavior. A perceptual analogy might be helpful. When we look at a printed page we see a set of clearly organized structures which have meaning. These do not have the same meaning for a newborn child. Our present perception obviously depends on a long process of learning. The fact that in the past we had to learn how to read detracts in no way from the psychological reality of our present percepts. In the same way, needs and goals become established as segregated, identifiable, and relatively independent systems. An interest in stamp collecting, an ambition to shoot an elephant, an intention to keep tomorrow's appointment with the dentist, may have a developmental history, but these are psychological facts that can be studied in their own right. It is with the contemporary motives of people that we deal in everyday social intercourse.

Autonomy means independence. It would be a mistake, of course, to argue that motivational systems can be completely autonomous, in the sense of being completely independent of other motivational systems, any more than the perceptual object can be considered as unrelated to the rest of the perceptual field. Some motivational systems are clearly less autonomous than are others. Human motivation may be thought of as a complex hierarchical organization of interrelated systems. These systems may vary in a number of different ways, e.g., in (1) strength of need, (2) precision of goal-directedness, (3) position in the hierarchy of superordination-subordination, (4) permanence, (5) degree of ego involvement, and (6) degree of segregation from other motivational systems. For instance, a food appetite or a craving for morphine may be temporarily so strong as to disrupt all other motivational systems. The ambition to become President, on the other hand, may at any given moment be weak, but it may endure for a lifetime, and it may serve as a silent initiator, director, and regulator of many other motivational systems, establishing interests, dictating decisions, and shaping the whole style of life. In one sense we may say that each individual is unique in his motivational pattern. If we are to understand him we must get inside his world and find out what needs are directed toward what goals. If each individual were completely unique, no science of social psychology would be possible. As we shall see, however, there are broad communalities. Many people have common needs, common goals, common attitudes, interests, opinions, and beliefs, and it is possible to study these communalities. What we must never forget, however, is that these communalities are never more than similarities; and that behind the communalities is individual uniqueness.

SYSTEMATIC SELF-REGULATION

This principle asserts that, once a motivational system has become established, it tends to maintain itself in spite of changing conditions. Again we have a perceptual analogy, the so-called constancy phenomenon. If we are to survive we must have a world that is, at least in its major properties, stable and dependable. If the color and brightness of an object were to change with every change in its illumination, or if its shape were to change with every change in orientation, we would never be able to recognize it as the same object. It is a law of perception that we systematically neglect the extraneous and irrelevant. We behave as though we were trying to keep the world as it is. We accept new things only insofar as we can incorporate them within the framework that we have, and if new things do not fit in they will be modified until they do.

The same principle applies in motivation. Once a system of need-goal tension has become established, it will behave in such a way as to maintain itself. A goal that has been accepted will continue to "look good" even after the initiating need has disappeared. We can observe this even on the level of food-directed behavior. We continue to eat long after hunger has been assuaged. The last piece of pie continues to entice us even when we know that to eat it would bring discomfort. The principle is most evident, however, in motivational systems that involve the self. The self is basically a perceptual structure that exemplifies the law of perceptual constancy; but its identity depends also on memory, and many of its essential characteristics, i.e., the ideal of self, are carried in imagination. To maintain its identity and stability the self must, as it were, defend itself against change. Thus when we are insulted our tendency is to disparage the person who has insulted us. When we fail in an examination we seek automatically for excuses that will explain the failure without injuring our self-respect. The so-called "mechanisms of ego defense" (repression, projection, rationalization, sublimation, identification, and so forth) are common ways in which the self maintains itself in the face of threats. When we rationalize an unethical act, what we are doing is finding a cause for the act that will make it unnecessary for us to accept the act as self-caused. When we "project" our feeling of guilt into someone else, the same rearrangement is taking place. The psychological field is being reorganized in such a way as to leave the self intact.

It is perhaps a mistake to call these "mechanisms of ego defense," because they operate to protect any strong structure in the psychological field; and sometimes it is the ego that makes the sacrifice. The parent of a delinquent child may literally feel the guilt in himself, thereby protecting his ideal of the child. We know all too little about the "confessions" in Communist political trials, but it seems plausible to assume that, whether or not the person who confessed was guilty, he may because of his deep belief in the rightness of the system have literally accepted guilt rather than recognize a flaw in the system. The history of religious inquisitions contains many similar examples, in which the integrity of the self is sacrificed to preserve the integrity of an objective ideal. It may be true that in our culture the ego is the structure that is most vigorously defended. The principle, however, is a much broader one. Any structure that is well established in the psychological field will resist change. If, for instance, someone presented evidence indicating that Lincoln had committed a petty theft, the reaction of the average American would be, not to revise his conception of Lincoln accordingly, but to challenge the plausibility of the evidence or the motives of the person presenting it. If we believe that all members of a particular racial group are stupid, dirty, lazy, and dishonest, and we are then shown a member of this group who is intelligent, clean, energetic, and of impeccable character, our tendency is not to revise our stereotype of the group but somehow or other to "explain away" the evidence. Where a strong psychological structure is threatened, whether it be an ideal of self, an ideal of another person, or an impersonal belief, we cannot rest content until the rest of the field has been sufficiently reorganized to take care of the conflict. We shall see how this principle is basic to an understanding of national, racial, and class prejudices.

THE DEVELOPMENT OF SOCIALIZATION

In politics and economics we speak of *socialization* as the assumption of social control over natural resources or public services, e.g., the socialization of the railways, socialized medicine. The educational or clinical psychologist may describe a person as well or badly socialized; this is really an ethical use of the term. In social psychology the word means something much more fundamental. Socialization is the process whereby a person comes to behave with reference to other people as people, to apprehend himself directly or symbolically as a member of a group, to live in a world that is structured in terms of persons. Socialization in this sense is an inescapable fact of psychological development. There are no well-authenticated cases of individuals who have grown up outside the context of human society, and we can only speculate as to what such people would be like. Literature contains a number of stories, some mythical and all inadequately documented, about children who grew up in animal societies or in isolation from human contact. No psychologist has ever had the opportunity to study such cases, or the temerity to perform such an experiment. What evidence we have, however, would suggest that a child brought up without human contacts would not be a human being as we understand the term. At present we must accept the fact that the only people we can study are those who have gone through a process of socialization. Our problem is to determine what variables affect what particular aspects of social growth.

Social Behavior in Animals

Can we learn anything about human socialization from the study of animals? Many animal species have societal organizations strikingly similar in certain aspects to those of human society, and we are often tempted to believe that we can find justification in these for particular kinds of social organization in man. The evident monogamy of some birds, for instance, has been hailed as proof that monogamy is a natural institution; the rigid class structure of insect societies would seem to suggest that societies operate best when there is a firm class organization: and the dominance-submission hierarchies in many animal forms are quoted in support of particular doctrines of leadership. Many of the earlier social theorists found comfort and inspiration in the study of animals. "Go to the ant, thou sluggard; consider her ways, and be wise." Unfortunately, however, such inferences are not justifiable. What is called social organization among the animals is not necessarily similar in kind to social behavior in man. The insects, who afford the most dramatic examples, are not our ancestors in the evolutionary scale, and they show only superficial similarities to human societies. When we study them experimentally we find little evidence that individuals interact with individuals as individuals. Their behavior is as nearly automatic as behavior can be. There is nothing in ant life analogous to the social world of man. We can learn more from the study of the higher vertebrates, especially monkeys and apes, since their structures are in many respects similar to our own. Even these relatively advanced animals, however, lack the capacity for linguistic symbolism, and are thus deficient in the one essential condition of human social life. Animals can teach us much about the laws of perception, motivation, and learning, but the superficial similarities between human and animal societies are apt to be thoroughly misleading.

The World of the Infant

The child at birth is not a social being. He is dependent on people, but he does not react to them as people because he cannot yet perceive them as people. We have no direct way of knowing what goes on in the world of the infant. All we can do is deduce from his behavior what probably is there for him. We have good reason for believing that the processes of growth and maturation that are responsible for his physical development are also responsible for his psychological development. In all probability the psychological world of the infant begins, not as a "blooming, buzzing confusion," as William James put it, but rather as a simple, relatively diffuse and undifferentiated field of experience, which gradually becomes organized and articulated as the organism develops and comes into contact with a wider variety of stimulating conditions. We can observe the baby responding to stimuli, but we have no way of knowing what sort of phenomenal object these stimuli represent and what sort of experience the baby goes through in responding. What is fairly clear, however, is that the objects of the world about him do not suddenly come into being for him as fully organized and meaningful. The perception of objects is a developing process that never stops. As the child grows and has experience his world becomes steadily richer in its differentiation, and at the same time more stably structured. The process of socialization must be considered in part as the process whereby the perceptual world becomes articulated and capable of carrying social meanings.

The Differentiation of the Self

The most important aspect of this development is the process of differentiation between subject and object, between the self and that which is not the self. In the newborn infant there is no self as we understand the term. The differentiation between self and not-self is probably a slowly developing process. Everyone is familiar with the example of the baby exercising his new tooth by chewing upon his toe, without apparently grasping the connection between the pain thus produced and the toe as a part of his body. Probably the developing feeling of selfhood is at first a function of a gradually differentiating percept of the body, paralleling the differentiation of the other perceptual objects in the field. The body percept depends to some extent on all the sense modalities, including vision and hearing, but its primary basis must be sought in the functioning of the receptor systems of the skin, of the muscles, tendons, and joints, and of the viscera. The perception of the world outside the body depends far more heavily on vision and hearing. These are the senses that give us the clearest and most stable of our percepts, the most pronounced constancy phenomena and the most elaborate organization of space. It is natural that in the developing perception of the child the objects outside his body should become organized for him more quickly than does the percept of his own body. The infant learns to identify objects about him more quickly than he learns to perceive his body as an entity. In other words, the objective takes precedence over the subjective in perceptual development. This is an important fact to establish. It means that the self is developing in a world that has already acquired some degree of stability and organization. The self does not project its properties into the objective world; rather, it conforms to a pattern that is already there.

The differentiation of self from not-self is, however, only part of the developmental story. Within the realm of not-self we have a similar differentiation between persons, or other selves, and things. At first glance the distinction between person and thing would seem to be simple and obvious. People are alive, expressive, capable of acting on their own volition; things are inanimate, inert, lacking feeling and volition. For the child, however, it is a distinction that must be learned. We tend to assume that the traditional primary and secondary qualities, size, shape, redness, sweetness, and so forth, are legitimate properties of things, but that the so-called tertiary or physiognomic qualities, like friendliness and angriness, are to be found only in living creatures. We are sometimes warned of the "pathetic fallacy," i.e., the fallacy of projecting our own feelings into inanimate things. The status of the primary, secondary, and tertiary qualities is an issue that need not concern us here. What is important to note is that in primitive perception, in the perceptions of children, of some preliterate peoples, and presumably, of some animals, the distinction is much less clear than it is for us. The child perceives his mother's face as friendly or angry, but he may react in the same way to the toy or to the stone that he has stumbled over; the stone is a "bad" stone. What has sometimes been called "animism" in preliterate people indicates a similar kind of perception. The apprehension of stones, trees, lakes, and the like as embodying friendly or malignant spirits suggests that for them these objects may possess humanlike qualities. Even our own behavior may reveal kindred phenomena. A mature adult may angrily throw a monkey wrench at a recalcitrant machine, as though the machine were a responsible agent; and it is difficult not to think of flowers as gentle and sensitive, music as gay or sad, and black thunder-clouds as threatening. Granted that when challenged we repudiate such anthropomorphism, the fact remains that the world of things is not for us completely neutral and impersonal.

It would seem that the process of psychological development involves a progressive depersonalization of some of our percepts and an accentuation of the dynamic qualities of others. We can observe this process of differentiation beginning in childhood and continuing throughout life, and we may assume that it is never complete. What is sometimes difficult for us to realize is that the pattern of differentiation may vary significantly from individual to individual and from culture to culture. When we try to understand the behavior of others we must remember that the concepts of "self," "person," and "thing" may not mean to them what they mean to us.

Roles, Attitudes, and Beliefs

The first persons the child comes into contact with are the members of his own immediate family, notably the mother. It is through the mother that the child gets its first rewards and punishments, and it is through mother, father, brother, and sister that the social world of the child receives its initial structure. Mother may be supportive, father may be remote and frightening, brother and sister may be rivals rather than friends. Whatever the structure of the family may be, this is the initial picture of society that the child will receive. And, since the structure of any given family tends to reflect the pattern of the culture, the child thus quickly learns to look at the world in accordance with the pattern of his culture. If father takes great care of his tools, tools become precious things, to be taken care of. If mother resents her housework, housework becomes something to be despised. If big brother is devoted to baseball, baseball becomes something supremely worth while, and so forth. The child sees the world at first through the eyes of the family. Since he has no opportunity for comparison, their world becomes his world.

Similarly, the concept of self conforms to the cultural pattern. In a society in which women play a subordinate role the little girl, as soon as she realizes that she is a girl, accepts a subordinate role. In a society with a rigid caste organization the child, as soon as he discovers that he is a member of a particular caste, unquestioningly accepts that position in society. As he continues to develop, and begins to have contact with a greater variety of people and things, new roles begin to present themselves. He sees himself in imagination as the street-corner policeman, as his favorite teacher, or as someone like his father. Much of early social development is a process of assuming different roles. This can be readily observed in children's play, in which the child may adopt successively a number of widely different roles. Fluctuation of role is one of the characteristics of childhood. As the child grows up the range of acceptable roles becomes narrowed, until finally one dominant role remains, with possibly a few latent alternative roles that may appear from time to time under special circumstances.

Throughout this process of social development the culture is steadily imposing its emphases on the world of the child. He perceives himself in accordance with the standards of his culture. He perceives other things, other individuals, and other groups as his culture dictates. By the time he has reached maturity he has developed a solid substructure of attitudes, opinions, and beliefs in conformity with the prevailing cultural pattern. He has gradually come to live in a world similar in structure to the world in which his friends and neighbors live.

The attitudes, opinions, and beliefs of an individual continue to develop and change throughout life, but for the normal person enough of them become sufficiently stable to provide a dependable framework for his conduct, and sufficiently consistent to permit us to predict his behavior. In general, the person who is conservative in politics is likely to be conservative in other respects, and the person who dislikes foreigners will probably dislike members of minority groups within his own nation. A belief defended today is likely to be defended a year hence. This fact of consistency makes it possible for us to apply scientific methods to the study of the attitudes, opinions, and beliefs of individuals; and the fact that people in a common cultural environment tend to become socialized in the same way makes it possible for us to study the psychological characteristics of groups.

PSYCHOLOGICAL GROUPS

Part of the process of socialization is the acquisition of membership in social groups, and much of one's social behavior and experience can be understood in terms of one's group memberships. In the broadest sense, a group is any clustering of individuals on the basis of at least one common differentiating characteristic. There are, however, two kinds of grouping that are important for psychology. In the study of perception, for instance, we recognize basic principles of group formation, e.g., proximity, similarity, good continuation, in accordance with which discrete stimulus processes lead to configured percepts. Such a configuration is psychologically not the sum of its parts, and if a part is abstracted from the configuration its properties change accordingly. Similarly, there are groups of people, e.g., a lynching mob, whose interactions are such that the group cannot be apprehended merely as a cluster of individuals in isolation. On the other hand, we may arbitrarily select a certain characteristic and group together all individuals possessing it. Thus we might group people according to age, sex, color of skin, size of income, or number of traffic violations, or we might consider as a group all people who during the past six months have bought a piano. Such groupings are essentially classifications, with no interaction implied.

Psychological and Sociological Group Membership

The first type of group (interactive) is defined psychologically, the second (noninteractive), sociologically; both are important. If we are to understand socialization in childhood, for instance, we must learn as much as possible about the characteristics of children at different age levels. Six-year-old children regarded merely as a class of individuals do not constitute a psychological group. Nevertheless we may define them sociologically as a group having a common age characteristic and find out how this is related to such characteristics as intelligence and emotional maturity. Similarly, we may select delinquency as our defining criterion and correlate it with income level, housing congestion or broken homes. The study of such sociologically defined groups is not only basic to the understanding of the structure and functioning of society, but it provides indispensable background information for the understanding of psychological groups. We must, however, keep the two categories distinct. Sociological group membership implies merely the possession of the formal defining characteristics of the group. Psychological group membership involves a feeling of belongingness in the group. Any wage earner is sociologically a member of the wage-earning class, but he may or may not feel himself identified with other wage earners. He is sociologically but not psychologically a member of the group. By contrast, a person may be psychologically a member of a group while lacking most of its defining characteristics. One of our most prominent Negro leaders, for instance, is blond and blue-eyed, physically indistinguishable from non-Negroes; yet he feels and behaves as a Negro.

Sociological group membership determines the way in which a person is apprehended by other people. Psychological group membership determines the way in which he apprehends himself. When we identify a person as a Negro, a German, a Mohammedan, or a Socialist, we are thereby imposing on him the characteristics of the racial, national, religious, or political group with which we identify him. These imposed characteristics correspond to the *stereotype* of the group, i.e., to the accumulated beliefs about the group, which may have stemmed from our own experience, but which are more likely to have been accepted uncritically from others. Thus, we may have a stereotype of the Negro as indolent and irresponsible. This means that we have a set of expectations which will inevitably influence our perception of any individual Negro. There are stereotypes for all identifiable social groups, some more rigid than others. Since it is virtually impossible to think of any person without classifying him in some conventional group or other, if only in an age or sex group, we must conclude that prejudgment is a normal component of the perceptual process. We are inclined to use the term *prejudice* when these prejudgments are really misjudgments, i.e., when they are inflexible and involve a disparagement of the individual or group in question. There is considerable evidence to indicate that people vary greatly in the rigidity of their stereotypes, and consequently in the strength of their prejudices.

The same mechanism of prejudgment operates in psychological group membership. When a person feels himself to be a member of a particular group, his own needs, goals, and frustrations conform to those of the group as he apprehends it, and his apprehension of other groups is correspondingly affected. Psychological group membership involves the extension of the feeling of selfhood to include other members of the group. Thus "being a Negro" is an experience of "we" rather than merely "I," and this experience tends to force all other people into a single "they" category of non-Negroes. The mechanisms of defense discussed above are thus just as pertinent to group behavior as they are to individual behavior.

Sociologically defined groups may, of course, become transformed into psychological groups. Wage earners may discover their membership in the wage-earning class and begin to develop class consciousness. When Hitler began his campaign to unify "Greater Germany" he succeeded through clever propaganda in persuading many people of German ancestry who lived in other countries that they were members of a great German race. In this process of transformation we have the key to the understanding of many of the conflicts that beset society.

Multiple Group Membership

Any one individual may have simultaneous membership in many different psychological groups, and the number and complexity of these memberships varies from person to person. He may be simultaneously a member of his family, of his tennis club, of his college alumni association, of the community welfare society, and of his church. Each of these group memberships imposes a particular loyalty on him and correspondingly determines his behavior. When he is at home he may think and behave as a family man. When he attends a committee of the welfare society he may think and behave as a member of the community. This fact of multiple group membership means that the psychological world of the individual contains a number of different interlocking frameworks within which he behaves. Much of what we call the personality of an individual can be understood in terms of the nature of and the relationships among these different group memberships. Such an interpretation is not incompatible with the concept of a central core of personality which is present in most if not all the roles of the individual.

For the most part our group memberships fit neatly together and support each other. There is seldom any conflict, for instance, between family and community membership, and loyalty to one's community may actually reinforce loyalty to one's country. It often happens, however, that different group memberships come into conflict with one another. The father may discover that loyalty to his country must draw him away from his family. Many sincerely religious people have found national loyalty incompatible with their religion. The nonnational ideal of science comes into conflict during wartime with the scientists' national group membership. Conflicts of group membership may lead to a number of different consequences: (1) In some cases they may result in neurotic or even psychotic breakdowns. The individual finds himself incapable of resolving the conflict in a normal way, and escapes into illness. (2) One of the conflicting group memberships may be suppressed. A conflict between patriotism and religious belief may lead to a denial of national group membership. (3) The individual may simply keep his incompatible group memberships in separate compartments. The respectable church member may be engaged in ruthless business practices that violate the tenets of his religion. He resolves the conflict by being a church member on Sundays and a businessman during the rest of the week. (4) The discovery of a superordinate group membership may alter the character of the memberships that were originally in conflict. When we accept the ideal of "One World," we do not deny the fact of national, racial, and other groupings, but we no longer see them as mutually incompatible.

Some Typical Psychological Groups

The structure, cohesiveness, and permanence of psychological groups will always depend on the interplay of many different factors. Rather than attempt a classification of such groups we shall present four typically different examples.

First, there is the *casual and temporary* group. A number of people (an aggregate) are waiting for a bus; this is not a psychological group. The bus, however, does not arrive on time. The common feeling of frustration is sufficient to transform this aggregate temporarily into a psychological group, and we find the members exchanging casual comments about the efficiency of the bus company. As soon as the bus arrives, however, the group as such disintegrates. Similarly, the passengers on an ocean vessel are initially an aggregate; but their common destination, their common interest in the voyage, and the fact that they cannot escape from the ship, unifies them for the duration of the voyage. Occasionally passengers discover other common interests which lead to lasting friendships; but more frequently a later reunion proves that what seemed to be a real group on board ship has no basis of permanence.

Secondly, there are *interest and action* groups. A number of mothers in a community become concerned about conditions in the children's ward of the local hospital. They meet to discuss ways and means of improving the situation. They develop plans, form an organization, exert pressure, and get results. The task has been accomplished, but in the process they have discovered the satisfaction of working together, and they agree to continue to work toward other objectives. The group has now achieved an existence that is independent of the originally initiating interest. Each individual member has become less an "I" and more a part of a "we." The group will maintain itself, however, only if it continues to discover new common interests and if the rewards of common action are understood as group rewards. Such a group will become even stronger if it meets with opposition. If as a group they have to fight back, each individual will become more thoroughly ego-involved in the group.

Thirdly, there are *involuntary or externally imposed* groupings. These are the sociologically defined groups, psychological membership in which is forced upon the individual by society. The natives of Africa do not think of themselves as dark-skinned until they have had contact with light-skinned people. Membership in the dark-skinned group is then, as it were, thrust upon them. They become a group because the rest of society sees them as a group, and they cannot escape. Each of us belongs to many such groups. We become aware of our membership only gradually as we begin to interact with the larger society about us, and in most cases we must accept this membership whether or not we like it. Membership in the family group is an example; we cannot choose our own families. Similarly we cannot choose our sex, nor in our present society can we easily escape being identified with a particular race. In this country, membership in a religious group is theoretically voluntary; but actually very few people ever really join a religious group through an act of choice. We are born Protestants, Roman Catholics, or Jews. The instances of "conversion" to another religious faith are so infrequent as to be noteworthy.

A fourth type of grouping might be called the *latent* psychological group. The scientist working in the isolation of his laboratory feels his affinity with other scientists in other parts of the world. He may not know them individually, or be able to identify them by name, but he knows they exist and he belongs with them. When the opportunity offers he is likely to seek them out, knowing in advance that they will have common interests. Collectors of stamps, angling enthusiasts, blind people, and so forth, may have this kind of group membership. The basis is an awareness in the individual that he is in a particular way different from other individuals and that elsewhere there are others who are different in the same way. Such people may come together physically or through communication develop into an organized interest or action group, but their feeling of group membership precedes the actual organization.

We can see in examples such as these some of the factors that contribute to and detract from psychological group formation. Physical proximity, similarity of personal characteristics and interests, easy identification on the basis of perceptual characteristics, and so forth, all favor group formation. A group will be more likely to maintain itself if the members are able to communicate readily with one another, if they have acquired a group name and a group history, if through group action they have achieved something which brings group rewards, if they have been welded together through resistance to common opposition. We shall now see how these factors operate in two concrete examples, namely, in national and racial groups.

NATIONAL GROUP MEMBERSHIP

The legal definition of nationality in terms of citizenship does not adequately define nationality. What is psychologically important is not what appears on the passport but the kind of national group membership the individual feels. The nation is not equivalent to the state. During its tempestuous history, Poland has been carved up in many different ways, and the citizenship of Poles has correspondingly fluctuated; yet the Poles continued to be a national group. The nation cannot be defined in terms of "race." Every one of the major nations is composed of different "races," and no "race" is confined to a single nation. There can be no linguistic definition of nation. Great Britain and the United States are different nations but have the same language. Nor can we identify nation with geographical boundaries as is traditionally done; the people who considered themselves Germans were not limited to the boundaries of the German state. Nationality is one of those psychological group memberships that draw support from many factors, but that are identifiable with none. The Jews are perhaps the most interesting example. The Jews have existed as a group for thousands of years. Until recently there was no Jewish state, and even now most Jews are not citizens of that state. In spite of Hitler's pronouncements, there is no Jewish race. The Jews are drawn from a wide variety of racial stocks. There is a Jewish religion, or rather several variants of the Jewish religion, but many people who are called Jews, and who think of themselves as Jews, do not profess the Jewish religion. There is no Jewish language; there is Hebrew which is spoken by many non-Jews. Yet the Jews are an identifiable group with a feeling of group membership. It might not be inappropriate to refer to them as a nation.

Since we cannot find a single criterion of nationality apart from the feeling of national group membership, we must look for multiple criteria. What contributes to national group membership? First, there is the *national label*. When we have words like *American, British, German, Jewish,* we have easy ways in which the individual can characterize himself, and simple categories into which someone else can put him.

Secondly, we have the *national home*, a geographically defined area that is an object of sentiment. When Canadians, Australians, and New Zealanders talk about "the Old Country," they are referring to Great Britain. For Poles the national home has fluctuating boundaries, but it is always the region between Germany and Russia. For many Jews, Palestine, however defined, is the home land, although most Jews have never seen it.

Thirdly, there is the factor of *historical continuity*. Continuity is probably the primary determinant of Jewish group membership. The Jews have been identifiable as Jews longer than has any other existing national group. Germany as a nation has only a brief history, dating back to the middle nineteenth century. Part of the success of Hitler's appeal to the German people lay in his ability to recreate for them a mythical history. By emphasizing the concept of *"Volk"* he gave them a feeling of membership in an ancient and continuous group. This tendency to seek for a history when no real history exists is very widespread. Even among preliterate groups, like some of the East African tribes that are known to have existed as tribes for a relatively short time, we find that in tribal mythology a history has been created. Where the known history of a group is none too flattering we find it gradually reshaped as it is handed on from generation to generation so as to conform to the national ideal.

Fourthly, we have the *national ideal* itself. One of the startling experiences of the young and naïve traveler is to discover that his own country is not universally admired, and that the people of each country he visits believe that in some important respect their country is the best. If a national group is to maintain its vigor, its individual members must believe in the essential superiority of that group. We find that each nation has an ideal of itself in terms of which other nations come off second best. The national ideal may provide an interesting study in rationalization. It is as though each nation had deliberately sought out those ways in which it might be considered to be superior to other nations, and had then attached supreme value to those particular superiorities. The national ideal may center about mere size and strength; it may emphasize ethical standards, artistic achievements, or even something as intangible as a way of living. In the United States we tend to be proud of our size, our wealth, our initiative, our resourcefulness, our toughness. We believe that we have a superior social system, democracy, and that we are more humanitarian than any other people. We tend to patronize the small, weak, and economically unproductive countries. In Great Britain the national ideal contains many of the same components, for the British and the Americans have in this respect a great deal in common. The Britisher, however, while conceding and admiring American superiority in some respects, is likely to suggest that in the essentials, namely in social stability, in basic common sense, in fundamental decency and good taste, in ability to survive reverses courageously, his people are superior. The Frenchman may cast many a wistful and envious glance at American wealth and comfort. He would like to have a fine motorcar and an electric refrigerator. For him, however, there is no question that in the essentials France is superior. The French, he asserts, are a people of intellectual and artistic refinement, who appreciate the finer things of life —good music, good paintings, good food, good wines, and stimulating conversation. The German will share the Frenchman's emphasis on intellectual and artistic values, but he will disparage the French as a superficial and disorderly people. For the Jewish nation, the national ideal centers about ethical and religious concepts, and includes a strong overtone of world mission. For the Indian there is no question that nations of the West are crude and materialistic, that his people are superior in the essentials, namely in social sensitivity and in spiritual insight. This list of examples might be extended indefinitely. It is important to note, however, that these are merely examples. There can be no disputing the fact of differences in national ideal, but it does not follow that every member of a national group shares to the same extent a single national ideal. Few nations are culturally so stable as to have no internal ideological differences, and during the course of history we may find the relative value emphasis within a national ideal undergoing radical change. Nor need we assume that the national ideal accepted by the members of a particular national group necessarily corresponds to the way in which that nation is apprehended by other nations. There may be a great discrepancy between a nation's self-rating and the ratings given that nation by others.

The foregoing are some of the internal factors that contribute to the formation and maintenance of national groups. But there are external factors as well. The feeling of national group membership depends in large measure on the awareness of the existence of other national groups. Many Americans do not really discover their nationality until they have begun to travel. In many parts of the United

States, Americans have little or no contact with foreigners, and seldom if ever hear a foreign language spoken. Nationality is not one of their primary group memberships. The same probably holds true for the remoter regions of other large countries. In contrast we note that small countries that are surrounded by other countries, like the Netherlands, Switzerland, and the various countries of the Balkans, have a strong national orientation. For the people of these countries the sight of a foreigner is an everyday experience, they are likely to speak at least one language other than their native tongue, and if they travel they soon come to a frontier. For such people nationality is one of the primary group memberships.

The mere awareness of other nationalities helps to maintain one's own awareness of nationality. If the other nationalities are apprehended as a threat, the effect is intensified. The feeling of nationality becomes then a chip-on-the-shoulder attitude. This is perhaps one of the reasons why the Balkan peninsula has been the scene of so many international conflicts. When nationality feeling becomes so strong as to wish to dominate other group memberships, we may speak of the attitude as one of nationalism. In a nationalistic state all the forces that normally contribute to cultural diversity tend to become coördinated in the service of national glorification. Group memberships that cut across national boundaries, e.g., religious and scientific memberships, may be either suppressed or nationalized. Potentially divisive subgroups, e.g., political parties and labor organizations, may be dissolved. Certain easily identifiable subgroups, e.g., racial and linguistic minorities, may be selected as "scapegoats" and persecuted. But, most important of all, other nations may be stereotyped as malignant and dangerous, and therefore as legitimate objects of attack.

Extreme nationalism has sometimes been compared to the psychosis known as paranoia. The paranoiac's delusions of grandeur are supported by delusions of persecution, and the combination may lead to dangerous forms of aggression. Nations do not become psychotic; but the analogy is apt. Nationalism involves both delusions of grandeur and delusions of persecution, and it represents the same kind of oversimplified restructuring of the psychological field. Any group membership that becomes dominant may present the same phenomena. If the group happens to control the implements of aggression it becomes correspondingly dangerous. In the world of today, the machinery of warfare is still under national control. This is why nationalism still presents the greatest psychological threat to world peace.

RACIAL GROUP MEMBERSHIP

The term *race* has been so loosely used that we must first clarify its meaning. The concept belongs properly to the science of physical anthropology, although, as we shall see, it has psychological implications. In biological classification we recognize various animal species. Among these is species *Homo,* a subgroup of the primate vertebrates. From time immemorial the obvious differences among humans have lent support to the theory that the human species itself can be broken down into further subgroups, or races, each race representing a separate biological entity and each with its own set of distinguishing characteristics. From these distinguishing characteristics physical anthropologists have attempted to derive sets of indices in terms of which races can be identified. Such indices are pigmentation of skin, eyes and hair, texture and distribution of hair, shape of head, shape of nose, conformation of jaw, and so forth. It is generally agreed that no single index is satisfactory in itself, but that some are more dependable than others and that better indices may yet be developed.

On the basis of anthropometric analysis various racial classifications have been proposed. One of the most popular of these gives us three major racial groups, the Caucasian or "white," the Mongoloid or "yellow," and the Negroid or "black," each of which can be further subdivided. Among the Caucasians, for instance, are such subgroups as Nordic, Alpine, and Mediterranean, and as well, some of the deeply pigmented groups of India. The words *Aryan* and *Semitic,* it may be mentioned at this point, refer to linguistic, not to racial groups.

The status of the concept of "race" is still being hotly debated. At one extreme there are those who contend that the races of man are evolutionary products, strictly analogous to the other animal forms, and that any attempt to understand man must take into account his specific racial heritage. At the other extreme it is argued that racial classifications are mere artifacts of our methods of measurement, that the skin-color index, for instance, would give us one set of races and the cephalic index another, that consequently races as such have no real existence. This debate need not concern us here. We may note merely that if primary racial groups were differentiated early in man's evolutionary history, they have now become so intermingled as to make it impossible for us to detect a pure strain; on the other hand, even if there were no originally different stocks certain recognizable characteristics have been so intensified in some groups as to make those groups stand out as "racially" different from other groups. The pygmies of the Belgian Congo, for instance, are recognizably different from all surrounding peoples. Thus, even if we abolish the term *race* as representing a biological entity, we may retain the adjective *racial* as a useful way of characterizing differences among groups that are due to heredity. Certain differences in skin, hair, bony structure, etc., may properly be called racial differences, even if we give up the notion of primary races. This leads to two important psychological questions: First, are these racial differences in any way related to fundamental psychological characteristics of people? Secondly, what is the role of racial differences in psychological group membership? Both questions are important for the understanding of social behavior, but unfortunately our research has sometimes failed to distinguish clearly between them.

Since the anthropologist cannot provide us with pure races, we cannot pick out a race and study its psychological characteristics. What we must do is work out correlations between racial indices and psychological variables. What is the relation, for instance, between skin color, texture of hair, and shape of head, on the one hand, and intelligence, temperament, or creativity on the other? The available evidence is inconclusive, but such evidence as we have all suggests that if there are fundamental psychological differences related to race these are at least very much smaller than the conventional racial stereotypes would have us believe.

The best studies have been in the field of intelligence measurement. During World War I the intelligence tests applied to American soldiers revealed a statistically reliable superiority in intelligence of whites over Negroes. This was hailed as proof of innate racial differences in intelligence. There was, of course, no control of educational opportunity, motivation, and similar social psychological variables. Subsequent studies have shown that the difference in IQ between Negro and white diminishes as the psychological environment of the Negro more closely approximates that of the white. There have been no similar large-scale studies of psychological characteristics other than intelligence. Until the evidence is in we cannot deny the possibility that, just as individuals vary in psychological capacities and traits, so groups of individuals may through a long process of natural selection have become differentiated in certain psychological ways. We have much to learn about the relation between temperament and physical constitution. There seems, however, to be a positive correlation between physical and temperamental types. It may well be, for instance, that life in the tropics tends to select constitutional and temperamental types that are different from those that would survive in colder regions. What we know at present is not sufficient to justify anyone in being dogmatic.

Even if races should prove to have no existence as biological entities, they do exist as psychological facts. People apprehend themselves as members of racial groups, and racial group membership constitutes one of the important influences that shape, not only ourselves, but also our appreciation of other people. It may be that if the anthropologists eventually explode the "myth" of race, racial membership will lose its psychological significance. So far they have not succeeded.

The distinctive thing about racial as compared with national group membership is that racial group memberships begin with a perceptual difference. This is why skin color, although not accepted by the anthropologists as the best index of race, is psychologically the most important. Differences in skin color are obvious, and it is consequently no accident that the most popular racial classification is in terms of white, yellow, and black skins. Natives of India, who are racially Caucasian rather than Negroid, may nevertheless find themselves treated as Negroes in the United States simply because their skins are dark. The fact of a perceptual difference operates in two ways. In the first place, it enables the members of a particular racial group to recognize each other, and consequently enhances their feeling of group membership. On the other hand, it makes the members of the group identifiable to people who are not in the group; and this fact of identification from without also contributes to the solidarity of the group. It is doubtful if racial distinctions, and consequently racial discrimination, could originate in the absence of some sort of perceptual differentiation.

Once a racial distinction has become established, however, it may maintain itself even in the absence of obvious perceptual differences. In the United States the Negroes are theoretically people with dark skins. In actual fact, however, a large proportion of American Negroes have relatively light skins. The intermixture between Negro and white has been so frequent in the history of this country that we can now find every shade of pigmentation from deepest black to what we call white. Nevertheless a clear line between Negro and white continues to be drawn, no longer on the basis of skin color alone but also on the basis of presumed inheritance. In some states anyone who has as little as one thirty-second of Negro "blood" is considered to be a Negro, and many people who are considered to be Negroes have no recognizable negroid characteristics. Where a racial distinction is to be maintained in the absence of an obvious perceptual differentiation we find that the distinction becomes reinforced by other criteria. Many light-skinned people of Negro parentage succeed in "passing" into white society. There are, however, two types of force that operate to prevent such "passing." In the first place, even a light-skinned child born into a Negro family grows up in a Negro community, attends Negro schools, and becomes identified to all who know him as a Negro. Unless he cuts away all his family and community associations, and starts life again as an unknown person in a new community, he will always be identified as a Negro. In the second place, the mere fact of being identified as a Negro generates within him a feeling of racial group membership, and his natural response is to develop a loyalty to his own group. Many light-skinned Negroes, who would have no trouble in "passing" if they so desired, have deliberately chosen to remain as Negroes, and to share the life of their fellow racial group members.

We find even better examples of the maintenance of existing racial lines in spite of the absence of perceptual differences in the recent history of the Jews. The Jews, as we have noted, are not a race in the correct sense of the term, yet they are treated as such. It has been repeatedly demonstrated that no existing anthropological technique can differentiate Jew from non-Jew. In some communities Jews may stand out as different from the rest of the population, because of the greater prevalence of their so-called Mediterranean characteristics, e.g., complexion and head shape. In the countries around the Mediterranean Sea the distinction does not hold. Here again we find that, in the absence of an obvious perceptual differentiation, artificial differences may be deliberately adopted by the group, or may be thrust upon the group by an outside agency. In many communities Jews have deliberately maintained a traditional form of dress, have clung to traditional Jewish names, and have retained and have transmitted to their offspring the Yiddish or Hebrew language, thereby making it easier for non-Jews to identify them as Jews. During the Nazi period in Germany Hitler found it necessary to invent obvious perceptual differentiations, forcing Jews to live by themselves in ghettos, to wear distinctive emblems, and to adopt certain specifically Jewish names. There were probably few young Germans, brought up in the Nazi tradition and exposed to anti-Semitic education, who did not honestly believe that there was something visibly distinctive about every Jew.

As mankind becomes more enlightened, racial group membership may become correspondingly less important. At present, race is still one of the great carriers of tradition and one of the common sources of social conflict. Racial group membership is felt by many people as even more fundamental, more intimate, more inescapable, than national group membership. Hitler succeeded in stiffening German nationalism by giving it roots in "blood and soil." In this country race is one of the most common bases for psychological and sociological group formation. Whenever we find prejudice, whether it be national, religious, or class prejudice, we are likely to find it reinforced by racial distinction; and when we probe for the sources of personal pride we are likely to find that some of our most cherished values are rooted in racial tradition. Thus, regardless of its anthropological status, "race" is one of the keys to the understanding of social behavior.

SOCIAL INTERACTION

However a psychological group may have been formed, it is still composed of individuals; and the maintenance of this group will depend on the interaction of these individuals. The study of the dynamics of groups is an important branch of social psychology, and the usefulness of the principles of group dynamics is being increasingly recognized in such fields of practical endeavor as education, industry, and government. We shall limit ourselves here to the three most important problems of group dynamics, namely, communication, persuasion, and leadership.

Communication

All social interaction depends on the fact that people can communicate with each other, and one important approach to the understanding of social relations is through the study of communication. Communication is not limited to language. The warning cry of an animal serves to communicate danger to the other members of the group. The cry of the baby communicates its state of hunger to the mother. In each case the reacting individual perceives a sound as a sign or indicator of something else. We say that the meaning of the sound is perceived, and behavior is regulated in accord with this perceived meaning. This is a kind of one-way communication, and it plays an important regulative role in human behavior. The stop sign at the street corner, the gathering clouds in the sky, and the angry expression on someone's face serve to indicate to us certain useful facts. They provide us with necessary information. In other words, much of what we perceive has sign character; it points beyond itself to something else.

There is much more to social communication however than the perception of signs. In social communication we use the sign intentionally to produce a particular effect. There is not only the perceived meaning but also the intended meaning. This can be conveyed through a facial or manual gesture, through speech or writing, through pictures or music, or even through the manipulation of a situation. The medium of communication places limits on that which can be communicated, but the full act of communication involves the communicator, the medium of communication, and the recipient of communication. For the sake of simplicity let us confine ourselves to communication through speech, and designate these three elements as the speaker, the language, and the hearer. Corresponding to these three units, we have the intention (of the speaker), the meaning (of the language), and the percept (of the hearer). When the percept of the hearer corresponds to the intention of the speaker, we say that communication has been complete. Complete communication is probably never achieved, but there are degrees of communication, and in social psychology we are interested in the factors which contribute to or detract from good communication.

We all know people with whom we can communicate easily, and people with whom we can never seem to reach mutual understanding; and we have watched with concern the successes and failures of communication in international conferences. There is possibly no more important problem of applied social psychology than that of discovering ways in which people can learn how to understand each other. There are two main reasons why communication can never be complete, first, because the speaker and the hearer are always two different people, and, secondly, because no language has ever evolved, or has ever been devised, that is capable of representing accurately all the variables in the psychological world of a person. In a sense these two variables are reciprocals. People who have lived together for a long time and have come to see the world in the same way require very little language for communication. On the other hand, a language that has become highly refined, like the language of mathematics, enables people of widely different backgrounds to communicate with each other.

Some meanings are easier to convey than others because they represent more nearly common experiences. All visually normal people have experienced the difference between red and blue; we have no difficulty in agreeing upon words for this difference. Similarly people of the same culture have no difficulty in conveying such meanings as "cow," "house," and "father." Even among people of our own culture, however, we are never sure that the hearer knows what we are talking about when we use words like *honesty, fair play,* and *decency.* These words refer not to simply and clearly organized structures in the perceptual environment but rather to complex and usually confused characteristics of the nonperceptual environment. In general, the farther removed our meanings are from simple perception the greater the difficulty in communication; and where cultural backgrounds are widely different even what seem to us to be simple and inescapable perceptual facts may prove to have a different meaning for the person to whom we are speaking. It has been demonstrated experimentally that even such tough and resistant perceptual properties as size and shape are in some degree a function of the attitudes, expectations, and value orientations of the perceiver.

Thus the first unit of the communicative act, the intended meaning, is a function of the psychological make-up of the speaker. It represents a structure in his psychological world. This meaning he now tries to convey to another person. But the success with which he does it will depend on his understanding of the psychological world of the other person. If the hearer has been blind from birth we cannot speak lightly of reds and blues, for these words cannot possibly have the same meaning for him as they have for us. If he is a moron we cannot use concepts like relativity; if he is an unregenerate thief he may not understand our concept of honesty. When we try to explain something to a child, we deliberately select those aspects of our world which we think are most likely to correspond to aspects of his world. If we have no insight into the psychological world of the hearer our communication may fail completely.

The hearer apprehends what we say in the context of his own psychological world, and he will understand only as much as will fit intelligibly into the structure of meanings that are already there. The meaning he perceives will be determined significantly by his own desires, interests, attitudes, and value orientations. It is unfortunately only too true that many of us hear only what we wish to hear. The meaning the hearer perceives is also a function of the way in which he apprehends the speaker. Two different people using exactly the same words may be understood as saying two different things, because the hearer has two different sets of expectations. In the act of communication there are thus, as it were, four people involved; two of them real and two fictitious. These are the real speaker, the hearer as apprehended by the speaker (the phenomenal hearer), the speaker as apprehended by the hearer (the phenomenal speaker), and the real hearer. All too frequently we find people talking at complete cross purposes with each other, simply because each is addressing himself to a nonexistent hearer and each is listening to a nonexistent speaker. Communication can be improved only as each participant develops a more nearly correct appreciation of the psychological reference points of the other person.

Communication thus involves the bringing together of two different psychological worlds. It may depend on nothing more than a simple overt act. I point to a bird; you see it; and to that extent we have experienced something in common. Most of social communication, however, depends on language, and language can be both a facilitator and an inhibitor. During the process of socialization, the assignment of names helps to organize and stabilize the structure of the psychological world; names become actually a part of the non-perceptual environment. Names are nouns, but language contains also verbs, adjectives, and adverbs, prepositions and conjunctions, and ways in which these are put together in sentences (syntax). Broadly speaking, nouns refer to things, verbs to action, adjectives and adverbs to properties of things and actions, prepositions and conjunctions to relationships. As soon as we begin to study language we realize, first, that no language represents completely and accurately all the variables in the psychological world, i.e., that linguistic structure is selective, and secondly, that no two languages represent exactly the same selection. Each language represents in a unique way one selection of the variables of the psychological world. In each language some meanings are incorporated in words, others in word combinations, and still others have to be conveyed by gesture, by intonation, or by context. No simple word-for-word translation from one language to another is ever possible. The meaning of the English word *knife,* for instance, is distributed in French between *canif* and *couteau.* The meaning of the German word *doch* can be conveyed in English only through an elaborate circumlocution. The English writer is always embarrassed by the lack of a neutral word for *he or she.* English has one word for *snow,* and the difference between *falling snow, snow on the ground,* and *hard-packed snow* is conveyed through word combinations. In the Eskimo languages each kind of snow has a separate word. A polite reference to a woman in English includes her marital status, *Mrs.* or *Miss*; but in *Mister* there is no distinction between the married and the unmarried male. In some languages it is impossible to speak of a person without indicating his age category. Such examples could be multiplied indefinitely. What is important to note is that when two people communicate with each other they must do so through a medium that automatically selects and defines different structures and characteristics of the world of each person. Thus while language extends immeasurably the range of meanings that can be communicated, it also creates obstacles which must be overcome. It is a veil through which we can apprehend only imperfectly what exists in the world of the other person. To this extent are the problems of semantics the problems of communication.

Various attempts have been made through the construction of artificial languages, like Esperanto and Ido, or through the simplification of existing languages, like Basic English, to develop a medium for universal communication. Worthy as such efforts are, we must recognize that, however faulty our existing languages are, they have at least evolved in the context of the requirements of human communication. Artificial languages, of which the best is mathematics, are excellent for the communication of certain restricted types of meaning. Until psychological analysis has progressed far beyond its present state of development, it seems unlikely that any artificial language will be able to provide a medium for complete communication.

Persuasion

Communication as a form of social interaction is seldom limited to the mere conveying of meanings from one person to another. Usually one person is trying to influence the other person, to change his opinions and attitudes, or to induce him to do something; and, even if he has no such conscious intention, the mere fact of social interaction is likely to produce such a result. Whenever we make use of one of the media of communication we are in effect exercising persuasion on the other person. We may recognize three kinds of persuasion: (1) the deliberate attempt to influence another person toward ends that are explicitly recognized and by methods that are accepted as legitimate; this is *education*; (2) the deliberate attempt to influence other people by techniques that are not fully recognized by the person being influenced; this may be called *intentional propaganda*; (3) the incidental influencing of other people by means that are not recognized as such; this may be called *unintentional or unconscious propaganda*.

We have seen how during the process of socialization the world of the individual gradually becomes organized, articulated, and stabilized in a way that roughly corresponds to the world as it is apprehended by other members of the same group. Much of this development depends on formal instruction. When we teach our children that the product of three and four is twelve we are deliberately revealing to them something that we believe to be true. It may be that we have never questioned the value of such knowledge, but so far as we are concerned the end is a good one, and in imparting such knowledge we are not trying to "trick" or "fool" the child. In education we try to impart knowledge, to develop habits and to mold attitudes that we believe are in the interest of the person who is being educated. We make no effort to conceal the goal or the means.

In general, we all know what we mean by education as distinguished from propaganda. When we get down to cases, however, we find that it is difficult to draw a clear line between the two. The term propaganda was originally used in connection with the missionary enterprise of the Roman Catholic Church. The missionaries were propagating the faith. In other words, they were engaged in what they considered to be education. More recently propaganda has come to mean almost the antithesis of education, i.e., the attempt to control people without revealing for what, in what way, and by whom they are being controlled. We are now inclined to think of propaganda as a way of deceiving people for sinister ends. During World War II we labeled as propaganda Goebbels' attempt to convince us that our cause was unjust and hopeless, whereas our efforts to give the truth to the German people was considered to be education. The social psychologist cannot be satisfied with two simple antithetical categories, education and propaganda, one good and the other bad. He is interested in determining the factors involved in the formation and alteration of attitudes and in the control of conduct. What has been called propaganda provides a rich source of evidence.

Some of our best examples of propaganda come from advertising. The advertiser wants us to buy a particular brand of cigarette. He may or may not believe that the brand he is advertising is the best; this is irrelevant. His immediate goal is to make us buy. If his brand were demonstrably the best, all he would have to do would be to lay the facts before us and trust to our judgment. He cannot do this, however, because no brand of cigarette is demonstrably superior to all other brands. His task is consequently that of persuading us not to look at the facts, but to make our selection on other than rational grounds. He purchases endorsements from glamorous movie stars, shows us pictures of pretty ladies and distinguished gentlemen smoking his cigarette, and invents ringing slogans. He may even make a concession to rationality by quoting supposedly scientific evidence in favor of his product. What he is doing is linking his product with existing attitudes and value orientations in the hope that the consumer will thus be led to buy it without actually scrutinizing it. Unfortunately the technique works all too well.

In political propaganda we can observe the same technique. Hitler frankly admitted that, however monstrous a lie, if it were repeated often enough it would be accepted. The political propagandist studies his people, assesses their hopes and their fears, discovers what they wish to believe, and then presents his message in such a way that it fits in with their existing attitudes. We have seen how the awareness of a common threat unifies people, how the discovery of a scapegoat enables them to free themselves from a feeling of guilt. The political propagandist who is clever enough to define the enemy and point to the scapegoat is likely to succeed. His technique is to persuade by making use of the existing psychological structure to further his own ends. A useful exercise for the American student is to analyze the propaganda in the contemporary American scene.

Intentional propaganda can usually be recognized and countered. Unintentional propaganda is far more difficult to identify. During World War II the rival countries flooded the neutrals with propaganda literature and propaganda films. These attempted to present their respective causes in the most favorable light. The enlightened individual, knowing the source and the purpose, could recognize this as propaganda. The same media, however, continuously carry propaganda which is all the more effective because it is unintentional. The film producer probably does not deliberately select those aspects of American life that he thinks should be emphasized. He is guided by his hunch as to what people will like to see. Nevertheless, when he presents a picture, in which people live in magnificent houses, in which men and women are chronically promiscuous, in which alcohol is consumed in great quantities, or in which firearms are used at the slightest provocation, he is unwittingly suggesting as right and proper certain modes of living. An American film to be successful must have a love interest. It is assumed that this is the theme to which Americans will respond, and each succeeding picture centered about a love interest reinforces the social pattern. Thus the movie producer is not only helping to mold American values, but he is also presenting America to the rest of the world in a particular way. Every moving picture, every newspaper editorial, every sermon preached from the pulpit, in fact every action performed by every individual, carries with it unintentional propaganda that may be of great influence. What is unexpressed, what is taken for granted, is conveyed in communication just as truly as that which is explicitly stated.

Leadership

Whenever a number of individuals become transformed into a psychological group we observe a process of differentiation of role. The number and kind of these roles will vary with the nature of the group. In organized associations we may have a president, a secretary, a treasurer, and chairmen of various committees. These roles are formally established by tradition. In a face-to-face group, formed on the basis of a common interest, even if there is no formal organization, we may find one person supplying the constructive ideas, another person translating those ideas into practical action, another person inconspicuously smoothing over difficulties, another serving as critic, and still another loyally shouldering the burden of work. The role of each individual becomes gradually established. In all groups, however, the most obvious differentiation of role is between leader and follower. Some individuals come to the top, others stay in the background. In every hen yard there is a hierarchy of dominance-submission, in every nursery-school play group some children will assume the position of leadership, and in every adult association, organization, or social movement we find the spotlight focused on some particular individuals. It is often said that leaders are born, not made, that the history of mankind is to be understood in terms of great men, that some are born great, others achieve greatness, and still others have greatness thrust upon them. These are mere literary clichés. If we are to understand leadership we must recognize that it is always a function, not only of the personal qualities of the individual, but also of the requirements of the situation. The kind of leader-follower relationship that develops will depend on the characteristics both of the individual and of the group. There is no such thing as the "quality of leadership" as such, and there are no rules of leadership that can be universally applied.

There are many ways of classifying types of leadership. One of these might be as follows: (1) There is leadership in an action group. This is the most primitive type, found in animal societies, in crowds, in mobs, and in other aggregates that have suddenly been transformed into congregate groups. The action leader stands out from the rest of the group in some obvious way. He may be taller and stronger, he may have a louder voice, he may beat down opposition through sheer physical domination. We find action leadership on the playground, on the battlefield, in the lynching mob. Many of the legendary heroes of the past, like King Arthur of the Round Table and Richard the Lion-Hearted, may have exercised this kind of leadership. In modern times action leadership has yielded place to other types.

(2) We may have leadership through persuasion. The persuasive leader is at his best in a face-to-face group. His instrument is language. Having sized up his audience, he selects his words, signs, and slogans in such a way as to elicit the appropriate response from his hearers. Hitler and Mussolini were persuasive leaders; so was the evangelist Whitefield, who was reported to have been able to pronounce a word like *Mesopotamia* in such a way as to bring tears to the eyes of his audience. The skilled diplomat, the street-corner

orator, and the labor-management arbitrator all exercise leadership through persuasion.

(3) The leader may operate inconspicuously through his organizational skill. As a person he remains in the background, but through his understanding of the group he is able to direct policy and practice in such a way as to accomplish his ends. Josef Stalin was an organizational leader long before he became a popular figure, and even then his personal traits were relatively unknown. The leader through organization may need at times to impress his immediate colleagues, but the secret of his leadership lies in his ability to understand his group, to see into the future, to plan in advance and to keep his own personal interests under control so that they will not influence his long-range plans.

(4) A person may merely through individual example become a leader. The historical records of Jesus of Nazareth are inadequate. It seems clear, however, that while he inspired the devotion of most of his immediate associates he failed during his lifetime to extend his leadership far beyond the face-to-face group, and even his immediate followers forsook him in a time of crisis. After the death of Jesus, however, he has come to be accepted as an example of a kind of life that is worth living. In this sense he is still a leader. In the same sense, Gautama Buddha, Mohammed, and Gandhi are to be considered as leaders, because through personal example they have demonstrated a kind of life that attracts followers.

(5) There can be leadership through cultural creation. Without personal dominance, skill in persuasion or organization, and without any real concern about the enlistment of followers, a person may through his sheer originality attract followers and become a leader. Aristotle, Kant, Newton, Debussy, Van Gogh, had their own private interests in the people about them. They were presumably leaders in their own immediate groups. As history views them, however, they are leaders because of their ideas. They were creators whose creations have been accepted by posterity, who have challenged and inspired followers who had no direct contact with them.

Leadership is always strengthened when the leader becomes invested with authority or prestige. Hitler began as a persuasive leader. He enlisted the support of skillful organizers and propagandists, who assisted him in securing power and in building up a myth about himself that made it progressively less necessary for him to appear before the people in the role of persuasive leader. His authority became such that his military experts accepted his judgments even when they knew these to be unsound, and his prestige became such that in the eyes of the great mass of Germans he could do no wrong. Authority and prestige may reinforce, or even at times create, leadership, but this leadership can be maintained only as long as the situation provides supports. The leadership of the army officer or the government official may disappear as soon as the individual in question has been divested of the authority and prestige of his position.

Galileo would probably not have been a successful leader of a mob; Lincoln was never regarded as a leader in any of the fields of science; Joe Louis could not give leadership to an international assembly of diplomats. Yet each of these has exercised leadership. Each has been outstanding in some particular respect. Each has demonstrated excellence, whether in science, in statesmanship, or in athletics, that is consonant with the value systems of identifiable groups of people. Each has consequently won followers. Thus leadership depends, not only on the characteristics of the individual as such, but also on the existence of a group that is capable of accepting leadership, and on the possibility of communication between the leader and the group. Beethoven on a desert island might have created truly great music, but he would not be listed as one of the shapers of the modern musical tradition had he not been able to communicate with an audience capable of understanding him. Thus by absolute standards the person who becomes leader is not necessarily the greatest of his generation. He is the one who is in some respect in advance of his group and is able to communicate with that group.

APPLICATIONS OF SOCIAL PSYCHOLOGY

Social psychology can not yet be considered as one of the applied sciences. Its principal contribution to the solution of practical problems still lies in the broad understanding it provides of the psychological bases of human relationships. Social psychology offers no simple and final answer to such problems as race prejudice, class conflict, and international tensions, although with social psychological training we can approach them in a more enlightened way. There are, however, a number of special areas in which the methods and results of social psychological research have proved particularly useful. A few of these may be briefly mentioned.

Industrial psychology is becoming increasingly a branch of applied social psychology. In addition to his interest in such topics as job analysis and selection, placement, and promotion of personnel, the industrial psychologist is paying more and more attention nowadays to problems of morale. The relation of a man to his job clearly involves his relations with his fellow workers, with his employers, and, to no inconsiderable extent, with his family and his neighbors at home. If we are to understand why men work hard, why some are more prone to accidents than others, under what conditions their work gives them satisfaction, and so forth, we must clearly consider them not merely as individuals but as members of social groups.

Government, insofar as it attempts to represent the needs and goals of the nation, is dependent for its guidance on indices of public opinion. Elections are at best unreliable indices. The well-known public opinion poll and the more refined methods of tapping the deeper attitudes and feelings of people are gradually gaining acceptance as legitimate tools of government. Whether or not this will make legislative representatives more responsible to the people, or merely make it easier for them to control public opinion, is still an open question. The fact remains, however, that the methods of social psychology are now being used as part of the process of government.

In *modern warfare,* social psychology is playing an increasingly large role. Psychological warfare represents the use of all methods other than the strictly military to impose our will on the enemy. The usefulness of psychological methods is now recognized both in strategic and in tactical planning. In offensive warfare it represents the attempt through propaganda and similar devices to confuse and demoralize the enemy. In defensive warfare it is directed toward increasing the morale among our own troops and on the home front. In both cases its effectiveness depends on the soundness of our psychological understanding of the individual and the group.

Education in its broadest sense always makes use of psychological principles, and most of these principles have to do with social behavior. In the family, in the school, and on the job the individual who is learning is usually learning in a social context. He is acquiring new attitudes, establishing new social relationships and assimilating a pattern of culture. His incentives are usually social incentives and his rewards social rewards. Thus, the principles on which any educational process rests are likely to be in part at least social principles.

Social psychology can be and is being applied in many other areas. It is important to realize, however, that no profitable application can be made without an understanding of basic principles. The purpose of social psychology will continue to be, not to find practical rules of thumb, but rather to gain scientific understanding.

SUGGESTED READINGS

1. Karpf, F. B., *American Social Psychology*. New York: McGraw-Hill, 1932. Covers both the European background of social psychology and the leading American contributors up to the date of publication. A history of social psychology.
2. Klineberg, O., *Social Psychology*. New York: Holt, 1940. Lays particular stress on the comparative study of social behavior in different cultures; revised edition to appear in the near future.

3. Krech, D., and Crutchfield, R. S., *Theory and Problems of Social Psychology*. New York: McGraw-Hill, 1948. Presents social psychology as a generalization from and an application of the basic psychological principles of perception, motivation, and learning.

4. McDougall, W., *An Introduction to Social Psychology*. Boston: Luce, original edition, 1908. Accepted as the classic statement of the doctrine of instinct and sentiment.

5. Mead, G. H., *Mind, Self and Society*. Chicago: University of Chicago Press, 1934. Particularly important for its analysis of the concepts of "self" and "role."

6. Murphy, G., Murphy, L. B., and Newcomb, T. M., *Experimental Social Psychology*. New York: Harper, 1937. Provides the best available review of the experimental literature in social psychology up to the date of its publication.

7. Newcomb, T. M., *Social Psychology*. New York: Dryden, 1950. Regards social psychology as distinct from both psychology and sociology, but draws more heavily than do most textbooks on the researches and theories of the sociologists.

8. Newcomb, T. M., and Hartley, E. L., *Readings in Social Psychology*. New York: Holt, 1947. A collection of reprinted studies representing the various fields of social psychological research.

9. Sherif, M., *An Outline of Social Psychology*. New York: Harper, 1948. A recent and systematic statement centered about the problem of socialization.

Chapter 7

Child Psychology

by LOIS B. MURPHY
and MEYER RABBAN

Backgrounds of Child Psychology

Methods

> OBSERVATIONS
> DIARY RECORDS
> PLAY SITUATIONS
> LEVELS OF QUESTIONS

Some Major Problems

> MATURATION AND LEARNING
> INTELLECTUAL DEVELOPMENT
> INFANT CARE AND PERSONALITY
> CULTURE AND THE INDIVIDUAL
> THE INDIVIDUAL PERSONALITY AS UNIQUE
> LANGUAGE DEVELOPMENT
> ASPECTS OF SOCIAL DEVELOPMENT
>> Aggression
>> Aggression, Sympathy, and Coöperation
>> Competition
> AUTHORITY
> THE WORLD OF THE CHILD
>> Religion, Values, and Beliefs
> PROBLEM CHILDREN AND CHILDREN'S PROBLEMS
> THE HEALTHY PERSONALITY

Suggested Readings

BACKGROUNDS OF CHILD PSYCHOLOGY

While rats are studied chiefly for their contributions to psychology as a science, children are studied because it is important to understand children and the adults they become. The psychological well-being of children and the consequences of the patterns of development laid down in their early years are important for the fate of humankind; whether early frustrations actually have something to do with later aggression, and therefore with the use of atom bombs, may actually be a question of life and death for the species.

Darwinian concepts of evolution reinforced the readiness of educators to think in terms of the growth of the immature organism, and the idea that growth during the period of immaturity may shape the pattern of mature behavior. Freud first offered serious evidence for the notion that in his emotional life "the child is father of the man." Stern's *Psychology of Early Childhood,* which we can take as an example of the integrated child psychology of the first quarter of this century, emphasized concepts of "development" and frequently used words and phrases like "formation of," "stages of," and other ideas related to the concept of growth. However, "personality growth" as a continuity, or a process by which the individual grows into a person, did not come into use until later, when the results of studies of individual children observed and tested over a period of years provided the necessary data. Similarly, the spread of the child guidance movement stressed through its clinical approach an attention on the individual child, and focused upon him all the techniques which would make clear his uniqueness.

In this field, as in many others, the scientist starts with a problem of significance but may soon get caught in the quicksand of his material, and become fascinated with problems which he had not thought of before he started. Thus a certain amount of research in the field of child psychology has become preoccupied with minute problems of infant and child behavior with little regard to the broad significance of this work for understanding human behavior. In the short space of this chapter we shall not discuss this type of work; but shall deal only with the materials which help us to understand people, that is ourselves, better than we could if there were no child psychology. But, first, we must discuss briefly some of the problems of method that confront us when we try to answer questions about children.

METHODS

In the world of minerals and plants, neither distance nor ethics limits man's ingenuity in devising experiments to test his hypotheses about the relationships between different things and events. In the world of stars and other heavenly bodies experiments have to yield largely to observations because distance prevents manipulation. In the world of animals and people, not distance, but respect for the living things, usually prevents us from inflicting serious pain and therefore from doing many kinds of experiments which might provide useful information. When we work with children we are in a way most limited in all the areas of science, because we not only do not wish to inflict pain but we also do not want to interfere in any way with the best development of the personality of the child. Consequently we again rely more on observations than on experiment, and the experiments which we do conduct are planned to contribute to the child's growth wherever possible. In the end, this often helps to focus our attention on problems of the greatest human importance. Actually we are not too limited because the child is a spontaneous creature, and acts out and tells us much when we let him do so; we have hardly begun to tap the resources available in the study of children, through the many possible kinds of observations which they could let us make.

An explanation of different methods used in the study of children, then, very nearly becomes a discussion of the different ways we plan, time, detect, organize and record our observations. We want to be objective in order to be accurate; that is, we do not want personal feelings and opinions to be mixed up with and to distort the data. At the same time, observations often need to give the quality of feeling or expression in a subtle way, and this requires sensitive perception and judgment. The emphasis on rigid objectivity as compared with subtle nuances of feeling-tone in behavior will depend on what we are trying to learn and what needs to be observed in order to answer the questions we are asking. Thus, a study of the amount of activity in play spaces of different sizes could be made with a rigidly objective technique, while a study of a child's feelings about his parents would require attention to shadings of mood and variations from one situation or day to another.

Observations

Observations may be made by an observer who sits or walks near the child, writing down words to describe behavior, or putting down check marks under selected headings, or making sketches of movement; or they may be made mechanically, as by a stabilimeter, which records the movements a baby makes, or they may be made by a camera focused on the child which obtains either still or motion records of the child's activity in selected or in planned situations. Records may include details of behavior alone, or behavior and language, depending on what is to be studied. Studies of of prehension are examples of studies focused on movement. Studies of any form of social behavior generally need an adequate record of behavior, feeling and language simultaneously. Since neither an observer nor a camera can pursue the child through a wide space, most-studies are made with the child confined to a small enough area for the observer or camera to keep him within easy focus for clear seeing and hearing. This means that many observations are made in test situations especially planned to elicit the behavior to be studied. Extremely few studies of children engaged in completely spontaneous activity have been made outside of nursery school or elementary schoolrooms, which also set certain physical limits to the area of activity.

Consequently, we have many more studies of specific aspects of physical and mental growth, than we have of the processes of social interplay in the child's own spontaneous world; and our knowledge of what really goes on between parents and children is mostly indirect, derived from what the children or their parents report, not from direct observations of what mothers say as they bathe their babies or tuck their children into bed.

It must be added that since most of the studies are made by students of child psychology in undergraduate or graduate courses, they are usually limited to what can be attempted by an individual student in order to satisfy the requirements for a term paper, or a dissertation. If we are really coöperative and democratic enough to plan our studies in terms of the importance of the questions that need to be answered, we will have more research carried on by teams of trained persons and groups of students under their supervision, building on and adding to previous knowledge.

These studies are generally made on children in or near the college or university area, and so we know much more about the middle-class and upper-middle-class child in university towns than we do about rural children in small one-class towns. Barker's recent study of "Richard" in his Kansas community of less than eight hundred people is a welcome addition, as is Claudia Lewis's picture of children in Cumberland, to our lopsided research picture of children, but we need much more material on the growing up of children in different subcultural groups, different kinds of families, different occupational and religious groups.

Generally, observational studies can be made either at a particular point in time or over a period of time. In the first, or *cross-sectional* method, we ask: "What are children of a particular age, grade, community, class, like? How, at a particular moment, does a child compare with other children of the same age, grade, sex?" In this way we learn about the characteristics of a group of children, and where any particular child stands in that group so that he can be compared against a plotted trend and an estimated norm. This method indiscriminately lumps all individuals together at a particular age level, whether or not they are at the same stage of development. With the second method, called the *longitudinal* method, we look for the pattern of growth of an individual child. We can see the uniqueness of his rate of growth in detail and when a number of children are studied by this method we can generalize about sequences of development and at the same time about interrelationships between growth processes.

Diary Records

Some very important studies of children have been made by the use of diary records, which generally concentrate on noting down the new items in behavior as they appear while the child is growing up. Stages in motor, emotional, language, and social development have been outlined on the basis of such observations. The advantage of records made in the home by the person closest to the child is that such a person is more likely to see the first time a child makes an effort to reach a new goal, or makes a new observation, while people who are testing a child at regular intervals, are able to observe only the well-crystallized forms of behavior rather than the moment of new achievement and what brings it about.

Diary records in a nursery school formed the basis for an important study on social development. These records were made from memory at the end of a day in school since there was no time for recording on the spot. For this reason they may lack precise detail at points, yet they are adequate enough to give a solid picture of the dynamics of aggressive behavior which has not been challenged by subsequent observers.

Very carefully controlled studies, in which there is agreement on the specific behavior to be observed and recorded, may not contribute much to knowledge if the context of the behavior is not filled in. Otherwise, we do not understand its meaning, for just to count "contacts" (symbolic or physical) between children does not tell us much unless we know the goal or intent of the contact and its result for the child who makes and the one who receives the contact. For this reason, when we want the greatest accuracy it is useful to have two recorders working together, one to note the time and event as accurately as possible, while the other records the total sequence of behavior reactions; or another way is to record the "objective" aspect of the behavior on one side of the record sheet with comments on the evident intent, feeling, and result on the other side. A few experienced observers who use shorthand and follow children's behavior easily have done this; beginners sometimes find it too much to attempt. The success of these studies lies in the care and thoroughness with which they were done and the mature perspectives of the observers who knew children well and had a sensitive eye to the meaning of the child's behavior.

Play Situations

Play and playlike situations of many sorts, as well as unfinished stories and requests to make up a story about a picture, have been used by many investigators as methods obviously natural and attractive to children, suitable for getting material on the child's feelings, or attitudes, or ways of looking at problems. The best examples of the use of these methods recognize the fact that we cannot substitute external standardization for inner feelings when we attempt to "control" an experiment. One investigator who tried to arrange a doll play experiment so that each child would start with equal familiarity with the material, proceeded to guide the child carefully through each room of the dollhouse only to find that some children became quite impatient with this formality, while others did not, and instead of starting at the same point emotionally, they had very different feelings. It is well to follow the procedure used by good Rorschach testers, who attempt to get rapport with each child, and put the child as much at ease as possible, since emotional blocks, such as may arise from anxiety or resistance to the tester's behavior, will obviously affect the behavior of the child and the results of any play experiment.

Levels of Questions

Questions may be asked at different levels: (1) at the level of immediate observation of behavior; (2) at the level of context in which the observed behavior appears; and (3) at the level of the inner significance of the behavior for the child's own personality. To illustrate the above three levels, we may want to know (1) how many new words children 12 years old can learn in a given space of time; (2) how the behavior of 12-year-olds toward their peers, or their parents, differs from that of 10-year-olds or 14-year-olds; whether 12-year-olds are especially negativistic or disorganized, whether this is true in all groups of American 12-year-olds, and also in groups of this age in other countries, or in primitive cultures, and also what other kinds of behavior are related to the behavior we are observing; and (3) at a deeper level, what feelings and goals are developing in the 12-year-olds which may underlie such disorganized behavior. The first two kinds of questions can be answered by making careful observations and counting them, then, where necessary, using statistical procedures to find relationships between different items of behavior or between behavior and different situations in which it occurs. The third type of question requires analysis of a different kind: one looks for underlying trends among the items of behavior in a given sequence. Here the work of the psychoanalyst is related to the analysis made by a historian or a biographer; each has a different vocabulary and is interested in different problems. But each in his own way looks for consistencies and inconsistencies and draws generalizations that represent the common denominator within the life-history data on an individual or a country. It is often the psychoanalyst who suggests, then, that the disorganization of the 12-year-old may be an important and necessary step to the reorganization of personality on a new and more mature level as the child grows into adulthood.

This deeper level of analysis developed by psychoanalysis paved the way for methods known as *projective techniques* whose intent is to show the inner drives, needs, feelings of a child which may be reflected indirectly in any given examples of his behavior. For instance, an inactive child may be inactive because of lack of energy or because of feelings which hold him back. These can be feelings of fear that he cannot keep up with others, or antagonism and resentment because at an earlier time someone took advantage of him, or guilt because he has hurt someone else and is anxious lest he do it again. It will not be possible to help this child successfully unless we know which feelings are responsible for his withdrawn behavior. Similarly, a very aggressive child may be aggressive out of sheer primitive energy, or because he feels he has to ward off possible attack, or because he wants to get back at the others for things they have done to him. In the first instance he merely needs to be patiently taught the limits within which he can use and the socially acceptable ways he may use his energy. In the latter instances he will need another kind of help toward feeling more friendly to other children.

No one method or type of method is suitable to answer all the important questions. The methods which are most relevant and economical depend upon the particular questions the psychologist wishes to answer. Sometimes this will mean objective methods alone, sometimes deep-level analysis will be required, and sometimes a combination of methods will bring the best answer.

SOME MAJOR PROBLEMS

Maturation and Learning

The complexity and often the unreasonableness of adult behavior can sometimes mislead us into a picture of humans as being rather undependable. However accurate this may be when adults are subjected to complex and conflicting demands and stimuli, they all go through dependable sequences of early growth. Gesell, McGraw, Shirley, and others have patiently recorded the steady, orderly character of the unfolding of early behavior. The baby holds up its head first, then its shoulders; then its back and arms develop, and it can begin to sit and to grasp. As development proceeds, it can crawl and finally walk. Babies do not walk alone before they can sit. The "cephalo-caudal" (head-to-tail) pattern of development parallels development which must take place in the central nervous system before more complex motor functioning is possible.

Each stage of development anticipates the next; it means the acquisition of skills essential for the accomplishment of the next stage of the sequence. Once a new stage is reached it comes into spontaneous use; there is an impulse to put the new power to work, and usually with vehement enthusiasm—an "all-out" absorption in the exercise of the new skill. Gradually, with mastery, the newness wears off and the skill becomes a bit of common everyday behavior. As the child develops, then he revises his habits, abandoning old ways despite their enthusiastic practice. As Jersild puts it: "The fact that he has practiced creeping assiduously does not mean that he will creep his way through life." Sometimes old ways do crop up even though they are no longer appropriate. In reacting to the new baby, a 4-year-old may regress to infantile behavior he had abandoned. Thus development is not a clear-cut, step-by-step progression, but rather in the nature of a spiral that winds its way upward from stage to stage. Here Gesell refers to the fact that the child seems to regress after the appearance of a more complex response, but although the child does go back toward "the region of departure" it is at a higher level. Much of this spiraling is the result of the interaction of all phases of development: motor skills make for wider social interests; social interaction involves emotional response; emotional response influences self-evaluation which in turn may impinge upon further motor and social development. Preoccupation with any one phase of development may mean that others are either slowed down or held in abeyance.

But the rate of development for each child within the orderly sequence of stages is a highly personal matter. When each stage will appear and how long it will take for the next one to come are

matters of individual tempo. Some children go through changes
no less remarkable than the changes we see as a tadpole grows into
a frog, or a caterpillar into a butterfly. Growth is sometimes gradual like the steady growth of a kitten into a cat; but sometimes
children blossom or reveal new aspects of their personality not
clearly foreshadowed by earlier observation. Each child has a
unique unfolding design for growing. Therefore "each child is
to be assisted in growing according to his natural design without
deprivation or forcing." The growth of the child as a whole, that
is, growth considering pattern, rate, and level of many different
aspects of growth, shows an underlying unity in structure, function, and achievement that marks the individual child.

Since different organs and functions mature at different ages,
we can never know the full potentialities of a person until adulthood, if then. A girl's voice may not exhibit qualities of special
beauty until after puberty; the same may be true of her figure or
face, and qualities of heterosexual attractiveness. Children with
limited coördination and poor musculature may appear less adequate as measured by the standards and physical demands of
8-year-old rough house than they do ten years later, when maturation has made it possible for the full range of their intellectual
and creative abilities to be made clear.

Much of this growth is a matter of learning. Perhaps it is more
correct to say that learning and growth go along together: growth
makes possible grasping, sitting, walking, yet we also learn to
reach for things, learn to walk, just as we learn to talk after the
repertoire of available sounds provides the possibility. There is
no one moment at which human beings begin to learn; they are
from the beginning adaptive organisms, responding to stimulation
even in utero and show definite conditioned responses during the
first days after birth, as shown, for example, in Marquis's study of
adaptation to feeding schedules.

Marquis wanted to find out whether infants could adapt to a
feeding schedule within the first ten days of life. In the experimental group were sixteen babies fed on a three-hour schedule

until the eighth day and then on the ninth day changed to a four-hour schedule. There were two control groups in the experiment: one a group of babies on a four-hour schedule and the second group on a self-demand schedule. The data she recorded were the percentage of half-minute intervals per ten minutes of general bodily activity recorded mechanically by a device that supported the infants' bassinets. After the experimental group was changed to a four-hour schedule the activity of these babies increased abruptly at the end of the third hour, the usual feeding time, and was much greater than either of the control groups. One of the control groups, the babies on the four-hour schedule first showed relatively more activity between the third and fourth hour, but this gradually decreased. The other control group, the self-demand babies, which required feeding approximately every three hours, did not change in activity level.

Since infants, as in the above experiment, and children are so amenable to learning, adults like to arrange things so that children will learn "properly"; many even believe children will learn little unless they "train" them. Gesell, on the other hand, has a profound respect for the capacity of any organism to learn the basic things it needs to learn on its own power if it is given a chance to do so when it is physiologically ready. To test the point of view that learning is at the mercy of growth level he and his coworkers conducted a series of experiments. One of the most famous of these sought to find out the effects of daily practice on the ability of one twin, called Twin T., to climb stairs. Her identical twin was kept for a control and given no practice during T.'s training period.

Beginning when she was 46 weeks old, T. was stimulated to engage in several activities every morning six days a week for six weeks. These included stair-climbing on a four-tread stairway leading to the crib, creeping to an interesting object placed near by, walking by holding on to the crib, or a chair, or the experimenter's hand. Stair-climbing was the most carefully controlled activity from an experimental point of view, so T. was enticed to climb the stairs as often as possible. Not until the twins were 53 weeks old did a similar training period start for Twin C. At 53 weeks, Twin T. climbed the stairs in seventeen seconds, while Twin C. despite her lack of training only took forty-five seconds. At 55 weeks Twin C (after two weeks of training) climbed more rapidly than had Twin T. at 52 weeks (after six weeks of training). At 79 weeks, T. climbed the stairs in seven seconds, C. in eight seconds; T. seemed more agile but her speed was about the same.

In other words, C. accomplished about as much as T. despite T.'s big head start. The moral of this is that if we wait until a child is physiologically ready for an activity he will learn much more economically. It should be noted that certain qualitative features (stair-climbing time is quantitative), e.g., willingness to try new tasks, suggest an advantage for twin T.

Although there is very little logic in such a distinction most people have tended to assume that children need to be "taught" skills like reading, writing, and arithmetic, whereas they are expected to "pick up" skills in sports and social relations without much adult help. A few important experiments have shown that training can help a child overcome social difficulties. Special training in certain games was given to the children who were the least active participants in a nursery school group. When tested subsequently with the children who had originally been most ascendant, the formerly shy children outdid the originally assertive group in ascendance. Others have similarly demonstrated the possibility of helping children to overcome unhealthy reactions to failure by training them to cope with experiences of failure. Probably many children go through unnecessarily long periods of insecure feelings when some well-timed coaching in needed social or athletic skills would give them confidence to assert themselves in the group. Children's peer group studies have shown the importance of "being good at games"; the value of this should not be underestimated.

While many adults remember painful music lessons and practice times with a feeling of regret for wasted energies, this does not mean that music cannot profitably and comfortably be taught. Preschool children can improve in rhythm and singing (with no evidence of discomfort, but with satisfaction) when they are given training periods suited to their level.

Our understanding of growth and learning from many such investigations points to the fact that the most effective nurture involves adaptation of training to the level of the child's growing abilities.

Intellectual Development

While a child's brain grows rapidly and reaches a size approximately that of an adult earlier than the rest of the body, intellectual development continues into adolescence and later; at least whatever we test with intelligence tests, and whatever it is that makes it possible for us to pass harder examinations in school from year to year, keeps on developing.

During infancy, tests actually measure motor development and these measurements have little relationship to verbal expressions of intelligence which are completely accessible only after the ability to handle abstractions has matured. Such findings are substantiated by Gesell's "eighty biographies" of the development of individual children. These include some children at a superior level during infancy who were below average later on, some who were inferior on the Gesell norms during infancy but superior later on, as well as some who maintained the same rate of development throughout the period of the study.

But after the ability to handle abstractions has matured we find that when ten thousand children are tested at successive intervals of a year or more, their relative position from brightest to dullest remains rather stable. For this reason we have believed that the level of intelligence tested by standard tests was essentially a measure of inborn ability. By and large it is true that children with intelligence quotients of 80 do not later attain intelligence quotients of 120. However, there may be emotional factors which can bring about marked changes in intelligence scores. Children who are shy, inhibited, or maladjusted obtain higher scores when their relation with people and their environment is improved. Children who remain in institutions over a period of years may decline in test scores. The kind of behavior expected in a particular social milieu can also affect an intelligence test score. In a study of the relationship between membership in a social class and intelligence score, it was discovered that vocabulary and problems in the tests are pitched at a middle-class level relating to customs and habits sometimes completely unheard of and bewildering to a lower-class or isolated rural child.

Tests do not guarantee that we are getting at the maximum potential ability of the child, but only at his performance under the conditions of the test, and this performance is affected by his ability to "give" in general, to draw on his resources to the best of his ability. Studies of test scores in large groups of children tested at one time do not tell the whole story of intellectual development in children as we obtain it from broader longitudinal studies. When individual children are followed during their whole growing-up period we find that some children improve steadily while others fall behind. Gains from 80 to 135, or 89 to 170 have been reported; in some of these cases we find the increase in test scores paralleled by an improvement in general outgoing responsive spontaneous behavior—the child becomes better able to "give" and to show what he can do.

Some children are unable to use their abilities in school in an efficient way because even though they have adequate ability they feel inadequate in comparison with the rest of their brilliant families. Some withdraw from the struggle, others become the class cutups with comments like this: "If I cut up all the time and don't study, then they won't know I'm dumb. They will think it's just because I don't study." Others compulsively indulge in delinquency, at least securing a reputation for bravery with their peers. Still others dully commit to memory without understanding materials with which they are confronted.

Infant Care and Personality

From the findings of a welter of studies about the effect of infant care routines on personality widespread contradictions appear to exist. For example, one study reports that bottle-fed babies are happier and healthier; while another study makes the same claim for breast-fed babies.

As for the importance of "mothering," so earnestly stressed by many, the Dennises found that without any specific stimulus from adults twin babies reared for seven months with minimal attention developed all the basic skills. It is important to note that while Mr. and Mrs. Dennis did not smile at a given baby until it smiled first of its own accord, and did not cuddle it or give it motor stimulation, the twins did presumably have the consistent dependable care of the adults in a stable family. This is what babies did *not* have when studied in foundling and hospital environments, and found to be greatly retarded.

There are at least two main points to be watched in the arguments about the importance of adult care for adequate growth in infants versus the claims that culture and mothering have little to do with the baby's development. Dennis worked with two babies. That is not a large sample; others might not have fared so well even in the Dennis household. And those babies had a dependable environment; institutional babies cared for by a series of nurses have no opportunity to establish stable emotional relations and obtain from them a feeling of trust in interpersonal relationships.

Indeed, such apparent contradictions between different studies of nature versus nurture can usually be resolved when we examine the conditions of each experiment carefully to see exactly what went on. Contradictory results are not actually so unless the same conditions existed in both experiments.

Another difficulty with our attempt to discover relationships of early experiences to the later development of personality arises from our failure to record all the factors influencing the child's development or even the major factors. We may find excellent case study

illustrations of the idea that unhappy feeding experiences may produce an overconcern with "oral needs" for the rest of the person's
life; or that excessive emphasis on toilet training may produce rigidity through the whole personality. But when we study a large sample
of run-of-the-mill children, it is hard to find such neat relationships;
rather, we learn that the personality and attitudes of the mother who
is weaning the child or instituting toilet training, the organic constitution of the individual child, and the full range of social context are operating together in the shaping of personality, and in
anything but a static manner that lends itself to simple correlation
studies. This search for one-to-one relationships actually distorts the
picture. Many influences have had an impact and a frustration in one
area may be balanced out by gratifications in other areas. Thus, an
examination of 135 children on whom we had data regarding infancy experience, and full records of behavior and personality at
the preschool level, failed to show clear and simple one-to-one relations in any except a few outstanding cases. For example, rigidity
in toilet training was found to be important only when extreme *and*
when reinforced by rigidity in other areas of handling. We must
watch the full richness and detail of a child's experience, and trace
out the many interacting factors in development.

Culture and the Individual

Every culture makes its own pattern of demands upon the people
who live in it and grow up in it. The Dobu infant grows up to be
a suspicious, distrustful, witchcraft-haunted adult; the Arapesh baby
becomes a coöperative, gentle, nonaggressive person; and the
Kwakiutl youngster can look to the day when he, too, will be able
to shame others by making a huge bonfire of his painstakingly collected blankets and canoes.

Yet in every society there are more or less wide differences between individuals and their ability to meet the standards of the culture. In a Puritanical period, a premium is placed upon capacities
for self-control; in a period of expanding individualism, the impor-

tant thing may be initiative and the ability to solve problems independently and to strike out for oneself. In this generation there has
been more and more emphasis upon the need for coöperation and
adjustment of an active, not inhibited sort. Each of these emphases
is easier for certain people to cope with than it is for others. When
coöperation or creativeness is demanded, solitary people or people
who are not very creative may feel pressures just as great as the
pressures felt by vigorous, virile people under restrictive laws dictating personal behavior.

Fortunately our culture still has room for a variety of personalities,
and we find certain typical patterns of personality developing among
children at different ages. In a study of adolescent personality in
children of a typical Midwest town, youngsters were grouped in such
categories as the self-directing personality, the adaptive, the defiant,
the submissive, and the maladjusted types.

While we all accept the statement that growth can only take place
in an environment, and that these different environments produce
or contribute to the development of different kinds of personalities,
we do not yet know much about the precise influences in the many
different environments or subcultures in our country. It has been
shown that children growing up in communities where parental
standards were at odds with those of the school could not develop
much consistency of behavior; they had to do what was expected in
each setting. Many children grow up in heterogeneous environments like this. Alison Davis has shown the futility of expecting
children from lower-class families to do well in schoolrooms taught
by teachers of completely different standards and ideals.

Heterogeneity in the community or subgroup in which a child
grows up may cause considerable confusion when families living
next door to one another have conflicting requirements about what
is allowed. Being different, whether as a member of a religious
or ethnic minority, can make for heartrending experiences for a
growing child, and may lead to anxiety and isolation when out of
suspicious attitudes and prejudice parents forbid children to play
with one another. In a homogeneous community, on the other hand,

class biases are hard to discover; children growing up in this sort of group would be expected to be more integrated and comfortable than children exposed to conflict and confusion in their earliest years.

The Individual Personality as Unique

If it were ethically desirable to breed human beings as we breed race horses, or apples, we might know much more about individual differences in temperament than we now know. We have already commented on differences in rate and pattern of growth which may affect a child's status in his group. And we have pointed out that depriving environments can do more harm to some babies than to others. What else do we know about the many big and small differences that make up the individual personality and its ways of selecting from, responding to, being satisfied or frustrated by any given environment?

It was shown some years ago that some babies in the first years of life were consistently given to smiling, others to somber expressions, others to variations between gaiety and sadness, while still others showed little expression at all. Acute sensory responsiveness, including sensitivity to color and to music, is observed in some babies who, it is believed, are more prone to be disturbed by their environments than babies with less sensitivity. Skin sensitivity and low thresholds for pain and for changes in heat and cold may make it harder for some babies and young children to adjust easily to the environment. Even in newborn babies variations in activity level range from very active and moderately active to quiet.

No one has attempted to use Sheldon's outline of differences in physique and temperament in relation to infants, although observation of a number of infants in normal families will readily show anyone differences between very active "kickers" and alert concentrated "lookers" and food-centered "suckers," who might well correspond to his "mesomorphs" or muscular type, his "ectomorphs" or nervous-system-centered type, and his "endomorphs" or visceral type. Of course, in any such grouping, most individuals are mixtures and cannot be neatly classified. Yet the differences in capacity to respond to one or another type of stimulus, which go with low or high thresholds in sensory, motor, intellectual, and emotional areas and which may be related to body build are important for the kinds of adjustment the child will make, the kinds of training he can use, and the kind of person it is possible for him to become. Toscanini and Jack Benny did not become what they are solely because of different environments.

Language Development

An important aspect of child psychology which is still understood only superficially is language. Everyone realizes its importance and many studies of the stages of development of language have been made, through studying the number and types of words children of different ages can use. We know that babies begin to babble and coo before they are 6 months old, and between the ages of 6 months and 1 year they "listen" to familiar words and respond to a few of them; by the age of a year or a little more they can use a few words like *bye-bye, mama, bow-wow,* and by 2 years they have a considerable vocabulary of words and short phrases which they can use to express wants, pleasure, displeasure, or recognition of familiar objects and people in their world. From this time on, they add words and integrate them rather slowly into sentences, refining their pronunciation and grammar until at 5 years there are few remnants of "baby talk," and they are using most of the parts of speech and some abstract as well as concrete words. Later language development may depend upon such a factor as bilingualism, but development results chiefly from the models provided by the family, by the stress on correct speech, on wide or exact vocabulary, on the presence of books and the reading of them in the home, and on the general support for the emphasis placed on language skills by the school. Then throughout life there are moments of struggle to find the word or phrase to communicate an exact shade of meaning.

But it remains for the next generation of psychologists to study the development of language in a more meaningful and subtle way so that we can understand the more intimate aspects of language, how words carry the culture to the child and contribute to the building up of an inner world of experience, fantasy and thought, which becomes each child's private universe. Objects and experiences are accepted or rejected after the age of 4 or 5, according to whether they carry invisible labels of good or bad, and as the child grows older, these verbal pigeonholes multiply as the child's value judgments become more complex. One does not do the things that might label one as a sissy, or as sentimental, or as a boor. The label in turn does something for one's own self-appraisal. Thus, language is a major force in the development of feelings about ourselves, our adequacy, our ability to like ourselves, to accept or disregard certain things in ourselves.

Language sustains class differences, sectional differences, religious differences: "we" don't talk that way, such words are snobbish, or uncultured, or blasphemous; if we use them we are waving signals that show that we "do not belong." These emotionally toned aspects of language are in part responsible for international misunderstandings, family feuds, and school fights. If you use a word innocently which has a threatening feeling for me, I am put on my guard, or I assume that you meant it in a threatening way and I am angry. Untangling disagreements is often a matter of clarifying language, of finding out what the other person really meant.

It is these emotional aspects of language which are the ones which have been studied least, and yet are the most important. If we could learn to recognize the inadequacy and relativity of words, and be alert to their ambiguities and different values for different people instead of taking them as substitutes for the realities they symbolize, we could avoid many conflicts between individuals and groups.

Aspects of Social Development

In a complex culture like ours, rural traditions mingle with concepts emerging from the industrialized living of today, and scientific assumptions of the post-Darwinian era thrust its values on religious ideology. The effort to achieve respect for the individual and coöperation between groups is matched only by the drive to outdo others and compete aggressively with them. It is thus inevitable that the study of social development would be a confusing task.

AGGRESSION

Every normal human being is born with the necessary equipment to solve his own problems and meet his own needs. He has hands to manipulate objects to feed and clothe himself, he has limbs for locomotion, brains to think and solve problems with, and the impulse to be active and do something when wants are not immediately satisfied. Every normal human being has the emotional equipment, in his autonomic nervous system and endocrine glands, to respond with anger, and aggression if need be, when he is frustrated in the effort to meet his needs. Probably just as some animals are more aggressive than others, there are also some innate differences between humans in this regard. But it is hard to know about this, since children are subjected to such varying experiences that we can never omit the possibility that a more aggressive child has become so as a result of what he has been through. Hostile, rejecting parents, aggressive punishment from adults, perennial frustrations in home and neighborhood life, may stimulate aggression in certain children, although other children who have had the same kinds of experiences may withdraw, and some others may find ways of handling their problems without becoming extremely aggressive or withdrawn.

Whatever the patern of behavior a child shows at a given age, it can generally be somewhat modified by changing the kind of treatment he receives. Autocratic treatment from adult leaders stimulates more aggressiveness with teasing, time wasting, and sabotaging of work, while democratic treatment promotes greater satisfaction in work and more friendly coöperation among children.

Susan Isaacs' study of aggression in young children is a well-balanced empirical study, based on anecdotes recorded at the end of each work day in a school for young children. Undoubtedly recording on the spot is preferable, provided that the context of the situation is described adequately, so that the causes of the child's behavior, or at least the immediate precipitating stimuli can be seen. Although the anecdotal record is usually a method susceptible to some distortion through inaccurate reporting and forgetting, Isaacs collected enough good data to enable her study to remain unchallenged with its rich details of children's aggressive behavior arising from rivalry, possessiveness, and jealousy.

Many other aspects of the situation will affect the amount of aggressiveness as well. A large number of children in a small space, with too little play equipment to meet their needs stimulates competition for the equipment; one fights for the tricycle or the swing or the wagon and if one has to fight every day in order to get what one wants, one gets practice in being aggressive.

While it is often true, as is said, that aggression is caused by frustration, it is by no means true that frustration always causes aggression. We know that tense dominating behavior of adults produces more aggressive behavior in children than friendly coöperative guidance; and frustration is doubtless an element here, because being dominated means that our freedom to move and decide for ourselves is interfered with. But there are many kinds and degrees of frustration and by no means all of them have been studied. If one is frustrated by a person weaker than oneself one behaves differently from the way one behaves if one is frustrated by a stronger person; if one is frustrated by an unpredictable "act of God"—a thunderstorm or a drought—one behaves differently from the way one behaves if one is frustrated by one's dog, which can be controlled more easily; if one is frustrated by someone one loves one feels differently from the way one feels if the frustrating person is nobody of special concern.

These differences have not been studied in detail, but one situation has been the subject of an experiment by Kurt Lewin and his collaborators: A group of children was shown some attractive toys and allowed to play with them for a short time after a half-hour of free play with toys not nearly so desirable. Then a screen was placed between the children and the toys so that they could see them but not reach them, and they were again given the not so desirable toys to play with. Defining constructivenes of play as the extent of creativity, elaboration, and complexity of an activity, scales were devised to evaluate the constructiveness of the play before and after the period of frustration. The authors found that play became less constructive after the experience of frustration. Together with this regression in the quality of the play activity, some of the children became passive, disorganized, or emotional. They also found that a few showed more constructive behavior; that is, the frustration acted as a challenge to bring out their resources more fully. Although there was no control group, with two periods of play with the old toys but without the frustration experience, the authors cite these findings to point out that the frustration was followed by regression rather than aggression in this situation (it would have probably been a different matter if the experiment had been staged by a mother at home) and that the responses of different personalities differed even here, some feeling defeated, some stimulated.

AGGRESSION, SYMPATHY, AND COÖPERATION

At the same time and among the same children we find aggression and also helpfulness, coöperation, and sympathy to the point where they will defend another child who is attacked. This positive correlation between aggression and sympathy is nearly as high as the correlation between sympathy and coöperation, that is, the children who are the most aggressive tend likewise to be the most sympathetic.

If this seems illogical to us, it is only because of the things we let words do to our picture of reality. Aggressiveness logically is the opposite of nonaggressiveness; therefore we assume that it does not appear side by side with behavior we do not think of as aggressive. But nothing could be further from the facts. Both aggressive and sympathetic behavior are aspects of outgoing response to other children at the preschool level, and for many people, later as well.

When we say that sympathy and coöperation come from socialization of the individual, what do we mean by socialization? If we look at the picture of children's behavior in a full account like that in *Child Life in School* we find that at 7, children's aggressive behavior is becoming patterned in socially acceptable ways. They are learning rules of social intercourse, rules of games like baseball; they imitate adult methods of expressing protests such as the sit-down strike. Aggression is not eliminated; it is shaped and toned down. The child submits to a referee instead of spitting or hitting or yelling, "I'll chop your head off," as does the 4-year-old.

This process of assimilating the structure and rules of the social group probably goes through the stages suggested by Piaget in his important studies of the child. At first the child is very rigid about the rules which he has accepted unilaterally from the authorities, the grownups. Then gradually he comes to feel himself capable, as a member of a group of equals, to help form rules for the group. While he still wants a definite structure, to control his behavior and that of the others, he can help create the structure and thus retain autonomy while accepting regulations at the same time.

COMPETITION

By the age of 5, children have begun to compete volubly and actively. The typical family situation in our middle-class culture seems ideally developed to stimulate this competition: often the child has no close ties with adults other than his father and mother, and competition for the affection of each is more or less inevitable. In our typical two-child families, the child does not have the opportunity to develop the feeling that he is part of a flock of children who share the care of the adults, but again he must compete with one other child—trying to keep up with the older one if he is the younger, or if he is the older sibling, trying to hold the attention of his parents when he feels displaced or dethroned by the baby.

In the many studies of the effect of order of birth upon personality, it has been hard to find consistent results that would make it possible to say: oldest children are so and so, much as we might like to find simple answers of that sort. There are too many different pigments in the painting. You may be a preferred or rejected older child; you may be of the sex your family wanted or not; you may look like or be like your mother or father, or completely different from anyone else in the family; you may be the picture of health or sickly from your earliest weeks. All these things will have a bearing on what it means to you to be the oldest child. But the fact that you are the oldest in a two-child family rather than a ten-child family will still be important and may influence your development more than the fact that you are the older per se.

The place of the child in the family structure is not the only major stimulus to a competitive attitude toward life. Middle-class America has been preoccupied with standards and norms; for instance, comparisons with the Gesell age levels are made by many parents from the child's earliest weeks. Good performance in comparison with what is expected for your age gets approval and excitement from the adults, and failing to come up to the norms is a cause for embarrassment or disappointment. Many children who grow up in an atmosphere of physical, intellectual, and social competition feel pressure both at school and at home to meet high standards for adjustment in any or all of these areas. This high demand-level of the culture doubtless has some good results in stimulating children to use all their resources, but it also dampens the spirits of many who feel that they cannot possibly live up to the expectations of the grownups. This is a common form of the beginning of what Horney has called the "neurotic personality of our time."

Authority

A study of the relation of parental authority to children's behavior and attitudes included interviews and questionnaires to parents about their own disciplinary techniques and those in turn of their parents. Individuals report that their disciplinary techniques are similar to those of their parents, but in the direction of less severe and less emotional discipline, and toward greater respect for the child's personality. Our skepticism about the accuracy of the parent's report is reinforced by the fact that data from the children show that the child perceives the parent as more severe than the parent perceives himself. Children may resent present-day interferences with their power and freedom as much as children of an earlier generation resented physical punishment. An adequate picture of parent-child authority patterns today would have to take into account the increasing effects of crowded city living and the tension it produces, the decrease in the number of relatives (and authorities) a child is close to, as frequent moving separates families from grandparents and uncles and aunts.

The child's experience of authority is seen from different angles by investigators with different interests. Lewin and his collaborators were interested in the changes which might be stimulated in the behavior of a group of boys by changing the social atmospheres, as in substituting democratic leaders for autocratic ones. With groups of boys, each exposed to a democratic and an autocratic leader, it was found that work was productive and at the same time more satisfying, and less bickering and aggression occurred under the democratic leader.

Taking prejudice as a mark of the authoritarian individual, Dr. Frenkel-Brunswik and coworkers analyzed interviews that were conducted with eighty persons, forty-five classified as prejudiced and thirty-five as unprejudiced by the various tests used. These two groups were divided equally between men and women, who were selected from the original 2,099 subjects. The following is a summary of the developmental pattern which she believes produces authoritarian and nonauthoritarian types, in at least the extreme 2 percent of the group:

When we consider the childhood situation of the most prejudiced subjects, we find reports of a tendency toward rigid discipline on the part of the parents, with affection which is conditional rather than unconditional, i.e., dependent upon approved behavior on the part of the child. Related to this is a tendency . . . to base inter-relationships on rather closely defined roles of dominance and submission, in contra-distinction to equalitarian policies. . . .

Forced into a surface submission to parental authority [because of this harsh discipline], the child develops hostility and aggression which are poorly channelized. The displacement of a repressed antagonism toward authority may be . . . the principal source of his antagonism toward outgroups. . . .

Fear and dependency seem to discourage the ethnocentric child from conscious criticism of the parents. It is especially the prejudiced man who seems intimidated by a threatening father figure. . . .

The fact that the negative feelings against the parents have to be excluded from consciousness may be considered as contributing to the general lack of insight, rigidity of defense, and narrowness of the ego so characteristic of [the prejudiced individuals]. Since the unprejudiced child as a rule does not seem to have to submit to stern authority . . . he can afford in later life to do without strong authority, and he does not need to assert his strength against those who are weaker. . . .

[The unprejudiced individual] is more capable of giving affection since he has received more real affection. He tends to judge people more on the basis of their intrinsic worth than on the basis of conformity to social mores. . . . He is able to express disagreement with, and resentment against, the parents more openly, thus achieving a much greater degree of independence from the parent and authorities in general. . . .[1]

Thus may hostility breed hostility, and aggression occurs where children feel rejected or dominated or are treated cruelly and aggressively by adults.

More subtle distortions of parental behavior such as overprotection, indulgence, and excessive restriction may also produce aggressive behavior in some children, but not in all, for each child responds in terms of his own needs and resources and the same treatment which produces aggressive behavior in one child may be related to shy, withdrawn behavior in another. What the parent does may have different results depending on the feeling-tone that goes with it—cold democratic behavior is not the same as warm

[1] T. W. Adorno et al., *The Authoritarian Personality*, Harper & Brothers, 1950, pp. 482–484.

democratic behavior in a parent; and a warm autocratic parent may be accepted much more comfortably by a child than a cold autocratic parent.

The World of the Child

The child world or peer group has long been recognized as important, but has been objectively studied only in recent years. The sociometric method used with variations by many investigators gave us a graphic device for describing the relationships within a given group. In essence, it consists simply of asking each individual with whom he would like best to work, to eat, to play, and then allowing them to group themselves as they have chosen. These choices are then graphically charted to show who is preferred by whom. A child chosen by many is seen as the center of a cluster, while one chosen by few appears as an isolate, without links to the others in the group.

When the reputation of children among their peers is studied over a period of years, we find children who have had relatively stable positions while other children vary sometimes quite dramatically from year to year. Children who have the continued support of their classmates are considered good-looking, friendly, good at games, popular, etc., by a sizable number of their classmates, while those less consistently liked are regarded as sissies, poor sports, quick-tempered, unfriendly, and poor at games.

The structure of one child's relationships may be very different from that of another: one child might be mentioned as the "best friend" of a third of the class; another might be in a compact little clique, all of whom mention each other; another might mention several children as his best friends and have the feeling completely unreciprocated; another might be mentioned by no one and in turn mention no one. Isolated children may vary greatly in the way they feel about their isolation, some being unhappy, others belligerent, and still others absorbed in their own fantasies and interests.

When dramatic shifts occur, they may be due to changes in the group's feelings about certain characteristics. One boy was very popular in the third grade (11 of 17 boys regarded him as their best friend), a member of a clique in the fifth grade, but mentioned only twice in the sixth grade. The fact that his family belonged to a minority group may be of significance. At different age levels the group felt differently about certain qualities of personality and behavior, so that the same quality which made a child popular at one age level might lead to unpopularity at another age level: being "quiet" is an asset in the first grade, but not in the fifth!

RELIGION, VALUES, AND BELIEFS

The majority of America's children learn something about religion at home and express religious attitudes at least in times of crisis or bereavement, and although half of the children in the United States go to Sunday school for at least some part of their growing-up period, psychologists have paid little attention to the contribution of religion to the formation of the inner values and beliefs about personality and life which to some extent guide their behavior. Along with this neglect has gone a general neglect of the cognitive factors—the way the child sees himself and the world—in relation to his social behavior and personal living. If it is found that Sunday-school children are not more honest than children who do not go to Sunday-school, the study is apt to conclude that religious education has no effect, and the total fabric of feelings, needs, longings, which interweave themselves with religious ideas are neglected. Plant, on the basis of more than twenty years of clinical experience with children comments:

In early years—perhaps by four—the child begins to hear and then to learn that the religious philosophy of the family or community contributes to his sense of belongingness—but now it is to the general scheme of things. He hears that God cares for him because of who he is and not fundamentally because of anything he has or anything he has not done. Until he is about seven such statements merely build up a framework for what will later take on meaning for the individual in so far as the envelope allows. It would be interesting to know whether belongingness in the Church is sought earlier or more insistently by children who are secure or those who are insecure in their own families—but I have no data. . . . From early adolescence on, the Church gives a great many children a sense of belongingness which has greater continuity and certainty for the individual than anything provided by his parents. This is true whether the individual looks to a personal God interested in him as one of His children, or finds in his religious experience an orientation to basic and everlasting "values." . . . As adolescence closes . . . the child frequently develops serious tensions from the fact that his culture constantly refuses to distinguish religious experiences from the formal symbols for these. Consequently, he has a more difficult time in fitting his non-attendance at church with his natural need to feel that he is a "regular" part of his culture, than he has in questioning the formal claims of the church he has attended. Children tell me rather easily, "I am really deeply religious—it's only that I can't believe what *they* teach." [2]

Problem Children and Children's Problems

The "problem child," more often than not, is a descriptive term contrived by an adult who finds a child is "difficult" or "hard to manage." Actually, the so-called maladjusted child may be seeking adjustment, attempting to meet his own needs.

The studies of problem children who have been brought to clinics find that in the background of these children there often are early disturbances in the relation between the mother and child, unfortunate experiences in feeding, or toilet training, or discipline in handling property and getting along with other children. It is sometimes assumed that it must follow that if children have a thoroughly good start, they will be able to take all the adjustments of life in their stride and will avoid maladjustments.

This is overoptimistic. A good start is a good start and every child needs the best foundation he can get. But as illustrated in the following, a child may be very well adjusted at one period and still become disturbed when the demands of another stage come along:

[2] J. S. Plant, *The Envelope,* The Commonwealth, 1950, pp. 25–27.

In the fifth grade Sam "radiated health. He seemed one of the favorites with boys and girls. He was anxious to have everything go just right and was out for all the wholesome fun and work that could be packed into each day." His cumulative record had reported him to be "cheerful and polite" in the first grade, a "well-rounded child" in the second, "an excellent pupil" in the third, and "a nice pupil" in the fourth grade. He came from a family of friendly, healthy, good-natured people, with a jolly father and pleasant mother, who belonged to an industrious group and were close to their kin. The parents love children and were proud of Sam.

By the sixth grade Sam had begun to change; at times he seemed in a dream. He "doesn't finish his work and doesn't listen to plans; he asks over what has been so recently agreed upon . . . he sometimes acts sullen and mumbles. Soon gets over this mood and laughs unnecessarily." He gained over ten pounds during the summer. He became moody, would avoid girls, sprawled and day-dreamed, ignored group agreements, was restless, and sometimes neglected his job as safety patrolman. In the spring he flew into a rage over a matter of looking up words in a dictionary, and protested that he would not take part in the dances for a field day program.

His thoughtful teacher realized that this formerly friendly, well-organized boy was going through a growth spurt when it was "normal for the pre-adolescent to sort of 'go to pieces' at this stage" and that it was her task to accept the "aggressive behavior as a normal phase of growth." With tact and understanding she helped him to participate as much as possible with the group.

By the end of seventh grade, Sam was again working pleasantly with the others, willing to give and receive help, participating in social activities and in the school band. He seemed to enjoy a feeling of social security with the boys, and was beginning to be interested in girls.[3]

Sam's "good start" did not prevent the period of early adolescence from being difficult, but it gave him the background of stability and good relationships which contributed to a quick recovery of his balance at a new level.

[3] Adapted from D. A. Prescott *et al., Helping Teachers to Understand Children,* American Council on Teacher Education, 1945, Chapter 8.

To find out what the "normal child" was like, a group of children was observed while they grew. The original group consisted of 252, and after fourteen years 224 children and their families were still in the study. This total group represented an unselected sample of the community from which they came, since every third child born from January, 1928, to July 1, 1929, was chosen. One of the outstanding findings is that normal children do have problems and if we are to say that the absence of "problems" is the mark of the "normal child" then that descriptive term could be only rarely, if ever, used.

In this study the average number of problems varies during the preschool years from four to six per child out of sixty-three descriptive or interpretive labels systematically covered at each level. Bedwetting and soiling decreased with age, while constipation, masturbation, and restlessness in sleep did not. Nail biting increased as thumb sucking decreased. Temper tantrums, fears, jealousy, and inferred oversensitiveness increased to around 4 and 4½ years and then began subsiding. Since these occur at one age level in more than 50 percent of the children they cannot sensibly be regarded as neurotic behavior, as so commonly assumed, but rather as evidences of tension or adjustment devices. And problems of this sort do not come singly: quarrelsomeness, negativism, temper tantrums, jealously, competitivenes, mood swings, and irritability (in the sense of reactivity) were a cluster suggesting a labile or disturbed organism. Another cluster—behavior withdrawn, introverted, submissive, shy, somber, and excessively reserved— was associated with underactivity.

Behavior problems, therefore, cannot be regarded as specific entities to be treated like a cold or the measles. The child with speech problems, or enuresis, or temper tantrums, is pretty sure to have other problems as well, all of which are expressions of tension of one sort or another: anxiety, insecurity, or resentment and hostility, and the like.

It was pointed out that even where there is a sound foundation of security, disasters such as those brought by the depression (or the war) could produce panicky, anxious types of reaction. It was also noted that in periods of stress for adults, whether financial difficulty, or fatigue, or worry, or illness, children may be temporarily unwanted, and show regressive behavior or an absorbing need for reassurance which disappears when the parental attitude disappears after father gets the needed job, or mother recovers from the operation. Feelings of rejection are much more rare, and are really present only when the mother can find nothing good to say about the child and blames it for "spoiling" the other nice children in the family, and for not responding to everything the parents try to do for him. Broken homes are important not just objectively but because the child feels that the parent could not care for him very much or he would not leave; aggressive or delinquent behavior is one expression of the emotional upset he feels.

No child completely escapes some periods of difficulty and we might say further that the frequency of problems is a measure of the cultural strain experienced by children in our culture. At the same time, it is important to note that in some cultures these kinds of behavior would not occur or would not be considered problems. As many psychologists and anthropologists have pointed out, what is a symptom in one culture is not a symptom in another culture. Many groups simply do not expect children to control their bodily functions at an early age or might take fears for granted, so that there is less fuss by the adult, and less stress on the child.

The study of the problems of the normal child also illustrates the important principle that a given kind of behavior may be due to different factors in different cases, just as the same conditions may produce different results in different children. For example, bed-wetting at 5 years in one child might be connected with poor muscle tonus, in another with little or no attempt at toilet training, and in a third might appear when the child had been exposed to drastic and severe toilet training before it was mature enough to be capable of the necessary muscular control.

An example of the different effects of a given physical condition appears in a discussion of the experience of undersized boys. If the father of the undersized boy played guard on his college football team and hoped for a son who would carry on the tradition, the boy's size has a different adjustive aspect than if his father were an intellectual who wanted his son to become a professor. Similarly, the undersized boy feels differently if his siblings are much larger and more successful in athletics than if they are also small and nonathletic. If he has other compensating gifts, and feels appreciated for other qualities of personality and ability, size may be less important. If he is not only small but also late in maturing, his position may become even more extreme, and his problems even greater. In other words, the meaning of any given condition to the child will depend on the total context of the situation the child is in, what is demanded and valued both in the adult group and among the child's own peers, and upon the total resources of the child including his view of himself in his group and his sense of security in coping one way or another with the problems of adjustment in his total situation.

"Privileged" children are not necessarily exempt from strains and problems. Marital discord is found to contribute twice as much to problems as lower educational or income status of the family. Sudden loss of income, inadequate income in comparison with the ambitions of the parents, and tension over the management of income, brought strains upon the children regardless of the actual size of the family income. This again illustrates the point made earlier that the objective situation is less important for adjustment than what it means to the child.

Many important questions are left unanswered: as yet we know little about the factors of resilience which account for finding stable children with little evidence of behavior disturbances in underprivileged and disturbed homes, while some poorly adjusted children were found in homes with good marital adjustment and superior educational and economic status.

We cannot overemphasize the conclusion that a home which is psychologically unfavorable in only one or two respects permits a youngster to adjust without much disturbance, provided the parents are themselves secure enough to give the child adequate security and affection.

The Healthy Personality

It is probably fruitless, then, to look for a formulation of what constitutes a normal personality. We can be more usefully concerned with how the working through of the problems of growing up makes for healthy personality. Erikson deals with just this problem in his outline of the sequence in which major qualities of healthy personality in our culture may be expected to develop:

In early infancy, when the child is completely dependent on adults, especially the mother, for every kind of care, stimulation and satisfaction, basic *trust* is established when the child's needs are adequately met.

As the child gains control of his muscles and develops the ability to control elimination, *autonomy* develops.

With the acquisition of motor skills, such as creeping, walking, etc., the child is able to move toward his own goals and can follow his own *initiative* in relation to people and things.

At the school-age period he learns to carry through a task and a responsibility, and thus develops a capacity for *industry*.

By puberty, cliques and gangs are becoming well-established, with leaders and followers, and he has acquired a sharper feeling of his own *identity*.

Adolescence brings more intense friendships and loves with a new level of *intimacy*.

Adulthood, with its acceptance of roles in job and a new family, brings *generativity* (as contrasted with egotism.) [4]

In the normal mature person these qualities contribute to a sense of reality in living, a feeling of independence, satisfaction in craftsmanship, responsibility, and integrity. Where the experiences of life

[4] Adapted from E. H. Erikson, *Childhood and Society*, W. W. Norton & Company, 1950, Chapter 7.

have failed to develop these qualities, the adult feels pervaded with a sense of doom, indifference, self-absorption, apathy, and despair.

This outline of feelings which a healthy personality may be expected to develop is focused chiefly on the feelings about oneself. Sometimes psychology has paid less attention to the self than to the child's use of his environment, his relations with other children and with adults. We need to learn more about how the child develops a feeling of security, a feeling of adequacy, of acceptance of the authority or reality of life which limits him and cannot be controlled by him; how the child develops a sense of integration both in terms of self-sufficiency and in terms of cohesion of parts within himself. Plant, interested in the impact of the social scene with its changing patterns of family, school, church, and industrial life, attempts to show at each point some of the possible effects of current trends as they permeate the "envelope" through which each growing child sifts the experiences in his subculture. One is deeply impressed by the importance of the individual personality of each child, with its own congenital temperament, its own absorption of meanings and symbols, its own way of sorting out and rejecting or absorbing what it can "afford" to pay attention to at any given time.

To learn more about how each very unique child can realize his optimum growth and capacity, future research in child psychology must continue to run down in all their complexity the many and varied forces at work at any moment of development, and over the years of growth. No one time, no one cause is all-determining.

We must learn more about the differences in growth rhythms and readinesses among children, to know better how to foster the development of individuals.

We can feel reassured when we find that the almost inevitable errors of handling have no dramatic consequences for the child in a total picture of happy, vital parent-child relationships, and when we see continued evidence of the child's amazing resilience in even trying situations.

SUGGESTED READINGS

1. Barker, Roger, Kounin, J. S., and Wright, H. F., *Child Behavior and Development*. New York: McGraw-Hill, 1943. The chapters in this book are concise presentations by the original investigators of some of the most important recent studies in various aspects of the field of child psychology.

2. Biber, B., Murphy, L. B., Woodcock, L. P., and Black, I. S., *Child Life in School*. New York: Basic Books, 1953. A multi-faceted, intensive study of how seven-year-old children behave and learn.

3. Carmichael, Leonard (ed.), *Manual of Child Psychology*. New York: Wiley, 1946. Each chapter exhaustively covers and critically evaluates the findings that have contributed to all the various areas of child psychology as a field of scientific investigation. An advanced text.

4. Davis, Allison, and Havighurst, R. J., *Father of the Man*. New York: Houghton-Mifflin, 1947. A simply and absorbingly written account of social and emotional development. There is considerable stress on the influences of social class membership.

5. Gesell, A., and Ilg, F., *Infant and Child in the Culture of Today*. New York: Harper, 1943. A popular account of the findings of these pioneer workers in child development.

6. Isaacs, Susan, *Social Development in Young Children*. New York: Harcourt, 1933. A perceptive, anecdotal account of social development during the preschool years.

7. Jones, H. E., *Development in Adolescence*. New York: Appleton-Century-Crofts, 1943. An account of the research conducted at the University of California that considers a vast array of influences on adolescent personality.

8. Lewis, Claudia, *Children of the Cumberland*. New York: Columbia University, 1946. An example of the greater understanding of child development that comes from the observation of children in one of America's nonmiddleclass subcultures.

9. Plant, J. S., *The Envelope*. New York: Commonwealth Fund, 1950. This veteran clinician writes a sensitive appreciation of individual

uniqueness and the way in which this uniqueness lends a particular meaning to social and emotional experiences.

10. Prescott, D. A. *et al., Helping Teachers to Understand Children.* Washington: American Council on Teacher Education, 1945. This book seeks to show teachers how education can become more effective with clearer, deeper understanding of children.

Chapter 8

Educational Psychology

by FRANK S. FREEMAN

Historical Background

Definition and Nature

Personality Development of Pupils

Psychology and Educational Measurement

Psychology of the Teacher

Counseling and Guidance

Psychology in the Construction of Curricula

Psychology of the Adult Learner

Individual Differences
        EXTENT OF INDIVIDUAL DIFFERENCES
        VARIATIONS WITHIN THE INDIVIDUAL
        INFLUENCE OF INHERITANCE
        INFLUENCE OF ENVIRONMENT
        RACIAL AND NATIONAL ORIGINS
        SEX DIFFERENCES
        THE AGE FACTOR
        PHYSIQUE AND INTELLECT
        SPECIAL ABILITIES AND DISABILITIES
        EXCEPTIONAL INDIVIDUALS
        CONCLUSION—INDIVIDUAL DIFFERENCES

Psychology of Learning Applied to Education
        LEARNING THEORY
        SPECIFIC PROBLEMS IN THE PSYCHOLOGY OF LEARNING

Other Areas in Educational Psychology

Conclusion

Suggested Readings

HISTORICAL BACKGROUND

Educational psychology is concerned, in a broad and most comprehensive sense, with learning and teaching. These two terms, it will be seen, are not restricted to the problems of classroom procedures and techniques; they include a complex of factors involving the whole individual and all the forces affecting his behavior at any given time. Thus it is that educational institutions and agencies have been and are the largest users of psychology. While the modern scientific period of the subject dates from about 1900, the writings on psychological topics relevant to educational practices and problems may be said to have begun at least with Aristotle's *De Memoria et Reminiscentia,* in which were stated the laws of learning by association: namely, similarity, contrast, and contiguity.

The first major impetus to the development of educational psychology came, however, with the establishment of normal schools. The first of such schools, as we have come to recognize them in their modern form, was established in 1804 by Johann Heinrich Pestalozzi in Switzerland. His school for the preparation of teachers of young children was distinguished by his insistence upon the psychological treatment of children and the application of psychological principles to the study of educational problems. Pestalozzi's teaching methods were what has come to be known as "child-centered"; that is, a knowledge of children as psychological, developing, and maturing organisms is essential before educational methods and materials can be properly used with them.

Johann Friedrich Herbart, who had met Pestalozzi and had been strongly influenced by him, is also recognized as one of the major figures in developing the subject of educational psychology during the early years of the nineteenth century. He based his educational practices upon psychological and ethical principles, having organized a practice school and conducted a seminar in pedagogy while a professor in Königsberg. So far as educational psychology is concerned, Herbart's main conceptions were that the mind is built up entirely by outside experiences, by the outside world; the mind thus develops elements of consciousness which he called ideas. The ideas within a person tend to maintain and consolidate themselves into what Herbart called the apperceptive mass. Each new experience or idea is received or rejected, evaluated, and interpreted according to its harmony or conflict with the apperceptive mass. According to this conception, a teacher can best arouse interest and attention in a pupil and can best get a pupil to retain experiences and ideas through making use of his body of related knowledge previously acquired and consolidated. The educational problem, then, becomes one of presenting new materials in such a way that they will be incorporated with the old; that is with the existing apperceptive masses. It is obvious that Herbart's concern was with the utilization of his psychological principles for purposes of classroom teaching in a much more restricted sense than Pestalozzi's principles, the latter being concerned more with what is now called the "whole child."

It so happened that an appreciable number of able American teachers and scholars were studying in Germany during the last two decades of the nineteenth century. They were so strongly influenced by Herbartian principles that they formed, in the United States, a Herbart Society to propagate their principles for the solution of educational problems.

While the adherents of the Herbart Society were among the most able and most forceful of American teachers and scholars concerned with the educative process, there were also many others who belonged to no particular "school" of thought but who were concerned with the more adequate psychological preparation of prospective teachers. They also helped to introduce the study of educational psychology in the flourishing normal schools and universities of their day.

Modern educational psychology, as an experimental, specialized field of study, dates from about 1900. Edward L. Thorndike published his first *Educational Psychology* in 1903, in which he applied to educational problems the methods of scientific research and in which he presented scientific findings on such topics as the measurement and distribution of mental traits, relationships between mental traits, original and acquired traits, the influence of environment, changes in mentality with increasing age, sex differences in mental traits, characteristics of exceptional children, and relationships between mental and physical traits. Compared with the earlier largely speculative publications in the field of educational psychology, Thorndike's was based upon scientific observation and experimentation, being factual and nonspeculative. In 1913 and 1914 Thorndike published his three-volume work on the subject: I, *The Original Nature of Man*; II, *The Psychology of Learning*; III, *Mental Work and Fatigue, and Individual Differences and Their Causes.*

Thorndike's 1903 volume and his later comprehensive and distinguished publications were among the first in the field and gave strong impetus to extensive research and publication by many others. Also, some of Thorndike's contemporaries were beginning to make the first of their many important contributions to the subject. For example, Charles H. Judd in 1903 published his *Genetic Psychology for Teachers*; Lewis M. Terman, shortly after 1900, had begun his researches which were to result in the publication, in 1916, of his very important volume, *The Measurement of Intelligence,* and the Stanford-Binet Intelligence Scale, which for many years was the most significant single psychological instrument used to determine general intelligence levels of children.

Although the foregoing writers on the applications of psychology to educational problems did give some attention to the nature and needs of children and adolescents as growing and developing biopsychological organisms, their principal concerns were with the learning process, as it might be applied to the classroom for the purpose of improving methods of teaching, and with individual differences in ability to learn. Notable contributions were made in the psychology of learning in general, in the learning and teaching of specific school subjects, in the diagnosis and remediation of general and specific learning difficulties, in the education of the mentally retarded (including the mentally deficient) and the mentally gifted, in nursery school and kindergarten practices, in the evaluation (by means of standardized tests) of educational attainments, and in the measurement of individual differences in abilities.

The development of behaviorism in the United States, during the second and third decades of the twentieth century, was encouraged by the conditioned reflex theory of Pavlov and his followers, and tended further to emphasize in educational psychology the nature, conditions, and mechanics of the learning process, with little or no attention given to what are now called needs, motives, and dynamics of behavior.

Beginning about 1930, however, emphasis in educational psychology began to shift from learning theory and learning mechanics (though these were not neglected) to investigations of aspects of behavior, development, and learning which deal with the learner (child, adolescent, or adult) as an organic unit. This approach is in contrast to most of those preceding it, which dealt with a small subunit of the organism (e.g., the reflex arc, and the stimulus-response connection), under controlled conditions of the experimental laboratory or under the uniform or nearly uniform conditions present in the investigation of large groups.

DEFINITION AND NATURE

Educational psychology may be defined as the application of the principles, facts, and techniques of individual and group psychology to human development in a more or less controlled situation. Some of the principles, facts, and techniques have been drawn from general psychology and from related fields, notably social psychology, clinical psychology, and social anthropology. Educational psychologists have also developed their own special principles, facts, and techniques in such areas as instructional methods in various school subjects, relationships between teachers and pupils, relationships among pupils themselves, remediation of special difficulties in school learning, the needs of school children with special talents and defects (both psychological and physical), techniques in group thinking and group activity of children, vocational and educational guidance, counseling on adjustment problems of pupils, the psychological and educational effects of various modes of pupil classification, methods and results of teaching by audio-visual means, methods of evaluating the results of instruction, effects of various disciplinary techniques, and the nature and development of interests.

It is thus clear that educational psychology is more than the application of general psychology, *per se,* and related fields, to educational practice. While educational psychologists test the validity of applications of general and social psychology and related subjects to education, they have developed in many areas psychological facts, principles, and techniques with which other branches of psychology do not deal adequately, if at all. The developing concepts of the psychology of personality, adjustment, and mental hygiene have changed teachers' practices in regard to classroom discipline and have modified their conceptions of classroom control and procedures. Teachers now are more alert to and concerned with the needs of children as social-emotional organisms than they were before. The development of educational and psychological tests, and of statistical methods, has emphasized the nature and extent of individual differences; and it has resulted in more concern with individualized instruction, the modification of learning materials, and the reëxamination of promotion schemes. The development of child psychology has focused attention upon the nonintellectual aspects of human growth; upon the child "as a whole." The result has been increasing attention to school experiences that might contribute to social and emotional maturation. The development of the psychology of learning has revealed the prime importance of motivation. It has also shown the desirability of curriculum organization other than the "logical" one, the function of experiences at the pupils' own levels, and the superiority of understanding and insight as contrasted with sheer memorization.

PERSONALITY DEVELOPMENT OF PUPILS

Concern with personality development and the mental health of children and adolescents is being emphasized in educational psychology and has become part of the daily work of enlightened teachers. They now apply in the classroom a number of well-recognized psychological principles, among them being that all human behavior is activated by fundamental motives; that a sound teacher respects the personalities of pupils; that the school (that is, the teachers, other pupils, curriculum, etc.) is one of the major factors in developing the mental health of children; that children's learning and other behaviors are based upon the functioning of the individual as a whole, involving his intellectual, emotional, social, and physical traits.

Each of these principles has certain important implications for educational practice. When it is realized that all children need the experience of successful and approved achievement, course materials are adjusted according to individual needs, and successful performance is emphasized rather than failure. Then goals and objectives are established which are within reach of the intended learners. The individual is thus evaluated in terms of his own abilities and potentialities rather than in terms of the group as a whole or in terms of objectives arbitrarily defined by educators or other adults. A second motive, or need, is recognition and approbation in one's group, frequently called status. Educators who recognize this fundamental need will provide conditions within which their pupils may achieve status within the various school situations. Emotional security is essential in the lives of children as well as adults. Educators who recognize and implement this fact will arrange disciplinary procedures and methods of control in such a way that no child loses his self-respect or feels himself rejected. Educators who understand and apply the psychology of human motivation are concerned with the causes of children's and adolescents' behavior, rather than with symptoms and overt manifestations alone.

The psychology of childhood and adolescence, while having much in common with the subjects of personality development and mental hygiene, has made some other specific contributions, widely incorporated into educational practice. From these fields have come the following conceptions, among others. In order to achieve optimal development of a child it is necessary to provide school experiences that will help develop not only his intellectual capacity (as usually conceived) but also his capacities in the arts, physical skills, and social participation. This principle gives implementation and concrete meaning to the conception of educating the child as a whole. Thus all school practices are viewed from the point of view of the impact they have upon the intellectual-social-emotional development of the individual.

Research has shown, also, that each child and adolescent may develop at a rate more or less different from the general trend, or average of his age, in respect to intellectual, social, emotional, and physical traits. A given individual's abilities and resources, at any time, may thus vary in either direction from what might be expected of him on the basis of his age or grade placement. These facts have emphasized the necessity of considering each person as an individual rather than merely as an anonymous member of a group.

It is commonplace now to recognize that differences among children and adolescents as regards school learning, behavior in school, and attitudes toward school are due to a complex of factors: physical, intellectual, emotional, and social. Each of these has its subdivisions; within each area numerous relevant facts may be found and observations made. Many of the facts and observations will cut across two or more of the areas. When the data have been assembled and the observations made, they must be interpreted with emphasis upon a meaningful, comprehensive picture of the child as a whole.

In dealing with a rather complex problem of development or behavior, in the handling and solution of problems of adjustment in school or out, isolated facts and observations have only limited usefulness, and at times none at all. The developmental and behavioral significance of facts and observations can be derived only by interrelating them into a meaningful whole. When, for example, a teacher attempts to interpret a child's attitudes, behavior, and performance in school subjects, it is often necessary to know his home status, his physical condition, the values of his social groups, and his status among his peers, as well as his intellectual capacity. Similarly, when parents attempt to understand a child's attitude toward school, it is necessary that they take into account, among other factors, the foregoing considerations and, in addition, the teacher's attitude toward the child as well as their own attitudes toward him and toward schooling in general. If we find a child who is overaggressive on the playground, the explanation might be uncovered in his unsatisfactory experiences in the classroom or in an inferior status imposed upon him in his community. Again, an excessively zealous child in the classroom might be overcompensating for feelings of inferiority or rejection outside of school.

PSYCHOLOGICAL AND EDUCATIONAL MEASUREMENT

In the field of measurement and statistics, educational psychology has made many significant contributions for the better understanding of individual differences, of how much has been learned, and of what specifically has been learned. Educational psychologists have, therefore, been very active in the development of tests of intelligence, educational achievement, special aptitudes, interests, and emotional adjustment. These types of tests are necessary for the sounder and more adequate understanding of the individual's mental maturity and readiness to learn certain school materials at certain levels, and for getting insight into his personality organization, since learning in school situations is a function of the total personality.

Measurements of the extent and nature of individual differences in general ability, special ability, achievement in specific school subjects, and personality have shown the need for differentiated instruction as to rate of progress, content of courses and curriculum, and methods of instruction. Also, the use of psychological and educational measuring instruments has been primarily responsible for the development of programs of diagnosis and remedial instruction. Difficulties and disabilities in learning are now more readily diagnosed through the use of standardized tests, especially in reading and arithmetic, two fundamental subjects in which handicaps often retard an individual's entire educational progress and may even create an emotional block to all learning. The use of diagnostic instruments has encouraged, in fact necessitated, the development of special methods of remedial instruction. Thus, there have been many experiments to determine the value of one instructional technique against another; and these experiments have added to the fund of knowledge on the psychology of learning.

The use of measuring instruments, in addition, has helped to define the several educational levels, and to determine and evaluate progress in learning from grade to grade. Without these instruments a sound program of guidance and counseling would be impossible.

PSYCHOLOGY OF THE TEACHER

Since parents and teachers are generally the most important adults in the lives of children, it is necessary to understand the psychological traits of these adults if we are to evaluate the behavior of the pupils. While various psychologists have been concerned with the study of personality traits of adults in general, educational psychologists have been concerned with traits of teachers in particular, since the impact of teachers' attitudes upon their pupils is strong. For example, one of the most valuable investigations has shown that dominative or coöperative teachers produce dominative or coöperative behavior and attitudes in their pupils.

In general, research on the psychology of teachers has dealt with the mental health of teachers as affected by the conditions of the profession, and with the qualities essential in a desirable teacher. As regards the problem of mental health, teachers are under pressures and demands that are not usually found in other professions: they are expected to participate in church and other community groups; they are expected to exhibit personality traits and conduct patterns which parents regard as the ideal but do not necessarily exhibit themselves; their activities, both professional and nonprofessional, are closely scrutinized, as those of other professional groups are not; they are often subjected to the rule of autocratic administrators (as are persons in other occupations). The foregoing situations often result in frustration and tensions. The mental health factors are not entirely of a negative kind; for prospective teachers as a group are somewhat above the average in mental health, and successful teachers often find the social values of their work to be compensating factors. There are, of course, many communities in which teachers are not subjected to the undesirable pressures and demands mentioned above. Educational psychology has, in this connection, been concerned with the conditions that contribute to or detract from optimal mental health of teachers.

In the matter of essential qualities of successful teachers and procedures in their selection, much work has been done, and much remains to be done, especially in regard to the more subtle emotional traits. It is known, for example, that among the more obvious traits desired are better than average academic ability, good physical health, freedom from disabling physical and sensory defects, a genuine interest in children and in the educative process, a genuine conviction with respect to the value of education especially in a democracy, and a strong interest in the subject matter being taught. Regarding other traits of personality less is known definitely. On the basis of present knowledge, however, it seems reasonably clear that certain other characteristics may be specified as essential for successful teaching. Satisfactory personal and social adjustment is necessary: that is, sound interpersonal relationships; insight into, or better still, solution of one's personal problems and anxieties; ability to take a course of action as well as being able to employ rational thought processes; coming to terms with one's environment and working by rational and emotionally mature means to effect changes that one deems necessary or desirable; a sense of humor about one's work and one's self; recognition of one's own assets and disabilities.

Teachers' feelings and attitudes can affect their pupils adversely or beneficially. A number of studies have revealed that there may be unwholesome consequences as a result of working with and under teachers whose lives show marked evidence of frustration and distortion. This situation is educationally significant because the teacher's own judgment of pupil behavior and the teacher's aims and goals for the pupils' development will depend upon his own values and attitudes. It has been found, for instance, that so-called behavior problems among children are much more prevalent in classrooms of emotionally unstable teachers than in the classes of better-adjusted teachers. It has been shown, also, that some teachers are prone to manifest concern, anxiety, or annoyance with the behavior of a child who by his failure to conform interferes with the routine and standards of the classroom. Routine and standards, in turn, are the products of teachers', supervisors', and administrators' own attitudes and values, and to a degree to those of society in general. What the adult—teacher or parent—considers good or bad, right or wrong, desirable or undesirable, is in part a product of his own life history and his consequent values, as well as of those values and standards with which society expects conformity. Thus, pupils are subject to and affected by the experiences and histories of their teachers whose feelings, attitudes, and responses are conditional upon their own past relations and the manner in which past situations were resolved. A teacher who, for example, has not solved his or her own conflicts in a given area of living cannot be of much help and may even be harmful to pupils having conflicts in the same area.

The resourceful, cheerful, and attractive teacher is emotionally as well as intellectually mature. The emotionally mature person is one who has had a reasonably adequate pattern of life, who has met and resolved life's situations and problems with insight, who does not transfer his own difficulties and deficiencies to others but who, on the contrary, is capable of sharing in the interests of others and of giving sympathy and understanding in his interpersonal relationships. The presence of such a teacher at all levels from the primary grades through the university gives the learners an opportunity to develop in a classroom atmosphere in which security, mutual respect, and chance for achievement are pervasive. Such a teacher gives direction and guidance, rather than dominating a group of submissive individuals.

COUNSELING AND GUIDANCE

This aspect of educational psychology, long practiced in schools, should be a form of clinical procedure. While it is true that, as now often practiced, counseling and guidance are principally educational fact finding and advice giving, the conception has been changing in recent years due to the development of dynamic (motivational) psychology, psychotherapeutic principles and practices, and the projective methods of testing and evaluating personality. These developments are making it necessary to distinguish between three different but somewhat overlapping professions in schools, all of which ideally are parts of general counseling and guidance procedures. First, there is the *psychometrist* (or *psychometrician*), whose principal duties are the giving, scoring, and reporting on individual and group tests of intelligence, special aptitudes, and achievement in the several school subjects. Second, there is the *guidance counselor,* whose principal tasks are to assist pupils in making educational and occupational decisions, utilizing whatever educational and psychological information is available. He uses, in addition, approved techniques of interviewing. Third, there is the *school psychologist* (and the psychologist in college and university), who, of the three, should represent the highest level of professional preparation. He should be one who can supervise and actually perform the work of the other two, and who, in addition is able to administer and interpret inventories of personality traits and projective tests. He should be able, also, to employ psychotherapeutic methods with pupils when such are indicated.

Through the utilization of principles of the dynamics of human behavior, evidence from projective methods of testing personality, and modern techniques of interviewing and psychotherapy, the approach to guidance and counseling in educational institutions now rests upon the following principles: the processes of guidance (and of therapy where needed) should activate and help develop the individual's own resources to solve his educational, vocational, and behavioral problems; the counselor or therapist should contribute to the development of a pupil's own inner strength and resources by practicing the principles of mental hygiene in his relationships with the pupil; the superficial giving of advice is generally futile; basically the pupil (or anyone else, for that matter) should be assisted in deciding upon a course of action which he feels is his own. Fundamentally, counseling and guidance, as an essential aspect of school practice, should make use of the principle that the pupil is at all times functioning as a psychological, biological, and social organism.

PSYCHOLOGY IN THE CONSTRUCTION OF CURRICULA

The construction of curricula involves the application of principles of educational philosophy, social philosophy, and psychology. In regard to the last of these the main consideration is this: Since it is the responsibility of schools to promote optimal development of each pupil and to advance his learning, the development of any curriculum must take into account the general course of child and adolescent development, and the universal fact of individual differences. In connection with the first of these—the general course of development—consideration must be given to such aspects as levels of sensory perception and motor development, language skills and development, capacities for abstract and conceptual thought processes, nature and strength of interests, social and emotional needs. In connection with individual differences, consideration must be given, within the general plans of a curriculum, to adaptations and adjustments necessitated by special abilities or disabilities, unusual interests, unusual general ability, and significant social or emotional factors operating at a given time.

Curricula, furthermore, should utilize the psychology of the learning process: e.g., the effectiveness of repetition and practice, the role of feeling and emotion in learning, the factors in remembering and forgetting, transfer of learning, the importance of organization in presentation and of insightful learning, activity versus passivity, coördination and interrelationship of materials, and the effects of reward and punishment. Thus, in organizing curricula, from the psychological viewpoint two major areas must be considered: the nature of general and of individual development, and the principles and factors involved in the learning process.

PSYCHOLOGY OF THE ADULT LEARNER

Beginning about twenty-five years ago, educational psychologists have been showing increased interest and activity in the learning processes of adults. This interest is prompted by at least two considerations: first, the scientific study of changes in psychological processes associated with increasing age; and second, the educability of adults as a most important aspect of their mental health. Since the average life span is increasing and our population is thus growing "older," the psychological problems of the employability, usefulness, status, capacity to learn, and morale of the adult have become increasingly significant and acute.

From birth onward, in the course of the average or longer life span, development is a process of maturation to maximum performance levels, followed by a period of stability (a "plateau" in learning and performance), and later by decline. That this is the sequence, there is no doubt. But concerning the general age levels of these three phases, the characteristics of development of the various psychological functions, and the detailed nature of decline, scientific information is not yet definitive, although much is known.

Adult behavior, like that of children and adolescents, depends upon physical and physiological changes, one's psychological history, and present conditions. While each developing function goes through the three phases mentioned above, each has its own rate. For example, hearing capacity reaches its maximum at about the age of 14 and declines slowly thereafter. Visual acuity increases up to about the age of 20, then declines slowly to about 45, followed by a much more rapid decline to the age of about 60. Speed of reaction increases until about the age of 30, then slows down gradually for the rest of the life span. Capacity to memorize and retain increases until the age of about 20 or later, remains level until 25 or later, then declines very slowly indeed to age 45. General ability (a composite and integration of psychological functions), as measured by adult tests of intelligence, increases to age 20 or higher, then declines very, very slowly until age 50, except in the case of speed of reaction, which declines more rapidly.

As adults grow older, there is not only some loss in visual and auditory acuity, and in speed of reaction, but their energy resources are also being reduced, so that their performances, in general, will suffer. It is necessary, therefore, to distinguish between an adult's *level of ability* and his *performance* which may be adversely affected by decline in the sensory capacities, in speed of response, and in energy level. Furthermore, adults often do not have a sufficiently strong purpose or need to learn, so that their performance is further affected adversely, as compared with level of ability.

The fact that speed of response and energy level generally decrease as age increases in adulthood is especially significant in the measurement of adult intelligence, especially after the age of about 45. Failure to eliminate or minimize the factor of speed in testing adult mental ability had, earlier, led to a misconception regarding abilities of persons of middle age and older; their decline was very much exaggerated.

The more recent and more valid research studies have demonstrated also that rate and amount of decline are associated with the individual's educational history and the demands made upon him by present conditions of his mode of living. It has been shown that of individuals who were initially equivalent in levels of mental functioning, those who had more schooling were more able intellectually throughout adulthood than those who had less. And, as might be expected, those persons who entered occupations requiring extensive formal education and continued study and mental alertness declined much more slowly than persons in other occupations. Performance in adulthood—i.e., level of mental activity—is, therefore, significantly associated with the extent of use or disuse of psychological functions.

These findings in regard to adult abilities and rate of loss mean that adult education and reëducation may go on effectively throughout practically the entire life span; that the success or failure of an adult to learn is related principally to his initial capacity, present interest and motivation, energy, and opportunity.

INDIVIDUAL DIFFERENCES

This subject is one of several that have been most thoroughly studied and investigated in the field of educational psychology. While observers for many centuries have recognized the fact that individuals vary among themselves in respect to psychological and physical traits, it is only about sixty years since differences in psychological traits have been intensively studied, although a few scientific investigations were made earlier, notably by Sir Francis Galton beginning in the 1860's.

The educational importance of scientific knowledge of individual differences in psychological traits is obvious; for if educational practices are to foster and develop the resources of all persons, they should not be subjected to educational uniformity, or what has been called, educational "lockstep," whereby every pupil proceeds through identical curricula and courses of study at identical rates, regardless of differences in abilities, interests, or needs.

Scientific study of individual differences, furthermore, is essential for the understanding of their causes, particularly in connection with the question of the roles of heredity and environment. The basic and very important question is this: Do environmental conditions significantly affect the development of human traits and differences, or must variations be accepted as biologically (genetically) predetermined facts with which at present little or nothing can be done? This is a fundamental question in a democracy in which we would seek to develop and foster human abilities and human resources, regardless of the social, racial, economic, or religious group in which they originate.

Extent of Individual Differences

It is impossible to represent a person, as a whole, by means of a single index. There is no psychological test or other device which will reveal the integration of all the facets of an individual's personality: his general intelligence, his mechanical or artistic ability, his emotional traits, his values and attitudes. What any test or device does is to measure or describe an aspect or a segment of the individual. The aspect measured may be relatively simple, as in the case of reaction times, or relatively complex as in the case of intelligence. Thus curves of distribution which portray human variations represent selected traits rather than distributions of total personalities.

Scientific doctrines of human abilities and differences are not in agreement with the rather popular notion that all persons fall naturally into one of several distinct types. According to this erroneous opinion a person is either "visual-minded" or "auditory-minded," "mechanical-minded" or "language-minded," musical or unmusical, intelligent or unintelligent, etc.

As a matter of fact, human beings in their range and complexity of variation can no more be correctly classified as members of one or another specific type than they can as giants or dwarfs, gen-

iuses or idiots. This does not mean, however, that there are no individuals at either extreme in these and other traits. It means that
when a representative population is measured or tested, it is found
that instead of two opposed types there is a continuous gradation
from one extreme to the other, with a concentration of individuals
about a central point (or score), while the frequency of cases decreases as the deviation from the central tendency increases. The
nature of this distribution is illustrated in Figure 8.1, which is
known as the theoretical normal frequency curve.

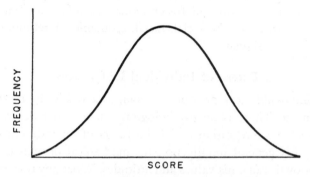

FIGURE 8.1.   A Normal Distribution Curve.

The readily discernible educational implications of the distribution of human abilities are very significant. First, since the general
population is not divisible into two or three ready-made classifications in any psychological traits, there are no readily available and
fixed categories which the school can employ for the purpose of
differentiated instruction. Second, the range of abilities, as shown
by the frequency curve, is such that differentiated educational procedures are imperative, whether in the form of acceleration or cur-
ricular enrichment, or both; and whether by homogeneous classes,
or by groupings and individualized instruction within a single heterogeneous class. Third, because individuals do not fall readily into
one type or another, the importance of the individual as the unit of
education, not of an alleged type, is emphasized.

The following two examples show how closely actual research data approach the theoretical normal frequency curve. Figure 8.2 is a distribution of intelligence quotients obtained by testing 1001 first-grade children with the Stanford Revision of the Binet-Simon Test. The range of intelligence quotients is from about 60, representing marked mental inferiority, to about 160, representing a very

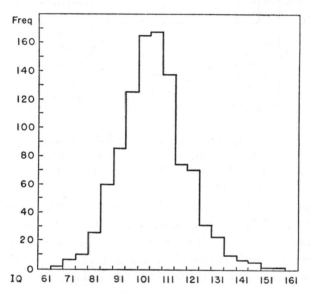

FIGURE 8.2. Distribution of Intelligence Quotients of 1001 First-Grade Children. (From M. M. Wentworth, *Individual Differences in the Intelligence of School Children*. Harvard University Press, 1926. By permission of the Harvard University Press.)

high degree of mental superiority, while the central tendency, representing the typical, is in the neighborhood of 100. Similar distributions are found when standardized tests are used with groups at all levels and ages, including college students and adults.

Figure 8.3 shows that a close approximation to the normal frequency curve may be obtained when we measure more limited mental processes than those involved in general intelligence. This

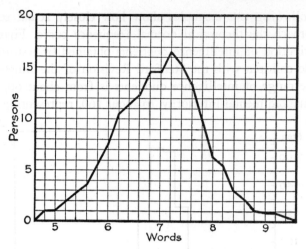

FIGURE 8.3. Distribution of Memory Scores, 173 University Students. (From D. Starch, *Educational Psychology,* Macmillan, 1924. By permission of The Macmillan Company.)

curve shows the distribution of scores made by 173 university students in a test of memory span for words. Much the same form of curve would be obtained if we were to measure some other specialized functions, such as those involved in copying digits or letters, cancellation tests, rate of tapping, and motor skills.

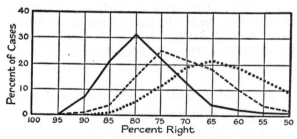

FIGURE 8.4. Distribution of Capacities in the Sense of Pitch. Solid and broken lines represent different age groups. (From C. E. Seashore, *The Psychology of Musical Talent,* copyright, 1919, by Silver Burdett Company, New York.)

There is some evidence, however, that in a few special instances, and under present environmental conditions of development, distributions do not conform with the normal probability curve. Two instances in point are the auditory senses of pitch and time. Figures 8.4 and 8.5 show curves for these two functions. The reasons for these and similar conditions are not entirely clear; but it is believed that marked differences in experience and training are chiefly responsible.

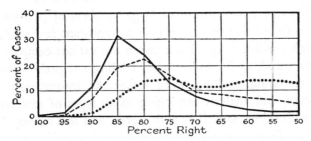

FIGURE 8.5. Distribution of Capacities in the Sense of Time. Solid and broken lines represent different age groups. (From C. E. Seashore, *The Psychology of Musical Talent,* copyright, 1919, by Silver Burdett Company, New York.)

Variations Within the Individual

While members of a group differ among themselves with regard to any given traits, it is necessary to know as much as possible about each person's characteristics for educational, guidance, or clinical purposes. Even though general trends and general principles concerning psychological traits and their interrelationships have been established, there are always individuals who are exceptions. Until an individual has been studied, we cannot assert that he is or is not consistent with a general trend or principle; nor, if discrepancies exist, can the degree be known without investigation. We need to have complete information with regard to the person himself if his individuality is to be recognized and suitable education made available. A complete psychological portrait would include details of

intellectual capacities, special abilities and disabilities, nonintellective traits of personality (i.e., temperament, emotions), attitudes
and values, interests, and environmental forces. We are here concerned primarily with intellectual capacities; yet we are constrained
to emphasize that manifestations of general intelligence and special
abilities or disabilities do not occur in isolation from one's other
psychological traits or from his physical traits.

The problem of variations within the individual has been studied
by measuring or otherwise evaluating and then correlating numerous abilities or performances of large numbers of persons. It has
thus been found that there is always a significant and sometimes a
quite high positive correlation between the various complex mental
processes tested, as in reading rate, reading comprehension, arithmetical reasoning, spelling, word definitions, information, tests of
construction and analysis employing many types of materials, reasoning with things as well as with words, and still others. The correlation coefficients are not perfect, nor are they uniform. There are
also a few types of performance that show only a low correlation
with capacities in other fields. Such are, for example, the elementary
sensory and motor capacities in music and graphic arts.

Figure 8.6 is a "profile of a pupil's school attainments," measured
as objectively as possible. Here we see very marked though not perfect consistency of performance, extreme disparities being absent.
In this pupil, the mental processes required in the various school
subjects are apparently highly consistent.

Significant inconsistencies in the usual school subjects are sometimes found in pupils. Their presence would be indicated in the
"profile" by appreciable fluctuations in the curve connecting the
points representing the levels of the several school subjects. More
marked inconsistencies are found between performance in ordinary
school subjects and general intelligence, on the one hand, and the
elemental sensory and motor capacities of music and graphic arts,
on the other. Figure 8.7 shows such a case: a child of very superior
intelligence, yet one who ranks very low in five tests of auditory

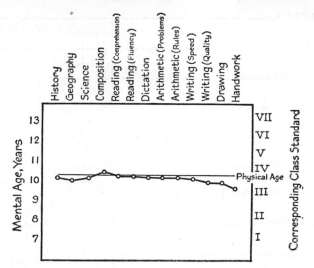

FIGURE 8.6. Profile of a Pupil's School Attainments. (From C. Burt, *Distribution and Relations of Educational Abilities,* P. S. King & Son, 1917. By permission of the London County Council.)

sensitivity required in music, and who is also below mediocrity in drawing.

The systematic study of the nature and extent of individual differences has, to the present, been largely *cross-sectional* in character, employing one variable at a time. By this method, a representative group of individuals is measured with respect to a given trait, such as intelligence, height, strength, and reading rate. The data are then arranged and analyzed, and the relative rank of an individual is determined by his position in the group. This type of study has been and still is very valuable, but we must realize that a single measure does not portray an individual. Nor is a series of such measures, taken at a given time, altogether satisfactory; for although such a series provides a psychological "profile," it does not show the dynamic interrelationships of an individual's various traits; it does not give the "organismic" picture that is so essential. No trait exists

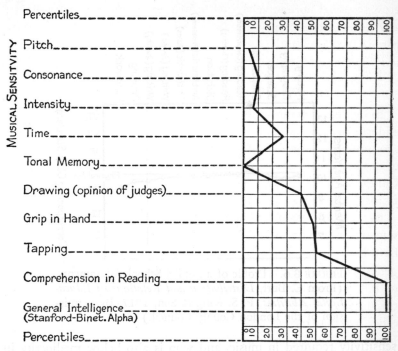

FIGURE 8.7. Psychograph of a Child of Very Superior Intelligence with a Special Defect in Music. (From L. S. Hollingsworth, *Special Talents and Defects*, Macmillan, 1923. By permission of The Macmillan Company.)

in isolation within a person; every trait is a dependent part in a larger whole that acts as a unit; it is this whole which gives every person his uniqueness. To portray this uniqueness, more recent investigations have been employing the *longitudinal* method, in which the same individual is measured and studied over a period of some years in respect to each of a variety of traits. Thus, each individual's tempo and peculiarities of development are portrayed. After this is done, it is essential to organize all the pertinent facts into a "case" and to attempt an interpretation of them in order best to understand how that person came to be what he is. In short, the cross-sectional normative study can be used to discover resemblance and differences among individuals, while the organized individual pattern, or case, can be used to explore and appraise more fully the individuality of each person.

Influence of Inheritance

Individual differences in mental abilities, as in other psychological and physical traits, have been analyzed to discover the causes responsible for variations. Fundamentally, the question reduces itself to the perennial one of heredity and environment, or as Sir Francis Galton so aptly called it, *nature and nurture*. These are the basic factors in individual differences; they are comprehensive.

By heredity we mean trait resemblances between parents (and sometimes grandparents or other ancestors) and children, which have been biologically transmitted, that is, transmitted through the genes. By environment we refer to conditions which are ascribed to the socioeconomic status of parents, the characteristics of the community, educational opportunities, conditions of health, and other external factors which operate from outside of but upon the individual. Other factors ordinarily analyzed in their relationships to human variations are racial membership (also called, at times, remote ancestry), national origins, sex membership, age, and physique. These factors, however, are really of a secondary character; for it is readily seen that they are particularized aspects of nature and nurture. Yet they are important enough to warrant separate analysis.

Insight into the nature-nurture problem is especially desirable since it is important to know what equipment a child starts with, how far environmental forces—including schooling—may be expected to develop and add to his equipment: whether a favorable environment can create or increase capacity, or whether the milieu can only supply the individual with materials to work on. It is doubtful whether biology and psychology can even now give unequivocal answers to these questions. Evidence, however, is extensive and thorough enough to free the answers from anecdote and biased speculation; and converging lines of evidence lead to very plausible conclusions. We shall summarize briefly the lines of evidence.

According to genetic theory, each individual starts with his own particular set of genetic elements—the *genes*—which in their diverse and numerous combinations yield varieties of structural, physiological, and psychological differences. Each germ cell of each parent (sperm and ovum) contains thousands of genes; there are gene diversities among the many germ cells of each parent; thus it is extremely improbable that any two children even in the same family will be developed from identical combinations of genes, except identical twins. Since all the germ cells within each parent do not carry identical trait potentialities and since the biological inheritance of a child is a biparental matter, we see the genetic reason for variations in traits among siblings, including nonidentical twins. Since some of the germ cells of parents contain genes of traits that have not appeared in themselves, we see, also, one reason why children often only partially resemble their parents. While there are gene diversities within the germ cells of each parent, there are also some genes that are identical. This fact is partially responsible for the trait similarities found among siblings.

Gene theory places emphasis upon the individual; it makes amply clear that a considerable degree of variation may occur among children of the same parents, and between parents and offspring, so far as genetic constitution is concerned. This is just as consistent with the gene theory of biological inheritance as are the resemblances between siblings, and between parents and children. The fact is, then, that the newly conceived individual need not necessarily fear relegation or look forward to the same intellectual level as that of his parents, as the case may be. Nor have his older siblings necessarily defined his mental status for him. In general, however, it is true that the new individual will tend to approach the levels of the other members of his immediate family. The significant positive correlations between abilities in members of the same family show this. Nevertheless, there are very marked deviates, as when an extremely brilliant or an extremely retarded child appears in a family where none such has appeared before—at least within memory or record.

Psychological studies of the factor of inheritance have been made by analyzing the following: degree of resemblance among parents and children, ordinary siblings, nonidentical twins, and identical twins. Occasionally degrees of resemblance between cousins and other familial relationships have been investigated; but the most important data pertain to relationships existing within the immediate family. Two comprehensive methods have been used: the study of family pedigrees, and correlations of measurements.

The tracing of family pedigrees with respect to complex human psychological traits and behavior has met with so many difficulties and valid scientific criticisms that the results of such investigations are of little value. This method had been extensively used in the first quarter of this century to investigate the hereditary factor in families having long and sordid histories of degeneracy and mental deficiency; but these reports are of little scientific significance because of the many unknown and uncontrollable factors involved, because of the extreme unreliability of the anecdotal evidence obtained, and because of the disregard of environmental conditions. The two most widely known reports of this kind are those dealing with the Kallikaks and the Jukes. In animal experiments, however, family pedigrees can be studied by means of selective breeding. These experiments have provided some evidence in support of the importance of biological inheritance in infrahuman animals in maze learning, although it is probable that the animals were bred for motor or sensory traits which may be used in solving a maze problem but these are not the equivalent of the complex human process called "intelligence."

Sir Francis Galton used the pedigree method with families of eminent men and women in his first book on the subject, *Hereditary Genius* (1869). His approach and conclusions were strongly hereditarian; for he concluded that eminence tends to run in families because of biological factors. Since the more extensive and scientific study of human differences, many writers on the subject of human differences have pointed out that Galton's interpretations cannot be accepted because he minimized the significance of large environmental differences, ignored great discrepancies existing in England in regard to educational advantages, health conditions, occupational opportunities, class status, and privileges—in short, the important environmental factors influencing learning, performance, and opportunities for achieving eminence.

Since the turn of the twentieth century the predominant method of studying family resemblances has been by the correlation of measurements of members of the same family. In particular, intelligence test results of siblings have been correlated. The coefficients for the most part, fall between $+.40$ and $+.60$, with a median of about $+.50$. There are extreme instances where the coefficient is as low as $+.30$ or as high as $+.70$; but $+.50$ may be regarded as representative. When intelligence test results of parents and children were correlated, it was found that the representative coefficient was also about $+.50$.

Twins provide superior data for study, as compared with ordinary siblings. The environments of twins are often more nearly alike; and if they are identical twins, genetic constitution is a constant factor. The constant genetic factor enables us to evaluate environmental influences.

When intelligence quotients of twins are correlated, the following coefficients are found to be typical:

Nonidentical twins	$+.60 - +.65$
Identical: reared together	$+.85 - +.90$
Identical: reared apart	$+.70 - +.75$

These coefficients should be compared with that found for ordinary siblings: namely $+.50$. Since nonidentical twins are genetically as alike and as different as ordinary siblings, the difference between the coefficients of these two groups must be attributed to environmental factors. Likewise the difference between the genetically identical twins reared together and those reared apart must be attributed to environmental factors. The possible influence of hereditary factors is indicated by the higher correlation existing between identical twins reared apart than between siblings or nonidentical twins reared together.

Concerning identical twins reared apart, differences between the members of pairs have been found in respect to intelligence, non-intellective traits of personality, and physique. The degree of differences in psychological traits is due in general to three factors: age of separation (the younger, the greater the probability of marked differences), the duration of the period of separation, the degree of environmental differences.

Influence of Environment

The separation of heredity and environment as influencing factors is artificial, because the two always function together. But it is desirable for present purposes to select some investigations that bear more directly upon nature or upon nurture.

Environmental influences, as they affect mental development, have been analyzed with regard to the following: educational and other developmental opportunities in childhood and adolescence; socio-economic groups, as represented by parental occupations and incomes; nursery school attendance; foster home; residence; institutional environment; specific training. The literature and technicalities of this subject are very considerable; so we shall present in brief only the general conclusions.

Since 1906, a number of significant studies have shown that achievements in scientific, scholarly, and other professions are attributable not only to the genetic potentialities of an individual, but to environmental opportunities, which constitute a major factor.

Attacking the problem from a different but related approach, psychologists have shown repeatedly that children who are brought up under conditions of very marked psychological impoverishment or in isolated areas not only rank low on tested psychological functions but drop in level of performance as they grow older.

Regarding socioeconomic status, it has been found that there is a significant correlation between parents' occupational ratings and their children's measured mental abilities. This correlation has too often been interpreted as being due only to the influence of heredity. In interpreting the findings as to cause and effect, it is necessary, however, to emphasize the extensive overlapping of the abilities found among children in the several socioeconomic groups, the differences in cultural and educational conditions from birth onward, and differences in physical as well as intellectual nurture.

Nursery school attendance appears to have an advantageous and permanent effect upon mental development as represented by results of psychological tests. The effect is, of course, not uniform with all children. Length of nursery school attendance is a factor; but more important is the discrepancy that exists between the home environment of the young child and the developmental advantages provided by the nursery school. Obviously, greater benefits will accrue to children from the less and the least advantaged homes.

The benefits that children derive from placement in a foster home or in an institution will depend in part upon the qualities of these. In general, children placed in superior foster homes will show an advantage in mental development over their siblings in poorer foster homes. Correlational studies show that siblings brought up in different foster homes do not resemble one another nearly so closely as do those brought up together. The coefficients varied from about +.20 to +.35, depending upon age and duration of separation, and differences in quality of foster homes. Then, too, correlations between mental abilities of "own" children and foster children in the same homes are positive and significant (+.30–+.35), indicating effects of common environmental factors. Also IQ's of unrelated foster children in the same foster homes yielded correlations ranging from +.25 to +.35. Since between "own" and foster children and between unrelated foster children there are no common genetic elements, we should expect an average correlation of zero, unless environmental factors were effective.

Finally, the effects of superior institutional care were shown thus: some illegitimate infants of mentally slow or retarded mothers were placed in such institutions. Those fathers who were known were, as a group, of less than average ability, as inferred from formal education completed. When the children were tested after several years, their intelligence ratings, as a group, were at "high average." Even more striking were the results obtained with children placed in superior adoptive homes. Variations on this type of investigation consisted in moving young children from inferior to superior institutions, and in noting effects produced by placements at different ages. Criticisms of findings of these studies—some of them quite severe—have been made by those who lean strongly to the hereditarian doctrine of human capacities and differences. Yet none of these criticisms can successfully negate the essential conclusion of the effects of changed environment: namely, that improved conditions, especially if experienced very early in life, do benefit the individual's psychological development.

The effects of specific practice and training upon individual differences in ability have been investigated experimentally. In general, it has been concluded that continued schooling does make a positive contribution to the development of measured mental processes. In regard to practice of specific skills and restricted areas of performance (as contrasted with general intelligences as tested), the effects of practice are positive also, and depend upon the stage of learning at which individuals are measured, the amount of practice between measurements, the group's similarity and dissimilarity in regard to other relevant traits, and the kind of learning and performance being measured. These researches indicate further that the nature-nurture problem is not an either-or proposition and that the generalized education of schooling and specific practice in limited operations contribute to the nature and extent of human differences in psychological traits.

Racial and National Origins

We have already stated that the heredity-environment problem is the fundamental one and that analyses in relation to other factors, though secondary, are still important and essential. Views regarding human differences in mental abilities attributable to racial and national membership have been undergoing marked change in the last twenty years. Although emphasized by many scientific writers in psychology it is only within relatively recent years that the scientific view has become rather widespread and has been adopted in other fields, such as political science. In 1950, the United Nations Scientific, Educational, and Cultural Organization issued a statement emphasizing the scientific doctrine: namely, that differences in mental abilities are not attributable primarily to membership in one or another race, or subracial group, or to being a member of a particular national group. The differences among racial and national groups are the results of differences in social, cultural, economic, and educational factors operating upon these groups; the range of variations within any one group is much greater and much more significant than the differences between any two groups.

There are at present no pure races, particularly in Europe and the United States. Anthropologists are agreed that at one time there were primeval races from which all others have been derived by crossing, so that contemporary groups have lost their definiteness through intermixture. As a consequence, there are no demonstrable innate intellectual differences to be found among the so-called "racial" groups—e.g., Alpine, Nordic, Mediterranean (really subgroups of the Caucasians)—where the cultural and other environmental factors are comparable.

Educational differentiation cannot rest upon racial or national membership. Instead, it becomes an individual matter. This doctrine applies to the North American Indian and the American Negro as well as to others; for although it is true that psychological measurements have shown them to be below white groups in *manifested* abilities, the disparities in social, economic, educational, cultural, and hygienic factors are so marked as to make impossible any direct comparison. What present data do show is that under existing conditions of very serious environmental inequality, they have, as groups, failed to reach the levels attained by contemporary whites. Nevertheless, mental test results have revealed that at least 25 percent of Negro schoolchildren reach or surpass the average performance of white children, even under present disparate conditions.

Some writers have sought to demonstrate that even though "pure" races are not to be found in this country or Europe, there are, nevertheless, within political units rather well-defined groups which, with time, have advanced toward uniformity of language, physical characteristics, and mental traits; and, they maintain, some of these "natio-racial" groups are innately superior to others in intellect. The notion of Nordic superiority is a case in point. To support their argument, the protagonists of this view cite the fact that mental tests of the foreign-born in this country show in general that immigrants from so-called Nordic countries rank higher than those from the Alpine or Mediterranean countries. It has been shown, however, that there is a very high correspondence between immigrants' intellectual ratings and the educational-cultural status of their native countries. This fact, rather than innate national differences, explains the low ratings of some groups and the higher ratings of others.

Several notable studies have been directed to the question of national differences. One was conducted in this country with 2,600 children as subjects; another was conducted in France, Germany, and Italy. Both of these demonstrated that differences in mental abilities are not associated with physical traits held by some to be characteristic of "racial" groups. The differences are appreciable when individuals are grouped according to environmental criteria. Finally, it has been demonstrated that the level of *effective* intelligence in nearly every person, regardless of "race" or national origin, may be raised through education.

Sex Differences

Whereas for centuries it was popularly believed that woman is by nature intellectually inferior to man, the large volume of presently available scientific evidence clearly established the fact that such is not the case. In regard to intelligence quotients, the averages for male and female groups are just about the expected 100. Standardized tests have shown female groups to be superior to male groups in linguistic development. In number concepts and arithmetical ability, there seems to be a slight advantage for male groups. In manual performance and in mechanical ability, males in general surpass females. There is, however, in every area of ability and performance, great overlapping between the sexes. For reasons as yet unexplained, there are more males at both extremes of the distribution. Finally the fact that there are many more men of great accomplishment than there are women, is due to a complex of social and biological factors, not to basic differences in intelligence.

The presence of a real, even though small, group difference may contribute to or give rise to interests, preferences, habits, and educational and vocational emphasis. Thus originally small differences may be developed into permanent, significant ones, such as those found between adult members of the two sexes. The disparities in the end results must, therefore, be attributed to an appreciable degree to cultural influences that differentiate between boys and girls, men and women.

The Age Factor

Everyone knows that individuals change with age during the course of the developmental cycle: that is, growth and decline. The following psychological principles have emerged from the scientific study of that cycle. Individual differences in rate of mental development are manifested in infancy, though development conforms to a defined order of succession. Children tend to maintain their relative rank in tested abilities after the age of 18 months or 2 years, investigations having yielded for the most part correlation coefficients of $+.75$ and higher. As already pointed out, in middle age and older adulthood, people suffer some decline in mental abilities; but the noteworthy fact for our purposes is that during decline individuals tend to retain their relative ranks with respect to their groups. Individual differences are not the result of haphazard growth. Provided there are no significant environmental changes, an individual tends to maintain his relative rank of mediocrity, superiority, or inferiority as determined by the integral character of his genetic constitution and the conditions of his development.

Physique and Intellect

The relationships between physique and intellect have been studied from three aspects: intellect and physical size, intellect and health, intellect and body types. Briefly, the conclusions are the following.

The correlation between *physical size* and mental ability, while positive, is so very small as to be negligible; any height and weight may be found in superior, average, and inferior groups of children. These physical indices do not furnish any clue to mental status. A more reliable and significant measure of physical development— not of size—is the anatomic index, obtained by determining skeletal ossification. But even this index is only negligibly associated with mental abilities at any given age. Thus physical size and development, and mental ability, are independent aspects of individuality.

When *health* has been investigated, as it affects mental ability, the factors studied were malnutrition, sensory handicaps, defective teeth, diseased tonsils, enlarged adenoids, simple goiter, hookworm, intestinal toxemia, etc. The defect of most of these researches is that their subjects were children already well along in development, in whom permanent damage might already have been done; for the period, duration, and intensity of the deleterious or pathological conditions are not accounted for. Aside from the question of permanent effects upon mental level produced by these and other defects, physical handicaps do affect mental efficiency and actual achievement; energy level and endurance are reduced, fatigue comes sooner, muscular development is adversely affected, it is more difficult to create and maintain interest and attention. Certain physical characteristics and defects—of face, head, body, sensory organs—may engender unfavorable attitudes in other persons; these attitudes may develop handicapping emotional behavior in the affected individual, involving a reduction in manifested mental level and performance.

As factors in individuality *body types* have been studied especially in regard to their relationships with temperaments and other nonintellectual traits. According to type theory (or typology) an individual is believed to be classifiable as a whole into one of a few groups, each group being essentially separate from the others. There have been many such attempts at classification; but even the most recent of them is of very doubtful validity. Essentially, the typologist maintains that body build is associated with certain social-emotional traits. For example, one of Kretschmer's types is the "pyknic" (thick-set, large trunk, short legs, round chest, rounded shoulders, short hands and feet) who is said to have a "cyclothyme" personality (friendly, sociable, animated, practical).

On the whole correlations between characteristics of body build, on the one hand, and various intellectual and social-emotional traits, on the other, have yielded very low correlation coefficients, showing that psychological and physical traits are not necessarily associated, except as certain physical characteristics have social and behavioral values of one kind or another and thus affect an individual's behavior and his conception of himself. If size, muscularity, agility, and body proportions affect one's activity, skills, and social relationships and status, then obviously certain physical traits will at times influence one's psychological development and status. But whatever relationship exists must be seen as resting fundamentally on the behaviors and values that give a person status in his culture and sub-cultural groups.

Special Abilities and Disabilities

A person's special talents and skills, if he has any, define his individuality more sharply and emphasize the importance of differentiated education in his case. It has already been indicated that although abilities within the individual are not perfectly correlated, the correspondence in the large majority of cases is sufficiently high to warrant the view that an individual's performances in the several academic subjects should not deviate seriously from one another. However, there are exceptions to the rule that a person is about equally good, mediocre, or poor in all mental abilities. Variations, when they occur, are found principally in arithmetical (and mathematical), linguistic, mechanical, graphic, or musical abilities. Of these, the musical and graphic have the least relationship to general intellectual level; the mechanical is more closely related, but the association is not nearly so marked as in the case of linguistic and arithmetical abilities.

Of these five, in fact, only the musical and graphic appear to have a legitimate claim to being *special abilities*. Their designation as such rests largely upon the fact that they require fortunate combinations of a number of specific mental factors which, within the individual, vary independently among themselves and independently of general ability. It is essential, however, if a person's achievements in these activities are to surpass the more mechanical aspects—such as reproduction or competent performance—that the specific factors of each ability be complemented by general intellect of an appropriate level.

It is true that in a very few cases there are special aptitudes in the linguistic, arithmetical, or mechanical fields which, as in the case of "lightning calculators," cannot be ascribed to external or accidental causes. To an explanation of these, psychology has relatively little to offer except to suggest unusual imagery of various kinds, well-developed mechanics, and short cuts. But in general, competence in arithmetical and linguistic abilities is highly correlated with general competence. It is sound to conclude, therefore, that ordinarily where an individual excels in a single ability other than music and drawing, the reason is to be found not primarily in innate mental inconsistencies but rather in such factors as interests, purpose, habits, motivation, and kind and extent of education.

In arithmetic and languaage, if disabilities exist in the case of otherwise able persons, the cause is usually one of poor habits, poor mechanics, physical handicaps, lack of interest, handicapping emotional traits, or poor teaching. As for mechanical ability or disability, barring sensory and motor defects, the principal causes may be ascribed to formal and informal education, nonintellectual traits of personality, and cultural emphasis, rather than to an innate special ability or disability.

In the study of individuals having special abilities (even of prodigies) and of those with special disabilities, one cannot but be impressed by the small initial handicaps from which serious disabilities may develop eventually, or by the small initial advantages which, combined with zeal and highly competent instruction, may eventuate in very large final differences such as to constitute, in effect, special abilities.

Exceptional Individuals

By the term "exceptional individual" we mean one who deviates so markedly from the average of a group in respect to traits of intellect, physique, or other aspects of personality as to create a special problem of education or adjustment. We shall be concerned here with the intellectually exceptional—both the mentally superior and mentally inferior—who present special educational problems and whose personality traits do not conform with some of the popular notions about them.

In terms of intelligence quotients, children with IQ's above 110 have been classified as "superior" in some degree, since the "normal" range of IQ's is commonly regarded as being between 90 and 110. When we speak of intellectually exceptional children, however, we refer usually to those of IQ's of 130 or higher. Indeed, some psychologists place the lower limit at 135 or 140. These individuals at the extreme upper level of the distribution need special educational consideration. It is necessary, therefore, to know not only their intellectual traits but their nonintellective characteristics as well.

As a group these children come from superior homes in regard to parental education and occupation, socioeconomic status, cultural opportunities, furnishings, and quality of community. In physical development, they are as a group, somewhat taller and heavier than the average. As for traits of character and emotional adjustment, they rate significantly in advance of an average control group. Their interests and play activities are more mature than those of ordinary groups of children. In school, they are accelerated for their age and they are capable of much more extensive and intensive learning than ordinary pupils even of their advanced grades. *Gifted children,* as a group, continue their formal education much longer than the average; and they enter the professions in larger proportions. And contrary to popular opinion of not many years ago, they do not level off to mediocrity in adulthood, they maintain their superior levels and performance.

On the whole, then, gifted children, as a group, present a picture of wholesome physical and personal development. Educationally, they have presented problems which have been variously met. Should they be accelerated in the schools, or should they be kept with their age groups and have an enriched curriculum? A categorical answer cannot be given. The handling of each individual will depend upon his social, emotional, and physical as well as his intellectual development. Should the gifted be taught in heterogeneous classes or in classes grouped according to ability? Practices differ; at present there is less emphasis upon ability sectioning than there was ten years or more ago; but unless the educational needs of gifted children can be met in a heterogeneous class, they should be grouped in special classes. Teaching geared to the gifted requires special methods and materials, best provided in a special class.

Mentally subnormal individuals present their own educational problems. They also may present serious social problems; for without sound training they are more likely to become social liabilities than are normal or superior persons. This is so because the mentally subnormal are lacking in judgment and discernment, learn slowly if at all, and often come from home and community environments that are not conducive to wholesome personal-social development.

Individuals having IQ's below 80 (borderline) are usually classified as mentally subnormal. Their degree of deficiency increases as they proceed from the simple sensory and motor functions to the complex mental processes, especially those dealing with language and number and abstractions in general. They are educable for the simpler routine occupations. Their behavior and performance in general—though more rigid and stereotyped than in normal persons—is capable of improvement through training by means of special methods and materials. For this reason we find special classes for the mentally subnormal in many of our public schools. In the more extreme cases, and in those having asocial tendencies which cannot be remedied in the home community, institutional care is indicated.

In making a diagnosis of mental subnormality, the psychologist must take into account the individual's health history, emotional condition, and developmental opportunities; for in each one of these categories of factors may be found reasons for regarding a low IQ, in a particular case, as evidence of spurious rather than unavoidable mental subnormality. In other words, a diagnosis of mental deficiency is not made on the basis of an intelligence quotient alone.

Conclusion—Individual Differences

The experimental studies and the other scientific investigations into the nature and causes of individual differences in mental abilities may be generalized in the form of a general principle, which follows.

The extent and form of mental development are dependent in part upon conditions of the individual's environment during his developmental period, and in particular during the years of infancy and early childhood. There is an optimal period for the nurture and utilization of genetic potentialities; unfavorable or impoverished environments during that period will retard or restrict mental development. This doctrine denies that mental development is a mere unfolding process or that mentality will develop in a vacuum. It denies also that environmental forces may only help or hinder the process of development. On the contrary, it states that conditions of nurture are themselves an integral part of the process of development. If this doctrine were not sound, it would be necessary to discard the principle that education is more than the absorption of information and the fixing of habits. On the contrary, however, educators are psychologically and biologically justified when they speak of education as growth, as the development of individuality, and as enabling the individual to approach the limits of his genetic potentialities.

PSYCHOLOGY OF LEARNING APPLIED TO EDUCATION

Learning Theory

Education is, among other things, the process whereby information is acquired; whereby skills, reasoning and thinking, values, attitudes, and social behavior are developed. Briefly, learning may be defined as the process of developing, improving, and refining behavior. It is quite understandable, therefore, that educational psychologists should be concerned with the learning process, as a primary problem, whereby the objectives of education may be achieved most effectively. As psychological theories of learning evolved from animal and human experimentation, they influenced actual classroom practices. There are several approaches to the learning process; each may be made operative in one or more learning situations; some are more effective than others in promoting the kind of mental development we seek to encourage in thinking citizens of a democratic society; some have been overemphasized, at one time or another, by certain educators. We shall briefly state several of the approaches to learning, with a brief evaluation of each.

Learning by *conditioning* is a process of shifting a response, already possessed by the learner, to a new substitute stimulus. It is a mechanical process, being controlled by the teacher and involving no necessary awareness or choice on the part of the learner. For example, an infant makes a response such as movements of withdrawal, accompanied by the feelings of fear, to a substitute stimulus (e.g., a white rat) when an originally unpleasant and fear-provoking stimulus (e.g., a sudden loud sound) has occurred simultaneously and often enough with the presentation of the white rat. The process of conditioning is useful mainly in infancy before the learner can communicate with adults or others by means of language, and while he must be under continual care of a nurse, usually his mother. At school age, conditioning may aid in overcoming handicapping emotional attitudes, such as dislike or fears of school, classmates, etc., which have been produced by unfavorable conditioning. But the conditioning process is not useful or applicable in the complex process of the usual school learning situation.

A second method of learning is *mechanical repetition* commonly known as rote memorization. It is an ancient schooling practice to have a student memorize, in an apparently mechanical manner, exact verbal responses (e.g., definitions, names, quotations) without regard to understanding of meanings. In this approach, unlike conditioning, the learner is aware of his task, its goal, and the teacher's direction. It is a method that is useful so far as conformity in spelling and the like are required. But it is still learning at a relatively low level because the learner is not given freedom to depart from the path laid down for him and because he is not given the responsibility of understanding meanings, nor of creative effort.

The theory of learning by *trial and chance* is based upon experiments in which the learner is confronted by an obstacle that prevents him from reaching a desired goal. For example, a cat is shut in a puzzle box from which he wishes to escape to reach food. The box is so equipped that the random pawing and clawing of the cat may by chance pull a cord attached to the latch that opens the exit. Likewise after many random trials a child or an adult may by chance solve a mechanical puzzle or a mathematical problem. Through repeated chance successes, the learner finally comes to make the required movement promptly, and thus reaches his goal. As an approach to learning, the trial and chance method is higher than the preceding two because the learner has more or less initiative and freedom of activity. But learning by this method—if it takes place at all—results in accidental solutions that the subject might or might not understand. An example in the classroom would be the "wild guess" in verbal responses. Learning by trial and chance success is not an optimal approach because it depends upon the accidental discovery of a solution (often a trick device) that promotes only slight understanding at best, or none at all; and progress is usually slow and irregular.

Retrial for motor skill is the process of developing sensory-motor coördination and precision in an act which the learner regards as his goal or as a means to other goals; e.g., walking, handwriting, using tools. The learner has in view a goal towards which he proceeds, at first awkwardly, modifying his movements as he perceives the relation of results attained to the desired goal. There is a marked contrast between such continual modification in developing motor skill, on the one hand, and conditioning, mechanical repetition, and trial and chance success, on the other. The learner is free to try new movements; his ability to feel his way into the necessary coördination may be supported by a teacher who demonstrates the process either incidentally or intentionally, who may make verbal suggestions during the procedure, but who does not require exact conformity in the early movements. The learner thus gains understanding in the process; he acts intelligently as he guides his own learning rather than having his activities dictated by rigidly fixed conditions in regard to which he may have no understanding or purpose.

A very different approach to learning from the first three discussed above is known as *insight through visual survey*. According to this method of learning, a transformation of a problem situation occurs for the learner because all at once he sees the direction to his goal; the situation becomes organized for him in his visual field. The solution may involve a direct approach, or the use of mediating implements, or a roundabout approach. The individual discovers for himself the means of circumventing the obstacle or bridging the gap between himself and the end he has in view. For example, a child separated from his objective by a wire fence perceives that he can reach the desired object by running around the open end of the fence. He has performed a roundabout movement which at an earlier age he was incapable of doing because he could not perceive the relationship of moving away from an objective to its ultimate attainment. Numerous experiments with apes and children have shown that they are capable of using and even creating mediating instruments as a means of obtaining an object not within direct reach; e.g., sticks, twigs, boxes, blankets, and ropes. The individual's learning here depends upon visual perception and the organization that occurs to him while he faces the problem. In learning by visual insight the relation of learner to teacher differs from that in the first three approaches; for now the teacher sets and arranges problems in such a way that insight may occur. Insight involves a relatively complete understanding of the process before it occurs and usually is transferable to other similar situations. The learner using insight guides his actions himself and is thus developing considered, responsible activity.

As an approach to learning, *reflective thinking* is recognized by all educators as a primary goal for living in a democratic society. It depends largely upon the use of language, bringing into the learning process and solution of problems many factors that cannot be seen visually. Thus language and thought greatly extend the possibilities of solving problems, circumventing obstacles, and reaching goals. Reflective thinking, like visual insight, may involve sudden transformations in the situation, but at the symbolic level. The learner scrutinizes and explores ideationally the new insights before attempting new overt action. In actual learning, children and adults employ inseparably visual insights and thinking in terms of language. Scientific method consists in testing insights (often called suggestions or hypotheses) by actual trial. Since insights come originally from some individual's experiences, these last two approaches to learning encourage individual responsibility in behavior usually associated with the free operation of intelligence.

This brief discussion of several approaches to learning will incate to the reader the nature and scope of some of the problems in the general theory of learning and its implementation in schools.

Specific Problems in the Psychology of Learning

We shall here indicate some representative specific problems, each of which deals with a more or less restricted aspect of the learning process. Since the number of aspects is large and the number of researches on them extremely numerous, we shall of necessity confine ourselves to brief general statements on each.

Many of the earlier experiments dealt with remembering and forgetting; principally the methods of memorizing. For educational purposes, it is significant to know, as research has shown, that distribution of practice periods is more efficient than concentration of periods and yields more lasting results; that learning by wholes of the proper length is superior to learning by parts, or the process of assembling those parts; that accurate first impressions promote learning and recall; that an active, purposeful attitude promotes learning and recall, whereas a passive attitude does not; that subjective factors such as interest and emotional tone affect the processes of learning and recall. Experiments have also shown that forgetting proceeds most rapidly in the period immediately succeeding learning and that, therefore, spaced and continual relearning is necessary. All the foregoing principles are directly applicable to teaching and learning.

Many experiments have also been performed on what we may call the conditions of learning. For example, what is the role of *repetition*? The old adage that 'practice makes perfect" is not necessarily true. Practice—that is, repetition—is helpful if it provides opportunities and conditions favorable to the selection of the correct response; or, in other instances, opportunities for the better apprehension of details, meanings, and relationships. Sheer repetition does not bring about learning; but if repeated efforts enrich the perceived materials, learning will be fuller and more lasting.

All observed situations, data, and behavior undergo change in the direction of more stabilized forms. Certain forms, like the circle and square, are intrinsically stable in perception. Other perceptions and experiences become, through frequent functional contact, rather well fixed "pieces" in the furnishings of one's environment. In general, what becomes precise and stabilized depends in part upon what is actually emphasized in an individual's early experiences in any given area. This process of fixing and stabilization has been called the *precision* factor. Unless learning and teaching proceed in a manner that encourages the emphasis and stability of certain aspects rather than others, the intended learner fumbles about indefinitely and uneconomically.

The factor of *primacy* simply signifies that first impressions are stronger than subsequent impressions of the same situation. In learning and teaching, therefore, it is essential that the correct responses should be established from the earliest stages. If first responses are fumbling or if first impressions are incorrectly apprehended, the errors of response and the distorted impressions may be a serious obstacle to later learning.

Recency as a factor in learning may be stated thus: other things being equal, recent perceptions are more readily recalled than remote ones. There are instances when such is not the case; but in those instances, unusual or exceptional conditions are operative. Exceptions are the forgetfulness of recent experiences in very old age, recall of highly emotional experiences of some time past, and differential recall of recent experiences depending upon degree of emotional intensity and upon pleasantness or unpleasantness.

In another connection, we discussed insight in learning. Applying this concept, we say that the ease of acquiring information and principles and concepts will depend in part upon the degree of meaning they have for the learner and upon how well they are organized into useful, or functional, patterns. The elements or parts of a learning situation must be perceived as members of an organized whole. This is what is meant by the factor of *organization* in learning.

Pleasantness-unpleasantness and *punishment-reward* as factors in learning are, of course, of basic interest to educators. The voluminous research on these problems shows that degrees of feeling are effective thus: mild degree of pleasantness is most facilitating; mild degree of unpleasantness is next; strong emotional feelings interfere; very strong emotional feelings are disruptive; emotional neutrality or indifference makes learning more difficult.

Studies on punishment-reward—another aspect of pleasantness-unpleasantness—show that effects differ according to the emotional and intellectual status of the learner. Individuals of superior ability and others who have had experiences of successful achievement and status in their groups seem to improve their performances after mild punishment (not corporal) whereas the performances of individuals of inferior abilities or inferior status suffer under even mild punishment, while they improve under reward. The effects produced on persons of average abilities are usually better after rewards; but their response to reward or punishment will depend upon the nature of the situation and their positions in it. It appears that the person who has security in a group can withstand or even benefit from mild punishment, whereas the insecure person, who has suffered defeats and frustrations, is set back by punishment and needs the evidence of approbation represented by reward. However, it should be remembered that a task may be performed because of the interest in the task itself apart from extraneous rewards.

One of the earliest of problems investigated was *transfer of training*. The question to be answered is this: does learning in one area or subject of study have a carryover value to other areas or subjects? In the latter part of the nineteenth century and early twentieth, many educators held the unsubstantiated view that some subject—e.g., Latin and mathematics—almost to the exclusion of all other fields of study, had considerable transfer value. Then the pendulum swung and it was believed by some that no transfer of learning took place, but that, on the contrary, all learning was highly specific; we learn what we specifically study; and no more.

The prevailing view at present, however, is that transfer, in varying degrees, does take place, depending upon the conditions of learning and teaching. First, the amount of transfer is greater in the case of more intelligent persons. Second, all subjects and activities can have transfer value if properly taught. Third, some subjects of study can have more transfer value than others because they can make greater demands upon logical, sequential, and accurate thinking; e.g., mathematics and scientific proof. If transfer is to take place, the teacher must teach for it; the attitude of the learner must be such as to promote it (as contrasted with rote learning and mechanical utilization); and the subject matter must be mastered. Transfer of learning does not occur in a vucuum, nor is it an automatic process.

OTHER AREAS IN EDUCATIONAL PSYCHOLOGY

There are several areas in educational psychology which are of wide interest at present, although some of them are by no means new to the subject. In concluding this chapter we shall only mention these areas to indicate several of the major paths being followed and to show more fully the range of topics and problems in educational psychology.

The learning of the *fundamental school subjects* has for some time held a major place: for example, the nature of the reading process, the optimal age to begin to learn reading, the correction of reading disabilities; arithmetical reasoning, learning the fundamental arithmetical processes, causes of difficulties in learning involved in spelling; development of handwriting skill, the application of principles of learning to social and physical sciences. Researches on these problems have sought to answer questions as to what should be taught, and when, and how in view of the school's stated educational objectives.

Recently, educational psychologists have been directing more attention and effort to understanding *how children actually proceed* in learning information and generalizations, interests and attitudes, personal and social adjustment, principles and techniques of problem solving, aesthetic responses and values. Also of major importance at present are the relation of motivation and of emotional behavior to learning, and the nature of language and meaning. Investigations into these questions take into account, of course, the environment of school, home, and community as factors in learning. The purpose in these areas is to apply to specific learning and teaching tasks our knowledge of the general learning process and conditions, and also to develop new techniques of research for the solution of problems especially relevant or peculiar to schooling.

The *measurement of educational achievement* has, of course, been a special province of educational psychologists. The test of educational achievement (as distinguished from the various other tests of mental abilities) is designed to measure what and how much an individual has learned in a course of instruction. There are also educational tests intended to reveal a learner's weaknesses and difficulties (as in reading and arithmetic); these are called diagnostic tests. A third type is devised for use as a predictor of future performance in a specific kind of school subject (foreign language, algebra, etc.) The reason for using educational tests is that they have been (or should have been) standardized according to recognized scientific procedures, and they thus eliminate the "personal equation" of the teacher in marking. Though many of the available achievement tests are poorly conceived and constructed, the sounder of them are valuable as *one* method of evaluating the performance of pupils and students. These tests, however, should not be used to the exclusion of other methods, including the older type of written examination and the judgments of teachers.

The first of these three kinds of instruments—tests of actual learning—has been most widely used. They are, for the most part, measures of acquired information, skills, and techniques. While these are certainly important, they have been criticized as being too limited in conception and as not getting at other educational objectives of primary importance, such as critical thinking, evaluation, attitudes, and values which are expected to develop and emerge from instruction. The result is that more attention is now being given to devising tests of these less tangible but more enduring outcomes of education.

CONCLUSION

We may define human psychology as the science of human experience and behavior. Educational psychology deals with many aspects of experience and behavior, some of which are relevant, in one way or another, to all branches of psychology, while others have particular or sole relevance to the schooling part of the educative process. The school receives a child, at age 5 or 6, who has already had a long personal-social-emotional history. Each child presents his own background of heredity and environment; yet all children have, psychologically, much in common as developing human beings. Children enter school at varying levels of development and learning. They become members of new and expanding groups; new skills, techniques, and habits have to be learned; information must be acquired. The pupils have been removed, as never before, from the custody of parents and from a familiar home to a new environment of peers—some hostile, some indifferent, some friendly—and teachers who themselves may be, in varying degrees, well or poorly adjusted.

The educative process is directive, purposeful and creative. It attempts to help develop individuals for satisfactory personal, social, vocational, and intellectual modes of living. While until about 1910, educators were concerned principally with children to the age of about 12 or 13 years, since the great majority then ended their schooling at grade six, at present educators and psychologists must deal with problems of learning and development of the entire life span. In the nineteenth century, all aspects of American society were relatively simple compared with the heterogeneous and complex American society which the schools now serve. Until about 1920, the United States lived and functioned in relative isolation. Now the schools must think and operate in terms of "one world" (hardly harmonized as yet) and in terms of international attitudes, values, and understandings. In view of expanding and increasingly complex responsibilities of the schools, it is apparent that educational psychology is a crucial aspect of the educative process and that its scope must be comprehensive.

SUGGESTED READINGS

1. Anderson, G. L., Educational psychology and teacher education, *J. educ. Psychol.*, 1949, 40:275–284. One article in a group on the nature, content, and role of educational psychology in the preparation of teachers.

2. Anderson, H. H., *et al.*, Studies in teachers' classroom personalities, I, II, and III, *App. psychol. Monogs.*, nos. 6 (1945), 8 (1946), 11 (1946). Three monographs reporting methods used in measuring the psychological environment of children in school and the effects of this environment upon their behavior. The principal factor in the classroom environment, here reported, is the teacher.

3. Bruce, W. F., and Freeman, F. S., *Development and Learning*. New York: Holt, 1942. A volume in developmental psychology, presenting the development of the individual as a whole. The second part of the volume deals with several approaches to learning and the value of each in contributing to human development.

4. Cole, L. E., and Bruce, W. F., *Educational Psychology*. New York: World Book, 1950. One of the most recent textbooks on the subject. It emphasizes learning in the current social scene, directed toward development of the mature personality.

5. Freeman, F. S., *Theory and Practice of Psychological Testing*. New York: Holt, 1950. Presents the psychological and statistical rationales and uses of tests of intelligence, specific aptitudes, personality, and educational achievement.

6. Klineberg, O., *Race Differences*. New York: Harper, 1935. A comprehensive summary of psychological and anthropometric research on the various aspects of the subject.

7. National Education Association, Department of Supervision and Directors of Instruction, *Mental Health in the Classroom*. 13th Year-

book, 1940. On the problems and practice of mental health in schools.

8. National Society for the Study of Education, *Intelligence: Its Nature and Nurture*. 39th Yearbook, 1940. Part I is devoted to a comparative and critical exposition of the psychological problems and of research. Part II contains reports of original research.

9. Skinner, E. (ed.), *Educational Psychology*. New York: Prentice-Hall, 1945. A textbook at the intermediate level, each chapter having been written by a specialist in the subject covered.

10. Tryon, R. C., Studies in selective breeding, *J. comp. Psychol.*, vols. 11 (1930), 12 (1931), 28 (1939), 30 (1940), 32 (1941) ; *passim*. Reports of a series of experiments with white rats, dealing with inheritance as a factor in maze learning.

11. Tyler, L. E., *The Psychology of Human Differences*. New York: Appleton-Century-Crofts, 1947. A text on individual differences summarizing some of the research on the several aspects of the subject.

12. Wallin, J. E. W., *Minor Mental Maladjustments in Normal People*. Durham, N. C.: Duke University, 1939. Deals with the problems of adjustment of the kinds frequently encountered in schools.

13. Wertheimer, M., *Productive Thinking*. New York: Harper, 1945. A study of the significant relationship between meaningful material and the development of insight in learning.

Chapter 9

Abnormal Psychology

by BÉLA MITTELMANN
and LAURA MALKENSON

Historical Background

Methods of Investigation—Causes, Classification, and Therapy
SOME INTERVIEW TECHNIQUES
                        Psychoanalysis
                        Hypnosis
CASE HISTORY
DYNAMICS   Unconscious Processes
                        Evaluation of Self and Environment
                        Conflict
                        Frustration
                        Coping Mechanisms
DEVELOPMENTAL FACTORS
THE INTEGRATED PERSONALITY
INTERPRETATION OF CASE HISTORY OF M. R.
SYNDROMES
                        Neuroses
                        Psychoses
                        Disturbances in Childhood and Old Age
THERAPY
                        Psychotherapy
                        Somatic Procedures

Psychological Test Procedures
STANDARDIZED TESTS
PROJECTIVE TESTS
                        Rorschach Test
                        Thematic Apperception Test

Experimental Methods of Investigation
    EXPERIMENTS WITH HUMAN SUBJECTS
        Hypnosis
        Interview
        Drugs
    EXPERIMENTS WITH ANIMALS
        Experimental Neurosis
        Ablation

Summary

Suggested Readings

As a starting point for our discussion, we shall describe a patient with a "psychosomatic" disorder.

The patient, M. R., a woman in her thirties, complained of attacks of pain in her fingers during which her fingers would turn blue (cyanosis). She had had these attacks over a period of five years. Recently, she had become aware that the attacks were initiated by fear.

The mother of three children, she had been twice married and divorced. She was in poor financial circumstances, living in a cold-water flat, and had hardly enough money for fuel. The attacks in her fingers started during her second marriage, when she was pregnant and while difficulties arose in her marriage. The symptoms she complained of are commonly known as Raynaud's Syndrome—named after the physician who first described it.

Although she complained of physical symptoms, the patient was suffering from an emotional disorder—the symptoms were initiated by fear and conflict.

How are we to understand the causes of the patient's illness? In order to understand them, more information about the patient is necessary. There are several techniques of getting such information.

In the following, three methods of investigation—clinical (included in the section on Methods of Investigation), experimental, and psychological testing—will be discussed along with the type of data they reveal and the implications of these data. Before doing so, however, a short historical statement, giving the more important steps in the development of the current approach to and understanding of abnormal psychology, will be made.

HISTORICAL BACKGROUND

"Insanity" was first recognized as a disease toward the end of the eighteenth century. Phillippe Pinel, a French physician, thought of mental disease as a primary illness of the brain reflected in personality impairment. He classified mental disorders on the basis of gross symptomatology. Emil Kraepelin (1896) worked out a system of classification, still largely current, based on symptomatology, but he also took into account the course of the illness. Bleuler differentiated between the underlying mental processes and the resultant symptoms. The splitting between various mental functions, which he called "schizophrenia," he assumed resulted in the symptoms which Kraepelin classified as "dementia praecox."

As regards less severe manifestations of mental illness, Liébeault and Bernheim expressed the view, in the nineteenth century, that hysterical symptoms were based on suggestion, thus explaining them on a psychological basis. Janet thought of hysterical symptoms as "dissociations"—i.e., psychic manifestations which were not integrated with the rest of the personality.

Sigmund Freud, who started his work toward the end of the nineteenth century, developed concepts of psychodynamics which revolutionized psychiatric thinking. He considered symptoms to be purposive, in that they were solutions to problems of adjustment. He stressed the importance of unconscious processes in motivation. The therapeutic technique of psychoanalysis, which he evolved along with his theory, was not only an epochal contribution in itself but also became the basis for other forms of psychoanalytically oriented interview techniques. Adolf Meyer, working at about the same time as Freud, independently came to somewhat similar general conclusions. He stated that symptoms represent characteristic "reaction types" representing the individual's reaction to stress situations. He emphasized that the personality functions as a whole—i.e., any behavior pattern represents the reaction of the total organism to a life situation. This concept of "holism" was stressed by Gestalt psychology also.

As the conception of emotional disorders broadened, the study of mental illness became integrated with other lines of development in medicine and psychology. Localization in the cerebral cortex was first established for the function of voluntary movements in the nineteenth century and soon after for speech. It was clearly established in the twentieth century that the prefrontal areas of the brain are closely connected with the diffuse functions of intellect and emotions as well as with vegetative reactions. Vegetative reactions occurring during normal emotional changes were first recorded toward the end of the nineteenth century, and experimentally induced pathological emotional changes were studied in the twentieth century. Pavlov, in his work with the conditioned response, was the first to produce neurotic reactions experimentally in animals. Liddell and his coworkers, by studying the totality of behavioral changes and the alterations in vegetative function which take place in animal neuroses, broadened the significance of this work for the understanding of abnormal psychological reactions.

Hypnosis, first developed by Mesmer, became important for the understanding of abnormal psychological phenomena when it was found, particularly by Liébeault and Bernheim, that hysterical symptoms could be removed by its use. Charcot, working in the nineteenth century, was the first to induce hysterical conversion phenomena (such as paralyses and vasomotor phenomena), through hypnosis. Projective testing started with the development of the association technique introduced by C. G. Jung as well as with the Rorschach Test developed by Hermann Rorschach (1921). Another landmark in the development of projective tests was the publication of the Thematic Apperception Test by H. A. Murray.

Since then, numerous testing techniques have been introduced. The first major development in somatic methods of treatment of mental disorders was the use of malarial fever for the treatment of general paresis (syphilis of the brain). States of unconsciousness, first induced by insulin (and later by other techniques), were introduced as a therapy in schizophrenic patients by Sakel in the 1930's.

Psychosomatic medicine, a term coined in 1939, in the broadest sense attempts to integrate data obtained by clinical, experimental, surgical, introspective, behavioral, and qualitative methods of observation.

METHODS OF INVESTIGATION—CAUSES, CLASSIFICATION, AND THERAPY

Some Interview Techniques

In psychiatric interviews, the patient is encouraged to talk about his problems and the day-to-day events in his life together with his reactions to them, his feelings, and his attitudes. The investigator may leave the patient free to talk about whatever he wishes or may guide him by asking questions or making comments, thus directing him towards topics which are likely to prove significant. The investigator is also able to observe the patient's reactions during the interviews. For a well-rounded picture of the patient and his functioning it is helpful to obtain as much data as possible. The parents can give information about the patient's early years which he cannot remember. They may be able to describe aspects of the patient's behavior which he does not speak of and which is not apparent in his behavior in the interview sessions. An overall picture may thus be gained of the subject's reaction patterns, his modes of aproaching life situations and of handling situations of stress, his needs and strivings, his interpersonal relationships, and his past history. Complex interrelationships among all of these aspects of the patient's emotional life are brought out.

PSYCHOANALYSIS

Although phychoanalysis is used primarily as a method of treatment, it elicits a great deal of material from patients regarding
their emotional life, and the material thus gained has been of great
importance not only in the understanding of individual patients
but also in leading to theoretical formulations regarding psychodynamics and personality development and organization. In this
technique, the patient is usually asked to lie on a couch and say
everything that comes to his mind (free association). He is told
not to withhold any thoughts or feelings no matter how unimportant, foolish, shameful, or reprehensible they may seem to be.

In thus saying everything that comes to mind, the patient tells
of events that have occurred together with his reactions to them.
At times he may experience emotional reactions which he is unable to explain. As he relates the details of the situation in which
such a reaction arose, a relationship between the two is discovered—a relationship of which the patient had not at first been
aware, which had been *unconscious*. A patient, for example, may
tell of an anxiety attack but be unable to explain the reason for
the attack. Upon being asked about the events which preceded
the attack, he may relate that his employer had criticized his
work. Although he felt resentment toward his employer because
of this, he said nothing. The meaning of the anxiety attack in
this instance was that he feared retaliation from his employer
because of his hostility and that he felt himself to be helpless to
defend himself against such an attack. Thus unconscious as well
as *conscious* material is revealed.

HYPNOSIS

Both of the procedures already described can be carried out
while the patient is in a hypnotic trance. The chief advantage of
doing this is that the patient may be able to reveal feelings and
attitudes of which he is normally unconscious and thus could not
relate during the waking state or may be able to recall memories

which have been repressed. Frequently, too, patients who do not talk freely may be induced to do so while under hypnosis. While the information revealed is essentially the same as that obtained by the other methods, unconscious material is more readily accessible. Not everybody, however, is hypnotizable.

Case History

The material gained in interviews may be organized into a "life history" with emphasis on the individual's emotional vicissitudes and adjustments during the course of his development. How he was treated by his parents; how he got along with his siblings and playmates; his school and later work adjustment; his sexual attitudes and behavior; his marital adjustment, etc.; these are all of major importance. The purpose of this type of organization of material is to help clarify how the individual's experiences helped to shape his emotional development and how his attitudes, expectations, and behavior helped determine the specific course of events in his life. The following is the life history of the patient described at the beginning of this chapter.

M. R. was the third of eight siblings. She had been a quiet, timid child, devoted to both her parents, particularly to her mother who was blind when the patient was born. She was sympathetic to her mother, helping her in managing the home and caring for the younger children. When she finished elementary school, she worked efficiently as an operator on children's dresses. She was poorly informed about menstruation and was very much frightened at its first occurrence.

At the age of 16 she married a man who mistreated and beat her. Before her marriage she had had no sexual enlightenment and had never masturbated. The patient became very resentful of her husband's treatment of her and on one occasion she drank iodine with suicidal intentions. She attributed a tubal pregnancy which occurred not long after the marriage to having been kicked in the abdomen by her husband. From this marriage she had one child. She divorced her husband after five years and worked as a professional dancer, having always danced well.

She married again some six years later at the age of 22 and was happy for the first four years of her second marriage. During her pregnancy (second in this marriage) her husband began to give her less money for the household. She then feared that he, too, would mistreat her. She was worried and enraged. It was at this time that she had the first painful attacks in her fingers, which were more frequent and more severe during exposure to cold. She became sexually frigid and refused intercourse. Her husband left her shortly after the birth of the child. The patient became "hysterical" when this happened and was hospitalized for a few days. Six months later she effected a reconciliation with her husband, became pregnant and gave birth to a fourth child. She again began having difficulties with her husband and he deserted her for the second time. She rejected his later attempts at reconciliation for fear that difficulties might start anew, that she would have to submit to intercourse, and that she might become pregnant again. Further, her child by her first husband got along poorly with the stepfather. M. R. earnestly wanted to take good care of her children but she frequently became angry with them and then would feel ashamed of her outbursts of anger.

Before attempting any analysis of the case of M. R., it is important to have some understanding of the *dynamics* of behavior that may be relevant in the development of her disturbed behavior.

Dynamics

UNCONSCIOUS PROCESSES

Many of the individual's attitudes, feelings, and impulses are unconscious because they are in some way painful or dangerous. Hostile and sexual impulses and excessive dependency longings are those which are most frequently unconscious because they are considered objectionable by others and because they clash with the individual's own moral standards and personal ideals or self-esteem. The patient therefore *represses* them (shuts them out of conscious awareness) and denies them in order to avoid anticipated condemnation, rejection, and punishment from others as well as feelings of guilt and unworthiness. Patients are usually unaware of the causes of their symptoms and emotional disturbance. In order to understand them, it is necessary to understand the nature of his unconscious impulses, strivings, attitudes, and feelings which influence, at least in part, practically all of his behavior and conscious attitudes.

EVALUATION OF SELF AND ENVIRONMENT

Basic to emotional illness are disturbances in the patient's evaluation of himself (self-esteem, feeling of moral worth) and of his environment (security feelings). He feels himself helpless to attain his major goals and to handle any difficult situation. He feels that he is unworthy because of his unacceptable sexual and aggressive impulses. At the same time, he feels that others are stronger than he and he fears injury, abandonment, and humiliation as retribution for his impulses. Such attitudes are frequently partially or entirely unconscious. The patient, for example, may consciously maintain an attitude of superiority to others in order to reassure himself against his fears: "I am better and stronger than they; they cannot hurt me." That this is ineffective, however, becomes evident when his superior status is threatened in any way. Such a threat becomes dangerous for him because it would serve to prove to him that his underlying fears were justified and he must therefore fight to maintain his superior status. Because of these disturbed attitudes, any realistic dangers or difficulties which the patient must face are exaggerated.

CONFLICT

The patient's needs and impulses may be in conflict with each other (e.g., dependency longings and hostile impulses directed toward the same person), with reality limitations or with his own moral standards. Conflicts are always painful, in part because they usually involve deprivation and frustration of one or both of the needs involved and a threat to the individual's integrated functioning. In that they represent unsolvable problems for him, they threaten his feeling of adequacy and self-esteem. When the patient is driven by the expectation of catastrophic helplessness and worthlessnes, by anger and fear of the stronger individual, and by the fear of abandonment and humiliation as described above, he frequently takes conflicting measures to relieve his distress. He may, for example, seek dependent and supportive relationships with others at the same time that he strives for superiority. Since both of these needs are of vital importance to him, he is unable to give up one for the other.

FRUSTRATION

Whenever a need remains ungratified, the individual feels distress. Such lack of gratification may arise from any one of several sources. Whenever conflict is present, some need must remain either partly or entirely ungratified. Frequently external factors are the cause. For example, a man with a limited income may have to give up a number of pleasurable activities because he cannot afford them. Most individuals are able to withstand a fair amount of such deprivation. Whenever vital needs are involved, however, the individual feels threatened by it. People who are potentially or actually emotionally ill, because many of their strivings represent desperate efforts to attain security and a feeling of adequacy, are likely to experience any deprivation as a threat. It tends to give reality to their fears of being helpless and of being injured. Resentment aroused by such frustration may further complicate the situation in that it increases their fears of retaliation on the part of persons towards whom their aggression is directed. In the face of such frustration, the individual may begin to feel that his situation is hopeless.

COPING MECHANISMS

The individual seeks by various means to gain some measure of security and some gratification of his needs despite his subjective and objective difficulties. The measures by which he attempts to achieve this are referred to as coping mechanisms. These coping mechanisms can be classified into three groups: attempts to diminish distress; attempts to strengthen oneself and thus diminish one's fears; attempts to reach one's goals or substitute goals despite one's fears.

In the first group are such methods as *avoidance* of the dangerous situation by giving up the dangerous—usually aggressive or sexual—activity or by developing *incapacitating symptoms* when faced with dangerous situations. An unacceptable impulse may be denied through *repression* or through *projection* ("I do not hate him; it is he who hates me"). The patient may deny responsibility for an impulse as in the case of obsessional ideas of a violent or obscene nature ("These are not my thoughts; they come to me from without") or for his behavior as when he blames others or external difficulties for his failures. He may attempt to *rationalize* his behavior by giving rational, acceptable grounds for it as when a mother explains her punishing her child by saying it is "for his own good" rather than because she feels hostile towards him. He may maintain an *emotional detachment* from people and from his activities so that rejection or failure cannot hurt him.

The individual may attempt to strengthen himself by seeking support from a stronger individual *(dependence)* whom he hopes will care for him and handle his difficulties for him. He may be submissive and ingratiating to others in order to ward off expected attack or rejection. He may be self-aggrandizing, feeling that he is superior to others, and may need always to be in a dominant relationship to others. He may develop the opposite attitude to an objectionable, repressed one *(reaction formation)* and thus enhance his moral self-evaluation through his exceptionally "virtuous" behavior. The patient may be elated and active, denying his fears and self-contempt. He may seek through *substitution* satisfaction through gratification of bodily urges, as when he eats excessively after experiencing disappointment.

Finally, the individual may attempt to reach his goal and obtain gratification by devious means. He may, for example, be able to pursue a goal if he limits in some way his participation in the activity involved, thus protecting himself from the dangerous consequences. He may do something to counteract the effect of a given act in order to eliminate the danger involved. He may be able to carry on certain activities only if he follows a rigid set of rules in so doing. He may substitute another, similar activity for the desired one or may react emotionally to a situation which is different from the one which aroused the emotion. He may *attack* the stronger individual in order to render him less dangerous or he may injure himself or submit to attack in order to assuage feelings of guilt and seek forgiveness. The individual may *regress* by giving up his mature goals in favor of earlier goals and/or by using earlier techniques for attaining his goals. Another means for gaining gratification is through *compromise formation*. The individual may seek to gratify in some measure two opposing needs by working out a solution which gratifies each partially though neither fully, or he may carry out an activity in such a way that it does not achieve its assumed purpose but in some way fulfills another need.

Developmental Factors

As the individual develops, the nature of his goals and strivings, his attitudes, and his techniques for obtaining goals change in accord with his developing functions and capacities. Freud, in his libido theory, described some of these changes, with particular reference to pleasure strivings and attitudes toward the environment. According to this theory, as the individual develops, different bodily organs become dominant as sources of pleasure. Thus, during the earliest stage, the mouth is the dominant source of pleasure. At about the age of 2 years, the anus becomes the main source of pleasure; and at 4 or 5 years, the genitals become the dominant pleasure zone and remain so through adolescence and adulthood.

Along with this development, there are corresponding shifts in the individual's emotional attitudes, different attitudes becoming dominant at each stage. During the earliest period, the child is completely dependent and seeks gratification for his needs in his contacts with others. Later he becomes ambivalent, manifesting self-assertion, destructiveness, and compliance. This is followed by a period during which ambitious striving predominates. Finally, tenderness comes to the fore; at first it is accompanied by self-centeredness but during late adolescence, it is directed largely toward others, particularly the heterosexual love object.

A special feature in the child's early development is the attachment to the mother. At about 6 months of age, he begins to want her presence quite apart from any special bodily gratifications received in contacts with her. The normal course of this development may be interfered with and any one or more of the "pregenital" levels of organization may persist into adulthood. Even if the individual's development continues through to the final genital stage, he may return to an earlier developmental level in the face of stress situations.

The development of the functions of intellect, motility, and speech are also of crucial importance. Speech enables the individual to communicate his demands to others; with the development of motility, aggressive and destructive acts, as well as mastery of the environment, become possible. As these functions develop, the individual's whole self-evaluation as well as his realistic capacities are altered. He is no longer helpless and completely dependent on others but becomes able to gratify his own needs as well as to influence others in a more active, directed manner. As the child becomes capable of manipulating his environment effectively, his self-esteem is heightened.

The Integrated Personality

The individual tends to react in an organized and consistent manner. Any individual, faced with a given situation, will interpret it (as potentially threatening or as potentially gratifying) and react to it in a manner which is consistent for him; this interpretation will be influenced by his past experiences as well as his current emotional needs, attitudes, and strivings. The person who reacts to one situation of stress by withdrawing from it will tend to react in the same way to other types of stress situations. Apparent inconsistencies in behavior and reaction patterns may occur, but if one looks beneath the surface at the underlying motivation, it will be found that the contradictory aspect of the behavior is only superficial. Thus, a man may be entirely submissive to his employer and at the same time be tyrannical in his treatment of his family. Such a person sees the world as hostile and threatening and believes that only by being stronger than others can he be safe. In situations where he feels he is the weaker individual, he hopes to gain some measure of security by submitting to and not antagonizing the other person. If he can attain complete domination in the family situation, he can better endure his inferior status at work. He feels that, since there are some persons who are weaker than he, he is not entirely helpless.

The individual tends to react as a whole. In any situation of stress, the entire resources of the *total organism* are mobilized. Physiological as well as emotional and overt behavioral reactions occur. When an individual experiences fear, for example, he may report that his heart is palpitating and that his perspiration is increased. Other physiological changes also take place, including increased supply of blood to the periphery of the body, decreased activity of the visceral organs, increase in tone of the voluntary musculature. All these changes prepare the organism for emergency action.

Interpretation of Case History of M. R.

At this point let us now return to M. R., the patient described earlier in this chapter, and try to understand the causes of her behavior and symptoms.

As a child, her dependency needs were never fully gratified; instead of being cared for, she had to take care of her blind mother. She felt resentment towards and disappointment in her parents. She also felt hostile toward her younger siblings because she was required to help care for them, because she felt their presence deprived her of her full share of parental affection, and because it was necessary for her to earn money and to contribute to their support. She experienced guilt feelings and feelings of worthlessness because of her resentment and hostility and therefore repressed these attitudes, was a "good" child, acceding willingly to the demands made upon her.

She sought gratification of her unfulfilled dependency longings as well as release from responsibility in an early marriage. At the same time, however, her feelings of guilt over her hostile impulses made her unable to accept the love and care she desired and she chose for a husband a man who mistreated (punished) her. Her self-injurious trend reached its most direct expression in her suicidal attempt—which at the same time represented a plea for love and forgiveness. (The unconscious idea behind this act was: "I am punishing myself and suffer for my sins; please forgive me. If you do not love me and treat me kindly, life is not worth living.")

When her second husband reduced her household allowance, she feared a repetition of the abuse she had received at the hands of her first husband—abuse which represented to her the retaliation she expected for her own hostile impulses. This fear of rejection was expressed in the symptom of pain in her fingers. The symptom also represented an expression of helplessness. The impairment of sexual function which occurred at this time represented a revival of her earlier sexual repression as well as self-directed aggression resulting from her guilt over her sexual impulses, which she had never fully accepted, and in addition, they represented a disguised expression of aggression toward her husband because of her disappointment in him.

Her displays of anger toward her children expressed her resentment over the demands they made upon her and constituted another source of guilt feelings. Once the underlying dynamisms were more fully understood the type of therapy required became more obvious.

Syndromes

Psychiatric symptoms represent the individual's attempts to handle stressful situations and are in this sense coping mechanisms. The symptoms developed are related to the individual's overall reaction pattern. Thus the person who has always been rigid and systematic in his work will be likely to develop compulsive symptoms consisting of complicated rituals which must be followed in the carrying out of any activity. His symptoms will, in turn, be quite different from those developed by a person who is, for example, dependent and submissive or one who seeks to avoid stressful situations. Thus any given syndrome (characteristic pattern of symptoms which make up a disease entity) will tend to have similar dynamics and etiology in all people who develop it, despite the many individual variations which occur, and to be different in etiological background from other syndromes, although a good deal of overlapping is present. Diagnosis of an illness, based as it is on major symptomatology as well as on etiology, is helpful in understanding the patient and his problems, but for thorough understanding much more information is needed.

Psychiatric illnesses are grouped into the categories of neurosis and psychosis. Psychoses, in fully developed form, are much more serious illnesses than the neuroses and are much more incapacitating. The psychotic patient's evaluation of reality is seriously impaired in a way that is not seen in neurotic patients. In the following, we shall briefly describe the symptomatology, dynamics, and etiology of the more common psychiatric syndromes.

NEUROSES

Patients with *hysterical neurosis* usually tend to react emotionally to most situations. Their strong emotional reactions may or may not be expressed overtly. If they are, the patient is likely to be socially outgoing and may behave impulsively; if not, the individual usually is quiet and unassertive. Such patients are usually infantile, feeling themselves to be helpless, seeking dependent ties, and desiring emotional closeness. They tend to repress their impulses, especially if they are of a hostile and sexual nature. Several types of symptom characterize this syndrome: anxiety attacks (states of intense fear—frequently there is fear of impending death or of going "insane"), phobia (irrational fear of a special situation), conversion symptoms (changes in bodily function without organic cause). The symptom frequently indirectly expresses the patient's unacceptable impulses as well as being a form of self-punishment. Thus a woman who unconsciously desires promiscuous sexual activity may be afraid of going out on the street alone. She thus blames the external situation rather than her own impulse for her fear and at the same time prevents herself from carrying out the impulse. The symptom also represents an appeal for help, and, by requiring a person close to her to accompany her whenever she leaves the house, it assures the patient of the desired care and protection. It also serves to express hostility towards the other person through the excessive demands made upon him.

In *neurotic depression* the patient's dominant mood is one of sadness and discouragement, although there may be periods of relative cheerfulness and he is able to respond appropriately by smiling even when he feels depressed. The symptom is usually a reaction to disappointment in a love relationship or to death of a loved one as in the case of prolonged mourning. Feelings of abandonment and hopelessness are dominant, but there may be unconscious guilt feelings and self-condemnation over repressed genital or hostile impulses, and the loss may be evaluated as a punishment for these impulses.

In *obsessive-compulsive neurosis,* the patient is troubled either by thoughts which come into his mind, which he cannot keep out of consciousness and which he claims do not express his feelings (obsessional ideas), or by the need to carry out acts which he cannot suppress although he does not want to perform them (compulsive acts). A common obsessional idea is the thought of killing someone close to the patient, such as the marital partner or a child, toward whom there is felt no conscious hostility. Such patients are frequently indecisive, always being filled with doubts whenever they must make a decision. They are usually orderly, excessively clean, inclined to be stubborn and stingy, idealistic and perfectionistic, conscientious in carrying out responsibilities and considerate of others. They tend to be orderly in their thinking as well as in their behavior, striving to be completely logical. These traits represent a reaction formation against hostility and against rebellion toward authority. Thus, as children they may have acquiesced to parental demands for control of eliminative functions and have repressed the desire to smear. Dirt and messiness still represent rebellion against parental authority to these patients. Their hostility gains some expression through obsessive thoughts which have aggressive content, through their intolerance of any interference with their ordered existence, and through their perfectionistic demands on others. The hostility is frequently displaced; the patient who unconsciously feels hostile towards his wife may have obsessive thoughts of killing his children. They gain security from their orderliness and perfectionism by structuring their world in such a way that everything is predictable and therefore can be coped with, by forestalling the consequences of unacceptable or inadequate behavior, and by obviating the necessity for making decisions through having a fixed, systematic way of carrying out all tasks. Their predominant fears are of enslavement, of injury and destruction from a hostile environment, and of moral disapproval for unacceptable impulses. Regression is seen in their frequent concern over eliminative functions. These patients frequently suffer from constipation or diarrhea.

The patient with a *psychosomatic disorder* complains of a disturbance in the function of a bodily organ. The dysfunction is based on physiological or structural changes. Usually the attacks occur in situations of emotional stress and at times the illness first develops in response to emotional stress. At other times, an illness which first developed as a result of organic causes later recurs during emotional disturbance. When the former is the case, the functional change may be the same as is usually found during emotional excitation but, because of the intensity and/or longevity of the disturbed emotional state, or because of organic tendencies which already exist, or as a result of a combination of both factors, the physiological changes are more intense and sustained than is usually the case. Eventually, the sustained dysfunction may lead to organic changes. The particular disorder which develops may be related to a more or less specific emotional constellation. Thus, patients who suffer from essential hypertension (chronically elevated blood pressure with no demonstrable organic cause) frequently have intense repressed hostile impulses together with anxiety and depression. Some of the more common psychosomatic disorders are peptic ulcers (small wounds in the stomach or in the duodenum), allergic reactions (characterized by a sensitiveness to an external protein which is ingested or inhaled and which leads to an attack of asthma, hay fever, hives, etc.), some endocrine disorders, and migraine (periodic severe headaches usually accompanied by nausea, vomiting, constipation, or diarrhea).

PSYCHOSES

Patients with *manic-depressive* psychosis may suffer from attacks of mania or of depression or from alternating attacks of depression and mania. Between such attacks, they are able to function quite adequately. In depressive attacks, the patient feels sad and unhappy and experiences feelings of guilt and unworthiness and may be self-accusatory, blaming himself for having injured others. This last may be expressed through delusions—the patient believing that he has committed some unpardonable sin. Such patients are likely to commit suicide as an act of self-punishment and as an expression of their feelings of hopelessness. Their behavior is generally slowed down (psychomotor retardation), as is also their physiological functioning and their thinking. In manic attacks, there is pressure of activity and of ideation. The patient is constantly doing something, takes little rest, and sleeps little. His mood may be elated, and he tends to be grandiose, feeling there is nothing that he cannot undertake successfully. Grandiose delusions may be present: for example, the patient may insist that he has a million dollars in the bank. His behavior is often impulsive and even rash and may, as a result, be counter to his own interests. Thus, he may make expensive purchases or invest money in unsound business ventures which he is sure will succeed.

In the periods between attacks, the patient may be outgoing and hard-driving in his behavior and cheerful and optimistic in his outlook (thus showing hypomanic features) or he may be worrisome, concerned, and anxious and inclined to be pessimistic (showing features of mild depression). Some patients vacillate between the two (are cyclothymic) in their adaptation. They are usually dependent in their emotional attachments. The depressive attack represents a turning of aggression, which was formerly felt towards another person close to the patient, against himself. He feels helpless and abandoned by the person on whom he is dependent and expects punishment from him. He feels guilt over and attempts to expiate for his hostile impulses. The dynamics of the manic attack are essentially the same as that of the depressive attack, only here the patient attempts to ward off the threatening depression and to deny his feeling of helplessness through the escape into activity and grandiose self-evaluation.

Involutional melancholia is a disorder associated with the period of intellectual and physical decline. It is often associated with the menopause in women. The patient becomes severely depressed and agitated with anxiety and guilt feelings. He may have delusions of sin or of persecution, that he has changed, that he has some dread disease. In addition to those dynamics present in other types of depression, this type of patient is reacting to the decline in functions with feelings of inadequacy and worthlessness. He feels that he no longer has any hope of achieving as yet unfulfilled goals.

Paranoia is a form of illness in which the patient presents a delusional idea (a fixed, unrealistic belief). He may, for example, believe that some one is intent upon injuring or murdering him or that some one is making sexual advances towards him. These ideas are held without realistic foundation, although, once the delusion is developed, the patient supports it by interpreting events in accordance with it. He is usually highly logical and frequently convincing in defense of his delusion. Such a patient, even prior to the development of the delusional ideas, is apt to be suspicious. Usually, his evaluation of reality is good in areas not touched by his delusion. He is likely to be rigid and compulsive in his general adaptation, not reacting with strong emotions, although he may become quite excited in defending his delusional idea. The delusion frequently represents a projection of repressed homosexual impulses (with the formula, "I don't love him; I hate him. I don't hate him; he hates me") or of hostile impulses. The patient fears rejection and injury; defensive hostility is seen in his accusatory, suspicious attitudes. Paranoia of jealously is the form most frequently seen.

Schizophrenia represents a severe maladjustment in which there is marked disturbance in the patient's evaluation of reality. His thinking is bizarre, determined by his inner needs while disregarding objective reality (autistic thinking). He is emotionally withdrawn and cannot form strong emotional relationships. His emotional responsiveness is dulled and is frequently inappropriate. The patient may be delusional or have hallucinations (abnormal sensory experiences without perceptual stimuli), and his behavior is apt to be peculiar and inexplicable to the observer. The following symptoms may dominate the condition at various times: loss of initiative and simple deterioration; delusions of persecution with auditory hallucinations; states of stupor and/or excitement; involved irrational philosophical and theoretical ideas with delusions of grandeur.

Dynamically, these symptoms represent the patient's attempts to escape and deny a painful reality and to repress his intensely painful emotional reactions. He feels completely helpless to cope with either the objective or the subjective dangers. Thus he distorts the meaning of events and his responses are then inappropriate to the actual situation. Inhibitory controls are given up and the patient may attempt to achieve direct satisfaction of sexual and hostile impulses. This results not only from his giving up efforts to adjust to reality but also from his attempt to derive some gratification from a painful existence.

In *organic reaction patterns* the primary cause of the illness is change in brain function. The change may be due to injury, to infectious disease, to toxic agents, or to the absence of a vital chemical. The patient's mental functioning is impaired as a direct result of the changed neural function, the nature of the impairment depending on the location and extent of the neurological changes. The altered functions include intellectual impairment, poor emotional control, and behavioral changes. This impaired function represents a threat to the patient and he mobilizes his resources in order to cope with the world and his own impulses with his remaining capacities. Many patients attempt to simplify and routinize their lives in order to prevent unforeseen situations which are beyond their capacities to cope with. They may deny their incapacity and assume a boastful, self-aggrandizing attitude. Or, in response to the frustration arising from their inadequacy, they may become irritable. The clinical picture is the outcome of a combination of these factors. It is frequently difficult to determine to what extent an emotional change such as irritability is due to the direct effects of the brain damage and to what extent it is the patient's reaction to his impaired capacities.

DISTURBANCES IN CHILDHOOD AND OLD AGE

Although some of the manifestations of psychiatric disturbances in children are similar to those in adults (anxiety reactions and phobias, for example, are relatively common in children and depression or depressionlike reactions are found at all age levels), many are different. Night terrors do not occur in adults. Enuresis, soiling, and feeding difficulties are frequent childhood symptoms. In other instances, although the manifestation is similar in both children and adults, the significance of the problem is different. Overly aggressive, destructive behavior in a child is not unusual and is not so serious in its implications as it is in adults.

In old age, decline in function and irreversible organic changes may complicate the picture. Impaired hearing, for example, is frequent in old age. The patient may react badly to this impairment, feeling helpless and becoming irritable and suspicious, believing that people are talking about him when he cannot hear. This reaction to the impairment represents a projection of the patient's own hostility and/or fear of retribution for his hostile impulses.

Therapy

PSYCHOTHERAPY

The techniques of psychiatric interview which have been described are at the same time methods of treatment. One fact which is peculiar to psychotherapy is that the treatment and the gathering of information are simultaneous—the gathering of information is part of the treatment and has therapeutic effects in several ways. In talking about his problems to the therapist, the patient feels that he can rely on a stronger individual who understands and is interested in him. He is allowed to express his unacceptable feelings and impulses without being condemned or punished; he is thus enabled to accept them with less self-condemnation and can evaluate himself more realistically and comes to feel the world to be less threatening. He finds that his symptoms do not represent mysterious, incomprehensible forces and foreign bodies within himself but that they they are related to his daily experiences, reactions, attitudes, and strivings. Insight into the complex interrelationships involved gradually develops. Talking about his problems and expressing his emotions is a way of "letting off steam" and he experiences relief and diminution of tension as a result. The patient's neurosis represents a complex interlocking, self-perpetuating system involving anxiety and guilt with which the patient copes as best he can. He does so, however, with faulty attitudes which reinstate the initial conflicts. In the therapeutic sessions these become disentangled and comprehended emotionally as well as intellectually and the faulty reactions diminish. In psychotherapeutic interviews, in general, any one or several of these aspects can be emphasized. In psychoanalytic therapy in particular, in addition to the above-mentioned events, the therapist attempts to combat faulty attitudes directly by consistently pointing out their persistence and their pernicious consequences.

Hypnosis may be used therapeutically as a way of quickly getting at unconscious material—either as an adjunct to regular interviews or in a treatment carried out entirely with the patient under hypnosis.

Psychotherapy can be carried out in groups as well as individually. Techniques of group therapy vary widely, including such methods as educational lectures by the therapist, inspirational speeches, and fairly free discussion of problems with expression of feelings and ideas by the members of the group. In the last, the mechanisms involved are similar to those operative in individual therapy. The special factor in group therapy is the relationship which develops among the members of the group. The members tend to identify with each other, lose their feelings of uniqueness, and are encouraged to express themselves when they hear the other members talk of their problems and experiences. Each member of the group should be seen individually at least once by the therapist after termination of the group sessions.

Raynaud's Syndrome (the complaint of M. R.) has been found to respond well to psychotherapy. In general, the effectiveness of the treatment varies in accordance with its intensiveness. The following results (see Fig 9.1) were obtained with four patients seen in psychotherapeutic interviews:

The first patient averaged three attacks a day during the two-year period preceding treatment; during the first two weeks of treatment the average number of attacks per day dropped to less than one. The second patient averaged four attacks per day over a period of four years before starting treatment. This decreased to two per day after treatment was begun and remained at that frequency during a prolonged interruption in the treatment. When treatment was resumed, the number of attacks decreased further to an average of less than one a day. The third patient had an average of eight attacks a day over a four-year period preceding psychotherapy. While undergoing treatment, which lasted about a year, she had an average of one attack a day. Following treatment she had an attack on an average of one every week. The fourth patient had an average of three attacks per day before treatment; this dropped to one attack every three days during three years of intensive therapy. On follow-up one year after completing treatment, she reported she had had no attacks since treatment terminated.

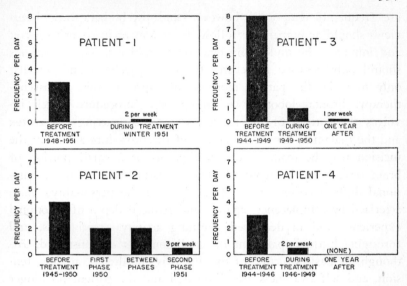

FIGURE 9.1. Number of Attacks of Raynaud's Disease Before, During, and After Treatment in Four Patients.

SOMATIC PROCEDURES

Emotional disorders can be treated by somatic methods as well as psychotherapeutically. The most extensively used somatic treatment is the administration of sedatives. In the ambulatory patient, this should be done sparingly and only as an adjunct to psychotherapy. In severely disturbed patients, sedatives may be used to cope with the immediate excitement.

Three somatic methods of more radical nature which have gained fairly wide acceptance are insulin coma treatment, electric convulsive treatment, and frontal lobotomy. In insulin therapy, a series of comas are induced by the administration of insulin which reduces the supply of sugar to the brain. In electric convulsive treatment, an electric current is passed through the brain, producing convulsions. Although it is not entirely clear just how these techniques produce their effects, they seem to reduce the emotional pressure behind the patient's symptoms. These effects are frequently temporary, however, and psychotherapeutic interviews should accompany or follow the treatment in order to get at and influence the underlying emotional problems. These methods should only be used in severer forms of psychosis and, ideally, only to make the patient more readily approachable in psychotherapy. Frontal lobotomy is an operative procedure which involves the cutting of the nerve pathways connecting the cortex and the thalamus. Several variations of the procedure are used; the incision may be made at different points or a small portion of brain tissue may be removed. The operation results in an emotional dulling (often called "bleaching" of the personality) characterized by complacency, apathy, and reduced depth of emotional experience and in decreased planning activity, creativeness, and foresight. Little impairment of intelligence is demonstrated. Although the basic structure of the illness is not altered, anxiety, tension, and self-awareness are eliminated and the patient no longer reacts to his difficulties. One might say, in an oversimplified way, that the patient adjusts to his illness. Obviously this technique should be used only in cases where less radical techniques have failed to produce results.

PSYCHOLOGICAL TEST PROCEDURES

A relatively rapid method of studying the individual is by the use of psychological tests. The subject's responses to standardized test situations are observed and evaluated. There are two types of psychological tests in common use—standardized tests and projective methods of examination.

Standardized Tests

Questionnaires and rating scales are usually referred to as standardized tests. The former usually consists of a series of multiple choice questions. These tests can be scored rapidly and the subject's score can be readily compared with those of other subjects.

The Cornell Selectee Index, a questionnaire designed to indicate the presence of emotional maladjustment, consists of a series of questions which can be answered "yes" or "no." Each question is pointed at revealing the presence of some emotional difficulty, maladjustive tendency, or psychosomatic reaction. Several of the items are so-called stop questions—questions which, if answered in the positive, indicate the presence of pathology. Emotional maladjustment is also suggested if more than a given number of items are answered "yes." This questionnaire was designed to facilitate brief psychiatric interviews. By noting the questions to which the subject has given a positive answer, the interviewer can predict what topics will prove most significant to pursue in interview examination. Or the test may be used to screen patients with severe neuroses from the rest of the population.

Projective Tests

In projective methods of examination, the subject is presented with a relatively unstructured test situation and asked to organize it. The rationale of such methods is the hypothesis that everything a person does is characteristic of him—that he will "project" himself into any situation he is confronted with. Since most life situations are fairly structured, the individual will tend to respond in a way that is called for by the situation, and the projective aspects of his behavior will be obscured. In projective test situations, on the other hand, the situation is relatively unstructured and because it is unfamiliar to him, the subject cannot fall back on habitual, learned social patterns and the projective aspects of his behavior are therefore highlighted. He must first organize the task and his mode of organizing it will be typical for him and based on his characteristic ways of perceiving. In addition, his habitual modes of expression—both verbal and motor—can be observed. While the subject's test performance on these tests can be compared with those of other subjects as when standardized tests are used, his full individuality is expressed in his test responses so that a refined personality picture can be derived from them.

RORSCHACH TEST

The projective method most widely used is the Rorschach Test. This consists of a series of ten standard, bilaterally symmetrical ink blots, five of which consist entirely of shades of gray and black and five of which use colors with or without gray areas. The subject is simply asked to tell what they might be or what they look like. His responses are recorded and scored. It is usually necessary for the examiner to ask questions about the responses in order to clarify the patient's meaning or to score them adequately. This is done during an inquiry period after the subject has given his spontaneous responses. In scoring, the following factors are considered: (1) *location:* the part of the blot used, whether the response takes in the whole blot or a part of it; (2) *determinant:* what perceptual features in the blot suggested the response to the subject. Here such blot qualities as form, color, shading, and texture, and movement impression are scored; (3) *content:* the conceptual area within which the response falls, such as animal, human, plant, etc.: (4) *popularity-originality*: whether a response is a frequently seen response (popular) or a very unusual one (original).

Briefly, the general significance of the various types of determinants are as follows: The extent to which form is used as a determinant in forming responses is related to the patient's control over his emotions and impulses; the more form is used, the greater is this control. Excessive use of form suggests repression and inhibition; too little use of form suggests highly emotional, perhaps impulsive reactions. Movement responses (e.g., two men bowing) indicate responsiveness to inner stimuli, intellectual creativity, and spontaneity. Color responses represent the person's emotionality, particularly in response to external stimuli. Responses in which shading play a role indicate anxiety and sensitivity. Color responses may be fused with form elements (e.g., a red butterfly, in which both the shape and the color of the blot are important)—pointing to adaptive affectivity—or considerations of form may be found on the inquiry to be secondary (a bouquet of flowers) or absent (water)—indicating impulsiveness or emotional outbursts. Shading responses may similarly occur in varied relation to form. In interpreting a record, the examiner must consider the *overall pattern* of the patient's responses. For example, not only does he want to know what determinants the subject uses, but he also wants to know the relative frequency with which each one occurs in the subject's protocol. This is true also of the location areas and the content. He also takes into account qualitative features of the record which are not scored.

We will now discuss very briefly some of the outstanding features of the Rorschach record of a patient with Raynaud's Syndrome to illustrate how a record can be interpreted.

The patient, a married woman of 31, gave a total of 20 responses. Only 4 of them were pure form responses (form as the only determinant), suggesting insufficient control over emotions. This hypothesis is borne out by her color responses: 1 FC (fusion of form and color) and 4 CF (determined primarily by color, form playing a secondary role), which suggests poorly controlled affectivity. The ratio of human movement responses (M) to color responses is 2M:4½C (the color responses are weighted, FC's counting ½, CF's 1), indicating that this patient is more responsive to outer emotional stimuli than to inner stimuli. Since this dominant affective responsiveness is poorly controlled, we would expect this woman to be emotionally labile, responding with strong feelings to the world about her. Such a picture is frequently found in hysterical persons.

One of her responses to the first card is the following:

"Could look like the backbone, the chest skeleton, rather distorted." On inquiry, she said, "Did I say that about this one? Whole thing. Don't ask me what these things are (pointing to small projections) unless the x-ray didn't show through clearly—or unless the person was wearing some pieces of metal that are showing. I've had lots of chest x-rays, maybe that's why it looks like that. Backbone in center, ribs on side."

This response is scored W F At: The subject has used the whole card (W), her response was determined by form alone (F), the content is anatomy (At). Anatomical responses, reflecting concern with bodily organs and their functions, are frequently given by persons with somatic symptoms. Careful scrutiny of this response reveals that there are obsessive-compulsive features in this woman's character make-up as well as the hysterical features already pointed out. She finds it necessary to account for all details of the blot carefully in finally structuring her response. The tendency to react impulsively is also seen. Although she does eventually work out the response in detail, her initial reaction was an overall one, disregarding details, and she showed a reluctance to concern herself with them: "Don't ask me what these things are."

It should be emphasized that no definite conclusions can be drawn from a single response taken out of context. The implications of a single response can only be seen adequately and with security in terms of the overall test picture.

THEMATIC APPERCEPTION TEST

Another widely used projective technique is the Thematic Apperception Test. This consists of a series of twenty pictures—some pictures of the series varying according to the subject's age and sex—about which the subject is asked to make up stories. The subject's stories are compared with the most usual themes elicited by each card and any deviation is considered significant. Recurrent themes in the record point to meaningful fantasies, wishes, fears, concerns, etc. The descriptions of the various characters in the stories are considered. Thus the main characters are considered to be projections of the subject's self-image, or, at times, his ideal self-image. Descriptions of other characters reflect his attitudes toward significant persons in his environment: parents and other authority figures, husband or wife, etc. The manner of reacting to and handling problem situations described are apt to reflect the subject's own reactions to stress and his coping mechanisms. Story endings may reveal his feelings of helplessness or adequacy, of hopelessness or hopefulness concerning his difficulties.

The patient whose Rorschach has been discussed gave the following story about a picture showing a woman lying unclothed on a bed and a man standing, turned away from her, with his arm shielding his eyes:

"This lady and this man are married. They went to school together, fell in love when they were young, and as they matured further they still loved each other. He's a doctor—studied to be a doctor. And the woman grows ill, more and more so, and he realizes that she has . . . mmmm . . . let's see, what's inoperable besides cancer? . . . Let's say that she has . . . pneumonia, and complications set in, and he can't—oh! I know a nice story. They're in South America, in a country where there's about to be an election, and there is much revolution going on, and he finds it impossible to obtain the necessary drugs for his wife to care for her. In this picture she had died, she's dead. He has studied to be a doctor for one purpose—to help people—and the one person he has wanted to keep alive as well as himself is his wife and he has failed. For a while he cares for . . . he doesn't want to go back to the States, to the town he had been practicing in. Instead he works there in South America and cares for the people who know nothing of medicine. He cares for them, and through them and through their great appreciation for the little that he does for them in medicine, he again finds gradually calm within himself and a passive adjustment. And he lives there all his life, becomes a benefactor, so to speak, of the town. Everyone loves him—he's happy."

The theme most frequently elicited by this picture is one of sexual aggression and/or promiscuity. The fact that this theme is not used suggests sexual conflicts. The main character of her story, the person with whom she is most concerned (the *identification figure*) is the man, indicating some degree of masculine identification. In constructing her story, she has, as in her Rorschach response cited above, worked out the details carefully (note how she goes to great lengths to explain the fact that the wife's illness is incurable), so again we see the possibility of an obsessive-compulsive personality component. Her concern with the theme of death is of significance in relation to her illness. Most patients with Raynaud's Syndrome are concerned with death and many identify with a person close to them who has died. The fact that the husband in the story is unable to cure his wife suggests that she thinks of men as being passive and ineffectual. This is supported by her statement towards the end that he makes a "passive adjustment."

Here again a cautionary statement should be made. One cannot interpret a single TAT story with security. It is with *repeated* themes, recurrent attitudes, etc., that the examiner works in interpreting a protocol. The illustration given here, however, illustrates the way a clinical psychologist can use test data in building up a personality description. For a thorough, detailed picture of an individual's personality functioning, several projective tests are necessary. This is so for several reasons. One is that each test is so designed that it highlights certain areas of personality so that several techniques must be used to get a well-rounded picture of the total functioning. The Rorschach, for example, is especially useful in revealing the personality *structure* of the subject, the functioning of and interrelationships among the structural components, and their relative strengths and weaknesses. The TAT on the other hand brings *content,* i.e., specific areas of conflict and deep-lying attitudes, into sharp focus.

EXPERIMENTAL METHODS OF INVESTIGATION

It is possible to study the effects of emotional conflicts on the individual through experimental techniques, showing the relationship between internal events and observable changes in physiological functions and in the action of voluntary and involuntary musculature.

Experiments with Human Subjects

In experimental investigations with human subjects, there are three methods by which the situation can be altered: (1) by hypnosis—while the subject is in a hypnotic trance, the investigator suggests a conflict situation to him; (2) by interview—the investigator, in an interview with the subject, discusses topics which are known to be conflict-laden for the subject; (3) by drugs—a drug which produces changes in neurophysiological functioning is administered to the subject.

HYPNOSIS

In a hypnotic experiment, the investigator suggested to the subject that he had stolen some money and was afraid he would be caught. When he was brought out of the hypnotic trance, the subject could not remember what happened during the trance. He complained of not feeling well, of feeling upset, but did not know why. When he was asked to associate to a list of words, his responses to stimulus words relating to the suggested situation were delayed. Voluntary and involuntary movements were recorded; tremor was shown when "conflict" words (those relating to the suggested conflict situation) were introduced and respiration was altered.

Another hypnotic technique frequently used is that of regression. The subject, in a deep trance, is given the suggestion that it is a particular period in his past—e.g., his tenth birthday or his first day of school. He then proceeds to act out events which occurred in the suggested situation and to behave as he did at that age. The regression is usually not complete, however, and remnants of "older" behavior are observed.

These experiments illustrate (1) the nature of unconscious processes and their influence on behavior; (2) the effects of conflict; (3) the operation of such mechanisms as repression, regression, compromise formation, and rationalization; and (4) the influence of the individual's emotional state on the skeletal musculature.

INTERVIEW

The patient, with Raynaud's Syndrome described earlier was studied during interview sessions. Changes in finger temperature were recorded while discussions of her difficulties were carried on. In one such session, when her domestic problems were discussed, she experienced tension, fear, anxiety, resentment, feelings of helplessness, frustration, and guilt. She complained of headache, of being in a cold sweat, of a sinking sensation in her abdomen and a bearing down pain in the pelvic region, with precordial pain, palpitation, and shortness of breath. Her finger temperature was observed to drop 8.2° C. In a similar interview carried out in a cool room, her finger temperature dropped 13.2° C. and she complained of tingling and pain in her fingers. A similar procedure was carried out a third time, again in a cool room, the patient being inadequately dressed. This time her skin temperature dropped 13.5° C., her fingers became deeply cyanosed, and she complained of severe pain (Fig. 9.2). Thus a typical attack of her disease was induced experimentally.

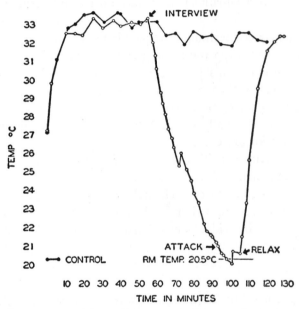

FIGURE 9.2.   Finger Temperature Changes in Patient M. R. (described here) Before, During, and After an Experimentally Induced Attack of Raynaud's Disease.

DRUGS

Psychological changes occur while the subject is under the influence of various drugs and poisons. Subjects administered synthetic mescaline exhibited mental changes of the type frequently found in schizophrenic patients. Visual hallucinations expressing wish-fulfilling fantasies and auditory hallucinations which started as an idea and then were projected and heard from the outside occurred. Somatic sensations such as alteration or loss of parts of the body were reported. Delusions, misinterpretation of environmental situations, depersonalization experiences, and thought disturbances occurred. It was found that the extent to which these described changes took place in a subject was related to his personality structure, to the presence or absence of emotional illness, and to the type of illness.

Whenever tension is induced by any method—by discussion of disturbing life situations, by suggested conflicts in hypnosis, by confronting the individual with a problem he cannot solve—diffuse somatic changes can be observed, involving the heart, lungs, gastrointestinal tract, bladder, eyes: in short, practically every organ of the body.

Experiments with Animals

EXPERIMENTAL NEUROSIS

Experimental studies have also been carried out on animals. The most commonly employed method is based on the conditioned response technique developed by Pavlov. In one such experiment, a sheep was trained to stand quietly on a platform in harness. In response to an electric shock (unconditioned stimulus) administered to his foreleg, the animal flexed his leg (unconditioned response) and then stood quietly again. This response was conditioned to the sound of a metronome (conditioned stimulus) which would be set going and, after the fifth beat, the shock would be administered. The animal would start to flex his foreleg (conditioned reaction) before the fifth beat until the shock occurred. The animal maintained his conditioning when the number of beats occurring before the administration of the shock was increased. With some animals, however, when the increase in the number of beats before the shock was large behavior changed profoundly. The animal would flex his leg too soon or too late; it became restless on the platform, repeatedly flexed its foreleg whether or not the metronome was beating, vigorously resisted being brought to the laboratory, and fought being put on the platform. Even outside the experimental situation, it showed changed behavior: it tended to be withdrawn, to crouch in a corner, and to be more submissive in case of attack. Its pulse became rapid and irregular.

This type of experiment illustrates (1) the role of psychogenic, particularly situational, factors in the development of neuroses; (2) the alteration of the total organism occurring in neurosis; (3) the role of conflicts in the development of neurosis and the effects of such conflicts; (4) such mechanisms as compromise formation, avoidance, and defensive hostility; and (5) changes in functions of various organ systems correlated with emotional stress.

Both the immediate emergency reaction to stress and the changes resulting from prolonged stress reactions can be observed. The emergency reaction results from the discharge of large amounts of adrenalin into the blood stream and from the activation of the sympathetic nervous system. The organismic changes which occur in response to chronic stress have been termed "general adaptation syndrome." The same changes have been observed to occur in response to all types of stress: infection, sustained physical effort, situational tension, etc. Some of the changes found in prolonged stress reactions include increase in blood pressure, ulcerations in the gastrointestinal tract, and changes in the endocrine system—particularly enlargement of the adrenal cortex.

ABLATION

Portions of the brains of animals have been removed in order to observe the behavioral changes which occur. An adolescent female chimpanzee was ordinarily affectionate, coöperative, and eager to work in problem situations. One of the problem situations used is the following: Food is placed under one of two cups.

An opaque screen is then placed in front of the cups. When the screen is raised a few minutes later, the chimpanzee is permitted to reach for the food. In order to choose correctly, she must remember under which of the cups the food was placed. The chimpanzee became very upset when she was unable to solve this problem. She flew into a temper tantrum during which she rolled on the floor, beat the grate, defecated and urinated, and showed signs of diffuse sympathetic discharge. She finally refused to go into the problem cage. After removal of both frontal lobe areas of the brain, the animal eagerly accepted the experimental situation, never showing any emotional disturbance no matter how many times she made a mistake.

Ablation experiments demonstrate the localization of some psychological functions. They also emphasize the integrated functioning of the total organism. In other words, one cannot speak simply of a psychological or of a physiological reaction or alteration. Any change which occurs within the individual is a change of the whole organism, and the reaction which takes place is a total, integrated one having both physiological and psychological components.

SUMMARY

The three methods of investigation (clinical, psychological, experimental) described complement each other in building up our knowledge of the total individual. More important in the use of several approaches in studying the individual is the fact that any one method may fail to reveal some important aspect of personality function. When experimental methods are used in studying the patient's reactions, physiological changes usually associated with anxiety—such as increased heart rate, and excessive perspiration—may take place without the patient's experiencing anxiety, even in a situation which may be expected to arouse anxiety. The projective tests may show evidence of schizophrenic thought disorder when clinical examination gives no evidence of psychotic impairment. At other times, an underlying psychotic coloring may be observed in clinical examination of a patient who presents a neurotic picture in the projective test findings. Any indication that a psychotic potential is present is important in determining the therapist's approach to the patient's problems. The therapist must be aware of the danger of a psychotic breakdown, be alerted to early signs of such a reaction in order to forestall it if possible, and be prepared to handle it if it does occur.

SUGGESTED READINGS

1. Brenman, M., and Gill, M. M., *Hypnotherapy*. New York: International Universities, 1947. This book indicates how hypnosis may be used in a constructive fashion and the text constitutes a good introduction to this particular area.

2. Freud, S., *A General Introduction to Psycho-Analysis*. New York: Liveright, 1935. A statement of the basic position taken by the psychoanalysts as indicated by Freud.

3. Kalinowsky, L. B., and Hoch, P. H., *Shock Treatment and Other Somatic Procedures in Psychiatry*. New York: Grune & Stratton, 1946. A straightforward factual account of present day organic therapies. This book includes a comprehensive view of the field as well as the author's own investigations.

4. Maslow, A. H., and Mittelmann, B., *Principles of Abnormal Psychology*. New York: Harper, rev. ed., 1951. A basic general text simply written and indicating the scope of abnormal psychology.

5. Meyer, A., *The Common Sense Psychiatry of Dr. Adolf Meyer*. New York: McGraw-Hill, 1948. A statement by the originator of the term *psychobiology*. This text contains fundamental concepts and represents advanced reading in the field of psychopathology.

6. Murray, H. A., *et al.*, *Explorations in Personality*. New York: Oxford, 1938. This book contains a summary of the experimental data as well as the description of the Thematic Apperception Test. In addition, it contains a description of a wide variety of other methods of personality analysis.

7. Pavlov, I. P., *Lectures on Conditioned Reflex*. New York: Interna-

tional Publishers, 1928. A rather detailed statement of the experiments and data of Pavlov, the Russian physiologist.

8. Rorschach, H., *Psychodiagnostics*. New York: Grune & Stratton, 1942. A description of the Rorschach test and the original experiments and data obtained from it by Rorschach himself.

9. Rosenzweig, S., and Kogan, K. L., *Psychodiagnosis*. New York: Grune & Stratton, 1949. A comprehensive account of the various projective methods of personality analysis.

10. Weiss, E., and English, O. S., *Psychosomatic Medicine*. Philadelphia: Saunders, 1943. A statement of the basic position of the psychosomatic approach. This text is illustrated by a number of case histories, is easily readable, and comprehensive in scope.

Chapter 10

Clinical Psychology

by BERNARD STEINZOR

Historical Sources of Modern Clinical Psychology
    THE SCIENTIFIC ATTITUDE
    THE EMPHASIS ON INDIVIDUAL DIFFERENCES
    THE HUMANISTIC INFLUENCE
    THE CONTINUITY OF THE RATIONAL AND
       NONRATIONAL
    WORLD WAR I AND WORLD WAR II

The Clinician and His Training
    THE PREPROFESSIONAL (UNDERGRADUATE)
       CURRICULUM
    THE PROFESSIONAL (GRADUATE) CURRICULUM
    SELF-EVALUATION

The Clinician and the Patient
    THE PROBLEM OF DIAGNOSIS
          Psychological Testing
    THE PROBLEM OF THERAPY

The Clinician and His Science
    SERVICE AND RESEARCH
    THE CLINICAL RESEARCH APPROACH
    GENERAL LAWS AND UNIQUENESS OF PERSONALITY
    SCIENCE AND VALUES
    SOME RESEARCH PROBLEMS
          An Illustrative Study
          The Normal Person
          The Type of Therapy
          The Clinician

The Clinician and His Profession

      TRAINING AND EXPERIENCE
      LEGAL RECOGNITION
      PROFESSIONAL CONDUCT

Conclusion

Suggested Readings

Clinical psychology is a rapidly growing profession. It is a field closely related to the other areas of psychology and to the social sciences in general. For these reasons, a description of this area of psychology must be highly selective. What then guided the choice of issues that are included? This field is engaged in a unique educational experiment in which the training of the clinician is geared not only in preparing him for service but for equipping him to build an experimental science. Such an attempt at combining these two functions in one curriculum raises many real problems. Some of these are only now being gradually solved by new approaches and techniques. But there is a frequently expressed point of view which holds that clinical practice is only an art and never can become a science. Therefore, the guiding idea for selection of topics in this discussion is that there is only an apparent opposition between service and science.

HISTORICAL SOURCES OF MODERN CLINICAL PSYCHOLOGY

A variety of historical circumstances has contributed to the setting of the atmosphere in which the clinician works. These will be described under headings which emphasize the important ideas and attitudes stemming from the particular era of history.

The Scientific Attitude

Whenever we are attempting to separate what we wish to see from what actually exists, we are adopting a scientific attitude. The history of science is replete with examples of man's struggle to become more realistic. On the one hand, man desires to see his world ever more clearly. But on the other there is an almost equally strong wish to hold on to his fantasies. Copernicus (born 1473) was of conservative temperament, yet his formulation of a heliocentric solar system taxed the beliefs of men and resulted in profound shock to the established culture of his day. Men were eventually asked to reëxamine their cherished idea that they and the earth were at the center of creation. Darwin's (born 1809) ideas on evolution again demanded that man reconsider his self-concept and face the fact of his kinship to all living forms. The march of science does involve the progressive disillusionment of humanity with its exaggerated and distorted ideas about itself.

As difficult as it has been in the physical sciences to evaluate personal bias in the light of empirical test, the task has been infinitely more so in the human sciences. Relatively speaking, the chemist can go rather far in his studies without concerning himself too greatly with his private hopes for the world. However when we study other humans we unavoidably and necessarily become involved with them. This greatly increases the potentiality for errors of observation. It is this very problem of establishing appropriate detachment when studying ourselves that largely explains the rather late development of the human sciences.

The task of clinical psychology is directly addressed to this difficulty. By becoming attentive to our private worlds we may yet develop a sufficiently objective attitude toward ourselves before we destroy the world in some mad chase after a vision of eternal perfection. When we thus describe the scientific attitude as one in which private desire is clearly separated from what is, we can recognize this is the central concern of the clinician as practitioner.

The Emphasis on Individual Differences

The founders of modern experimental psychology, Weber, Fechner, and Wundt, were steeped in the methods of physics and physiology. These disciplines influenced them to seek general laws about individual functions by carrying out very strictly controlled experiments with few subjects. They assumed that a careful and thorough analysis of the data on a single individual, would yield results true for all. However, not long after the first psychology laboratory was opened in Leipzig, another approach was taken to this problem of human fallibility. Sir Francis Galton published in 1883, *Inquiries into Human Faculty and Its Development,* and this marked the emergence of what is the most unique feature of psychological science, the study of individual differences. Galton's work on psychometrics and his invention of special tests was a forerunner of the entire testing movement. In America, the work of Cattell also spurred psychologists to turn their attention from human uniformities to individual differences. However, not until A. Binet in France was asked to devise a method for placing children in school on the basis of their ability, did testing of differences really get under way. After the publication of the Binet-Simon Scale in 1905, mental testing mushroomed so rapidly that even today many believe that clinical psychology and giving tests are synonymous. Quantification is a major criterion of a scientific approach. The psychological test seemed to fulfill this requirement so admirably that for a long time some psychologists even believed they had discovered the way to become respectable even among their scientific colleagues in physics and chemistry.

A particular development in mental testing, that of projective techniques, has given clinical psychology its most recent stamp. Rorschach published his classic Ink Blot Test in 1921, but even before, many investigators made use of unstructured material as a method of understanding the person's way of interpreting the world. Many other techniques besides ink blots have since been developed such as the Thematic Apperception Test, sentence completion devices, finger painting, and doll play. All are based on the assumption that the meaning the subject gives these stimuli reveals something about the inner states determining the individual's behavior. These projective methods combined a testing approach with a dynamic point of view and thus made available to the clinician powerful tools for personality study.

The Humanistic Influence

In 1896, Lightner Witmer started the first psychological clinic. The clinic, at the University of Pennsylvania, was dedicated to the practical investigation and solution of problems of schoolchildren. Witmer gave psychology its first clinical stamp by his readiness to use qualitative approaches. We can today recognize the importance and courage of his step since Witmer's efforts were not too well received by other psychologists who, as indicated, were "aping" the physical sciences. While the study of individual differences did give psychology its special flavor, the person could well have been and often was lost in the mass of statistics that accompanied the proliferation of mental testing. The clinical approach to individual differences was affirmed by Witmer in the face of criticism that his work was not scientific.

There were other places where humanitarian values were applied in psychology. At the beginning of this century a training school for the feeble-minded was established at Vineland, New Jersey, and a few years later, the first behavior clinic to deal with juvenile delinquents was established at Chicago. Shortly after World War I, many child guidance clinics got their start through the help of the Commonwealth Fund. This action reinforced an increasing emphasis on prevention through early treatment as it was recognized that adult difficulties have their springs in childhood. The work with child guidance clinics repeatedly demonstrated the extreme importance of a historical developmental approach to understanding the disturbance of grownups. Still another important stream was contributed by the mental hygiene movement. Clifford Beer's autobiography, *The Mind That Found*

Itself, sparked the work of educating the public about mental health.

The Continuity of the Rational and Nonrational

Since the turn of the century, when Sigmund Freud first began to publish his observations, psychoanalysis has proven to be a rich storehouse of ideas and hypotheses for all students of human behavior. Of the many major concepts developed by Freud two were especially influential in the development of clinical psychology. The first, the theory of infantile and childhood origins of neuroses, has been briefly mentioned. The second, that of the unconscious and its nonrational aspects, had the most widespread effect on all of human thought. Freud's formulations of the relationship between logical and illogical thought and normal and abnormal phenomena were unusually radical ideas. They faced man with the necessity of changing his view of himself and thus were in line with all great scientific discovery. The notion of the relationship between sickness and health was itself not unique in biology and medicine. However, when dealing with human affairs, the connections of everyday behavior and dreams and their relation to the delusions of the mentally disturbed seemed to be a most improbable doctrine. Psychoanalytic thinking did again confront man with his vanity. This time the challenge was to his wish to deny his essential brotherhood to all men; the brotherhood of the primitive and the civilized, the sane and the mentally ill, the dreamer and the man of affairs.

World War I and World War II

During World War I, the practical usefulness of the mental test for rapid classification and assignment of human resources was demonstrated. The psychologist during World War II expanded this line of inquiry to many other problems besides general aptitude. He guided the selection of candidates for many of the highly specialized positions necessary to fight a modern war. In the emergency, the psychologist found himself working on many problems and sharpening many tools which he would only have slowly approached under ordinary circumstances. Psychologists took on responsibility for appraisal and treatment of the psychological casualty. After the war, the continued need for care of the veterans prompted the Veterans Administration to establish a program for training clinical psychologists. This close cooperation of government and private institutions in planning for the solution of a social problem was quite unique. The United States Public Health Service has also stimulated the expansion of clinical psychology by providing funds for research and training. These recent developments of the last decade have given the final impetus to the professionalization of psychology in the field of mental health.

THE CLINICIAN AND HIS TRAINING

We began the task of delineating the field of clinical psychology by a brief view of the historical forces which have set the atmosphere in which the clinician functions. We can approach this from another direction. Let us examine the formal training which contributes to the development of a clinician. Primarily what gives a profession its character are the goals and principles guides the education of its members. Through the university a group can move independently and shape itself as close as possible to its professional ideal.

A recognized and formalized training program is only a product of the last decade when clinical psychology became a legitimate field of concentration for the potential Ph.D. The tremendous demand for psychological services galvanized the universities into action. The American Psychological Association established various committees which have studied and debated policies for guiding the training of the clinician. Within the last few years crucial decisions have been reached and they may be summarized as follows. The first was that the basic training of the clinical psychologist was to have much in common with the other psychological specialties such as social, industrial, experimental, and child study.

The second decision stems directly from the first. Though the clinician was to be trained in diagnostic work and therapy, the special and unique contribution of the clinical psychologist was the design and execution of systematic research. The third decision reached was that the course of study be ordinarily set at four years of graduate work leading to a Ph.D. Finally, the training program was to be related as much as possible to the work of other disciplines. That the patient is a whole person was to be emphasized in the content of all courses. The clinician must be trained in an inter-disciplinary approach to the understanding and solution of social problems. On the job, the clinician would most likely serve as a member of a team including a psychiatrist, a social worker, and others engaged in the care of patients.

The Preprofessional (Undergraduate) Curriculum

How should the undergraduate student, considering psychology as a field of study, prepare himself for graduate work? The student can best prepare himself for advanced study of man's most intimate experiences by developing a broad background in the liberal arts and sciences. This would mean that the student take work in the humanities, and the social, biological, and physical sciences. He would deal with scientific principles not only in experimental psychology but in his study of physics, mathematics, and statistics. Furthermore, work in the philosophy and history of science would be invaluable for an understanding of the development of a scientific attitude. Biology would impress him with the experience of the continuity of life and with the "wisdom of the body." Sociology, anthropology, and economics would reveal to the student the effect on personal development of the complex institutions man has evolved. Courses in the history of civilization would help the student in attaining a more objective perspective of the society in which he lives. In reading the great works of literature, the student would be immersed in sensitive portrayals of human tragedy and grandeur. The great novel would provide an excellent model for detailed and dramatic study of lives in progress. Courses in educational theory and practice would make it possible to translate principles of learning into living terms. The neophyte psychologist would recognize how we must qualify generalizations about human behavior when we apply them to a specific person. He would learn to develop a flexibility of approach, warmth, and sense of responsibility so necessary for anyone attempting to release the creative potentials in another person. In a real sense, the preprofessional studies of a would-be clinical psychologist should be largely directed toward the attainment of a liberal, humanistic education.

The Professional (Graduate) Curriculum

Table 10.1 is an adaptation of the training program recommended by the Committee on Training in Clinical Psychology of the American Psychological Association. The titles describe content area rather than specific courses. This program is suggested only as a guide, since experimentation with a variety of training procedures is necessary to insure healthy professional growth. Each university must have the freedom to establish its own pattern for training its students.

Self-Evaluation

The further he progresses, the more aware the clinician becomes of himself as the most important instrument in clinical work. The clinician is constantly attempting to tune his sensitivities to understanding the patient. However, the paradox of sensitivity is that it also can prevent us from finding truth as well as directing our attention toward it. Our capacity for compassion and warmth of feeling for others can help us more fully experience another being's conflict and lead us toward its amelioration. It can also overwhelm us so that sympathy becomes pity, warmth becomes sentimentality, and a desire to help becomes overprotectiveness. The edge between a helping and an interfering attitude is often quite a narrow one, especially in the subtle relationship between client and clinician. In those dramatic moments when the clinician has only his own resources to draw upon and when he finds it difficult to compre-

TABLE 10.1. Content Areas in Graduate Training in Clinical Psychology
(Internship: One Year)

Area	General Theory	Diagnosis	Therapy	Research
Biological Area	Physiology-genetics Neuroanatomy Endocrinology Physiological psychology Comparative psychology	Clinical medicine Psychosomatic disease Drugs and their behavioral effects		(The problem of verification constantly underlined in all courses)
Sociological Area	Anthropology Social theory Culture and personality	Social organization and social pathology (crime, delinquency)	Community resources Educational methods	Methods of social research
Psychological Area	Social psychology Developmental Individual differences History of psychology Systematic and contemporary schools of psychology Psychodynamics of behavior	Psychopathology Techniques of observation Interviewing and history taking Objective and projective tests	Remedial techniques Vocational guidance Therapeutic approaches: psychoanalytic, client centered etc.	Theory of tests and test construction Experimental dynamic psychology Statistics Clinical research
Application	Professional problems Ethics of profession	Practicums	Self-evaluation (personal therapy?) Individual and group therapy Play therapy	Individual research projects Dissertation

hend and respect the patient, he can become aware of the need for self-understanding. The clinician through the deepest possible self-appraisal will learn what are his strengths, weaknesses, and biases in responding to the patient's needs. He will also come to understand more critically why he wants to help people. Unless he can be in free touch with himself the clinician will fail others at the very moment when the best help he can give emerges from the direct spontaneity of the human situation. Sole dependence on an accumulation of facts and ideas will not serve the psychologist when he is asked to help another. His own creativity must be freed so that the clinician can make his knowledge a meaningful vehicle for communication with another person.

The adequacy of a clinical training program will be ultimately measured by how well it provides the clinician with a depth of self-understanding. Self-knowledge may be obtained at various levels, ranging from the insight one develops while dealing with case material to that obtained in a personal analysis. Though personal therapy is not at present a requirement in the training of the clinical psychologist, being a patient is frequently recommended as the best way of achieving a deep respect for all patients.

THE CLINICIAN AND THE PATIENT

Another way of portraying the field of clinical psychology is by discussing some of the practical problems that may confront the clinician. In this way we will reveal something about him and the aims he has in his service work.

The Problem of Diagnosis

As a diagnostician, the clinician's aim is to discover rapidly as much as he can about the patient's symptoms and the personality which has set the stage for the development of the symptoms. He wants to know as much as he can so that an adequate treatment program can be planned. This does not mean that the clinician discovers all there is to know about the patient and then tells him what to do. Rather, in identifying the patient's major problems and in learning to some degree how they have developed out of life experiences, the clinician and the patient can collaborate in arriving at wiser decisions as to the direction the treatment will take. The kind of psychotherapy to be utilized, whether the patient is to be treated initially by a period of hospitalization, the part the patient's relatives are to play in the treatment, and the possible length of treatment and its cost are some of the significant issues that can be decided on the basis of a diagnostic study.

The diagnostic role of the clinical psychologist has been, in the past, defined as the reporting of IQ scores. But as the clinician began to recognize the interrelationship between intellect and emotions and began to consider the total functioning human being, he became more concerned with finding answers to three questions: What is the person like? How did he come to be this way? What is he likely to become? The clinician recognized that such subject matter divisions of psychology as intelligence, motivation, perception, and emotions were helpful only as analytic categories. In the laboratory, it was relatively simple to measure one or another of these dimensions of personality. But when the psychologist was faced with a bright individual who was failing in school, or a successful student unable to get along with his friends, or a socially active person who was terribly unhappy, he found it impossible to divide up the person into neat categories. Suggestions as to how to help the patient did not emerge from this categorial procedure. The task of diagnosis thus changed from a mere inventory of traits to an attempt to organize a living description of a person. Labeling people as superior or inferior intellectually, or as neurotic or psychotic, has become a relatively minor part of diagnosis. Assessment of the personality involves not only measurement through the use of specialized techniques, but a creative synthesis in which the clinician relies heavily on his own resources for understanding the person.

Psychodiagnosis is, thus, that phase of the curative process in which the clinician uses special aids for a limited period of time with the goal of developing a program of therapy. It is important, however, to indicate that diagnosis and therapy have become less and less separate entities. Experience has taught the clinician that the greater the involvement of the patient in planning for treatment, the greater the chances for a successful outcome. Increasing attention is now being paid to the very procedures of referring the patient for diagnostic study, the appraisal with the patient of his wish to be helped and his readiness for it. The clinician thus from the very beginning focuses attention on the relationship between the patient and himself. He must always remember that the patient is suffering and sensitive to questions which touch on problems long avoided. In psychological disease, treatment begins from the first meeting of clinician and patient and the first attempt to ascertain what is wrong.

PSYCHOLOGICAL TESTING

Basically, there are three methods available to the clinician in his study of personality. These are the case history, clinical observation, and testing. Roughly speaking, the development of the case history approach has been the primary effort of the social worker and clinical observation the special work of the psychiatrist. Testing procedures have been the unique contribution of the clinical psychologist. Though knowledge of all three methods is necessary for the full functioning of the clinical psychologist, the present discussion will evaluate the strength and limits of testing.

1. *Controlling the factor of subjectivity.* Limiting the observer's bias is a crucial requirement of science. In the human sciences, moreover, the subject himself is undoubtedly distorting, largely unconsciously, the very facts that are being reported. More than any other technique, testing controls the problem of subjective distortion of results. By introducing standardized stimuli and standardized scoring methods, comparisons among individuals can be more exact. The reliability of the observer can be more readily checked by comparing his findings on a test with those obtained by another examiner.

2. *More accurate and complete appraisal of intraindividual patterns.* The assessment of people by means of tests makes possible a more objective study of intraindividual personality organization. When the clinician attempts to predict the outcome of therapy, he wants to assess strengths and weaknesses of the patient. The evaluation of personality strength is made more feasible since the tests the clinician selects have been designed to tap different personality levels. This is particularly true of the projective techniques. The most complete appraisal of the individual is obtained when the clinician uses a battery of tests such as the Wechsler-Bellevue, Rorschach, Thematic Apperception Test, and a word association test.

3. *Ability to tap more unconscious levels of the personality.* The test stimuli, particularly those that form the basis of projective techniques, tend to elicit responses from the more central layers of the patient's personality. They reveal facets ordinarily not available to observation except over long periods of time. In asking the patient, for example, to make up a story to a picture, the things he tells us in symbolic forms are less subject to influence by momentary conditions and by conscious or unconscious attempts to hide them.

4. *Standard basis for measuring personality change.* The use of tests in research on the outcome of therapy has become more prevalent. With standardized test conditions, the clinician has more stable points for measuring change. Since the tests also provide scores on a number of personality variables, it is also possible to more objectively estimate how a therapeutic procedure would affect one function more than another.

5. *Usefulness in neurological examination.* The possibility of organic correlates to psychological difficulties must always be determined. Objective tests, especially those more sensitive to factors interfering with intellectual functioning, have provided an important adjunct to the neurologist in the detection of nervous system damage. There are also occasions when psychological tests may reveal organic deficit not detectable by neurological examination.

These are the major assets of the approach to the diagnostic problem through the use of tests. The limits of tests have yet to be fully determined by research. One thing is certain, however. They will never become crystal balls which reveal everything about every recess of the personality. They can't reveal the content of the critical experiences of the past which have shaped the person's views of reality and thus continue to live on repetitively in daily action. The case history gives us more information on the question of how the person became what he is. The three basic diagnostic approaches (case history, clinical observation, testing) need to be integrated for a complete study. Each method provides material which supplements that obtained from the others. Each method raises questions about the individual which can be better answered through another approach. Another limitation of tests relates to the problem of predicting behavior. Tests are designed primarily to help define the individual's private orientations. This they can do fairly well. But to expect that they can directly predict future behavior from inner attitudes, is asking too much. Actually, all fields of psychology are confronted with this issue. We do know, on the one hand, that different forms of behavior are often expressive of the same attitude and that differing attitudes quite frequently reveal themselves in one kind of behavior. There is still much to learn about the correlation of the private world and social behavior. The complexity and infinite intricacy of human personality negate the existence of a one-to-one correlation between thought and action. Certainly the clinician's daily work convinces him of this.

The Problem of Therapy

There is a wide variety of theoretical orientations to the practice of therapy and an even greater assortment of techniques. Within the psychoanalytic framework, there are differing interpretations of the curative process described by Freud, Adler, Jung, Horney, Fromm, Sullivan, and Alexander. In the last decade, the client-centered orientation has been emphasized by Carl Rogers and his students. Important work also has developed in the treatment of special categories of mental illness such as schizophrenia. The special issues in the treatment of children through play techniques as well as group methods of treatment with both youngsters and adults have become a significant focus for study.

When we examine psychotherapeutic practice, we begin to think that there are as many kinds of therapy as there are therapists. On the face of it, this would appear to be a confused and unwholesome situation. Actually, this is an inevitable condition that grows out of the very dynamics of psychotherapy. We must remember that the basic aspect of the therapeutic situation is the development of an interpersonal situation within which the patient feels free to express himself. How may we identify the major features of psychotherapy? One way this can be done is by describing how the patient and clinician meet each other and the respective attitudes toward human beings they bring into the consultation room.

The patient generally comes with very mixed feelings about seeking help, for he feels that even if coming for help is necessary, doing so means he is a failure. Squeezed by his deep conflicts and upset by his sense of failure in not having himself solved his problems, the patient can hardly recognize the tremendous courage it takes to embark on a voyage of self-examination and self-discovery. The very lack of self-respect, which is such a significant feature of his symptoms, is expressed by the feeling that he is a coward. This attitude is reinforced by a cultural ideal of independence in which men and women are expected to stand on their own feet under all circumstances. The patient's self-beratement for being so dependent is accompanied by seemingly opposite expectations. The patient often strongly demands that the therapist be an all-seeing and all-knowing individual who can fathom by some magical procedures the causes of his distress. Furthermore, the patient likens his suffering to a thorn in his side that the clinician is expected to excise in very short order. In short, the distressed individual expresses his low self-esteem by believing himself to be a coward and by viewing the clinician as a worker of quick miracles.

How does the clinician view the patient and respond to these expectancies? Primarily by a respect for the individual compounded of knowledge about people obtained from his repeated witnessing of the struggle human beings have made for a more dignified way of life. He has become convinced that people are heroic when given the opportunity to join an alliance against illness. The therapist knows that the human personality is the most complex development man can study and he approaches the person with the humility necessary in the face of complexity. The patient, impatient with himself, tries to deny the truth of his own intricacy by driving for simple answers and by denying the meaningfulness of his conflicts. The clinician knows that tension, striving, and conflict are the very qualities that define living. The very forces the patient wants so much "to get rid of" are the forces that ultimately will be used in taking initiative and responsibility. The clinician reveals his respect by his deep patience with the difficulties that stand in the way of self-knowledge. The infant has become a human being through a long period of development in which biological, familial, and cultural forces have joined together. A tremendous amount of energy has gone into the formation of the person's character. Many experiences, long forgotten, have contributed to the emergence of the person as he is today. To assume simple, quick, ready and permanent solutions for the human situation is itself the crudest insult man can direct at himself. He is repeatedly searching for certainty. But his very nature and potentiality for reason and intelligence tells him too that the seemingly easy path is the false one. The clinician shows his deepest respect for the individual by helping him turn toward the many sources of his excessive and impeding conflicts. He takes an objective approach to the problem by, in effect, saying to the patient, "Let us explore yourself, let us together discover the beliefs you have made which are true and the beliefs that are false. Let us learn how you have denied parts of yourself and how you have clung to other parts which have led to distress. This isn't an easy undertaking and it often is seemingly protracted. You will become discouraged by this task and at moments may even feel alone in it. But the strength you will find in yourself to do this work will be renewing and liberating." Perhaps the most significant way in which the clinician reveals his respect for the patient is in the recognition that there is great pain in self-discovery, and hesitation in self-revelation. Change and growth of any kind are always accompanied by anxiety and pain in some degree. The emergence of both painful and liberating feelings which the patient has worked so hard through his life to deny, comes about through struggle and in the face of strong resistance. The therapist trusts the individual in his capacity to develop the confidence to face the self he has in fear so long avoided. The manner of revelation is determined by the very necessity of his own individuality and is the patient's to demonstrate in his own way and his own rate. Through these various facets which mark the attitude of respect for the person, the clinician and the patient learn to meet the most difficult challenge ever uttered by one man to another, "Know thyself."

THE CLINICIAN AND HIS SCIENCE

The clinician applying his knowledge to a practical problem is confronted with a number of issues. These problems stem partly from the nature of science and partly from the attempt to combine a service with a research orientation.

Service and Research

When the clinician pauses to assay the validity of the skills and tools he is using in practice and applies the yardstick of experimental methods, he often feels that his practice rests on shaky ground. Though he may have personal confidence in the usefulness of the Rorschach Test, for example, he is also aware of the relative paucity of more strictly controlled studies which would support the interpretations he makes of the patient's ink blot productions. He is, so to speak, caught between the wish to serve as it is expressed in a willingness to use a practical tool with all its limitations, and his research training which has bred in him a low tolerance for untested guesswork. At the moment of service he is aware that some of the ideas, even very cherished ones, which now influence his practice may turn out in the near future to be misleading if not downright false. In fact, he is dedicated to the discovery of new insight and to the establishment of firmer foundations for knowledge through research, even though it often makes his practice outdated. He is helping people and is also searching so that what he finds may reflect on the adequacy of practice. This dual attitude is a very difficult one to maintain. Yet it is crucial for those whose faith resides in the inexhaustibility of things to be discovered. Such people are not easily shaken by the double need to make do what we have and at the same time, entertaining new ideas and repeatedly learning new things from their patients and their colleagues. On the face of it there seems to be a contradiction between a service and a scientific point of view. However, we may more readily see this outlook as one of the fundamental requirements of good practice, whether experimental or clinical. The clinician demonstrates a courage in the face of uncertainty, which is also the key to any scientific undertaking. The practitioners' attitude of repeatedly attempting to objectify, conveys itself to the patient and helps him face the future, which is so much more uncertain than the past.

The Clinical Research Approach

The aim of science, as of all forms of inquiry, is the formulation of general laws which in explaining the past, provide a base for predicting the future. The scientist, in his search for generalization, has more recently recognized that laws defining cause and effect relationships can't be stated in absolute terms. Modern science has come to mistrust statements which deal with absolute truths and established facts. The results of observation and test, the special stamp of science, are put in the form of statements of probability and not of certainty.

The psychologist is concerned with the "facts" and "laws" of human behavior. When he wishes to predict behavior he must decide which kind of data should be used in making predictions. He can't avoid formulating a theory about human nature. Without some idea as to what he was looking for, the psychologist would see very little in his attempt to see everything. The clinical psychologist makes inferences about the individual's inner states or his private world such as unconscious anxiety, levels of frustration, conflict, self-perception, patterns of defense, and resolution of conflict. These concepts are not easily defined. They refer to experiences which are not directly observable, which are difficult to quantify, and even more difficult to isolate and vary in the traditional experimental method. Isolating single factors and manipulating one variable at a time seems to the clinical psychologist to do violence to the essential nature of personality. This attitude makes some sigh with impatience and exclaim that the clinician is defensively resorting to vague and mysterious entities as an excuse for not being more systematic and rigorous. The clinician has a number of answers to this argument, one being that often what is most impressive about people is the very nature of a creative act and the apparently simple fact of growth and change.

The clinician in doing research, can, of course, abandon the theories about personality which deal with elusive ideas in favor of a system which calls for more easily quantified data. This he isn't willing to do. He rather chooses to do a number of things to help him objectify and validate his theories. For example, (1) the clinician spends a great deal of time in checking his interpretations with others. This is done through seminars and consultation with his colleagues where different points of view on case data are thoroughly discussed. (2) He attempts to constantly reformulate his theories so they become more communicable to others and thus more susceptible to test. At first sight, many of his hunches may seem unrelated to the idea of others but more precise definition and further amplification leads to better communication with his fellow scientists. (3) The clinician also attempts to apply the insights he obtains in the consulting room to the explanation and prediction of behavior. This involves him in coöperative research with other social scientists. Such coöperative attempts frequently take the clinician back to the laboratory. Here, after careful analysis of clinical postulates, he develops methods for experimental testing of the organizing factors in personality. He can, for example, demonstrate how different types of people will differ in the way they express a similar physiological drive. (4) He looks intensively at the task of developing different devices for gathering diagnostic and therapeutic data. This includes such things as the use of sound recordings of therapy hours, the formulation of new projective tests, and the use of various scoring and rating techniques. He seeks the assistance of statisticians who can devise methods for analysis of patterns found in single cases. (5) Finally, and perhaps most importantly, we must again mention and emphasize the central significance of the clinician. The awareness of the need for self-evaluation and the recognition of one's own projections are of importance. Continuing work in improving the clinician's training and the evaluation of the factors within himself that make for successful service is a crucial area for research. The clinician's personal attitudes determine more than other factors what theory he acts upon in his work with human beings.

General Laws and Uniqueness of Personality

In the student's first brush with statistics he is likely to have been puzzled by the interpretation of a correlation coefficient. If, for example, it has been found that a significant relationship exists between the IQ and grades in college, he may conclude that given a certain IQ we can know what grades the person will make. He soon learns, however, that a statistical law does not tell us what the degree of correlation is between two factors for any specific person in the population. He learns that a statistical statement refers to groups and not to individuals. The student interested in a single individual's behavior may then wonder about the utility of such laws. He may become even more discouraged with any search for mathematical statements of cause and effect relationships when he is taught in personality courses about the uniqueness of each individual. He may very well conclude that since each person is unique, then generalizations about people are impossible. Clinical scientists have been concerned with this methodological issue and have called it the nomethetic (science of general laws)-idiographic (science of the individual case) problem. How can this apparent dilemma be understood and recognized as a false one?

An examination of the meaning of the term *uniqueness* may clarify the problem. (1) We need to remember that communication is made possible by the fact we invent symbols to stand for a class of events. We could not begin to talk with one another unless we used ideas with some level of abstraction. Classification of events, each one of course being somewhat unique in the sense of different, is a step that can't be circumvented in any form of description. Your first impact on me is my recognition that you are a human being different than others, yes, but having enough similarity so that we can learn to share with each other. (2) We can't really assimilate or recognize a new event until we can bring it into some relationship with what is known. The novel event, when it forces itself upon our attention, does so because we measure its difference from a relatively known class of events. Saying this is unlike what I have known before, implies a general statement comprehending the known. In other words, uniqueness itself can't be recognized without recognizing general laws. (3) When we speak of a person's trait as unique, we often mean that as yet it is undiscovered in others. This is mainly due to insufficiently refined analysis. We may at a later date discover the same attribute, to a lesser degree, in other people. For example, some of our deepest insight about everyday normal behavior comes from research on the abnormal individual who has a particular tendency common to all, but more extremely developed. (4) Since all of an individual's attributes are functionally interrelated, uniqueness often refers to the particular way these attributes are organized. What gives us our individuality, then, is not that we are composed of differing qualities, but the patterning of these traits is different for all of us. From the observer's point of view, he identifies the traits through analytic procedures. However, his task also involves a synthesis of his observations into a meaningful whole. The creative act, as a reorganization of existing quantities into a fresh experience, is as important a function of the scientist as of the artist. It is basically in this sense of creative synthesis that we can accurately speak of uniqueness.

This brief discussion of the relationship between the search for general laws and the uniqueness of personality may be summed up by answering the question, Is clinical psychology an art or a science? If we recognize that advance in knowledge always involves both the analytic and synthetic act the question becomes unnecessary. Idiographic and nomethetic approaches to the study of human beings are not in opposition but are complementary and inextricably bound up in the very nature of objective thought.

Science and Values

Until recently, science and ethics were considered to be independent spheres of inquiry. The objectivity required of the scientist, it was held, prohibited his making value judgments. This view is clearly based on a misconception of the scientist's work, as has been brought home to us by recent events in the field of atomic energy and by scientists themselves reporting on the process of their own work. They have pointed out that the very problem chosen for investigation itself involves a value judgment. However, for the clinical psychologist, the issue of the relationship between science and value is a moot one. The clinician chooses to concern himself with the problems of human adjustment and with the alleviation of pain and distress. In doing so he makes a most critical value judgment about the worth of the individual. Moreover, in talking about adjustment, he must perforce answer the question, Adjustment to what? What does the psychologist have in mind when he speaks of mental health and the mature personality? His answers to these questions are the very criteria against which the entire fabric of the clinical psychologist's work is to be validated. Yet, it is only recently that clinicians have begun to state more positively the goals toward which the healthy personality moves. It is from his studies of the human struggle against disease that the clinician can define the specific aspirations and ideals which mark man as the only form of life consciously shaping his destiny. Without taking into account human efforts toward a better way of life, the clinician will only develop a theory of adjustment marked by sheer contentment and selfish isolation from other men. The clinician must also coöperate in the solution of social as well as personal problems, not only as a citizen but as a specialist, who constantly witnesses the costs in human suffering of neglect, callousness, and rampant expression of competitive and dominating urges.

Some Research Problems

In validating psychological instruments, the knottiest problem is the establishment of reliable and meaningful criteria which represent the variable to be predicted by the test. For example, a large proportion of studies on the validity of tests have taken as the validating criteria, classifications of psychopathology such as schizophrenia and the neuroses. These categories have been seriously challenged because of the low reliability from one classifier to another and the wide variability in symptomatic expression of the diseases. However, extensive clinical experience and research in the problems of pathology have made it possible to slowly improve the usefulness of psychological tests and the refinement of criteria of personality disturbance. Certainly many clinicians express strong confidence in the tests they use, which of course by itself doesn't prove validity.

AN ILLUSTRATIVE STUDY

When introducing a standardized test into the clinical situation, the psychologist assumes that the behavior of the patient in the testing situation is a valid indicator of his behavior and its determinants in every day life. The patient often is quite dubious—and common sense supports his querulousness—about the meaningfulness of responses to a series of blots or a series of pictures. He wonders, "How can you tell anything about my difficulties in getting along on the job from the fact that I say that this ink blot is a whirling top or that one a skinned animal with the head off?" Here the clinician has two related answers. One is a statement of theory. In principle, he tells us that the private world of the individual revealed in the samples of his fantasies and mental processes elicited by the tests is a basic determinant of behavior. The theoretical problem is to work out a series of hypotheses as to the connections between the real inner life of fantasy and the acted out life of reality. The second related approach stems from empirical research and practical experience. By means of controlled research, the clinician has discovered that some sets of responses tend to have certain meanings. Through experience, for example, he has found that an individual giving a number of ink blot responses in which people or objects fall, is responding like those who often are significantly concerned with feelings of loss of support, rejection, or desertion.

Ideally, the clinician begins research with a theoretical scheme defining the dimensions of personality he believes important. He infers a set of common needs and the common ways in which human strivings are translated into action as well as the major consequences of the frustration of these strivings. He must have in mind a picture of normal-abnormal processes of adaptation to inner and outer stress. With such a framework, he thus can put to the test of research, the adequacy of the data elicited by his instruments and techniques.

An illustration of this research orientation is a recent study by G. Blum, titled, "A study of the psychoanalytic theory of psychosexual development." The design of the research is atypical of most current research in diagnosis as it is concerned with validating a theory rather than a test. In doing so, Blum did develop a semi-projective device called "The Adventures of Blacky" which may yet prove to be an important addition to the clinician's diagnostic armamentarium. The Blacky Test was primarily created to investigate a major phase of psychoanalysis, the libido theory. In one way or another, many practicing clinical psychologists utilize conceptions that are closely related to psychosexual theory. Blum's work makes the attempt to evaluate this aspect of the clinician's orientation to the patient.

An outline of the design of this study can provide a picture of the different steps involved in carrying on systematic research in clinical psychology. (1) He had a series of cartoons drawn which portrayed a dog Blacky in various kinds of poses and situations with his family. These situations were assumed to represent the psychosexual problems of oral eroticism (Blacky is suckling), oral sadism (Blacky is chewing on a dog collar labeled "Mama"), guilt, castration anxiety, penis envy, positive identification, sibling rivalry, guilt feelings, positive ego ideal, and love objects. (2) The test was then given to groups of men and women who were asked to write a short paragraph telling what was happening in the picture and then to answer some multiple choice questions about each picture. (3) A system of scoring the qualitative responses and the answers to the questions was evolved. (4) The results were then subject to statistical test in terms of sex differences and the degree of correlation among the different psychosexual variables. (5) He examined the literature for formulations of psychosexual theory especially as advanced by Sigmund Freud and Otto Fenichel. He then compared these statements with the statistical results of his study.

The general findings were that in a large majority of instances the significant statistical results were significantly in agreement with the theoretical point of view propounded in the literature. More specifically, agreement between theory and test was found to occur in such areas as these: Females tend to be more oral sadistic than males and their relation to the mother is more ambivalent than the boy's relation to the father; the aim of being loved is more important to the woman than the aim of loving. Blum cautions against overgeneralization of the results for three reasons: the test itself has no clinical validity, the analysis was confined to statistically significant results, and the population of the research was restricted to college men and women. However, further work with the Blacky Test has begun to show favorable results when used as a clinical instrument.

THE NORMAL PERSON

When the clinical research worker approaches the task of predicting normal functioning, say, success in a profession, he is faced with even more formidable problems. The more normally operating personality appears to be much more elusive of description. We can say more about ill health than health. A most significant and comprehensive study has been recently carried out by a coöperating group of clinicians on just such a question of normal functioning. In this instance, an unusually exhaustive list of the clinician's favorite instruments was applied to the problem of predicting the performance of clinical psychologists themselves. The report covers a five-year project carried on in connection with the four-year doctoral training program sponsored by the Veterans Administration. The subjects numbered some three hundred graduate students in clinical training in about forty universities.

The techniques of the interview, autobiography, credentials of applicants, situation tests, and projective test devices, in which they had most confidence, appeared to be less adequate for predicting success in clinical psychology than some relatively simple objective test scores. This does not mean that these clinical methods should be discarded. What it does point up is that knowledge about everyday personality functioning is less detailed than that about pathology. Further, clinical techniques haven't been developed sufficiently to make accurate predictions of specific behavior and this problem is quite far from solution even when the clinician deals with psychopathology. Valid prognosis, or the prediction of future behavior of the patient, based on test results, has still to be attained. Describing the underlying problems of the patient is much less difficult than saying, for example, that the patient will profit from a certain form of psychotherapy.

THE TYPE OF THERAPY

Much of the richest material for students of personality has been contributed by psychotherapists' description and analysis of the search for a healthy self. These case reports have provided a wealth of hypothesis and knowledge about the inner life of human beings. However, in comparison with case material, there exists a real paucity of more systematic research on the psychotherapeutic process, on the relative effects of different forms of therapy and on the relative success of any specific technique. There are many reasons for this. Such problems as the difficulty and expense of collecting the raw data of the therapeutic interviews; the highly personal nature of the material; the difficulty in reaching agreement on the criteria for successful therapy; the issue of having a relatively constant situation from one case to another since the very nature of interpersonal relationships requires flexibility; the question of adequate control groups; the problem of collecting adequate data on a large enough sample of homogeneous cases; and finally the intricacy and complexity of the therapeutic situation, are stumbling blocks to systematic study. There also has been a great deal of resistance on the part of therapists to such a research approach. Many are convinced that the psychotherapeutic relationship just does not lend itself to statistical study and that case discussion is the only way for discovering the facts and improving method. As of the present, there is some justification for this point of view. Carl Rogers and his group who have been doing the most organized and comprehensive study of client-centered psychotherapy have recognized that their researches have as yet not had any direct influence on their therapeutic convictions or practice.

Let us then outline the design of an ambitious and systematic research program on the adequacy of therapy being carried on at the Counseling Center of the University of Chicago by Carl Rogers and his group. The overall design of the research includes the following steps: (1) Complete phonographic recordings are made of all interviews of clients in the research group. (2) A battery of psychological tests is administered before, immediately at the conclusion of, and six months after therapy. These tests include one in which the client, by sorting statements, can describe how he sees himself, how he would like to be, and what he thinks the ordinary person is like. This test is administered while the client is in therapy. At the same time, the therapist can also sort the statements in terms of how he thinks the client would arrange them. (3) The counselor makes a set of ratings on his impression of the outcome of therapy and the nature of the therapeutic relationship. (4) Interviews and questionnaires are used in a follow-up study.

The data are still being collected. Rogers, however, does illustrate the study by reporting the results of all the techniques used on one case which was successfully treated, as determined by the results of the tests. Some of the hypotheses being investigated are: (1) As measured by the Thematic Apperception Test, the number and intensity of conflicts will decrease and the TAT clinical diagnosis of the client will be more congruent with the client's own self-knowledge. This hypothesis does point to the problem of measuring depth of insight. (2) The individual's self-picture and his picture of what he would like to be will become more congruent as therapy proceeds. (3) The client's behavior, as perceived by himself, will move toward what experts would define as emotional maturity. (4) The client's attitudes, as measured by a paper and pencil test, will become less prejudiced, more democratic, with a lessened desire to change others.

Results of previous studies on client-centered therapy indicated that as measured by some physiological concomitants of frustration, clients do become less easily frustrated, or, as measured by indices of neuroticism on the Rorschach test, clients after therapy have significantly fewer such indications. It has also been demonstrated that as positive feelings about self increase, so do feelings about others. Again, much of these hypotheses and results do fit with what one would expect as a correlate of helpful treatment. However, the accumulation of objective verifications of these beliefs makes for a body of fact and data upon which a more insightful theory of personality may be erected. The work of these investigators has brought into sharper focus an important way of thinking about personality. The attention to the self-concept as a major determinant of behavior is a product of client-centered research and practice.

Another important study, by Fiedler, starts with the question of whether a particular school of therapy or the experience of the therapist was more influential in the way the therapeutic relationship proceeded. The results of this study indicated that the more experienced and better-trained therapists were in more agreement with experienced practitioners of other schools than with less qualified therapists of their own system. In other words, experts more closely succeed in establishing a relationship in which understanding, rapport, and free communication exist between patient and therapist. This work does raise a doubt about the usefulness of all the heated polemics among the defenders of this or that orthodoxy. We apparently need to attend more to the qualities in the individual that make him successful in the most intricate of human relationships.

THE CLINICIAN

What are some of the qualities that make for successful clinical work? We can turn to a study carried out by L. Luborsky as part of a larger project on the selection of psychiatrists. Since Luborsky worked on the problem of "The personalities of more and less successful psychotherapists," we might assume that his findings would apply to the clinical psychologist as well. Luborsky studied two groups of psychiatric residents, a "high" and "low" group, as evaluated for their clinical work by supervisors. He then used a variety of material as a basis for comparing these groups, such as test reports, background information, patient's opinions, and the process notes of psychotherapy. Forty qualities were found which differentiated the good therapists from the poor ones. Luborsky summarizes these findings by stating:

The better therapists are considerably more sensitive, and show more independence of thinking and judgment. They attract more respect from people; most people like them. They express themselves more appropriately. On the other hand, poor therapists either try to shut off all expressions of impulse, especially hostility, and this brittle control can rupture suddenly; or, oppositely, they are under-controlled, extremely insecure, spontaneous, and impulsive. The better therapists are also personally happier, more interested in their work, and can learn more easily to do it. They are self-developing people.[1]

One unexpected finding was that the highs were more subdued in the way they expressed their warmth so that they often impressed others as being quiet. Altogether, Luborsky's study cast a sharp challenge to a frequently expressed picture of the psychotherapists as it appears in the cartoons of popular humor magazines.

THE CLINICIAN AND HIS PROFESSION

A profession is also identified by its concern with its duties and responsibilities to the public. The increasing group consciousness of clinical psychology is being expressed in the development of stand- ards of training and practice, in the formulation of an ethical code, and in the definition of legal relationships. All these features are largely products of the post-World War II period.

Training and Experience

We have already discussed the recommended training program of the Committee on Training in Clinical Psychology. This com- mittee, initiated in March, 1947, by the American Psychological Association, has been also exercising another function with impor- tant implications. Primarily as a consequence of coöperation of the universities and the government in training clinicians the commit- tee has been evaluating the quality of the doctoral programs of the different schools. Each university has been rated on a three-point scale and a list of approved schools is published periodically in the *American Psychologist,* the "house organ" of the American Psychological Association. The effect of this activity is to introduce a degree of pressure on the schools to develop their programs along the lines conceived by the profession as a whole. However, the

[1] L. Luborsky, "The Personalities of More and Less Successful Psychotherapists," paper presented to American Psychological Association Meeting, Washington, Sep- tember, 1952, p. 6.

pressure has been very light and informal because the committee has seen its work as providing the opportunity for the entire profession to become acquainted with a variety of training procedures and thus discover how things might be done better. It was felt that imposing strict uniform practices would stifle the experimental approach in education, a value and practice the scientist does not yield very readily.

Another important development in establishing standards of training and practice has been the creation by the APA of the American Board of Examiners in Professional Psychology, incorporated in April, 1947. ABEPP administers examinations leading to the status of diplomate in three applied areas, Clinical, Counseling and Guidance, and Industrial. The candidates who apply need to have five years of postdoctoral experience, a major portion of which is in the area of specialization. The names of successful candidates are published annually in the *American Psychologist*. The full effect of the work of ABEPP will not be clear for some years to come. It is certain, however, that the diplomate status will become more valued as an indication of a level of training, experience, and practice toward which all members of the profession will aspire and that it will carry with it professional and economic rewards.

Legal Recognition

Quacks and charlatans have always attempted to capitalize on people's difficulties. Unfortunately, at present, the category psychologist, as listed, for example, in the yellow pages of the telephone directory, includes many unqualified individuals. This is largely so because there is no legal restriction on the use of the term *psychologist*. As the profession of clinical psychology has come of age, it has begun to press for incorporation into law of standards of professional competency. Social control of the activities of special groups always has been a recognized principle in a democracy, the test of the extent of regulation being the social effects of the practice. As we have learned more about the private worlds of individuals, it has become clear that unregulated tampering is damaging and destructive to the personal and social welfare of the individual. There are some who believe that in the long run, self-regulation through methods described above is the best and only sound way to educate the public in recognizing the able practitioner. This question is only one of the facets of the broader issue faced by a democracy, namely, just what combination of legal force and education should be used in effecting social change. Of course, a major portion of the responsibility must be accepted by the profession itself and acted upon through the daily work of its members. However, most do agree that some kind of legal safeguards must be established. This should be done not only for the protection of society, but primarily because certification and licensing is a potent device for directing the public's attention to the requirements for adequate professional care. It is also true that as a society becomes more complex, the public becomes less able to judge the adequacy of the "expert." The widening gap between the common sense of the man on the street and the sense of the student of special affairs is one of the real dilemmas of modern society. Legal safeguards are thus set up to protect the public from incompetency and from the impossible demands it makes in the attempt to free itself from the anxieties of everyday life.

Our form of government gives the right of regulation of professions to the states. State psychological associations have been at work attempting to initiate and formulate bills which would legally restrict the use of the term *psychologist*. Only those who have demonstrated a standard of training and experience conforming to the level of professional training incorporated in the universities would be permitted to call themselves psychologists. At present, only a few states have passed bills restricting the use of the term *psychologist*. It is quite likely that in the next decade a majority of states will have given some form of legal attention to the practice of clinical psychology. This will certainly occur if the profession itself expands and solidifies its own experience with increasing self regulation.

Space prohibits a fuller discussion of the question of interprofessional relations. However, it should be noted that it is particularly at the point of legal recognition that many of the problems of collaboration with other professional groups, such as psychiatry and social work, come most sharply into focus. The problem of defining and restricting psychotherapeutic practice has been extremely knotty. As a relatively new profession, clinical psychology has only begun to learn how to work together with other, more established groups and to learn how to define its role without defensiveness.

Professional Conduct

Any group serving people can't escape becoming involved in ethical problems. A profession is under real obligation to human beings to define its aspirations and to describe its rules. In 1947, the APA established a Committee on Ethical Standards in Psychology. This group, after investigating various methods for the formulation of an ethical code, decided to approach the question empirically. The entire membership of the association was requested to submit descriptions of incidents in which a psychologist made a decision having ethical implications. Over a thousand such incidents were subjected to analysis. The main categories of ethical standards that emerged from this work relate to the psychologist and the public, to the client, to the clinician's role as a teacher, to his research work, to his writing and publishing, and to his professional relationship. In September, 1952, the code was published and the APA voted to try the system for three years before official adoption. A study of the published code will richly reward the student with real insight as to how psychologists have translated their understanding of the complexities of human behavior into a guide for their own practical action.

CONCLUSION

This portrait of the field of clinical psychology has been drawn from various vantage points. The historical conditions which have provided the background of ideas for the clinician's work were first described. The program of training of the clinician was briefly summarized with special emphasis on self knowledge as central to his task. The clinician's relationship to his patient and to his science was then examined. Finally, the growth of clinical psychology as a definable profession was highlighted by a short sketch of the steps recently taken which are indicative of group consciousness on the one hand and a strong sense of responsibility to the public interest on the other.

One point of view has run through all of the material. The scientist and the clinician are not at opposite poles in their work but have the same basic attitude toward the problems they study. Certainly the clinical psychologist has developed other techniques besides the classical experimental procedures, in order to objectify his observations. Some have then concluded that the clinician is unscientific. Such criticism has not recognized that the quality of individual personality, its complexity and interdependence of its many aspects, demands different approaches to its study. The above qualification does not mean the absence of a rigorous scientific methodology but merely the use of a different type.

We can summarize this point in another way. Many of the most significant advances in the understanding of human beings have come out of the "living laboratory," in which the "subject" and "investigator" have collaborated in an attempt to bring about change in the subject. Detachment is a hallmark of the scientist. Yet we have seen that the role of participating observer, though very difficult to maintain, brings one closer to the very heart of human experience. Psychoanalysis, for example, is both a theory of personality and a form of therapy. Its significant contribution to mental science stems in large part from this very fact, that from the beginning of its development it was both. In his attempt to alleviate suffering, the clinician discovers what has contributed to man's being so much against himself. The help the clinical psychologist provides can well be called action research. This concept is borrowed from the field of social psychology where it was coined as a description of new approaches to the study of race prejudice through experiments in improving race relations. The term does highlight the fact that in the attempt to act upon social and personal disequilibrium the clinician-scientist comes to grips with the essential pieces in the puzzle of human conflict.

SUGGESTED READINGS

1. American Psychological Association, *Ethical Standards for Psychologists*. Washington: American Psychological Association, 1952, vol. II. This volume includes the ethical principles and illustrative problems and incidents used to develop the code.

2. Blum, G. S., A study of the psychoanalytic theory of psychosexual development, *Genet. psychol. Monogr.*, 1949, 39:3–99. An unusual study in its attempt to evaluate an important concept of clinical theory. It is especially valuable for its research method and for the introduction of another projective technique, the "Blacky Test."

3. Erikson, E., *Childhood and Society*. New York: Norton, 1950. An excellent presentation of psychoanalytic psychology. It is especially noteworthy for the author's tying in of values to developmental stages.

4. Fiedler, F., A comparison of therapeutic relationship in psychoanalytic nondirective and Adlerian therapy, *J. consult. Psychol.*, 1950, 14:436–445. One of a number of research reports on the question of the relative significance of the system of experience of the therapist in defining the ideal therapeutic relationship.

5. Kelly, E., and Fiske, D., *The Prediction of Performance in Clinical Psychology*. Ann Arbor: University of Michigan, 1951. An unusually comprehensive and carefully planned study on the problems of determining factors which make for successful performance. It serves as an excellent source book for those interested in a definition of the field of clinical psychology.

6. Louttit, C. M., The nature of clinical psychology, *Psychol. Bull.*, 1939, 36:361–389. An excellent brief account of historical sources and some of the major problems of modern clinical psychology.

7. Luborsky, L., The personalities of more and less successful psychotherapists, paper presented to American Psychological Association Meeting, Washington, September, 1952. The title of this study well expresses its content. It is one of the first more systematic attempts at defining the able therapist.

8. Maslow, A., Self-actualizing people: a study of psychological health, *Personality-Symposium,* No. 1, "Psychology of Values," April, 1950. A report of research in process on the dissection of the healthy personality. The description of the positive orientations of such people to themselves and to others is exceptional for its clarity and detail.

9. Raimy, V. C. (ed.), *Training in Clinical Psychology.* New York: Prentice-Hall, 1950. The report of a conference attended by seventy clinical psychologists involved in professional training. Their formulations very well provide a set of guiding principles for the developing profession.

10. Rapaport, D., *Diagnostic Psychological Testing.* Chicago: Year Book Publishers, 1945, 1946, vols. I, II. Though published as a report on extensive research on the clinical usefulness of a battery of tests, the major contribution is the richness of clinical hypothesis and the attempt at systematic statement of theory underlying the tests. Both volumes can serve as primary references for major clinical tools.

11. Research Staff, Counseling Center, *Studies in Client Centered Therapy.* Washington: Psychological Service Center Press, 1952. A preliminary report on a very large scale and long range program in research on psychotherapy, planned by Carl Rogers and his associates.

12. Watson, R., *The Clinical Method in Psychology.* New York: Harper, 1951. A very comprehensive treatment of the wide variety of methods and theories used in clinical practice. An excellent source book.

Chapter 11

Physiological Psychology

by BERNARD F. REISS

Orientation
  PHILOSOPHICAL ASSUMPTIONS
    Double-Aspect Concepts
    Interactionism
    Materialism

The Methodology of Physiological Psychology

Fundamental Biochemical Concepts and Their Psychological Significance
  AMINOS
  PROTEINS
  ENZYMES
  HORMONES
  VITAMINS

Fundamental Neurological Concepts and Their Psychological Significance
  THE NEURON
  THE SYNAPSE
  NEURAL CIRCUITS

Recent Trends in Physiological Psychology
  PSYCHOPHYSIOLOGY OF LEARNING
    Conditioning
    Cell-Assembly Theory and Learning
  ABNORMAL BEHAVIOR AND PSYCHOPHYSIOLOGY
    The General Adaptation Syndrome

Conclusion

Suggested Readings

ORIENTATION

Although the words *physiological psychology* seem to indicate a clear and easily understood combination, just what this field is and how it differs on the one hand from physiology and on the other from psychology, is by no means easy to ascertain. The term physiological psychology has occurred repeatedly in the history of psychological thought and experimentation. As will be seen shortly during the consideration of historical trends in the area, the words have remained the same but their meaning has been frequently changed and is still in a state of flux. Let us trace some of these changes in interpretation, since they reflect the rise and fall of new attitudes and approaches to a basic psychological problem, the relationship of so-called mental to overt behavior.

In the last quarter of the nineteenth century when psychology took its place as a separate and independent discipline in the structure of universities, physiological psychology was its baptismal designation. However at that time, the word *physiological* was used to indicate that the methods of the psychologist were similar to those of the more respected and orthodox science rather than to denote the content of the subject. The problems to be examined by these methods were those originating mainly from philosophical speculation. In other words, physiological psychology was neither physiology nor psychology as we know these sciences today but rather an attitude and a program. As psychology increased the territory which it claimed, and as it began to enlarge the scope of its descriptions to include more and more aspects of behavior, both program and attitude changed. The former became circumscribed and paid less attention to the larger areas of thought, language, and reasoning and more to the type of activity which was obviously neural in causation. This meant an emphasis on sensation, motor reactions, fatigue, and the like. So too, the attitude moved from a simple acceptance of physiological methods toward the postulation of what has been called psychophysical dualism or parallelism. This is a philosophical concept in which physiological events were seen as existing parallel to but not causal to behavioral events. The two were regarded as distinct but as exhibiting different phases of the same problem. In effect, psychologists therefore minimized physiological data and concentrated on mental or sensory operations.

With the rise of social science in the hierarchy of college and university studies, psychology also moved toward a new level of integration in which behavior was viewed as part of a broad social and cultural field. The resulting emphasis on environmental and cultural determinism brought physiological psychology to a minor place in both research and teaching. This period, which coincided roughly with the interval between the two World Wars, was characterized by the ascendancy of psychometry and social psychology. Theorizing and research on the physiological mechanisms of behavior were not generally considered of major importance.

It has been only in comparatively recent years that interest in physiological psychology has emerged from the doldrums. Several factors contribute to this change in status, not the least of which is the practical research work done on the demand of the armed services and allied agencies during World War II. The emergence of new methods and data in neurology also stimulated thinking in physiological psychology and helped to fertilize the productive activities of many psychologists. Today some of the most exciting research in psychology lies in its borderlands with neurology and physiology. We shall have cause to detail these lines of work as we proceed with our survey of the activities of the present period.

Philosophical Assumptions

A few words must be said about the underlying philosophical axioms of the field of our interest. It is a general observation in the evolution of a science that interest in the unexpressed assumptions of the science is low during its infancy. As the science becomes more sophisticated and develops beyond the point of description and cataloguing of data, recognition of the need for philosophizing comes to the fore. Further research and the derivation of general principles are seen to be dependent upon making explicit the basic assumptions previously either not acknowledged or not stated. So too in psychology, many experimentalists long felt compelled to assert their independence of any special philosophical bias or set of assumptions. It was held to be unnecessary and actually unhealthy for psychological research to concern itself with philosophical considerations. In part, this attitude resulted from the felt need to deny the original derivation of psychological problems from their philosophical ancestors. Another reason for the antispeculative attitude was the absence of sufficient, well-established data on which to base general theorems. Critical examination of the work of many psychologists however reveals the acceptance, without acknowledgment thereof, of definite assumptions and tenets.

Nowhere in psychology is there more need for evaluation of basic philosophy than in the area of physiological research. From the beginning of interest in the field, quite unique philosophical attitudes characterized the selection of what was to be studied, the method of investigation, and the interpretation of obtained data. It is possible to classify the basic positions that have been here taken into two general formulations. In the first place, the physiological psychologist has used as his focal point of departure the age-old problem of body-mind relationships. In the very statement of the relationship, there is implied a set of basic assumptions about the disjunctiveness of mental and physiological data. The combination, body-mind, asserts that there is both a difference and a relatedness which requires study.

The second source of ideological difficulty arises in part from the insecurity of psychologists as scientists in competition with practitioners of other disciplines. In order to demonstrate that psychology is really as precise and objective as are physics and chemistry, the experimentalist tried to adopt the methods of the physical scientists.

As a result, a trend has occurred which may be called *reductionism* or the explanation of complex psychological events by simple concepts derived from mechanical physics and atomistic chemistry.

In dealing with the first set of questions, those centering around the body-mind problem, three positions are possible. For the moment these will be called the double-aspect view; interactionism; and materialism. Other labels will be introduced as the discussion proceeds and as they are used by psychologists who have addressed themselves to the problem.

DOUBLE-ASPECT CONCEPTS

Historically seen, this viewpoint stems from the ancient Greek writer, Aristotle. In his system, form and matter constitute an inseparable but distinguishable combination. To translate this into modern terminology it is necessary merely to substitute mind for form and body for matter. Rephrased to bring Aristotle up to date, the system holds that mind is the functional aspect of the body organ, the brain. The effect of this theory on the methodology of physiological psychology has been to concentrate the effort of the experimenter on the laws governing the functioning part, the mind, and to minimize speculation and research on the organic phase. Where attention has been paid to the brain, there has been evolved a rather static picture of that organ, i.e., the brain was viewed as a kind of container for the mind with special compartments designated for special mental functions. Researchers looked for brain foci of vision, thinking, and other "mental" activities. Cellular structure and brain geography were thought of as the determining elements in such localization of function. Although research did provide a few identifications, in general the rich behavior equipment of the organism was left without an organic basis.

INTERACTIONISM

Second in terms of historical sequence is the variety of *dualism* called interactionism. It reached its most classical expression in the writings of the famous French mathematician-philosopher, René

Descartes (1596–1650). Here the separation of body and mind was clearly recognized and indeed was only a part of a much broader biological dualism. To Descartes, man was the only rational animal, all other biological forms existing on a mechanical basis, incapable of reason and the so-called mental faculties. "I reason, therefore I exist." So Descartes asserted the primacy of mind. In the second place, the philosopher separated the mind from the body not only schematically but also in terms of the laws under which each operated. Descartes, however, saw that some relationship had to be established for the parallel functioning of the two unities. He held that this took place through the control of the mind over the body by the pineal gland, which he believed operated as the master organ. The mind determined how the pineal gland controlled the mechanical forces or substances coursing through the nerves and blood vessels. Two effects of Cartesian thinking on physiological psychology are obvious. Since infrahuman animals are automata, they can be studied by the principles of physics and scientific experimentation, whereas logical analysis and philosophical reasoning furnish the methodology of research on human mental functioning. The problem of the existence of mind versus body was settled. They were two and distinct. All that remained was to show how one influenced the other. The effect of this type of thinking on present-day psychology has been tremendous although not many workers in the field are willing openly to admit the interactionist nature of their assumptions.

As an example of a current dualistic system, we may profitably spend some time on the thinking of the Gestalt psychologists. Köhler, Koffka, and other "field" theorists have devoted considerable time and space to expositions of their philosophical orientation. Underlying all Gestalt considerations is the relationship of "molar" or large, organized groups to "molecular" or specific, elemental determinants. In dealing with the body-mind problem, Wertheimer, Koffka, and Köhler have proposed to solve the antithesis by the formulation of a concept called *isomorphism*. Literally translated, this means equality of form or structure. In the frame of reference of physiological psychology, isomorphism implies that physiological events are the same as behavioral data but operative at a different level. What happens in the nervous system, receptor organs, and effectors is basically a duplicate of what happens in the perceptual experience of the subject. The Gestaltists argue that their finding of patterns, fields, or principles of organization of mental events requires a similar organization in the physiological field. The two fields, psychological and physiological, are separate in terms of content but identical in structure. The Gestalt that exists in behavior on the psychological side necessitates the same type of Gestalt explanation on the physiological level. In terms of practical work, this point of view makes physiological research interesting but not essential. The psychologist is left to operate in his own area without the need to undertake any correlations between physiological and psychological research.

When this approach is examined historically, it can be shown that the concept of psychological fields has been developed from previously existing concepts in the neurophysiological world. Hence, if the latter cannot be shown to exist, the psychological structure also falls. Köhler's early theories depended upon the demonstration of physical gestalten. In his more recent thinking, he postulates neural fields but does not give any independent evidence for their existence. Hence, we are at the present time on the horns of a dilemma. The isomorphic position cannot be validated because one-half of the necessary data is absent. The Gestalt psychologists who have concentrated their research almost wholly on the facts of psychological behavior, therefore, in practice, operate as if they were as nonphysiological as other double aspect theorists (dualists).

MATERIALISM

As can be seen from the name, the materialist position holds that all phenomena of behavior are to be explained in terms of the operation of material concepts. It is here that we find the original antithesis of the Gestalt psychologists, namely the distinction between "molecular" and "molar," a source of much debate. Watson, the founder of the behaviorist or *mechanistic materialist* movement, was a firm proponent of the molecular viewpoint in that he believed in an atomic analysis of behavior. In other words, all behavior can be reduced to the operation of simple elements which Watson found to be reflexes. These were described materialistically in terms of neural arcs and sensorimotor connections. Consciousness was ruled out altogether by denying its relevance to psychological study. At the present time such a reductionist and absolutist denial of the importance of organization is inconsistent with recent facts both in neurophysiology and psychology.

In contrast to Watsonian mechanistic materialism is a group of attitudes which can best be brought together under the label of *somatic determinism.* The so-called mental data in this viewpoint are epiphenomena or by-products of the somatic factors or processes. Consciousness is a result of the operation of the brain, nervous system, bodily biochemistry, and other physiological processes. For the somatic determinist, research involves first the study of the basic causal events, the somatic phase, and only secondarily if at all the phenomena of the effect, namely the "mental" material. It is argued that mental happenings do not exist in a never-never land of their own but must have a reality in something material and organic. The latter must be the physiological functioning of the organism. A conscious behavioral act may be described in purely psychological terms but such a description does little more than serve as a definition which delimits what is being studied. That is to say, thinking as a purely psychological act is only a description of behavior in terms that allow the experimenter to carry on. In order to explain thinking, to construct laws of thinking, hypotheses, or constructs, it is necessary to assume that the psychological event not only goes off in a physiological frame of reference but is in actuality a physiological process. An electric light may be described as glowing when a switch is turned. Its glow as well as its dependence upon the switch can be explained only if the glow and the ignition are understood to be electrical phenomena. So in psychology, we can describe the behavior of the rat in a maze in terms of its relationship to the

reward received in the goal box. The explanation for error elimination, however, requires some statement of what takes place in
the organization of the physiological processes in the animal, specifically in its nervous and endocrine system.

Certain dangers are inherent in the position of the somatic deter-
minists despite the generally sound emphasis on materialism. One
of the pitfalls is the tendency to *reductionism,* to see all behavior
as describable in terms of simple physiological constructs such as
the cell. This is the error which was basic in Watson's position and
is no less dangerous when restated in more modern dress. A botanist
long ago pointed out that the cells do not make the plant but the
plant makes the cells. Now while it is true that the nature of the
whole sometimes determines the nature of the parts, that the plant
makes the cells, it is also true that this organizing function is made
possible by properties of the elements. There are chemical com-
pounds within the cell which are necessary for the existence of the
plant which makes the cells. In other words there is no possibility
of a twofold relationship. Scientific thinking must recognize the
existence of paradoxical or antithetical possibilities within the same
system. The whole is not independent of the nature of its parts nor
are the parts sufficient to explain all the qualities of the whole. A
scientist must seek the interrelationships of parts and wholes. Physiological psychology must understand the nature of the neural element as well as the new qualities that emerge when these elements
are combined in certain ways. The new qualities that are produced
when elements combine have both a continuity with their components and a discontinuity which is novel. Understanding or insisting
on a molar explanation or on a molecular explanation alone will
not suffice for a modern theoretical system nor for current research.
A conceptual scheme which will see continuity and discontinuity as
two interdependent aspects of the same problem is the only solution.
Such a view has been set forth recently under the heading of levels
of integration. How may it apply to physiological psychology?

The concept of *integrative levels* starts with the assumption that
new levels of complexity in the continual evolution of matter are

superimposed on individual units by the organization and integration of these units into a single system. Wholes on one level may become parts on a higher one. Knowledge of the laws governing behavior at one level, although necessary for the understanding of behavior at a higher level, does not usually make prediction of higher-level phenomena possible simply on the basis of data from the lower level. Each level is in many respects a unique organization which requires appropriate techniques of research and examination. The principles of organization in a lower-level situation do not apply to behavior at a higher level. Between higher and lower levels are intermediate stages called *mesoforms*. In these, one can see the origins of higher forms and the prerequisite changes in the lower ones.

Part-whole relationships are seen as dependent upon the level of organization. *Both the isolation of parts of a whole and their integration into a new system are equally essential problems for scientific investigation.* The concept of integrative levels does not assert the primacy of the whole over the part nor vice versa. Neither reductionism nor vaguely defined integrative approaches such as dynamics or holism can be used exclusively. The parts must be studied but complex phenomena have unique characteristics not predictable from the structure of the parts. However, the novel features of the complex cannot be explained by a mystic, nonmaterial assertion of inherent wholeness independent of the organizing properties of the parts. The properties of the whole are never independent of those of the component parts. Nor do the boundaries of lower and higher levels form tightly segmented compartments. The mesoforms exist in their own right and are the more interesting since they show properties of both higher and lower levels, thus pointing the way to the transformations which occur in the transition from level to level.

In the field of biological events, to cite a concrete example, the conception of integrative levels does not regard a living organism simply as a machine composed of parts whose descriptions can be summated into a description of the organism. Cells present a problem not encountered in test-tube experimentation upon the elements which compose a cell. The molecules composing a cell are affected in their behavior by their participation in the integration of cellular activity. In the organism, what we know about the behavior of an individual cell is interesting and helpful but research shows that such functions are vitally changed by the integration of cells into a system or organism. For instance, the ectoderm cells which normally form the belly skin tissue can be translated from an embryo salamander to a place over the organizer for the mouth of a frog in a frog embryo. These transplanted cells then develop as mouth parts such as teeth rather than skin. They are, of course, salamander and not frog teeth.

The same argument runs over into the higher levels of organized matter, the psychological and social. An organism in isolation behaves quite differently when it is a member of a population. Schneirla, working in the field of animal psychology, has demonstrated that the behavior of a colony of army ants is much more than the sum of the behaviors of its constituent members. One cannot predict the behavior of an ant in a colony from data gathered on the ant in isolation. It can almost be said that the individual ant has no behavior outside of its interrelations within the colony. Studies now in progress show that what is called maternal behavior or maternal "instinct" in the white rat is dependent upon the experience of the mother in a material and social environment. When prevented from seeing cage mates and even from becoming acquainted with a large section of its own body, nursing and retrieving of the young, newly born animals disappears. Similarly, access to food pellets, nesting material, and other manipulable objects is necessary for complete care of offspring. When these environmental variables are absent, the young are not suckled nor are nests built. If one were to describe maternal behavior in terms of its endocrine elements alone or if one were to assume that an animal brought up by itself was an experimental unit, it would be difficult to conceive of the experimental designs described above. Only when the individual organism is seen as a part of an integrated group can the researcher approach an adequate experimental treatment of behavior. In other words, the properties of the lower level and of the higher level must both be considered.

In a sense, physiological psychology is a mesoform stage of biological science. The data from physiological study of cells, organs, tissues, and systems represent the lower level. The psychological behavior of the organism in its material-social environment may be conceived as structurally higher. Within physiological psychology we may expect to see new physiological phenomena as we work on the one hand with animals in their daily routine within the population of their species mates and on the other with man within the organized society which is his distinguishing characteristic. What the eye sees may be quite different from what the person, the I, sees while functioning on a social, integrative level. The neurological processes in the two situations, the organ and the organism situation, may be somewhat different and require different research techniques and interpretations.

THE METHODOLOGY OF PHYSIOLOGICAL PSYCHOLOGY

It is sometimes said that the way in which a scientist works determines the nature of his science. Nowhere is this statement as misleading as in physiological psychology. Because of its position as a mesoform, its research methods must include those valid for the investigation of the lower or simpler levels as well as the new techniques required by the more complex and emergent higher level. The study of behavior is dependent in the first place on the nature of the response systems of the organism, its sensory, nervous, and motor machinery. However these systems operate in a double environmental setting, internal and external. By internal environment is meant the fluid and biochemical substances necessary for adequate functioning both of organs and organism. Here are included mainly the metabolic and hormonal processes and secretions. The external environment consists of the material social and nonsocial conditions for effective behavior.

In general, the methodological preference of physiological psychologists is for experimentation. A hypothesis is set up and the variables involved in its testing are explicated. Experimentation then proceeds by the controlled study of the variables both in isolation and in combination. The experimenter is able to manipulate the variables and to correlate the results of his manipulation with the behavioral outcomes. It is at this stage that a serious difficulty arises. Since experimentation in many instances requires interference with the physiological status of the organism, human beings may not be accessible as subjects and the work is done on animals. Can generalization be made from animal to human? Within the limits of experimentation, this question can be only partially answered. If the hypothesis is tested on a wide range of animal types and the conclusions are consistent from level to level, continuity into the human can be postulated with some reasonableness. Another approach is also possible. Where it has been already established that there is a structural or functional identity between a human characteristic and a specific animal form, that characteristic can be used as the basis for experimentation on the lower forms and extrapolated to the human. For instance, it is fairly well established that the basic amino acid requirements of the white rat and the human being are comparable. Hence we can use this identity for further work on the rat with the expectation that it will allow applicability to the human.

Where this type of extrapolation is not possible, it is necessary to resort to what has been called the clinical method. Here one is faced with the initial fact of physiological disorder. It is not relevant at this point to determine whether the disorder is the result of organic or environmental factors. The starting point is the disorder and the end result is the relationship between the malfunctioning patient and the locus of the difficulty. One of the early illustrations of this approach is the case of a man studied in 1861 by a physician, Broca. The presenting symptom was inability to talk. Nothing else showed up on rigorous examination. The patient died shortly after the initial examination. Postmortem study of the brain showed a lesion or injury in the third frontal convolution and the correlation of speech with brain locus was made.

In more recent years, the clinician has been responsible for the appearance of a new medical field, psychosomatic medicine. Here the correlation is between environmental factors and disorder states. Many patients seen by medical practitioners develop symptoms because of the conditions of their living relationships with other humans. The study of psychosomatic medicine has provided many interesting correlations between a precipitating environmental stimulus and physiological dysfunction. However, little information is at present available about the intervening mechanism which translates experienced difficulty into organic disorder such as stomach ulcer or headache.

One other method deserves special mention. This may properly be called the comparative approach. It seeks, like the rest of the methods, to correlate structure with function. Variation in structures such as nerves, sense organs, muscles, and glands occur as a result of evolutionary change. If one observes the behavioral differences in the animals showing evolutionary structural changes, one may reach conclusions comparable to those arrived at by surgical techniques which correlate structure and function. The difficulties in this method lie in the analysis of the separation of the structural variable dependent on evolution. An illustration may be given here. It has been shown in the animal world that as the importance of the frontal cortex grows, the degree of dependence of sexual behavior on the endocrine gland products decreases. Sexual activities such as mating become less fixed, more variable, and less dependent upon specific hormones as the animal evolves more forebrain. Such correlations between level of behavior and the evolutionary status of the nervous system are limited for the present to studies of mammalian forms. Occasionally one can see a direct relationship between a phase of behavior and nervous system but our knowledge is still restricted both on the psychological and physiological side. For instance, the pony is known to be very sensitive to olfactory (smell) stimuli. It examines the world nasally. The representation of the olfactory nerve in the cerebral cortex is likewise extensive. Although we can see several large differences in the type of nervous system evolved through the zoological realm, we do not see any systematic concomitant changes in behavior. There are invertebrates which do better on adaptational tests than lower vertebrates. The comparative method is stimulating but at present still young in its inclusiveness.

FUNDAMENTAL BIOCHEMICAL CONCEPTS AND THEIR PSYCHOLOGICAL SIGNIFICANCE

In viewing the behavior of organisms as evolving along lines or levels of integration, it was apparent that complete understanding of behavior involved both a knowledge of lower or simpler levels as well as the phenomena of the psychological level. The contribution of biochemistry, seen here as a lower-level study, is a necessary component of the understanding of the functioning of the internal environment and the nervous system. The term *lower* must not be misunderstood. The biochemistery of gland and nervous system is indeed complex but its complexity is only a part of the manifold which we are studying. It is therefore a prior part which we call a lower level. The total mass of data pertinent to psychology in the area of biochemistry is tremendous and it will be possible here merely to sketch some ways in which the material affects psychology.

Aminos

The life, death, and reproduction of organisms is dependent upon the transformation of food into bioelectrical energy. In this process, certain substances are of fundamental importance. The amino acids are the building blocks of which one of the major dietary requirements, protein, is made. Within the body, the amino acids can be divided into essential and nonessential groups. Essential amino acids are those which are not synthesized directly by mammals but must be present in dietary protein in order to allow growth and maintenance of health. Ten essential amino acids have been identified. In one study it was shown that diets which were deficient in a specific essential amino acid caused an impairment in the learning of a maze by the rat. Glutamic acid, a nonessential amino, has recently been found to reduce fatalities from sound-induced shock in male mice.

Various changes may affect the amino acid composition of the organism and thereby produce new products of fundamental importance to behavior. For instance, adrenalin and ephedrine are products of amino acids. Adrenalin is, of course, the hormone secreted by the adrenal gland and is of importance in the control of emergency functions of the organism and in emotions. Spermine, an amino derivative, is present in semen and gives it a characteristic odor. Research on rats indicates that this and other sex-specific odors are important determinants of various so-called instinctive acts. A female rat, prevented from smelling her own sexual areas from an early age to maturation, pays no attention to her young after parturition. In other words, experience with the odor of a part of the organism is an important element in what is commonly looked upon as instinctive maternal and sexual behavior. The amino acid is the specific cause of the odor and hence an element in the complete understanding of the behavior in question.

Proteins

Amino acids constitute the basic material of the important dietary element called protein. Proteins can be grouped into two major classes, the simple and the conjugated. The former consists chiefly of arrangements of amino acid units. The second group is formed by the combination of amino acid and an inactive chemical necessary for the effective action of the protein. Examples of simple proteins are the albumins, such as insulin, and the globulins, which include neuroglobulin, necessary for nerve activity, and thyroglobulin, a component of thyroid tissue. Conjugated proteins are particularly important constituents of such body elements as blood cells (hemoglobin), the male sex hormone stimulator (gonadotropin), and the cell-nuclei proteins. Studies have shown the importance of general protein, as a part of the diet, in the behavior of a variety of animals. High protein diets make animals more sensitive to a wide variety of shock-producing stimuli. Inheritance is also basically a protein process. Genes are nucleoprotein complexes whose rearrangements during reproduction are accompanied by chemical changes. Knowledge of the chemical processes in inheritance is getting to be a fundamental part of our basic information about behavior of the developing organism.

Enzymes

An enzyme is a catalyst, produced by living cells, which initiates and organizes complex chemical change in cells. This change is called metabolism. A catalyst, it will be remembered, is a substance which alters the speed of a chemical reaction without itself being destroyed or permanently changed. Enzymes can be recognized chemically by their names which predominately carry the suffix -*ase*. Among the factors which affect the efficiency of enzymes are temperature, hydrogen ion concentration, which is a measure of acidity or alkalinity, the concentration of the enzyme, and such external elements as x-rays, light, and other forms of radiant energy. In man, a recessive gene inhibits the action of an enzyme which oxydizes phenylpyruvic acid. The result of this inhibition is feeble-mindedness known as phenylpyruvic oligophrenia. Thus enzyme activity is of direct interest to the physiological psychologist.

Hormones

The endocrine or ductless glands secrete their chemical products directly into the bloodstream. These products are called hormones and exert their influence on behavior in a multiplicity of ways although, characteristically, they affect organs and tissues at a distance from the gland which liberates them. Some substances have been called hormones which are not manufactured by the endocrine glands. The nerve endings produce acetylcholine and sympathin and embryonic tissues manufacture substances, all of which behave like hormones. Like the enzymes, hormones play an important role in regulating metabolism.

Many individual facts about the various hormones and their effects are known but possibly the most important phase of hormone activity is the interrelationship and interdependence of functioning of many endocrine products. The term tropic hormone has been used to describe the situation. By it is meant a hormone which stimulates another endocrine gland to produce its specific secretion. This typifies one kind of interrelationship. Another type of interaction is the multiple stimulation of an organ by hormones from different glands. From the standpoint of the physiological psychologist, the complex, interlocking linkages among hormones present experimental problems of great difficulty. It is not possible to speak in most instances of single causation but one must deal with an integrated system composed of many parts. For this reason, we shall illustrate the role of the internal environment in various fields as we go along rather than point out specific relationships at this point.

Vitamins

Here again we deal with substances that act as catalysts in various metabolic and growth processes as well as in psychological actions. Vitamins are not synthesized by the organism but must be supplied in the diet. They exist in minute quantities in certain foods and are generally divided into two groups, the fat-soluble and water-soluble. Table 11.1 indicates the literal and chemical designation and some facts about their function.

Vitamins are necessary for the general healthy functioning of the organism and consequently for all psychological processes. Studies of specific relationships between behavioral data and vitamin deficiency have been made. A group of young rats was made vitamin B–deficient during their first two weeks of life by feeding their mothers a vitamin-deficient diet. This was continued until the rats were weaned and then the diet of the young rats themselves was made vitamin B–deficient. After a one-week return to a normal diet, the animals were trained in a water maze. Their results were compared with two other groups. One was bred and fed on a normal diet. The other was brought up with a thiamin deficiency (vitamin B_1). It turned out that the thiamin-deficient and the vitamin B complex–deficient groups were both inferior to the normal group in maze

TABLE 11.1. Some Vitamins and Their Behavioral Effects

Letter Designation	Chemical Designation	Behavioral Effect
A	Carotene or Axerophthol	Anti-night blindness. Plays a role in photochemical processes
B_1	Thiamin	Antineuritis
B_2	Riboflavin	Growth
B_6	Pyridoxin	Causes convulsions in dogs, rats, and pigs
	p-Aminobenzoic acid	Causes promotion of growth in chicks, lactation in rats
E	Tocopherol	Antisterility. Causes degeneration of sperm-producing male tissue, resorption of fetus in female
H	Biotin	Causes loss of appetite, fatigue, and muscle pain
P-P	Niacin or nicotinic acid	Antipellegra and accompanying symptoms of anxiety, confusion, and dementia

learning and relearning. So here again the interrelation among biochemical factors is seen to be of significance for a complete explanation of behavioral processes.

FUNDAMENTAL NEUROLOGICAL CONCEPTS AND THEIR PSYCHOLOGICAL SIGNIFICANCE

The previous section has described basic concepts for the psychologist in what may be called the metabolic system. Of equal importance are the events of the neuromuscular system. This complex is a systematic interrelation of mechanisms which translate stimuli from the internal and external environment into action. Three major divisions of the system are generally recognized: the receptor, adjustor, and effector processes. External energy in the form of light (radiant energy), sound (kinetic energy), temperature, and chemical change acts upon specially constructed selectors known as sense organs which, in their turn, transform stimulus-energy into bioelectric change or "nervous" energy. Thereupon, under certain conditions, nerves, activitated by the receptors, propagate the bioelectric changes to the spinal cord and brain. In these areas, multiple changes and adjustments of energy direction are made. The changes are further propagated along other nerves to the effector organs, the glands and muscles. At this stage, a retransformation of bioelectric to kinetic energy produces action or response. This is a much oversimplified description of an immensely complex system. In an effort to understand some of its intricacies, it is necessary to have a few basic concepts well in hand.

The Neuron

Like all other physiological systems, the neuromuscular system is built upon the organization and interrelation of elements, cells called neurons. Structurally, a neuron consists of dendrites, a cell body, and an axon with its correlates. Typically the dendrites are cellipetal: that is, when under stimulation, they carry electric changes toward the cell body. The axon is cellifugal, or conductive away from the cell body. Two coats, one cellular (myelin) and the other noncellular (neurilemma) are found to cover some, if not all, neurons. Substances like ether and alcohol are soluble in myelin. Hence the anesthetic effect of these drugs may be a sheath rather than a neuron function.

Under stimulation, the neuron is characterized by a series of electrochemical changes called nerve impulses. Recent advances in technology have made possible minute studies both of the electrical and enzymatic properties of the neural tissue. The result has been to emphasize the inextricably close relationships of electrical and chemical properties of nerve tissue. To start with, we shall describe some of the more basic electrical phenomena since they are historically older in the study of nerve physiology. The nerve fiber or axon is characterized in its resting state by a distribution of positive electric charges or ions along its outer surface and by negative charges along its inner surface. This polarization creates an electric potential which can be measured in thousandths of a volt. Disturbance to the equilibrium of charge within the neuron fiber sets off an action potential which is the basis of the nerve impulse.

When the external stimulus is strong enough, it causes a collapse of the polarization of the membrane, a process called depolarization. The change in the distribution of electrical charges in the membrane causes a circuit or flow of energy from within the membrane to its exterior and back again into the membrane. As a section of the membrane is depolarized, currents from the depolarized area move ahead to stimulate and depolarize sections ahead of the first area. Each depolarization stage produces current. Thus changes are propagated along and through the whole membrane and an action current is set up. The chief characteristic of this series of changes is called the spike potential or a sharp drop in the normal, resting, positive potential of the tissue. Since the spike potential cannot arise until the stimulus has a minimum intensity and since the spike potential always has the same size because of its dependence upon the size of the resting potential, it operates in accordance with what has been called the all-or-none law. Different fibers have different size spike potentials, but within one fiber the spike is as large as the membrane charge will permit. The spike potential, once initiated, continues to move along the fiber without the need for repeated external stimulation. Two other potentials have been described as following the spike. These are the negative and positive after-potentials. The positive after-potential is certainly related to fatigue and prolonged exposure to stimulation. During the negative after-potential phase, the fiber is in a state of increased excitability during which a subthreshold stimulus can produce a response. Another phase of excitability is known as the absolute refractory period. This represents a post-spike depression during which no stimulus can elicit a fiber response.

So far we have discussed the electrical aspects of neuronal activity. Electrical work, like all action, consumes energy. The metabolic system previously described must be the source of this energy. Although the picture is not complete, there seems little doubt that among the substances necessary for the electrical activity of the nervous system is a group of enzyme products called acetylcholine. The acetylcholine in free form depolarizes the nerve fiber and causes a sudden drop in resistance parallel to the spike potential. An enzyme (choline esterase) then breaks down the acetylcholine, thus permitting repolarization of the nerve. Finally, another enzyme (choline acetylase) rebuilds the acetylcholine content of the membrane and thus restores the potentiality for further activity. In recent studies of convulsive behavior in rats, local application of choline esterase caused a lessening of convulsive activity. This effect is presumably the result of the release of acetylcholine with a consequent repolarization of nerve tissue and redirection of nerve discharge into specific rather than diffuse channels. Physiological psychologists are becoming increasingly aware of the need to incorporate the biochemical as well as electrical phenomena in their experimentation.

The Synapse

The concepts pertaining to the functioning of neurons in groups are not basically different from those that apply to the functioning of a single neuron. Two types of neuronal combinations exist in living organisms. In one, the neurons are arranged in end-to-end form. Where the axon of one neuron in this arrangement impinges on the dendritic termination of another, the junction is called a synapse. The second grouping consists of neurons lying paralled to each other and side by side. This relationship is spoken of as an ephapse. Under certain conditions, in each arrangement, impulses originating in one neuron may stimulate current formation in the contiguous neuron.

What are the peculiar properties of the synapse which makes it of significance to the psychologist? In the first place, the synapse acts as a type of valve allowing transmission of impulse in only one direction. Whereas in a single, isolated neuron, stimulation may produce spike potentials and action current moving in either direction, i.e., to or from the cell body, when neurons are in synaptic junction, the direction of impulse is from the cell body and axon of one neuron to the dendritic ends and cell body of the other. The second factor is the delay in rate of conduction at the synapse. This seems to be a function of the relative size differences of the ends of the neurons, since speed is proportional to tissue diameter. In the third place is the so-called "optional" nature of synaptic transmission. In a neuron once stimulated, electrical change always takes place provided that the stimulation does not occur during the absolute refractory period. At a synapse, on the other hand, the continuation of an impulse over the synapse depends upon the state of each neuron and relationships among the neurons. This last function of the synapse is one of the most important facts in neurophysiology since it is the mechanism for the complexity of the behavior of organisms. Since axons from two neurons may terminate around the cell body of a third neuron, summation may arise from the simultaneous stimulation of the two axons discharging into it at about the same time. In the synapse and its properties we must seek for the explanation of learning, forgetting discrimination, and selection.

Neural Circuits

The concept of a neuromuscular arc as the basis of reflex action is old in the history of physiological psychology. There are many textbooks today which still picture the two- or three-component neuron reflex arc. Classically, the central nervous system was conceived as a self-contained mechanism, receiving signals from sense organs and discharging into the muscles and glands. The reflex arc with its three neurons arranged in sequence is the pseudo-materialistic basis for this concept. However, the neurological advances of the twentieth century have completely disproven this mechanistic picture. In reality, there are very few neurons with but one axon termination and one synaptic junction. Most neurons have several correlates or axon branches and therefore make synaptic connection with a number of secondary neurons. In addition, new types of circuits have been discovered which make possible the continuation of action after the initiating stimulus for that action has been removed. Figure 11.1 shows some of these complex arrangements

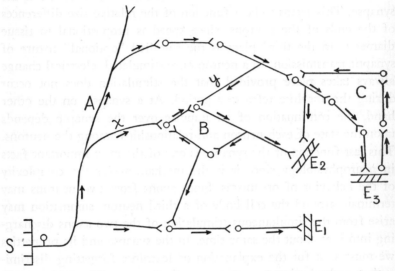

FIGURE 11.1.   Diagrammatic Representation of Various Neural Circuits: S, stimulated receptor; A, usual neuronal sequences; B, reverberatory circuit; C, feed-back circuit; E_1, E_2, E_3, effectors.

of neurons. In addition to the multibranched axon circuits of type A, two circular arrangements are shown at B and C. It will be easily seen that at B an impulse coming in over either neuron X or Y may stimulate the circuit in such a way that impulses will travel over the circular or *reverberatory* pathway surrounding B. This makes it possible for activity once set up to continue for a long time since impulses will stimulate the circuit B before passing over to the effectors at E_1, E_2.

A circular pattern of a slightly different type is shown in the diagram at *C*. Here the process involves the stimulation of an effector, a gland or muscle, as indicated at E_3. As the effector reacts, it innervates an afferent neuron chain which synapses with a returning, efferent system to reactivate the gland or muscle. This type of circuit has been called a *feedback* system. Feedback circuits have recently been found at various points in the neuromuscular apparatus. Among the important features of these arrangements is the possibility of repeated muscular or glandular action upon the cessation of the original, initiating stimulus. For instance, the act of picking up an object is initiated by a temporally limited stimulus. The act continues and can be corrected during its process if the object to be picked up is moved. The existence of feedback circuits makes possible the neural understanding of such self-initiated, regulatory behavior. An analogy can be made with the self-regulatory activity of the governor in a motor. Much of the current interest in reverberatory and feedback circuits has arisen because of the employment of these arrangements in the electrically operated calculating or "thinking" machines which were so useful during World War II. Industry makes use of the circuits in processes known as *servomechanisms* or self-correcting and directing machines. In communication and calculation, mathematicians and physicists have coöperated in the development of a new science called *cybernetics* which is based on feedback and reverberatory circuits. From their research, analogies to the nervous system and human behavior have, in turn, stimulated research into the regulatory and adaptive phases of human behavior and physiology.

RECENT TRENDS IN PHYSIOLOGICAL PSYCHOLOGY

Up to this point physiological psychology as a discipline in its own right has been somewhat in the background of our discussion. From the baselines of biochemistry and neurophysiology, it is now possible to see some of the problems that face the psychologist and how he is trying to solve them. It will be possible to examine only a few samples of psychophysiological research and those will be selected because they seem to point the way to new theoretical positions and to larger generalizations. It will be helpful to think of the general manner in which problems present themselves for consideration by the psychologist interested in physiological research. In most research of this type, both the stimulus (S) and the response (R) side of the psychological formula, S-O-R, have been determined. The locus of the physiological aspect (O) is also generally known but its mode of functioning remains to be investigated.

As an example, the field of audition presents itself. Here, the facts of sound were fairly well established many years ago, although new discoveries in electronics made refinements of technique possible. The psychological phenomena were known. The relation of wave frequency to pitch, of wave amplitude to loudness, just noticeable differences and limens or threshold points for hearing were included in elementary texts. In addition, there was a well-defined mechanical apparatus for conducting disturbances from the external environment through the outer and middle ear to the recesses of the inner ear. It was clear that transformation of mechanical to bioelectric energy must take place somewhere within the cochlea where the endpoints of the auditory nerve were found. The problem at this level is complex. What transforms the energy and how does it function so that the complex airwave is translated into nerve discharges that enable us to differentiate tones, sounds, and loudnesses? Here the use of new techniques in electronics and microsurgery came into play and it was possible to place electrodes directly into the cochlea and to amplify the electrical discharge so that it could be recorded. The result was the discovery of the cochlear microphonic potential. In other words, the microphonic potential represents the transduction of mechanical to electrical energy. Although there is some conflicting evidence, the organs responsible for this seem to be the hair cells of the organ of Corti. The situation within the auditory nerve itself is more complex. At least four sets of synaptic junctions are to be found between the basilar membrane and the auditory cortex. With the use of micro-

surgical techniques and extremely fine electrodes, it has been possible to study the discharges of single neurons in the group just
above the neurons leaving the basilar membrane. These single,
second-order neurons seem to be tuned separately for separate vibra-
tion rates. Some seem to be tuned, in addition, for intensity differences. The total picture, then, appears to be that the neurons of the
auditory chain are separately tuned for frequency and that the
fibers of the basilar membrane participate in the placing of frequency discharges. This is the place hypothesis. Intensity is a combination of the total number of volleys discharged per unit of time
plus the selective operation of a special class of neuron. This is a
variant of the volley hypothesis. Through the combined research of
physicists, physiologists, and psychologists the mechanism of auditory behavior is thus beginning to be determined.

A second type of approach for the physiological psychologist is
to start with a problem in which the response (R) is very complex and where the initiating stimulus or stimuli (S) is not known.
Changes in the physiological condition of the organism (O) may
then throw light upon both the stimulus and the resulting behavior.
An example of this procedure is to be found in the studies of
migration in salmon. The basic facts as established by coöperative
research are these: It is known that salmon are spawned and develop for some time far up in the headwaters of a stream. When
about 2 years of age, the young fish swim downstream to the ocean
where they spend two to three years. Then they return to the
stream from which they entered the ocean and proceed upward to
its headwaters where they spawn and die. Research has shown
physiological factors control some of this complex behavior. Light
operates to determine the initial downstream migration. Young
salmon have sensitive photoreceptors deep in the skin. As the
young fish grows, the pigment covering the receptors is lost and
light can stimulate the end organs. A light-avoidance reaction takes
place which moves the salmon downstream into ever and ever
deeper water where light rays penetrate with less intensity. Temperature and gonadal secretion seem to determine the return to the

headwaters of the stream. As the sex glands secrete more effectively, metabolism increases and more highly oxygenated and colder water is necessary. This leads the fish to the upper reaches of the streams. An additional factor of unknown physiology is the tendency of the fish to swim against the current. This is called rheotropism but its cause has not been established. So, in this series of researches on migration, we see how what used to be called by the mystic label "instinct" is now a matter of behavioral response to physiological changes dependent upon environmental stimulation.

Psychophysiology of Learning

In view of the importance of learning in the economy of human existence, it is not surprising that a great amount of psychophysiological research has been done to determine its neural and brain components. The search for a generalized theory is complicated by several factors. In the first place, there is large-scale variation in what has been termed learning. Conditioning, sensory discrimination, relational, and field or Gestalt learning have all been treated as separate phenomena with presumably separate neurophysiological mechanisms at work. Second is the difficulty of experimentation. Direct information on the role of the nervous system in human learning has come from two sources. One is the use of accidental brain injuries to determine their effect on learning. The other has been the study of surgical interference with various parts of the nervous system. Most of these data have been acquired incidental to such operations as prefrontal lobotomy and topectomy in the control of schizophrenia and incurable pain. Systematic exploration of various levels of neurological examination has not been possible with the normal human. For more precise information, it has been necessary to rely upon animal experimentation. This carries with it doubt as to the validity of extrapolation from infrahuman to human levels. It will be necessary, therefore, to describe what is being done with animals and then to state, in outline, a current theory which seeks to integrate the available information at both the human and animal level.

CONDITIONING

There is some evidence that conditioning can take place in organisms without a central nervous system, for instance, the paramecium. Certainly, when we come to a level of organization as high as the insect, we find conditioning despite the absence of a brain. Because of the universality of the conditioned response, it is thought of as a basic property of living animals. Although Pavlov believed in the brain as essential for this form of learning, there is some evidence that, even in the forms possessing that organ, it is not necessary for simple conditioned responses. At the moment, there is debate as to whether conditioning at the spinal cord level is possible. That conditioning can take place in decorticate animals was first established by a colleague of Pavlov. His experiments have been repeated and the results substantiated. A study of conditioning that deserves mention here was carried out by two researchers working in the Pavlovian Laboratory in Leningrad. First they produced a conditioned secretion of the kidney to a bright light. When the kidney was then surgically separated from all nervous innervation, the conditioned response still persisted. It was as if a free-floating kidney could retain a learned response once established. However, when the adrenal gland in turn was cut off from neural stimulation, the kidney secretion was abolished. Hence it seems that conditioning can take place via a humoral route as well as over nerve systems.

CELL-ASSEMBLY THEORY AND LEARNING

D. O. Hebb has recently attempted to draw under the heading of a single theory many of the established data of complex learning, memory, and attention. The following paragraphs will try to summarize the theory and to cite some of the material on which it is based.

On the psychological side, Hebb starts with the fields of perception and learning. Here there are two investigations which are basic to the theory. In one, some chimpanzees were raised in darkness by shrouding their heads in hoods during the first months of life. Upon removal of the hoods, the behavior of the animals was compared to that of chimpanzees of the same age, reared normally. Striking differences were found. Although the eyes of the hooded animals were responsive to light as manifest by reflex action, the chimpanzees failed to see even the simplest objects. When conditioned by electric shock to avoid a visual stimulus, many trials were necessary as compared to the single presentation required by the normal apes. Even the eye-blink response to an object before the face was absent and had to be acquired by learning. This finding with primates has been paralleled in humans when the visual behavior of adults, surgically freed from blindness due to congenital cataract, was studied. Although these subjects saw some figure-ground relationships, they had to learn to discriminate between triangles and squares. Some actually had to count the corners before they were able to say that the seen object was a square or a triangle. Counting the corners is dependent on eye movements. It follows then, that visual perception of simple wholes is built up through learning and through a multiple series of eye fixations.

Another psychological datum on which Hebb rests his theory is what has been called perceptual generalization. This can be illustrated by an experiment of Lashley's in which rats were trained to go to a black horizontal bar and to avoid a black vertical stimulus. When the bars were then presented as a series of squares or when the animal had to choose between two circles in a horizontal versus a vertical arrangement, the choice was always for the horizontal. Thus the animal seemed to generalize from its initial training to stimuli never before perceived.

Considering now, the physiological requirements for an explanation of the psychological phenomena, Hebb starts with the assumption that learning must involve changes in the nervous system. Since learning brings about more or less permanent changes in behavior, the alterations in the nervous system must also be more or less permanent. Secondly, current research has shown that the brain does not consist solely of a linear arrangement of neurons, synapting end-to-end. Reverberatory and feedback circuits (previously discussed) make possible a mechanism for more complex behavior than was conceivable under the linear hypothesis. Finally, as already indicated, a neuron may be fired by a spatial summation of impulses arriving at a synapse from several preceding neurons terminating at the same point. The time phase of the summed impulses can vary so as to produce both stimulation and inhibition. Putting all these facts together, the theory postulates that repetition of a perceptible stimulus will cause a growth of end knobs of neurons, particularly in those cortical areas which are known to have associational functions. The growth and increase in synapses makes possible the development of reverberatory and feedback circuits, each of which is specific for a given learned percept. These patterns of neural organization are known as cell assemblies. Further stimulation by larger units on the stimulus side causes a temporal arrangement of cell assemblies called a phase sequence.

Hebb has also pointed out some striking differences between the learning of young and adult organisms which seem to be best explained by his theory of neural action. Immature primates, including man, learn in a very slow manner as contrasted with the behavior of full-grown organisms. In addition, early learning is relatively fixed and unchangeable, resembling, in some aspects, reflex acts. (It can not be argued that motivation accounts for the differences, since the apes used in the study seemed to be highly motivated.) Also, Hebb believes that it is only in the more highly evolved forms of life that the difference between early and later learning is striking. Insect behavior, even shortly after birth, shows rapid learning such as that involved in getting to recognize the home hive of the honey bee. What appear to be instinctive acts have been shown upon closer scrutiny to be rapidly acquired behavior. As one goes up the phylogenetic scale, infant learning becomes slower and adult learning more efficient and complex. So too, insight is characteristically an adult phenomenon while conditioning and the slow growth of competence occurs during early life.

On the neurological side, Hebb suggests that what happens in early learning is the production of cell assemblies by repeated stimulation and then the recruitment of new neurons and cell assemblies both by continuation of environmental changes and by the use of reverberatory circuits. The increased speed of learning of lower organisms as compared to higher organisms is a function of the relative paucity of association areas in the lower phylogenetic scale. The greater the amount of association area, the slower the process of establishing cell assemblies. In turn, the superiority of adult learning depends on the existence of already made cell assemblies. Adult learning is, therefore, mainly a process of recombination of established neural complexes.

Abnormal Behavior and Psychophysiology

A psychiatrist once stated that it was more important to know what kind of person a disease had than what kind of disease the person had. It is certainly essential today to be aware of the personality aspects of behavior since many studies have shown the dependence of action on the total organization of the individual. With the tremendous rise in the demand for clinical psychologists and the resultant interest in that field, research on behavior and personality disorder has reached an all-time high. Here too, the influence of psychoanalytic thinking has made serious consideration of the relationship between physiological status, personality, and behavior disorder a necessity. The distinction between functional and organic, psychogenic and somatogenic, must be clarified in the light of recent developments. The prevailing emphasis in the field of psychopathology has been to maximize the importance of environment in the causation of disorder and to stress the causal influence of anxiety and emotional conflict. No matter how this discussion ends, one question remains. Regardless of the causation of a symptom complex or disease, the disorder manifests itself in action by the body. Ulcers of the gastrointerestinal tract may be a symptom or a result of a frustrated mother-love. Hysterical paralysis may be stimulated by fear of sexuality. In all cases, however, something in the organism translates the external stress into a

symptom of disorder. What is the physiological mechanism responsible for the localization of the symptom in the body? The answer
to this question certainly involves careful psychophysiological research because it will supply the missing link between the psychic
and somatic components of disease. To stress the importance of
this intervening variable is by no means to deëmphasize the need
to look to societal and social causation for mental disorder. It
simply expresses a need for completion of a picture. Calling a
disease "psycho-somatic" is an advance over the unitary concepts
of older days but the hyphen still represents an unknown, namely,
the mechanism by means of which the psychic cause expresses itself
in somatic terms.

THE GENERAL ADAPTATION SYNDROME

One attempt to solve the problem alluded to above has been
made by a group of researchers working with a concept called the
general adaptation syndrome (G.A.S.). This term was first used
by Hans Selye to describe the results of a large body of investigations on a great many animal forms. Basically the G.A.S. refers
to the response of the body to protracted stress situations. In
Selye's words, the G.A.S. is the sum of all the nonspecific, systemic
reactions of the body which ensue upon continued exposure to a
wide variety of stress-producing stimuli. By nonspecific is meant
the fact that the changes are not direct resultants of the stimulus.
For instance, exposure to extreme cold for a period of time produces symptoms in the stomach such as ulcers as well as changes
in blood pressure. These are not specific to cold but may be produced by any or all stress situations. In similar fashion, the term
systemic refers to the breadth and multiplicity of symptoms.

What is a stress-producing situation? The experimental investigations in man and animal have varied from surgical, through
chemical, to purely psychological stresses. At one extreme are such
situations as exposure to temperature extremes, occlusion of a blood
vessel, hanging of an animal by the hind legs. Chemical stresses
have included exposure to short-wave radiations and injection of

estrogenic hormones and other substances. In the psychological sphere, prolonged mental examinations, fears, anxieties, and conditioned neurotic responses have been used as well as electrocortical shock and convulsive seizures in rats. The unifying common denominator in all these varied stimuli has been a manifold of physiological disturbances including such symptoms as changes in blood pressure, erosions of gastrointestinal mucosa, and loss of appetite.

Characteristically the G.A.S. evolves through three stages: (1) The *alarm reaction* is divided into two substages: shock and countershock. In these phases, the initial responses are severe, involving gross anatomical alterations, lesions, changes in vascular permeability, etc. (2) The *resistance stage* is the one in which adaptive reaction to stress injuries takes place. Most of the alterations of the shock stage are reversed. It seems that, during this period, the body manufactures defenses against the mechanisms producing injury. Both hormonal and nervous agents play a part in the recovery manifested here. (3) During the *exhaustion stage* all defensive reactions fail. The adaptational energy of the organism is exhausted and, if the stress situation is prolonged, the animal dies. A graphic picturization of the G.A.S. is seen in Figure 11.2. Continued exposure to stress, then, is shown to develop a systematically changing picture of damage and repair. What symptoms are shown depends upon the stage of adaptation.

Some illustrations of the experimental and clinical evidence are in point here. Selye has given an example from war pathology of the aviators who, working under nervous tension such as combat flying, were found to collapse after a period of apparent immunity to damage. The breakdown referred to in aviation medicine as "exhaustion of nervous energy reserves," was characterized by gastrointestinal disturbances, nephrosclerosis, pneumonic edema, and high blood pressure. In another clinical example, sufferers from extreme burns start with the manifestation of shock, edema, congestion of the brain, hemorrhages, etc., and then show a relief of symptomatology as the resistance period occurs. The same course of

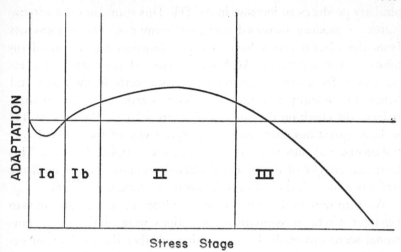

FIGURE 11.2. Course of the General Adaptation Syndrome: Horizontal line represents normal adaptation: Ia, shock phase; Ib, countershock phase; II, resistance stage; III, exhaustion stage. (From Hans Selye, *The Physiology and Pathology of Exposure to Stress*, Montreal, Acta Inc., 1950.)

events characterizes experimental animals. Repeated exposure to electrocortical shock in rats yields essentially the same data.

The next problem in considering the G.A.S. is to isolate the mechanism responsible for the symptomatology. Here Selye has been joined by a large group of investigators. It has been established with fair certainty that the physiological locus lies in the interrelationship of the pituitary and adrenal glands through the manufacture by the former of a powerful adrenal-cortex accelerant, adrenocorticotrophic hormone (ACTH). This hormone has been much popularized lately as an adjuvant in the treatment of arthritis and other diseases. The total picture is quite complicated but for our purposes it can be stated as follows. The stressor, although it affects some tissue directly, carries its effects to distant organs and tissues through two great mechanisms, the blood circulation and the nervous system. One or both of these may be the carrier of the damaging and defensive products. During stress, the anterior pituitary produces an increase in ACTH. This stimulates the adrenal cortex to produce increased corticoid hormones. These hormones from the adrenal cortex have as a part-function the reciprocal inhibition of the pituitary ACTH production. Under stress, the requirement for cortical hormones by tissue cells is increased and hence, the quantity in circulating blood is reduced. This, in turn, reduces the check on the anterior pituitary which elaborates ACTH in large quantities. Increased secretory activity of the adrenal cortex occurs, and thus meets the needs of the peripheral tissues. This increased activity of the pituitary-adrenal system continues until the stress is removed, the cells break down or adaptation occurs.

We turn now to the experimental evidence on animal and human behavior where stress-producing situations were used and the hormonal secretions studied to determine whether the mechanism described above was at work. In a series of studies, the indices of adrenal cortex secretion were the number of circulating blood lymphocytes and the excretion of 17-ketosteroid hormone in urine. As stress stimuli, the investigators used exposure to heat and to a pursuit-meter test which involves concentrated attention, muscle set and hand-eye coördination. Subjects were a group of normal men and a group of schizophrenic males. On both stress tests, the results showed that the schizophrenics failed to respond with increased adrenal output whereas the normals did. In contrast, a group of neurotic subjects overproduced as compared with normals. A second stress test with the neurotic group consisted of a deep-probing psychiatric interview as compared with a routine, nonprobing conversation. The stress interview again produced increased hormonal secretion. Although the evidence is not clinching, there are fertile suggestions for further research here.

CONCLUSION

The attempt has been made to indicate the far-reaching developments in physiological psychology. It is becoming clear that any worker in the field must acquaint himself not only with the material of the experimental and clinical psychologist, but also with the contributions of the workers in the most closely allied fields, namely, neurophysiology, endocrinology, and metabolic chemistry. Progress in psychophysiology will occur only as we recognize that the physiological mechanism must be studied from all relevant approaches.

SUGGESTED READINGS

1. Beach, F. A., *Hormone and Behavior*. New York: Hoeber, 1948. This is the best survey of the relationship of hormones to animal and human behavior now available. Written by a psychologist who has done extensive research in the field, it covers a tremendous range of exciting material.

2. Freeman, G. L., *The Energetics of Human Behavior*. Ithaca, N. Y.: Cornell, 1948. A textbook in physiological psychology from the point of view of homeostatic control.

3. Hebb, D. O., *Organization of Behavior*. New York: Wiley, 1949. A most exciting treatment of a novel attempt to elaborate an inclusive neurophysiological basis for psychology. This is a must for all students of the field.

4. Morgan, C. T., and Stellar, E., *Physiological Psychology*. New York: McGraw-Hill, 1950. An up-to-date and comprehensive treatment of the field. It contains summaries and critical evaluations of all important experimental studies in physiological psychology.

5. Selye, H., *Stress*. Montreal: Acta Endocrinologica, 1950. The extensive presentation of the general adaptation syndrome and related findings.

6. Stevens, S. S. (ed.), *Handbook of Experimental Psychology*. New York: Wiley, 1951. The chapters on physiological psychology, neurology, and sensory phenomena are required reading for all physiological psychologists.

Chapter 12

Comparative Psychology

by HERBERT G. BIRCH

The Field of Comparative Psychology
GENERAL CONSIDERATIONS
ANECDOTALISM AND PARSIMONY
THE WORLD OF ANIMALS

The Problem of Instincts

The Nature of Modifiability
CONDITIONING
SELECTIVE LEARNING
INSIGHT
SUMMARY

The Evolution of Social Life
INVERTEBRATES
Insect Societies
Communication
VERTEBRATES

Abnormal Behavior

Conclusion

Suggested Readings

THE FIELD OF COMPARATIVE PSYCHOLOGY

General Considerations

Man's interest in animal behavior is as old as man. From the earliest times his very survival has depended upon his ability to predict and in part, to modify and to control the activities of lower organisms. It is from raiding beasts of prey that man had to be defended, and as a predator himself the maintenance of his food supply was often based upon his ability to capture and to consume other animals. In the course of history animals were domesticated and through their directed activities man's labors were lightened, his food supply guaranteed, and his understanding of himself and of nature vastly extended. Thus man's relation with the lower animals is both ancient and intimate, and his efforts to understand their behavior universal and persistent features of human activity. Comparative psychology is the continuation of this attempt to explain the behavior of lower animals by applying to their study man's keenest instrument of inquiry, the scientific method.

The scientific study of animal behavior essentially begins with the elaboration of the theory of evolution by Darwin. Animal behavior was most certainly studied in the pre-Darwinian period, but not in any systematic manner. The theory of evolution had two fundamental aspects. On the one hand it sought to establish the developmental continuity of living organisms; to demonstrate how, in the course of time, more advanced organisms were descended from lower organisms. This feature of evolution, therefore, established the conception of the common ancestral origins of living organisms. The second aspect of evolution theory involved the principle of discontinuity of species characteristics. It pointed to the fact that in the course of time different kinds of organisms, having characteristics different both from each other and from their common ancestors, had evolved by a process of natural selection. Evolution theory, therefore, points both to the continuity and discontinuity of organisms, and causes us to focalize simultaneously upon resemblance and divergence, similarity and difference, inheritance and mutation. As Mayer, one of the most productive students of evolution, has put it, the evolution process is one of "continuous discontinuity."

The study of evolution has consisted of the investigation of several problems, each of which has endowed biologic science with a new field of specialized inquiry. The attempt to determine the laws of inheritance in reproduction has led to the development of genetics. The analysis of the emergence of new structures has enriched and renovated comparative anatomy, developmental embryology, and taxonomy. The efforts to examine the emergence of psychological capacity, of behavioral mechanisms for coping with the demands of life, produced the field of specialization called comparative psychology. Comparative psychology may, therefore, be defined as the study of the evolution of behavior mechanisms.

Since fossils do not behave, it is impossible to study directly the behavioral capacities of the varieties of organism that existed in the course of evolution. For this reason one must examine the behavioral capacities of the different varieties of existing organisms and by analyzing the behaviors which appear, together with their structural bases, draw inferences as to the process of behavioral evolution. This basic methodological principle determines the course of comparative psychological investigation, and leads ideally to the systematic comparison of the behavioral capacities of the animal phyla and of the structural changes which underlie the appearance of different behaviors.

How does one make comparisons? Obviously the first principle is that one can only compare comparables. This is to say that only to the degree that phenomena have certain characteristics or features in common can they be compared. If they have no such common attributes then they may be said to be incomparable. An example in point is an attempted comparison of the moon and green cheese. They may be compared as geometrical shapes or as masses but cannot be compared either as cheeses or as moons, because in these respects they lack common attributes and are incomparable. Therefore a comparison always involves the existence of similarities. Moreover, the process of comparison is the hunt for dissimilarities or differences. It is the attempt to determine the identity or nonidentity of two or more phenomenally similar events by an intensive examination of their characteristics. If no non-identities are discovered the phenomena are duplicates one of the other; if nonidentities are discovered the phenomena are similar in some senses but different in others.

In the analysis of animal behavior comparisons are facilitated by the fact that the fundamental vital processes of all living organisms are very much alike. To survive an individual animal must ingest food, engage in respiration, and in general behave in such ways as to promote its preservation, while for species survival, reproductive activities, and general interindividual relations must occur. All animals may be considered to be similar in the sense that they engage in a variety of activities which have survival consequences. Yet it should be noted that the similarities which exist are in terms of the end results of actions rather than in the sense that the mechanisms of behavior which underlie the reactions are the same. The rat and the human being may both learn to escape from a puzzle box, or the salmon and the human nomad may each engage in migratory behavior, but the causes for the behavior in each case are basically different despite the superficial similarity in end result. The rat and the human both escape from the problem box, but how they escape, what it is that they learn, and the potentialities for behaving which underlie the learnings may be quite different. The salmon migrates, on an endocrinological and biochemical basis, while the nomadic human migrates as a result of his culture, particularly expressed in the way he produces his food supply. The amoeba extending its pseudopod in the direction of a food particle and Oliver Twist extending his porridge bowl are not identities. The uncovering of the different mechanisms capable of producing seemingly similar behaviors is one of the tasks of comparative psychology. It is search for the *how* and *what* in behavioral events that distinguishes comparative psychology as a science from casual and analogic descriptions of animal behavior. The history of comparative psychology is the story of the struggle to develop a causal understanding of the organic and psychological processes underlying *phenomenally* similar behaviors at different animal levels. The progress of this program has been impeded by repeated tendencies to concentrate upon end results and surface similarities in behavior and to ignore differences in behavior mechanisms.

Anecdotalism and Parsimony

In the early years of evolution theory it was necessary to establish the concept of both structural and behavioral continuity. The anecdotalists then set themselves the task of combatting this resistance to the notion of continuity in descent by finding instances in the behavior of subhuman organisms that had a marked resemblance to human behavior. Their starting point was a popularized conception of human psychological characteristics, and they interpreted the behaviors of lower organisms in terms of human experience. Through their efforts the evolutionary conception of continuity in descent was made more palatable in that it converted the problem from one of seeing man as a special variety of beast into one of seeing the lower animals as possessing in a rudimentary form the intellectual, emotional, and social characteristics of men.

The data used by the typical anecdotalist like Romanes, Espinas, and Kropotkin were essentially collections of stories of the observations of humanlike behavior such as sympathy, mother-love, or intelligence in lower animals. These stories characteristically were isolated observations which were never examined in the context of either the situation or of the background experiences of the animal, but rather were taken as instances of human behavior in lower animals, sought for and found by untrained observers, who were basically motivated to find such occurrences. The expression, "Seek and ye shall find!" is nowhere as true as in the study of animal behavior.

It should be noted that anecdotalism was a one-sided, *anthropomorphic* view of the evolutionary process, and as such was a distortion which emphasized continuity. This distortion could be sustained only by depending upon unchecked and uncheckable reports, by ignoring negative instances, and by observing only fragments of behavior the interpretation of which is possible only if one permits free rein to one's prejudices. It was in opposition to these antiscientific tendencies in anecdotalism that C. Lloyd Morgan began his work and enunciated the fundamental principle to be used in the field of animal behavior, the principle of parsimony.

Morgan illustrated his views by certain observations on the behavior of a dog. He chose this animal deliberately because a goodly number of the anecdotalists' stories were concerned with the brilliance of reasoning in dogs, who opened complicated gates, etc. He pointed out that the conclusions regarding the dog's reasoning ability stemmed from the observation of dogs who already knew how to open gates, and that such observation does not tell us *how the animal acquired the observed behavior*. Further, no tests were made to determine the effects which would be produced by making small changes in the situation, like moving the gate latch to a new height, or changing the hinges to the other side. Therefore, no real basis existed for deciding upon the psychological capacities used by the dog in solving his problem, and any interpretation consistent with the preconceptions of the observer could be advanced with impunity. Morgan made such situational changes and his studies revealed that such skills as balanced stick carrying and gate opening in dogs developed out of a long and tedious process of trial-and-error learning and could not be attributed to reasoning or other intellective processes utilized by the human adult. On this basis Morgan advanced his principle of parsimony in psychology, which was an extension of the celebrated philosophical "razor of William of Occam" into behavior theory. This principle, now called Morgan's Canon, states that "in no case may we interpret an action as the outcome of the exercise of a higher psychical faculty, if it can be interpreted as the outcome of the exercise of one which stands lower in the psychological scale."

The application of Morgan's Canon to a concrete problem is

revealed in Pfungst's study of the horse Clever Hans. This remarkable animal could by tapping out a "code" with his hooves "solve" problems in mental arithmetic, and perform many other marvelous feats. The trainer, a thoroughly honest man, truly believed in the "intelligence" of his protégé and encouraged its study by skilled observers. Pfungst found that the animal could indeed perform adequately when the trainer was in the same room and in the view of the animal. However, when problems were presented in the trainer's absence, or when the trainer was in the room but was unaware of the problem presented by the psychologist, the horse tapped at random and gave no correct answers. It appeared that Clever Hans was responding to nearly imperceptible nods made by his trainer or by other observers when they were present and not to the problems presented. The questioner was not even aware that he was providing cues for the animal's response. Other stories of gifted animals, such as the Elberfeld horses who "could extract" sixth roots by mental arithmetic, or of wise dogs, may be explained in a similar manner. The features of the situation to which the animal is responding need not be assumed to be the same as those to which a human being would respond; rather these features of the situation and their relevance to the animal's behavior must be determined before an interpretation of the performance is advanced.

Not only did anecdotalism assume that a similarity existed between the behavior of human beings and other animals lower in the biological scale, but it also indicated that the *intentions* or *motivations* producing the behaviors were the same. This error is most clearly revealed in the analysis of "purpose." By purpose it is usually meant that the cause of the behavior or its intent is determined by the end result of the behavior. Thus a paramecium is said to move toward a small particle of organic matter "to obtain food," or a scallop to move from the vicinity of an approaching starfish "because it is fleeing from its enemy." It is probable that at the level of the adult higher mammal *some* behaviors are engaged in with the anticipation that they will yield certain consequences, but to assume that this is the case in the instances mentioned simply because the usual

end result *happens* to be the obtaining of food by the paramecium
or the avoidance of the starfish by the scallop is unwarranted. It
represents a *teleological* approach in that it substitutes the end result
of the behavior for an explanation of its cause without showing how
the end result is related to the causal process. A detailed analysis of
the behavior of the paramecium reveals that it moves not toward
food but toward any weak chemical stimulation. Thus if a minute
particle of $KMnO_4$ (potassium permanganate) is substituted for the
food particle, it too is ingested by the organism, which then dies.
Further, an extract of starfish broth is sufficient to elicit "flight" in
the scallop, which appears to be responding to the chemical characteristics of the starfish and not to its presence as an "enemy." Certainly the behaviors of lower animals are adaptive in the sense that
they function to promote survival in a given environment. It would,
indeed, be strange if this were not the case, because the very process
of natural selection in evolution is based upon the survival of organic
forms which have adaptive behaviors. But bioligical adaptation does
not depend upon the anticipation of end results by the behaving
organism and so is not to be considered as identical with purpose.
Another striking example is to be found in the behavior of the
octopus, which is said to creep into rock crevices and "lurk" there
out of sight of the animals upon which it preys. The assumption is
that the octopus has entered the crevice in order to hide from its
victims. However, it has been shown that the octopus will "lurk"
just as readily between two pieces of transparent plate glass, and
that its entry into small spaces is determined not by its desire to hide
but by its need for contact stimulation in the maintenance of its
general equilibrium.

The World of Animals

It is apparent from the previous discussion that to understand the
psychological significance of any performance it is necessary to come
to know the world of the performing organism and not to assume on
an empathic basis that its world and ours are similar. The first step
in this direction is made when we begin to study the sensory capaci-

ties of different animals. As a consequence of such analysis many behaviors cease to be mysterious or astoundingly intelligent and become instead fascinating examples of the way in which the receptive equipment of organisms function.

Even our fellow mammals do not have sensory capacities which are identical with man's. It is common practice to use a whistle to signal hunting and sentry dogs which is clearly heard by the dog but entirely inaudible to human beings. The reason for this lies in the fact that the human ear is relatively insensitive to sounds of over 20,000 c.p.s. (cycles per second), whereas the dog has an auditory spectrum which goes to over the 30,000 c.p.s. mark. The ability of the bat to avoid obstacles in the dark provides another striking example of unique sensitivity in a mammal. For many years it was thought that this avoidance was based on actual sensitivity. However, it was found that if the ears of bats were stopped up they were incapable of avoiding obstacles, that were otherwise readily dodged. Further, if the ears were left open and the mouth tied shut the bat again lost its ability to proceed without hitting into objects. These facts led to an inquiry which revealed that the bat avoided obstacles by emitting very high-pitched sounds (approximately 50,000 c.p.s.) which when reflected back to it from surrounding objects provided the basis for accurate avoidance. For obvious reasons this pattern is sometimes referred to as "bat radar."

Attempts to treat the world of animals as analogous to our own meet even greater difficulties when we consider the sensory capacities of nonmammals. Some examples drawn from the visual life of the honeybee should suffice to make the point. Try for a moment to imagine the visual world of the bee. Its eyes are composed of hundreds of facets each of which functions as a minor "eye" with its own retina and connections to the central nervous system. Simultaneously, images from facet upon facet representing contrasting views of the environment are being received by the bee. The complexity of its impressions are almost too great for us to conceptualize. Now then what do we know about the bee's perceptions when we say that they can learn to distinguish between two geometric forms?

A triangle most certainly does not look the same as it does to the human. Most probably it represents a given kind of flicker pattern.

Not only does the bee have this type of eye (a compound eye), but its visual apparatus is capable of responding to characteristics of light energy to which many other animals, including most humans, are insensitive. Bees respond not only to the intensity, wave length, and direction of light, but to its polarization characteristics as well. Thus a honeybee forager is able to maintain its orientation to the feeding place so long as it can see a patch of (to us) blue sky. The reason for this, von Frisch has shown, stems from the fact that to the bee this is not a patch of blue sky, at all, but rather a patterned arrangement of brightnesses. This pattern develops as a consequence of the animal's sensitivity to the polarization characteristics of light.

Certain studies of discrimination learning in mammals highlight the problem still further. It has been found that a rat can be trained to differentiate between members of a pair of geometric figures in a jumping apparatus. Moreover, once the discrimination is learned it is carried over to other pairs of figures which do not look similar to the original training pair from our point of view. However, the new figures are, for the rat, equivalent to the pair upon which it was originally trained.

THE PROBLEM OF INSTINCTS

Nowhere is a knowledge of the world of the animal so important as in the analysis of "so-called" instinctive behavior. For many years some psychologists have sought to eliminate the term instinct from the science because it created the false impression that by being given a name a behavior was being explained, e.g., social behavior is the result of a mating instinct, etc. However, in recent years there has been a revival of instinctivist ideas as a result of the work of Lorenz, Tinbergen, and their supporters. Despite certain differences in detail both the older and the newer instinctivism deal with a common core of behaviors. The theories arise as a result of the fact that there are certain complex adaptive patterns of behavior which are common to all members of a species and which typically occur under given environmental circumstances. Further, it appears that these behaviors develop independently of "learning." The patterns are then variously "explained" as the result of instincts, which are thought of as chain reflexes, or as neural patterns with energy reservoirs that build up to spontaneous discharge points, or even as inherent awarenesses of "purpose."

While it is undoubtedly true that complex unlearned patterns of adaptation exist, it is doubtful if the instinct concept old or new contributes very much to our understanding of the processes which produce such behaviors. If instinct is defined as that variety of adaptive behavior which occurs as the direct consequence of the interaction of the organism's inherited structure and physiology with the environment the task of comparative psychology is clearly to make explicit the ways in which organisms and environment interact and not merely to reaffirm and to label the fact of interaction. Since much of the discussion of instinct derives from a consideration of insect behavior it is appropriate to examine a typical pattern of insect behavior in this connection.

Many insect species are predatory and both feed on and lay their eggs upon the larvae of other insects. One such organism is the ichneumon fly (Nemeritis) which lays its eggs upon the larvae of the flour moth. Successive generations of ichneumon flies characteristically select the flour moth larvae as the organisms upon which to lay their eggs. Apparently the behavior is unlearned, common to the species, and the direct consequence of the way in which the characteristics of the flour moth larvae affect an organism like the ichneumon fly when it is ready to oviposit. Further, since the behavior has appeared reliably in many successive generations of ichneumon flies it is presumably inherited. However, certain experiments make this entire interpretation of the behavior dubious. It has been shown, that if ichneumon fly larvae are not permitted to feed upon larval flour moths, but are instead placed upon and made to eat larval bee-wax moths, later as adults the ichneumons so raised lay eggs upon bee-wax moth larvae. Thus a change in larval food has modified an "instinct." The same investigator has also shown that the larval hosts of other parasitic insects may be changed by causing the larvae to feed upon "strange" materials. In a general sense the above work suggests that an understanding of species-typical behavior requires a detailed analysis of the circumstances under which the given organism and its sensitivities develop. When such an analysis is made it becomes clear that the adult behavior is the end result of a complex developmental process including larval habituation as well as structure, organic state, and immediate environmental circumstance. It is, however, an unfortunate fact that very few species-typical behaviors have been subjected to the kind of searching scrutiny just described. Consequently, there remain fragmentary and partially understood descriptions of behavior which can be, and are, hastily labeled as instinctive.

The use of the instinct concept has not been restricted to insects. Much of the behavior of the lower vertebrates has been discussed in a similar manner. The migration of salmon, the movement of newly hatched loggerhead turtles to the sea, the pecking of chicks, the migration of birds, and even the mating and maternal behavior of lower mammals have all been classified as instinctive. All these phenomena have in common the characteristics of being only partially understood, and incompletely described. When any of these behaviors have been subjected to detailed analysis it has been found that the adaptive component depends upon a complicated organism-environment relationship that is only obscured by using an instinct concept. One such example can be drawn from Rowan's study of bird migration.

As is well known, many species of birds engage in large-scale migrations which are related to seasonal changes. Rowan studied the migratory behavior of one such bird, the junco, which moves south in the autumn and returns to the northern regions in the spring of the year. He found that the only reliable physiological change to accompany this migratory pattern was an increase in gonadal size during the early spring months and a decline in gonadal prominence during the fall. He next studied the environment and found that the amount of daylight per day was the situational variable to change most consistently over the year. He therefore hypothesized that the growth and development of the birds' gonads were determined by the changing nature of daily illumination. As the spring approached the days grew gradually longer, increased the general activity level of the birds, and thus produced increased gonad growth. During the fall each day had slightly less daylight time than the preceding day, the activity level of the juncoes dropped, and gonadal retrogression occurred.

As a result of this hypothesis he raised birds under circumstances in which he could control the amount of daily illumination. Under these conditions he found that even in midwinter birds, which had been subjected to daily increases in amount of illumination, when released flew northward. It thus became clear that the determiner of the bird migration was not a purpose—a desire to reach a good climate—but rather a forced pattern of action determined by the way in which gonadal growth was affected by diurnal variations in light. Just what further environmental factors the birds are sensitive to, and which cause them to fly in one or another direction as a consequence of their hormonal state is not as yet known.

Limitations of space prevent the detailed exploration of other instinctive manifestations, but even the present cursory view of the problem permits one to arrive at some general conclusions. In the first instance it should be clear that there is a variety of behaviors which are directly determined by the nature of the structure of the organism and the environmental situation in which it lives. Many of these behaviors are adaptive and represent the end result of a long process of evolutionary selection. The name which one applies to such behavior patterns is not important so long as it is clearly understood that naming and explaining are not the same thing.

An examination of the animal kingdom shows that such directly determined behavior is most typical of the invertebrate organisms and of the lower vertebrates, but that as one begins to consider the behavior of mammals it is found that variability and individually acquired patterns of action grow ever more important. Emphasis shifts from the fixity of behavior to the process of change, and an interest in the problem of individual development and of individual learning is not accidental but is necessary in analyzing mammalian behavior.

THE NATURE OF MODIFIABILITY

It is only fair to state at the outset that there is no generally accepted theory of learning. One of the reasons for this situation lies in the failure of psychology to approach the problem of modifiability in a phylogenetic manner. Rather, it has long been the custom to develop theories of learning on the basis of a partial consideration of the behavior of a particular animal, usually either of the rat or of man, and then to generalize to all animals from this restrictive standpoint. This tendency to avoid phylogenetic comparison has grown increasingly strong, and, recently, both Schneirla and Beach have drawn attention to the ratio of kinds of organisms used to studies that have been made. These investigations reveal that in the first two decades of the twentieth century a wide range of animals was studied, but that in recent years the ubiquitous white rat has come to be the most popular experimental subject. While it is true that the rat is a very convenient animal, which breeds readily and is economical to stock and care for, it is not necessarily an animal whose behavior can be taken as typical. When such an assumption of typicality is erroneously made, generalizations are developed which can obscure fundamental phylogenetic differences.

In a phylogenetic examination it is preferable to start with a consideration of the general question of modifiability rather than with "learning" as such. Starting in this manner, one can try to arrive at a definition of learning and can try to avoid the pitfalls that beset the unwary who initiate their inquiries with a firmly held opinion based on one species on what constitutes learning. Further, this approach makes it unnecessary to assume that different animals use the same mechanism in changing their responses to environmental circumstances.

It is well known that changes in behavior can occur for many different reasons. Growth changes in nerves and muscles, as Coghill has shown, can fundamentally alter the patterns of action of the larval amblystoma. Such structural changes underlie the development of swimming in the amblystoma and provide the basic framework for many of the reflexlike activities typical of the amphibian organism. In an insect like the honeybee growth changes in the salivary glands and wax glands are held to determine the social functions of the young adult. The young worker feeds larvae for about two weeks, but ceases this activity as the salivary glands atrophy and the wax glands begin active functioning. During the period of active wax secretion the young worker is engaged in comb construction. Changes in behavior may also occur in animals as the result of alterations produced in the sense organs as a consequence of previous stimulation. However, when one refers to changes produced by learning neither the modifications in behavior attendant upon growth nor the variations in sensitivity occurring as a consequence of adaptation are meant. However, this is a negative statement, and is not an adequate definition of learning. A positive approach can be achieved through the analysis of a concrete instance of learning.

Conditioning

Although learning has been said to occur in protozoa, the alterations in behavior described are capable of being accounted for by sensory adaptation and by peripheral chemical changes. The common earthworm is the lowest form of animal that has been shown to be capable of "true" learning. Yerkes has shown that the earthworm when placed in a T-maze is capable of learning to avoid the arm of the maze in which it was given an electric shock. In his maze, the left arm of the T contained electrodes that delivered a shock when the animal encountered them. On the maze floor a short distance before it reached the electrodes was a rough sandpaper surface over which the animal had to travel. When the earthworm was first placed in the maze it moved up the long arm, turned left, passed over the rough surface, and touched the electrodes. The shock which ensued produced a violent avoidance reaction. After a number of trials the animal began to exhibit the avoidance reaction as soon as it encountered the sandpaper, and *before it reached the electrodes.* Now the sandpaper, which originally was a neutral stimulus, has begun to acquire new arousal properties. It has apparently begun to take on some of the stimulational characteristics of the electric shock as a consequence of being associated with it in space and time. In the first instance, then, learning represents that phenomenon whereby a stimulus acquires new properties as the result of being temporally and spatially contiguous with another stimulus. This type of learning in which the arousal properties of one stimulus are changed because of its association with another stimulus is called conditioning.

Conditioning of a simple kind has been shown to occur in marine worms, in animals like snails, in insects, and in all the vertebrate forms. However, in the insects, in the vertebrates, and in particular in the mammals, simple contiguity of stimuli is only one of the conditions leading to learning. The evolution of the nervous system involves the complication of central conduction processes and the appearance of new mechanisms of organization. This development provides the conditions for new mechanisms of modifiability, which can best be appreciated through the comparative study of vertebrate learning.

As long ago as 1880 the physician-naturalist Abbott tried to study learning in a frog. The problem he selected was the determination of whether a frog could be taught to inhibit its natural tendency to strike at small moving objects such as flies. He placed the frog on a stand and immediately in front of it he presented a moving fly impaled on a pin stuck through the center of a mica sheet. Surrounding the fly was a palisade of sharp points. Thus, when the frog struck at the fly its tongue would be cut by the palisade. After many trials the frog continued to strike even though it never obtained the food and despite the fact that its tongue had been literally shredded by the sharp points. Apparently the frog was incapable of learning to inhibit its visually determined striking response. Or, more correctly, it was incapable of learning such an inhibition under the conditions established by Abbott, as was shown by Schaeffer in a later study.

Schaeffer found that a frog could learn very quickly to inhibit its strike at a bitter, hairy caterpillar. After the frog had struck a relatively small number of times at such prey, the caterpillar ceased to be an adequate stimulus for eliciting the striking response. Apparently, then, negative chemical stimulation can influence the visually determined striking response, whereas combining the visual stimulus with a tactual tissue-damaging stimulus is an ineffective procedure.

The foregoing example is illustrative of a general characteristic found in the learning of lower vertebrates. In these animals the various special senses are largely effectively isolated from each other and possessed of relatively independent motor nerve organizations. The behavior of the animals tends to be dominated by one or another sensory system, and to be influenced only with marked difficulty by stimuli affecting the other sensoria. Consequently, behavior is markedly stereotyped and learning, while present, functions in a subsidiary role in determining the animal's activities. It is only with the appearance of a new kind of nervous tissue, the new cortex, that learning comes into prominence as the main determiner of behavior. This tissue which first is found in a rudimentary form in reptiles achieves its highest development in man. In it stimuli from all sense organs converge and intermingle and are integrated into a unitary organized pattern. Further, in the cortex there exists a common motor projection system. As a consequence the domination of behavior by a single sensory system gives way to behavior which is conditioned by the totality of sensory events. Here, as is not the case with lower vertebrates, any sensory system can affect any other, and variability and learning come to replace reflexlike stereotypy as characteristic behavior. It is, therefore, in mammals that learning comes to be the most important determinant of behavior.

In the mammal it is possible to develop conditioning with great ease, as Pavlov has so successfully demonstrated. However, almost inevitably, in the mammal the simple factor of stimulus contiguity begins rapidly to be merged with a new problem. This is the consideration of the way in which the consequences of actions affect learning, a phenomenon which can best be approached by analyzing the behavior of a mammal in a problem box.

Selective Learning

Thorndike extensively investigated the manner in which hungry cats learned to escape from the confines of a problem box to reach food. When the hungry cat was first placed in the box it behaved in a highly excitable manner and with much variability. Different portions of the box were clawed at, pushed, and rubbed against. In the course of this varying activity the cat chanced to strike the string which released the latch and managed to leave the box. On subsequent trials the animal was much less excited, and more and more began to limit its activities to the neighborhood of the latch string. Eventually, the cat, when placed in the box, went directly to the latch string, pulled it and walked out the door. In successive trials variability of behavior is diminished and action comes to be restricted to those aspects which are required to escape from confinement. Such learning is apparently dependent upon at least three factors. In the first place, the animal must be one which behaves in a variable manner. Secondly, the animal's repertoire of responses, as revealed in its varying action, must include the appropriate response pattern. Finally, the consequences of the appropriate actions function to fixate the frequency with which they occur, while inappropriate responses are eliminated. This kind of learning has been called either trial and error learning or selective learning.

Although selective learning is most characteristic of the mammal it is not the exclusive possession of this animal form. Arthropods as well as lower vertebrates also exhibit the ability to learn selectively, but to a limited extent. Thus, a bird can learn to press a string and escape from a puzzle box. But, if the string is moved to another part of the cage, the bird spends an enormous amount of time in the region where the string was formerly present instead of shifting locus and working on the string in its new position as would a mammal.

The maze has also been used as an instrument for the study of selective learning. In general the task in the maze consists of learning to avoid entering blind alleys and of fixating progression along the "true" path to the goal box. A variety of animals has been observed in mazes, and their behavior reveals certain differences between the learning of mammals and of lower forms. The differences do not lie merely in the number of trials required to learn the maze, because, as has been shown, rats can learn certain mazes faster than can men. It is mainly in qualitative features of performance that differences are revealed. An insect like the ant tends to learn a maze piecemeal, with the elimination of the blind alleys occurring as independent and isolated events. The mammal such as the rat eliminates blind alleys in an interdependent manner, and shows much greater flexibility in readjustment when changes in specific blinds are introduced. Further, the rat comes to anticipate the goal box and is able to utilize short cuts and to ignore the previously learned paths when such possibilities are introduced by the experimenter.

While selective learning is characteristic of mammals it is not the highest form of learning of which they are capable. At the turn of the century, it was indicated that higher mammals, particularly primates, exhibited a kind of learning which was apparently not dependent on trial and error. This ability, which consisted of dealing with the related and relational features of the environment directly, was called "practical judgment." This area has been most fully explored by the Gestalt psychologists in their studies of insight.

Insight

The tool using of monkeys and apes exemplifies the kind of behavioral modifications that have been called insightful. In Köhler's experiments certain chimpanzees were found to be able to use sticks to obtain food that was out of reach, to move and to stack boxes to get at suspended food, and even to join two short sticks together to make a single long stick for reaching at distant objects. Although such behavior often is abrupt and sudden, it should not be considered to occur independently of previous learning. In one of my own studies, I showed that young chimpanzees who had had no experience with sticks could not use them as problem-solving tools. However, after only a short period of experience with sticks in the course of spontaneous play, the animals were able to use them as instruments in problem solving. Once the chimpanzee begins to use sticks as a tool it spontaneously expands its environmental manipulations—sometimes to the annoyance of the experimenter. One of my animals persisted in thrusting her stick through the cage bars and flicking the electric light switch on and off. When this was prevented, she proceeded to use the stick to unscrew the electric light bulb. Such spontaneous extensions and reorganizations of mastered behaviors are not characteristic of selective learning.

It is probable that the suddenness of problem solutions in primates occurs as the result of the reorganization of previous learning. In one study I investigated this problem by means of using a cage which had an enclosed inner compartment which could be reached only through a small trap door in one of its solid walls. An animal placed in the outer cage could not see into the inner cage. First a stick was placed on a shelf in the inner cage and shown to the chimpanzee. Then the experimenter took the animal for a roundabout walk and led it into the outer cage through an outside door. Food was then placed outside the cage and beyond the reach of the animal. The chimpanzee first reached for the food with its hand and was unsuccessful. He then paused, wandered about the cage, and gazed fixedly at the food. Suddenly he stopped and then ran to the trapdoor, leaped into the inner cage, and with no hesitation seized the stick and hurried with it to the food place. There he speedily swept the food into reach and ate. This behavior appeared to be based upon the reorganization and integration of two previous but separately acquired experiences, (1) the experience in using sticks, and (2) the knowledge that a stick was in the inner cage. These previous experiences provided the raw materials out of which the animal fabricated a response appropriate to the demands of the situation. Maier's studies of reasoning show that such reorganization may also occur in a much less complicated manner in lower mammals like the rat. However, reorganizational behavior is found most frequently in the primates, and is particularly prominent in human creative activity.

Over the years investigators have attempted to create test situations which could be used to determine the comparative intelligence of animals. In this connection, the delayed response deserves some mention. In the direct delayed response procedure an animal is shown food being placed in one of a number of containers and then after a delay period is permitted to make its choice. In the indirect delayed response procedure the animal is first trained to associate food with a light. Then it is shown a number of doors with a light over one of them. The light is extinguished and the animal chooses from among the doors. Obviously, a correct response consists of going to the door which had been illuminated. Lower mammals can perform successfully if the delay interval is not longer than a few minutes. However, the primates can sustain considerably longer delays—in one report up to several hours. Further, the primate can apparently anticipate the contents of the container, for as it was reported a monkey flew into a tantrum when lettuce was substituted for a banana during a delay interval. This ability to sustain long delays and to anticipate contents is probably very useful to the primate in its problem solving, a fact which is apparent in the example of chimpanzee reorganizational capacity given earlier in this chapter.

Summary

In summary it may be noted that a phylogenetic examination of learning indicates that learning is not a unitary phenomenon, but may consist of stimulus substitution (conditioning), act selection (trial and error), reorganization of previously selected patterns (insight), or all of these in combination. It was also found that different characteristic modes of learning occurred at different animal levels, with contiguity learning typical of the invertebrates and lower vertebrates, selective learning prominent in the lower mammals, and insight or reorganization learning characteristic of primate forms. It was also noted that the kind of problem presented to the animal played a role in the type of response encountered. It is clear from these facts that no single animal may be safely chosen as the ideal subject for learning experiments, but that the study of learning in a wide range of organisms enriches our comprehension of the vagaries and complexities of the learning process.

THE EVOLUTION OF SOCIAL LIFE

Invertebrates

Up to this point we have been concerned with individual animals and have mentioned social groupings only in passing. However, one of the most important determiners of survival in the course of evolution has been the salutary effect of aggregation. Consequently, a large area of comparative psychology is devoted to the study of animal social life and to the attempt to understand the forces leading to the formation of animal societies. In a sense Darwinian theory made a negative contribution to such study, because in its emphasis on the tooth-and-claw aspects of the struggle for survival it lost sight of the positive contributions to survival made by the coöperative relations among animals. It remained for the anecdotalists to enunciate the principle of mutual aid as a primary aspect of animal life. Although the evidence advanced was largely anecdotal, it was no more so than the evidence offered to "prove" the tooth-and-claw doctrine, and it served to focus attention on a serious gap in evolution theory.

The survival of even unicellular organisms is promoted by aggregation. Allee in a series of studies has demonstrated that certain unicellular forms live longer under adverse conditions when they are present in large aggregations than when they are exposed to the noxious situation as individuals. Of course such aggregations are "social" only in the broadest sense of the term, and more properly should be referred to as accumulations. The latter term is preferable since the animals come together as a result of individual responses to environmental pressures and not because of a specific interindividual relationship. In a sense then the accumulations are the result of an environmental trap phenomenon. However, even such an ability to be "trapped" promotes species survival. The value of aggregation in protozoans appears to depend on the facilitative effects of accumulated metabolic waste products.

INSECT SOCIETIES

Insect societies have probably received more protracted attention than those of any other form. Even Solomon was an intermittent student of ant society, and later philosophers and statesmen have frequently sought in insect societies for moral and social values that could profitably be applied to man. The consequences of so much interest have not been particularly helpful in the development of a real understanding of insect society. Analogy to human affairs has frequently replaced the analysis of insect life, and a picture of insect societies as excellent or horrible models for human society has been substituted for the consideration of the dynamic processes which produce the complex social organizations found among the insects. It is in the work of Wheeler that the key to an understanding of insect societies can be found.

Wheeler has demonstrated that in the course of evolution some two dozen insect societies have been independently developed out of originally solitary, nonsocial forms. The reason for the development lies in the structure of the social insects and in the way in which this structure promotes the development of learned interindividual relationships. According to Wheeler, social insects develop as a result of three things. First, the parent organism must be one which has a life span which overlaps the appearance of its offspring. Second, the eggs and larval young must have physical and chemical characteristics which cause the parent organism to lick and to manipulate them. Finally, the adults and the young must exchange food products—the adult licks fatty exudates from the young and the young stimulates regurgitation in the adult. The totality of social relations appearing around the exchange of food, or the exchange of stimuli related to food, has been named *trophalaxis* by

Wheeler. The life of a typical ant colony illustrates these relationships very nicely.

On a warm summer day we can often observe winged ants flying above a meadow. These ants are either males or fertile females known as virgin queens, and they are engaged in the so-called "marriage" flight. The males fertilize the females who then descend to the ground. Fertilization changes the light sensitivity of the female and she becomes negatively phototropic. She burrows deeply, bites off her wings, and hibernates through the winter. In the following spring she lays her eggs. These are gathered together, licked, and in some cases many eggs may be eaten. When the remaining eggs hatch and larvae appear the queen licks the larvae, and they in turn stimulate her to regurgitate food droplets which they ingest. The larvae develop, become pupae, and later adult workers who continue to exhibit the food interchange pattern with the queen, with other workers in the colony, and with new generations of young. Once a colony is established in this way it becomes self-sustaining. Different tasks are carried out by the colony members on the basis of their structural characteristics. Thus castes of workers, soldiers, and males exist in the colony as a result of the fact that the offspring of the queen are polymorphic, and the ensuing specific differences in structure *permanently* determine the roles played by individuals in the colony. As a result the division of labor in an ant colony is anatomically determined and immutable, in contrast with human society in which the social role of the individual is historically and culturally defined.

Adult ants from different colonies attack one another if they meet. This fact has been fancifully interpreted as being a manifestation of social awareness, consciousness of kind, and as a defense of territory against an intruder. However, such fighting does not occur if the ants are habituated to the same colony chemical. Fields raised a heterogeneous collection of ants in a single nest and found that they lived together peaceably, and it was found that "foreign" ants dipped in an extract of a colony's chemical were accepted by the colony.

COMMUNICATION

An aspect of insect social life that has recently received a great deal of attention as a result of the publication of certain researches of Von Frisch on the honeybee is communication. A worker bee, after taking nectar at a flower, returns to the nest and shortly afterward a number of secondary finder bees may be observed in the same flower patch. Three factors are involved in this behavior. The first finder bee upon its return to the nest sensitizes other bees to the flower chemical. Secondly, the finder bee does a dance which has two components, the first round and the second wiggle-waggle. The round dance excites secondary bees who then orient toward the original finder, while the waggle dance causes them to orient in the direction from the hive in which the food was found. This orientation is based on the sensitivity of the bee to polarized light and once the orientation is developed it is maintained by the environmental polarization gradient. As a consequence secondary bees whose orientation has been preëstablished by their responses to the activities and chemical characteristics of the original finder bee move in the direction of the food place when they fly from the hive. No interpretation based upon "intelligence," "language," etc., needs to be applied to these phenomena. In "communication," as indeed in their entire social life, the insects are limited by their restricted learning capacity and by the structurally determined stereotypy of their actions.

Vertebrates

The social life of vertebrate animals has not, on the whole, been given the same kind of detailed consideration by scientists as has that of insects. In part this derives from the tendency of psychologists to use the vertebrates as the testing ground for hypotheses derived from human social life. As a consequence the investigations have tended to be "problem-centered" rather than "organism-centered" and behaviors have been described in vertebrates in isolation from the general pattern of social life for the given organism. This tendency is most obviously seen in the study of dominance-submission relationships, which have been used by a large number of investigators as the typical form of social interaction in vertebrate animals. For example, it has repeatedly been demonstrated that "peck" orders come to exist in a variety of birds. In the simplest cases these dominance hierarchies are linear and bird 1 pecks bird 2 and 3, bird 2 pecks bird 3, etc., but 3 never pecks 2 or 1, and 2 never pecks 1. In other cases the hierarchies are not linear, and may sometimes assume very complicated patterns. However, such dominance orders give us little basis for understanding positive social relations like feeding young offspring and caring for chicks. Nor does the dominance hierarchy bear any predictive relation to flock leadership, since it is not the dominant bird which characteristically first enters new territory or leads the flock in flight.

Dominance and aggressive relationships have been demonstrated to exist in other vertebrates ranging from fish and reptiles to mammals and even primates. But, as Schneirla has pointed out, dominance hierarchies appear under rather special conditions, "particularly when groups of birds or primates are confined within a small space, when incentives (i.e., food and drink) are restricted in quantity or in accessibility, or when sexual responsiveness is high." Further, as Carpenter has shown, there are primates like the howler monkey in which no indications of dominance hierarchy formation have been found. As a consequence it is doubtful if the dominance conception is an adequate basis for describing vertebrate social relations in general. It should rather be viewed as a form of social interaction which characterizes groups living under suboptimal conditions, and as a symptom of the disintegration of positive social relations rather than as a feature of their maintenance. This latter point is clearly evident in the report of a baboon colony which was placed on a small island in a London zoo. Under these constrictive conditions, dominance-submission and aggressive relations grew so intense that the animals destroyed themselves through continual fighting.

Moreover, as several investigators have pointed out, as we ascend the scale from lower vertebrates to the higher ones, aggression becomes a less prominent feature of social life and coöperative inter-relations appear to be the more characteristic type of interaction. In no animal form is positive social behavior more clearly present than in the primate, and it is desirable to examine the social behavior of this vertebrate grouping in some detail. The study of primate social relations is important, too, because it provides us with some notion of the biological prototypes from which human societies originated.

Primate societies range in size from simple pairings and offspring to large hordes of several hundred members. In almost all instances the social grouping devolves from the biological family. However, family organization is not homogeneous and may consist in one primate form of a single adult mating pair and their offspring, in another of a mature male, a number of mature females and a miscellany of younger animals, or in still another of several adult males and females together with adolescents and young. Mating behavior is varied and may range from "monogamy" to complete "promiscuity" in sexual behavior. The societies may exhibit a great deal of aggressive behavior and hierarchical structure as in the baboon, or be almost entirely coöperative and peaceful as in the howler monkey. However, in all cases the attachment of the individual to the group is very strong and there are literally no nonsocial species of primates. The social character of the primate is so pronounced that Köhler was led to remark that a chimpanzee in isolation from his fellows is not a chimpanzee at all.

The strength of social attachment in primates probably derives from the prolonged period of infantile helplessness and childhood dependency, as a consequence of which a deep and abiding relation is established through a long series of mutual satisfactions and interstimulations. As the infant grows it comes into contact with other young organisms, plays with them, grooms and is groomed, and gives and receives food. The resulting tie to the group is so strong that a hungry howler monkey will stop eating and move after his group if it begins to leave the feeding place. In a group of six young chimpanzees that I observed almost daily for two years, one animal would not drink his milk if another member did not come to the feeding place. He would first go to the absent individual and pull him to the feeding place, after which he would eat.

The result of such strong social cohesion in organisms as intelligent as the primate is the emergence of rudimentary forms of coöperative activity. Thus Carpenter has observed howler monkey adults help young across large gaps in the trees by either bridging the gap with their bodies, bending the branches into reach of the youngster, or by carrying the young animal over the gap. Similar occurrences among the chimpanzees in the African jungle have been reported. It is, therefore, not surprising that in the laboratory situation young chimpanzees can be trained to work coöperatively in the solving of a variety of problems.

In the coöperative problem-solving situation the chimpanzees engage in a rather large amount of communication, and cause one another to act in appropriate ways through gestures, posturings, and grunting vocalizations. Thus coöperation in the primate is at a high psychological level, and involves the ability of the organism to anticipate the effects of its actions upon its fellows in the pursuit of a common objective. These facts have led Schneirla to call primate coöperation "psychosocial" in contrast with the "biosocial" facilitations of lower forms such as the insects. It is out of the psychosocial coöperation of primates that the enormously more advanced societies of the highest primate, man, take their origin. However, man has something that is essentially new and which makes him human, *culture*. The tendency of the older generation to transmit its individually acquired and socially inherited experience to the younger generation is the essence of culture. It exists only in the most fragmentary form in primate societies, where each generation, in the main, must individually and painfully acquire the same stock of knowledge that was accumulated by its parents. As a result each succeeding generation of primates has substantially the same level of control and mastery of the environment as did its ancestors. The social accumulation and transmission of understanding is absent, and changes which do occur are primarily the consequence of a leisurely process of biological evolution. In brief, biological societies are essentially conservative, in that each generation reproduces itself, while culturally organized societies are progressive, in that each generation accumulates understanding which lays the basis for new competencies in its offspring. Culture affects not only the general structure and dynamics of a society but also the nature of interindividual relationships. Thus while social status and social role in the lower primates is determined by individual skill and biological structure, in human societies status and role are determined by genealogy, property or other institutionalized forms. Because of these differences it is inadvisable to seek for direct analogues of human social life in primate societies.

ABNORMAL BEHAVIOR

A name frequently given to atypical or disturbed behavior in animals is "experimental neurosis," experimental because the behavior is deliberately induced, neurosis because the behavior is different from that which we think to be normal for the particular animal under investigation. It may be asked why we do not call the behavior observed "experimental psychosis" (in humans this term refers to the major mental illnesses which generally require hospitalization). To this question it might be answered that at the present time we do not have conclusive evidence that the animal's behavior is seriously or permanently disturbed, points which generally characterize psychosis. In evaluating animal studies of abnormal behavior, be the animal cockroach or chimpanzee, it is important to know something about its normal behavior. Such a study of normal behavior should include the animal's behavior in wild as well as in domesticated (cage) life. Only in this way can one understand what is meant by behavior deviations in a particular species. However, a comparison of disturbed animal behavior to disturbed human behavior on the basis of similarity alone is not sufficient. Science stresses both *similarities* and *differences*. Certainly there is a similarity in the kinds of situations which may cause a breakdown in man or animal and in the kinds of behavior that may be elicited. At the same time there are definite differences. We do not speak of the aspiration level of a cockroach, the Oedipus complex of a rat, or the attitude of a cat. In short, our culture with its overt directives and subtle nuances does not affect the animal as it does the human and consequently does not contribute as much to disturbed behavior in the former. This does not imply that study of disturbed animal behavior is wasteful and unproductive but merely that we must be careful in reasoning from lower animals to man. Mental disorder as we understand it today is in many ways peculiar to humans.

The terminology applied to disturbed behavior in animals is varied and there is no general agreement as to what type of behavior is to be called by what name. The subjective whim of the investigator may in practice determine the classification used. Thus one comes across such terms as *experimental neurosis, tantrum behavior, so-called animal hypnosis, convulsive seizures, borderline neurosis,* etc. Situations in which disturbed behavior may appear are also varied and it is not yet clear what the relative importance is of the many involved factors. Disturbed behavior may be found where there is restriction of activity, difficult discrimination, routine conditioning, vitamin deficiency, etc. The organisms affected by any of the above procedures are numerous and they include the cockroach, cat, rat, dog, sheep, pig, chimpanzee, etc. It might be mentioned at this point that identical procedures even with litter mates will not necessarily disturb the animals equally. While life among animals is not as complex as that among humans, this does not preclude the existence of individual differences in ability to withstand stress. It would seem that one rat, chicken, or pig should not be considered identical to the next rat, chicken, or pig. The next question concerns the type of responses or symptoms elicited. Here again the variety of symptoms, both physiological and psychological, is baffling. This list includes insomnia, cyanosis (condition of the body in which its surface becomes blue due to insufficient aeration of the blood), loss of pupillary reflex, loss of previous discriminatory ability, lack of gregariousness, significant change in heart rate, ejaculation, refusal to eat in the experimental situation, ticks, immobility, anesthesia, etc. Therapeutic procedures which have been attempted with animals (though with little success) include the use of: drugs, rest, activity outlets, and operative procedures such as lobotomy and thyroidectomy.

The limitations in the use of animals for the study of abnormal behavior have been noted. There are advantages as well. One can seldom use humans for this type of experiment. Furthermore it can be argued that one is frequently able to use large numbers of animals and consequently experimental conclusions derived are more soundly based. Another advantage is that one can more easily control the internal and external environment and genetic background as well. In the final analysis three conclusions may be reached about research on abnormal behavior in animals: (1) the data obtained provide us with information both about normal and abnormal behavior at different levels in the evolutionary scale, (2) scientific precautions are necessary to avoid rash generalizations from animal to man, and finally (3) it may be said that the study of disturbed animal behavior may represent a valuable approach to the puzzling problems that confront one in studying human psychopathology.

CONCLUSION

When a single chapter attempts to encompass a field it is necessarily synoptic. Abstractions must often be presented in the place of a richly detailed portrait of living organisms. The writer can only hope that this synopsis has whetted an appetite for greater knowledge and that the abstractions have posed questions and not repulsed inquiry. The field of comparative psychology, embracing as it does the life of all organisms, is really much more interesting than this chapter.

SUGGESTED READINGS

1. Maier, N. R. F., and Schneirla, T. C., *Principles of Animal Psychology*. New York: McGraw-Hill, 1935. A systematic and comprehensive discussion of behavior throughout the animal series. Clearly written, it is used extensively in courses in comparative psychology. At the end of each chapter there is a list of suggested readings.

2. Moss, F. A. (ed.), *Comparative Psychology*. New York: Prentice-Hall, rev. ed., 1946. This book presents a number of current problems in the field of comparative psychology. This text includes discussion by specialists of such questions as the effects of drugs, the neurology of learning, and the social behavior of animals.

3. Schneirla, T. C., Comparative psychology, *Encyclopaedia Britannica*, 1948. This article contains within its twenty pages an excellent and simply written survey of the history, problems, and procedures in animal psychology, evaluated from a modern point of view.

4. Tinbergen, N., *The Study of Instinct*. London: Oxford, 1951. An important book indicating the broader interpretation of comparative psychology held by European psychologists (as compared with American psychologists). This book is mainly concerned with a study of conditions responsible for innate behavior in a wide variety of species.

5. Von Frisch, K., *Bees: Their Vision, Chemical Senses, and Language*. Ithaca, N.Y.: Cornell, 1950. A challenging and interesting series of studies of sensory processes and communication in the bee. Findings are presented about which Von Frisch himself states, "No competent scientist ought to believe these things on first hearing."

6. Washburn, Margaret F., *The Animal Mind*. New York: Macmillan, 1908. A classic in the field of comparative psychology. This book represents one of the first attempts to interpret the data of animal behavior objectively and to utilize experimental methods in the study of comparative psychology.

Chapter 13

Psychology and Aesthetics

by RALPH H. GUNDLACH

Society and Aesthetics
      FOUNDING OF EXPERIMENTAL AESTHETICS
      PHASES OF LIFE INVOLVED IN AESTHETICS

The Psychological Nature of Aesthetics
      THE ARTIST
      THE PRODUCT
      THE AUDIENCE
      DIFFERENT ATTITUDINAL APPROACHES

A Classification of the Arts—The Product
      MUSIC
               Sounds and Their Stimuli
               Organization of Music
               The Aesthetic Response
      THE DANCE
               Motion as a Stimulus
               Organization of the Dance
               The Aesthetic Response
      PAINTING
               Color and Form as Stimuli
               Organization of Painting
               The Aesthetic Response
      ARCHITECTURE
      LITERATURE

Art Appreciation—The Audience
LEARNING TO APPRECIATE
CHILDREN AND THE VISUAL ARTS
DANCE AND DRAMA

Art and Society—The Artist
FUNCTION—A PRINCIPLE OF SOCIAL INTERACTION
STRUCTURE—A PRINCIPLE OF SOCIAL INTERACTION
The Cultural Tradition
The Class Tradition
The Art Tradition
The Unique Individual

Creative Activity

Suggested Readings

SOCIETY AND AESTHETICS

Persons, societies, and cultures display a bewildering variety of approaches to the meaning and objectives of their existence. Life's successes are thought of by many in terms of the accumulation of material property and wealth, or of the amount of consumer goods they conspicuously or inconspicuously consume. The exercise of power and domination over others is the driving goal of some, achieved often at great expense. Still others have moved to seek "salvation," perhaps by renunciation and denial; and others talk of human fellowship. Compare the cultural values of American manufacturers and businessmen with those of the fops of Restoration England, those of the monks in a medieval monastery, those of da Vinci and his contemporaries, and those of the villagers in Bali. In all of these the arts have some role to play—minor in some, major in others.

The arts tend to thrive in societies whose high-priority values look toward the welfare and happiness, and the rich fulfillment of the individual members of the society.

Another way of saying this is that those persons or societies whose lives are centered about war and conquest or about gaining control over people and things are building attitudes which are in large part incompatible with the contemplative, evaluative moods or the creative activities that inhere in aesthetics. In modern times, for example, it is clear to see that the Nazi leaders were quick to repress and destroy those artists and their products who could not be changed toward their fascist, restrictive, controlled social order. The wholesale censorship and direction of artists (and of scientists and teachers) in any society is a sign that the society is moving away from the goal of democratic institutions and moving toward the opposite pole of autocratic, fascist, enslaving institutions.

Participation in artistic activities is an enriching experience. The arts come out of the rich full feelings of people in song and dance, in story and legend, in ballad and drama, and in the style of construction of tools for living.

In our world today there is a tendency to play down the arts. Within our own society the arts have a clearly subordinate role. Just as the arts are subordinate in the values of contemporary society, so too, this important area for psychological study is peripheral in the field of psychology.

Founding of Experimental Aesthetics

Experimental psychology was born of the same parents as experimental aesthetics—H. L. F. von Helmholtz and Gustav Fechner. Helmholtz was one of the greatest scientists of the nineteenth century. His work on the sensation of tone, first published in 1863 and revised many times since then, was a monumental volume. In this book he formulated his famous theory of hearing, that there are resonators in the ear; and developed a theory of consonance and dissonance, a theoretical basis for musical harmony, and an account of the development of musical scales, instruments, and of music. Psychological work on tone sensations and music was continued as the major area of interest of Carl Stumpf, who for years was director of the psychological laboratories in Berlin.

Fechner's contribution was actually more influential on psychology. Although Wilhelm Wundt is credited with establishing the first experimental laboratory in psychology at Leipzig, 1879, the ground for this laboratory was the experimental approach to psychological problems developed thirty years earlier by Fechner, called psychophysics. Fechner's psychophysics showed a way to measure aspects of the "mental" world. The world of physics is measured in centimeters, grams, and seconds (cgs), but parallel measurement of sensory intensity in the "mental" world must be made, said Fechner, in units of just noticeable differences (jnd). This remarkable contribution was the resultant of several ways of quantifying sensory experience. Now that it had these methods of sensory measurement, and on the motor side the measurement of reaction time (from Helmholtz), psychology could at last become an experimental science.

Fechner extended his psychophysical methods to aesthetic matters. He took certain assertions about the basis of beauty as hypotheses to be tested experimentally. There was the idea, for instance, that the key to beauty in the visual arts is a certain proportion, the "golden section." That is, a proportion exists between two members such that the relation of the smaller to the larger is the same as that of the larger to the whole. Parts of a body, the parts of a line, the sides of a square will have the golden section, if $A:B::B:A + B$. The ratio is roughly 0.62. Fechner's elaborate and careful experimental approach resulted in many ingenious ways of testing the various questions raised. He not only worked with masterpieces of art, but he also constructed a series of rectangles, crosses, elipses, and other simplifications and controls and found that judgments of beauty or preference were scattered. Some people preferred one relationship while others went to the other extreme. In a number of cases the average value approximated the golden section, in others it did not. Fechner himself was looking for *the* artistically correct proportion, the "one best form" in each situation, and he looked upon the distribution of judgments about a mean value as indications of error and fallibility of his judges. The importance of individual values and the falseness of the supposition that there is *a* best form regardless of function or configuration, only became clear much later.

Two things are important to note in connection with the work of Fechner and the early traditional psychologists; one is constructive and the other is critical. The good thing that Fechner initiated was the experimental approach. He saw the fact of beauty and value in artistic products as a nest of problems that could be explored experimentally. He invented many ingenious ways of testing the various questions. This was a tremendous contribution. Fechner, as indicated, laid the basis for modern experimental work in psychology and in aesthetics. It would be much better in the foregoing sentence just to say in psychology, for in Fechner's view aesthetic problems were hardly another "field" but an integral part of the problems of perception and judgment. The second important point is a commentary on some assumptions underlying the approach of Fechner and most of the scientists that preceded him and that followed him in the next fifty to seventy-five years. This is the unquestioned assumption that it is possible to break down the experience of objects and events into "elemental" components. From this approach one would search for a key proportion which would give unity to painting, sculpture, architecture. One would think it fruitful to study the mood effect and expressiveness of each isolated color and the elemental combinations as a basis for determining aesthetic reactions to pictures; one would think the solution to design would be found in the reactions to isolated lines varied in size, direction, and breadth; in poetry one would ask what words are beautiful; and in music the approach would be to experiment with the emotion-arousing quality of separate tones or other sounds; and so on for other "elements." As a matter of fact, this was almost exactly the direction taken by experimental aesthetics. The outcome was largely negative: the response to a simple sound is not the same as to that sound in a melody or in a word. Even responses to these "elements" were not uniform or consistent. The atomistic approach, as is now well-known, was a long and well-explored cul-de-sac for experimental psychology and for aesthetics.

Nearly forty years ago the Gestalt school sharply criticized their contemporaries and predecessors for following erroneous assumptions such as the "constancy hypothesis" of a one-to-one relation between stimulus and response, and the "atomistic hypothesis" that rich experiences such as those arising from viewing a painting or hearing a symphony are nothing more than the summation of the responses to each individual spot or note. The beauty and expressiveness is a function of the total organization.

In the United States psychological interest centered about the development of the applied areas. Few of the many thousands of American psychologists were concerned with or interested in the problems of art and art appreciation.

Phases of Life Involved in Aesthetics

How many persons do you know who paint their own pictures, or who ever painted a picture? Photographs and reproductions do not count. How many people do you know who ever wrote a poem, or made up a meaningful song—except as a school class exercise?

A machine-oriented society where articles are standardized, mass-produced, and sold by national and local advertising may have only a limited place for the skills of the artist; or from the viewpoint of the consumer, for developing individual tastes and appreciations. In our society, "art" is remote from life and tends to be confined to "odd" characters and locations. Artists are viewed as eccentrics, and their products are "caged" in museums and galleries, or are displayed for an evening's entertainment from a concert stage. Museums and concerts, it is true, may be found in most of the large cities; but few people attend and fewer participate. Art as we experience it today does not have much impact upon the lives of the people of the community.

In primitive societies, in tribal groups, one finds that aesthetic productions and artistic activities are integral parts of daily living. There are the songs and legends about how the world is run, about the seasons and climate, about heroes, gods, and their deeds; there are ceremonials and dances around the major events of one's life—

birth, puberty, marriage, sickness, death; there may be artistry around the dress, style of living quarters, the cooking, hunting, fighting tools, and instruments. In many economically simple societies, the routines of living have an artistic flavor, and the performances include many or most of the members of the society.

The comparison of western Europe and American culture with that of other groups demonstrates the division in our society of art into two parts: a "class" art and a "folk" art, both of which are largely removed from the core of social living. The "folk" art includes the lively, the vulgar levels, where the values of living are savored. In our society, these would include folk songs, popular dance music, and jokes; dress and make-up; perhaps some parades and athletic spectacles. The "class" art has developed only within the last few hundred years. In the specialization of occupations the artist became differentiated from other citizens. The artist's product became confined to the concert hall or the display museum, which call for a passive role from the audiences. The separation has grown so far between art and life, that a new occupation has developed— the *critic*. The official critic is a commercial middleman whose job it is to bridge the gap between the artist and his audience, and evaluate the qualities and virtues of the artist.

In our society many people do not realize that there are aesthetic questions concerning public buildings and factories; offices and stores; homes, apartments, and community organization; and the very design of objects and tools of daily living.

THE PSYCHOLOGICAL NATURE OF AESTHETICS

From the point of view of psychology, many of the problems of the arts are similar to those of fields usually looked upon as quite different. In these days, the psychologist does not start with the smallest fragment he can find. On the contrary, he tries to get the whole picture in its setting. A schematic representation of what is involved appears in Figure 13.1. The figure is clearly circular, and this is a defect that in fact is remedied by the dynamics of events.

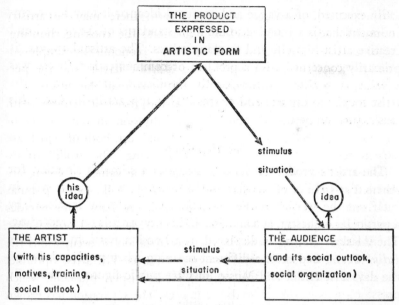

FIGURE 13.1.   The Artist and His Product in Relation to Society.

The circular figure can still represent the superposition of processes that do occur in time.

The Artist

Because the diagram is circular, one could start at any point. The artist, for instance, does not emerge out of a vacuum. He is a person with capacities, skills, and training who was born and brought up in some society, and his outlook about people, about what people want, and the world has been shaped by these factors. This is obvious, as one can see by noting the background of, say, Milton, Picasso, or the architect for the Taj Mahal. Nor does the artist start his own particular creative activity without some reason, some initiating, stimulating situation. Many persons including artists may get a vague idea, and let it drop there. Other ideas may become clear, and may get expressed in some artistic form. In the end it may not be the same idea; or it may be a poor expression, badly executed, of a vague and confused idea; or it may be an embodiment that is acceptable to the high standards of the critical and creative artist himself, and to many others. The artist, however, is primarily concerned with a problem of communication. There was a value, a quality, an emotionally significant episode which the artist sought to capture and express. This appears in his book, his music, painting, etc.

The Product

The artist's product in its turn becomes a stimulus situation for others, for publics of various kinds. But the artist's creation is in itself not the whole stimulus situation. A symphony is played by a particular orchestra, at some date in history; or it is on a recording. The Alaskan carving is displayed in a London museum. The play *Julius Caesar* had quite a different meaning when produced during the days that Hitler and Mussolini were public figures in the daily press.

The Audience

An audience—one person or many—may catch some kind of an idea from the presentation to him of the work of art. But the artist's production, as already indicated, comes in a context; and it also is presented to a person who brings with himself a set of values and expectancies, a level of sophistication, and a limited desire or motive regarding the object presented. As an illustration of this latter point, Freud one time commented on the meaning of Michelangelo's famous "David," and showed that various art critics evaluating this sculpture had assumed at least three sharply contrasting interpretations of what was going on. Similarly, there is more than one interpretation of *Hamlet*.

The artist's creation has some sort of effect upon some public. The effect upon the public may be small, or as great as the impact upon world history of the Bible or the writings of Confucius. And as the values of society are modified, as people's understandings and feelings are sharpened and changed by these and other creative works, so changes occur in the whole social pattern, the whole culture. This completes the circle of Figure 13.1, for the next artist comes out of such a revised society, and in his turn aids the perpetuation and revision of the succeeding generations. He is part of it, made of it; and in return, makes his contribution to society's culture.

Such a diagram, however, will fit almost equally well a great many patterns of human interrelationship. With minor changes it would hold for the relations to society of scientists and inventors, teachers, ministers, advertisers, and many others. It is basically the pattern of communication. What distinguishes the artist from others, in such a relationship, is not the pattern of the interplay nor the materials involved. Essentially the distinguishing feature has to do with attitudes.

Different Attitudinal Approaches

It is possible to formulate various attitudes or points of view which persons can take. This does not mean that one's attitudes may not be mixed; nor does it mean that any single person keeps the same attitude all his life. It is true, however, that in some societies one attitude may predominate and in other societies a different attitude is customary.

The attitude most current in our society is that of use or practicality. "What is it good for? What do I get out of it? How can it be used? Where will it get me?" are typical questions. In academic circles the practical question is asked by the engineer, the doctor, dentist, pharmacist, agronomist, home economist, and educator. These practical technologists may invent and discover new things; but their aim and orientation is toward the solution of some practical, immediate, specific problem. Another attitude characterizes the scientist, whose attitude is generalizing rather than specific. "What is it? How does it operate?" are his questions, and they are concerned with knowledge. A third attitude is concerned with values and questions of ethics. "What should I do? What is my obligation?"

The aesthetic attitude is also evaluating, but not in a moral sense. Suppose you look at a picture. You can look at it in various ways, with various attitudes. You may be interested in the technique and the materials; or whether the shape and composition would be appropriate for your living room wall; what it reminds you of; what it would cost. Aesthetic appreciation, however, requires a kind of a psychological relaxation on the part of the observer which permits the picture to move him. This receptivity, this passive-but-sensitive attitude is foreign to much of American life. The typical American is always on the alert to master and dominate, to control and manage—often for fear that if he doesn't, he will be controlled and bested. But in aesthetic areas the only way to experience the rich emotional values is by relaxing, by abandoning the hard, suspicious, competitive, and dominating attitudes. As a girl learns to follow the lead of her dancing partner, so the observer must learn to be led by the art object.

Clearly, aesthetic appreciation is a high skill to be achieved only with much practice. The rudiments of it, however, can be found in those grand situations in nature—an expanse of great ocean beach, a sunset, the Grand Canyon—where the mass, volume, and extent of the situation may provoke even "city-bred toughs" into a moment of exalted appreciating contemplation. It takes effort to be receptively attuned: pictures in a gallery can quickly develop "museum fatigue" in the unskilled visitor.

To sum up: aesthetics has as its distinguishing characteristic a kind of evaluating attitude which sets it off from other attitudes that are common in life. But the fundamental fact is that the relations between the artist and his product, his audience and his society, are much like the relations of anyone else singled out from society: the relations are mutual, with a certain loose play between the parts due to the difficulties of communication. People rarely if ever see, hear, or smell exactly what is focused on their sense organs: they always carry a preconception with them, a projected frame and setting, an anticipating interpretation.

A CLASSIFICATION OF THE ARTS—THE PRODUCT

There was no problem of classifying the arts in earlier days, for there were no arts, artists, critics, or scientists as such. Specialization and differentiation of occupation and function are a recent development, and so is the tendency to relegate art and art appreciation to the concert hall and the museum.

Apparently music, dance, and poetry and the theater were all one to the primitive peoples attempting to control their environment and their futures by magical practices, by the hypnotic ecstasy of the sung dance, by the protecting and controlling power of ritual and mummery and the magic of expressed wishful-thinking fantasy. A witch doctor simply organized and led the group, and became the spokesman pacing the way with a background of the echoing chorus. Every man was more or less a poet-singer-dancer, and the arts were the work of the people. Even the Greeks in the height of their civilization had no separate art forms for instrumental music alone, nor for verse apart from song. Of course oil painting is only about five hundred years old and novel writing is more recent than the printing press. The novel has given up poetic rhythm for other features; and concert music, moving toward rich rhythmic and tonal development, has lost its integration with dance and poetry.

Although the arts have been classified in many ways, and probably there is no one best way, it is worth while to consider the arts in relation to certain psychological functions. The functions in-

A MOOD (sensuous and perceptual)	AN OBJECT (sensuous and repre- sentational)	AN IDEA (representational and conceptual)

music ↔ dance ↔ architecture ↔ sculpture ↔ painting ↔ poetry ↔ prose

chants ↔ pantomime ↔ photography ↔ movies ↔ drama ↔ cartoons

FIGURE 13.2. A Classification of the Arts.

volved are primarily three: the perceptual, the representational, and the conceptual. These processes are involved in the appreciation of every art, but some arts are predominantly on the sensual-perceptual level, some are predominantly representational, and some are conceptual. Art products represent a continuum with music most often reflecting a mood and prose most often conveying an idea. A scheme of classifying the arts is presented in Figure 13.2.

A sample of five of the above arts will be briefly discussed in terms of the sensory materials they employ, how the materials are organized, and their impact as aesthetic experience.

Music

SOUNDS AND THEIR STIMULI

The stimulus for hearing consists in fairly rapid alternations in air pressure, affecting the ears. This mechanical energy, as transformed by the sense organs and central nervous system, is experienced as sound. Sounds are conventionally classed into three groups: tones, noises, and between these extremes, vocables. Tones are elicited by relatively periodic vibrations of atmospheric pressure, ranging from about 20 to 20,000 per second, figuratively referred to as "sound waves," and noises by aperiodic shifts in pressure. The vocables seem related to a whole pitch region.

All of the auditory experiences, whether tones, vocables, or noises, vary in certain respects that used to be called "sensory attributes" but now are more properly called dimensions of the experience. The idea of "attribute" was invented in those days of atomistic thinking when experience was said to be made of mental elements (sensations), after the analogy of physical elements (atoms). But then it became clear that what was actually meant by "a sensation" was simply an abstractive perception and not a structure.

Sounds vary in four directions, some of which have fairly simple relations to the physical stimulus, and some seem related to factors not only of the stimulus but also of the inner ear. The intensity of the stimulus is roughly related to the *loudness* or softness of the sound. The frequency of the vibrations are roughly translated into high or low *pitch*. From here on the terms employed are not universally systematized and accepted. Another dimension is called *volume,* sometimes referred to as brightness. This is related both to pitch (with loudness held constant) and to loudness (with pitch held constant). Low tones seem massive, spread out; high tones, as of a soprano or of a piccolo, are small. The remaining quality, *density,* may be understood by the difference between the compact, penetrating, piercing tone, in contrast to the diffuse qualities at the other extreme. It is with pitch, of course, that the major complications arise. The auditory mechanism is in many respects like a series of resonators, and it is this feature which gives hearing some of its most distinctive characteristics. One of these is the importance of the overtone series. The overtones (multiples of the fundamental frequency) of a music instrument give that instrument its unique quality, its *timbre*. Other characteristics of sounds, such as beat tones, difference and summation tones, masking, consonance and dissonance, or the effects of attenuating high or low frequencies as found in telephonic communication, recording, radio, and the like, will have to be omitted from this discussion.

ORGANIZATION OF MUSIC

Basically, music, like dance and theater. is a temporal art as opposed to the plastic arts and painting. The rhythmic patterns and various themes provide the easiest way to describe music. However, the qualitative fusion of sounds at any one time provides a significant difference from the parallel instantaneous presentation of a visual pattern of stimulation. The visual field is spatially laid out, and one can see only a single object at the same place at the same time. The auditory field is not spatial in the same sense, but is a qualitative fusion. Out of the mass of sound the components may be selectively attended to, if the listener has sufficient skill and training, and can follow various "voices" as well as note the harmonic texture.

Typical musical organization of a simple variety is seen in contemporary songs. The pattern is essentially a continuous melody line (rhythmical succession of tones) supported by a sequence of chords. Melody and chords are serially related in a system of harmony (combination of tones) so well worked out in hymns and "barbershop" singing. There are quite different ways of organizing sound into music, even within our own culture. In the days leading up through Bach, several voices, each having a linear melody, were set against one another in such a way that interesting harmonic and textural qualities emerged. In modern times, too, the musicians have moved off in many directions from the romantic tradition, seeking new kinds of sounds and new ways to organize them. They have gone from the traditional tempered scale to the quarter-tone scale; they have tried various modes other than major and minor, and with use of half-tone chromatic scales or whole-tone scales have abandoned even the stabilizing convention of "key"; they have shifted away from harmonic sequences to an interest in sound mass and tonal "color." Music of the East, India, China, the South Pacific, has an entirely different convention, being melodic and rhythmic rather than harmonic.

THE AESTHETIC RESPONSE

Some studies have shown that there are subcortical responses to sounds which affect adrenal secretions and circulatory and respiratory changes, and sometimes get a startle effect which changes the tonicity in the musculature. Visceral responses may be involved as part of the aesthetic experience. Such findings account in part for the effects of music as an energizer and as a stimulant to morale in factories, on the athletic field, and with marching groups. Music has also been successfully used in hospitals to facilitate recovery. Among primitive groups songs are employed in many ways including curative rituals.

Other studies have been made to find out what music means to people, what it can convey. Many of the findings indicate that the auditor uses the period of listening to let himself daydream either in dependence upon the music, or completely on his own. Some seem only to watch the players and conductor. Others listen to the music analytically and try to take it apart structurally, or listen for flaws in playing. A simpler phase of experience is the mood qualities which are a part of the musical ideas. Interesting studies have been conducted to determine the consistent mood meaning which a given musical phrase has to any considerable audience; and the characteristics in pitch, range, mode, melody line, loudness, rhythmic pattern, and many other variables which are most usually associated with any given mood quality.

Though the aesthetic effect of music is not symbolic or representational, it is possible, with musical instruments, to make sounds like a train or a bird or other object; and it is possible to work out conventions such that a particular set of sounds mean "get up" or "come to lunch," "captains, assemble" or "pick me up" What music conveys, on its own, is neither representational of objects, nor conceptual ideas on the level of workaday ideas. Language is ill adapted to indicate what are essentially musical ideas. The materials of music have become a part of external reality. For one equipped and trained to listen, there is tremendous delight in the statement and development of a theme, in the intricacies of contrast, tension and resolution, in the flow of the music.

Unless the listener has some background of experience listening to music, and has some idea of what the composer aims to do, he is in no position to fully enjoy or adequately evaluate what he hears. In this sense, appreciation is a skill that cannot be forced; the novice can be presented with a graded series of products, can be coached and skilled in performance and expression, and can have pointed out for his attention the differences, similarities, and complexities of music literature. But it is *his* appreciation.

The Dance

MOTION AS A STIMULUS

The materials used in the dance are expressive bodily movements which may be observed visually, but which carry their meaning in large part through the associated bodily movements of the observer. Members of an audience of a modern dance program may be heard to comment, laughingly, that they too had a physical workout, having been so moved by the dancing.

Little children learn very soon the "meaning" of the facial expressions and actions of the adults about them. These expressions and movements lead up to caresses, feeding, petting, punishing, dressing, cautioning, and so on. The child learns to identify, even before he has words with which to label and note, the permissive tolerance of the friend or the signals of rising tension and the irritation which precede a family quarrel. So unconscious are we of the actual shifts in facial expression and bodily tonus that the vague term "atmosphere" is often used for such situations. The circumstances in the families of many children encourage their learning through literal imitation of emotional expression of adults; thus the child may develop considerable skill in mimicry. This parallels learning to imitate sounds. The movements of dance, however, are effective directly or intuitively, and not through arbitrary intermediaries, as are the symbols of language.

The utilization of movements as symbols is illustrated by the wigwag use of flags in transmitting Morse code. A language of gestures, it is reported, is so well standardized in India that persons unable to understand each other's dialects may communicate through the use of dance symbols. In such a situation, the dance movement is no longer expressive in itself; it has become symbolic of an idea or concept in the same way that any spoken word, e.g., "Halt!" has lost its primary auditory quality and signifies an object or an act.

ORGANIZATION OF THE DANCE

Music, dance, and poetry (as chanted) are sometimes grouped as temporal arts, opposed to the spatial arts of painting, sculpture and architecture. One consequence of this difference is reflected in how an observer can manage the perceptual organization of the artistic product. One can study a painting or a building at his leisure; may look here and there, comparing line and color, mass and form, or what he wills, at his own pace. He can take his time to group the intricacies or organization and design. Not so with music and dance. Here an essential feature of the organization of the art object is the temporal, rhythmic, climactic sequence.

This rhythmic character contributes another primary difference. Where painting, sculpture, and architecture are most successful as explorations and revelations of objective reality, the rhythmic arts of music, poetry, and dance are highly personal and intimate. The rhythmic pattern may be auditory, but it sets up motor reverberations within the body. It asserts a body tempo and movement. One's physical activity in participating is highly intimate and personal, but at the same time one is keyed up to a social, group unifying experience. In this vital rhythmic respect, the whole group lives and moves as one. Such an experience can be both highly personal and group-identifying, a truly moving experience.

THE AESTHETIC RESPONSE

In the area of concert dancing it is revealing to compare some of the features of ballet and modern dance as found today in America, to understand the nature of the responses they may engender. Classical ballet was developed primarily for the entertainment of the royal court in Czarist Russia and other European monarchies, especially France and Italy. The female was the important figure, and her dress and movements were removed from the conventional world. Both in content and technique the ballet moved away from reality. The themes of the dances were often mere devices for the succession of solos and group work in different glorified and heroic settings, using fairytale figures, nobles, princesses, and other flattering, improbable materials in contrived situations. The ballet technique became systematized and stylized. The limited number of steps, turns, and leaps became almost athletic stunts, "virtuosity." A dance composition might consist in a number of such exercises strung together. In a dance sequence which requires a spectacular series of leaps or spins, the audience usually applauds immediately after the display of skill, regardless of any dramatic sequence and continuity the ballet might possess. Despite these flaws of content and dramatic integration, the beauty, grace, and charm of ballet has won a large and enthusiastic concert audience.

In revolt against the sterile bric-a-brac of conventional ballet came the dancing of Isadora Duncan (circa 1900), who was interested in the expression of feelings of ordinary people. There is no royalty, no noble class, no king's court in a democracy. Ballet was imported and was interesting as a spectacle, but it was foreign to the culture and had to change its very nature to endure here. Miss Duncan expressed the drive toward a new style of dance that could grow out of American culture. A new technique had to be created, however, and new subjects found for dance that had a bearing on the lives of the audiences. The depression days had their impact on the development of modern dance in America, and now both modern musical comedies and American ballet are being invigorated by the choreographic skills of artists under the influence of such individuals as Martha Graham, Doris Humphrey, Charles Weidman, and Hanya Holm.

The modern dance, in contrast to ballet, does not make the learning of a particular "alphabet" of movement its specific technical objective. The purpose of technique is to prepare and maintain the dancer's body as a thoroughly flexible instrument, capable of meeting all physical demands that may be placed on it. The movements of a dance, then, flow out of the central idea of the dance. The basis for appreciation of the dance is the individual's understanding of, and the sensitivity with which he responds to, the expressive movements of another.

Painting

COLOR AND FORM AS STIMULI

Where the ear is a mechanical sense organ, best adapted for distinguishing time differences and intervals and capable of some analysis of the fusion of sense impressions, the eye is a chemical sense, adapted for space. Because the sense organs for vision—rods and cones—are stimulated to chemical change by that energy called light rays, there is a lag and a slowness to vision. There is so much lag that "moving pictures" move. As with all sensory qualities, the lights and colors which we see are in part a product of the sense organs and their mode of reaction. What comes off the surface of the fields, the walls, the fabric, is reflected light of wave lengths measured in ten-thousandths of a millimeter. These, of course, are not black, white, colored, or even extended. Some of the sense organs (rods) in the eye act like ordinary camera film, and respond only to the intensity of the light; others (cones) have a different kind of response to different wave lengths, and this differential response involves the experience of "color."

The visual field has a central area, represented by the fovea, which is the point of concentration of sense organs for color vision; and as stimulation moves out from the fovea toward the periphery, the sense organs get fewer and the capacity to discriminate color lessens. The objects imaged at the point of vision may be fairly clear, but peripheral vision is vague and blurred, and loses both color and shape. That is why the eye is continually roving, turning the fovea hither and thither to get a clearer image. During the nineteenth century a school of painters, impressionists, attempted to paint pictures that would have the quality of a single glance: not photographlike overall accuracy of detail of the whole field, but a focal point of clearness with a vague impressionistic periphery.

In sound there is the phenomenon of octaves. In vision there is the phenomenon of complementary colors. Although the range of stimulating light waves shifts simply from short to long—a one-dimensional continuum—the colors may be depicted in a circle with the complementary colors placed opposite each other. The outer band of such a figure shifts in hue, and the progressively grayed qualities of the same hue vary in saturation. The after-image of a color is its complementary. If the stimuli for complementary colors are mixed in the right proportions, the resultant color will be a neutral gray, with the hues canceled out. "Mixture of the stimulus," however, is not the same as mixing the pigments. The stimulus would be the actual pattern of light reflected from the two surfaces. Pigments, however, are materials that selectively absorb some wave lengths more than others, and their color is a result of this selective absorption. Mixing two pigments, then, as painters do, is not the same as mixing the light from the two separately. The materials of the pigments will cancel each other in some respects but enhance each other in different respects; the resultant will be what they both reflect and do not absorb.

Because the eye reacts to reflected light, and because of its peculiarity of complementary colors, two interesting factors emerge for art. One is that it is difficult to find any extended surface which is uniform in color. Roof, wall, table top, or whatever it may be, has a play of light and shadow which makes its surface rich and variable. Furthermore, differences with morning, noon, and night, or artificial light, show that the colors do not remain the same from moment to moment. The other factor is called simultaneous or successive contrast. Complementary colors, like the reds and greens of Christmas, when placed side by side, tend to enhance each other. This is true to a lesser degree for noncomplementary colors. As a consequence a space that has no color at all but is a gray surrounded by light of some color, will appear the complementary of that color. In the yellow glare of snow fields, the shadows are blue. Colors in one place modify the values of the surrounding areas, and these facts are utilized by artists.

Some of the schools of the last century were very interested in different uses of pigments and color. The Pointillists, to get a richer color, applied spots of pigment to the canvas such that on close inspection one can barely make out the design for the myriad-colored pigment points. But if one moves back so that the separate spots can no longer be seen the rich and vivid coloring of sharply delineated objects appears.

ORGANIZATION OF PAINTING

The painter is using light and color, shapes, lines, and patterns, on a two-dimensional surface. How does he organize the form? Analyses show that some painters have organized patterns which can be analyzed in terms of lines—whether diagonal, triangular, spiral, or other. Another basis of analysis shows a treatment in terms of masses—simple or complex, static or rhythmic. Another approach has to do with the concept of space and distance and the various ways of indicating mood and feeling.

There have been many different approaches to the subject of the artist: representational, impressionistic, seeking the "real thing" below the surface appearance, a generalized nonrepresentational product, or a formalized account disinterested in the subject as such. All of these, and more, have been "schools" of art. The major break from the classical painting came with the Impressionists of the last century. The older, classic painting was naturalistic in style, and emphasized heroic or religious scenes as the subject matter of most importance, and devalued, in descending order, portraits, landscapes, and still lifes.

The break from religious and political monarchies and landed aristocracies was signalized by the American and the French revolutions, and the industrial revolution. Painting, in its turn, broke from its traditions in the nineteenth century; in content the new schools shifted to landscapes, character studies of socially "low" life, and still lifes, dropping the heroic, deific, allegorical, and religious topics.

The various nonnaturalistic schools that have flourished and waned during the last seventy-five years have been sectarian rivals and splinter groups disagreeing mainly about technique and form. The Impressionists tended to paint from the viewpoint of a single glance with one's eye, and thus take account of the optical feature of central clearness and peripheral vagueness in vision; or the quality of atmosphere; or the character qualities of close-ups. Some typical painters include Degas (1834–1917), Monet (1840–1926), and Pissarro (1830–1903). Around 1885 to 1905 there arose three new groups. Pointillists or Luminists, like Seurat (1859–1891) and Signac (1863–1935), put their colors on in separate spots so that the fusion occurred not in the painter's pigments, but with the light itself before it reached the eye of the viewer. The rational balancing of geometrical shapes and lines for their own sake deëmphasized content by moving toward painting still lifes; this is typified by the work of Cézanne (1839–1906). The third direction was antirational, i.e., primarily emotional, and sought the simple primitive expression of feelings, as with Van Gogh (1853–1890) and Gauguin (1848–1903). The next development, in the rationalistic direction, was Cubism (1905) with such painters as Braque and Picasso. The Cubists thought to get behind ordinary space to the significant forms somehow lying back of everything. Their "logical" static patterns, in another decade, led to the Futurist movement which insisted on the acceptance of the "machine age," and tried to paint forces, movement, action. Formal, rationalist, abstract schools sprang up in various countries, and are known as Suprematists, Constructivists, Purists, and the German Bauhaus school, with such artists as Gabo, Mondrian, Le Corbusier, and Ozenfant.

More recent movements of the times include the antirationalist and post-War I mockery of Dada and Surrealism (Picabia, Dali, Miro.) Exasperated and irresponsible, and dispensing with logic, they emphasized unconscious and personalistic associations. Less fantastic are the expressionistic painters such as Klee and Kandinsky. The great depression and the beginnings of the Second World War brought an emphasis again upon the social bearing of art. Just as Daumier and Goya in the nineteenth century picked up the social conflict and revolution of their times, so Kollwitz and Grosz expressed some of the feelings toward the causes and consequences of the First World War; and so do social conflicts find outlet in the Mexican painters Rivera, and Orozco, in the Guernica of Picasso, in the Deep South paintings within our own country of Gwathmey, and in Shahn's and Gropper's depictions of working people.

The term abstract art has been applied by some artists and critics to the work of a group of painters. It is a poor term to employ, since every picture is a particular, a unique individual object, and hence just the opposite of abstract. Other modern paintings are called "nonobjective" or "nonrepresentational." These terms are used ambiguously. For some these mean a fruitful emphasis away from photographic reality, away from the pictorial representation of objects and persons and scenes. But to others it is an attempt to escape content—an effort that seems futile. It is impossible to organize a design that has *no* meaning, that means "nothing." People who view any object have had a lifetime of looking and listening, and feeling about what they see and handle. There are many residuals of emotional conditioning that are carried along with them, and are evoked by the details of the painting. Even ink blots like those of the Rorschach Test, or clouds, are invested with meaning. Every shape and sound and smell sets off in the individual some chain of reactions, some organizing responses out of the person's experiences. The effective nonrepresentational composition depends on just these generalized emotional reactions for its effectiveness. The artist seeks to gain more power in his communication, not by striving for unique remoteness, but by freeing it of the limiting peculiarities of the emotional reactions to some specific object, and hence making it possible to play upon a wider, more profound range from the wealth of generalized common experiences.

The inventive and creative capacity of people is operating in the arts, and any attempt to lay down a limiting formulation consequently will be overrun within a short time. The variety of ways for presenting a composition is infinite. What can be said, then, is that artistic productions are effective because they select, abstract, distort, exaggerate, and organize the materials in a significant way; and present the material within the limits of principles of human perception. Such principles include the relations of figure and ground, of whole and part, of integration of contrasting members.

THE AESTHETIC RESPONSE

Various levels of communication have been achieved in painting from the capture of a vague feeling or mood; the quality of a person or a situation; or even a critical or approving commentary upon what is presented. Art is concerned with the particular, and every artistic product is itself unique. But art is not concerned with finding and presenting the unique as such, for the simply unique has no significance. A work of art is the embodiment in a particular form of some general truth, some pervasive emotion, some insight of wide relevancy.

Architecture

In architectural products we live and move, we work and play, sleep, eat and die. Architecture is a most social art.

Dealing with three-dimensional structures, architecture handles sensory-perceptual materials that are not only visual in the sense of surface and color, but spatial in the sense of distance, height, mass, volume, enclosure, and light. Since these structures are lived in, there are important tactile qualities of roughness, smoothness, and warmth, and of sound as well, whether from the echo of walking feet, or from a concert in the shell of a theater platform.

The task for the builder is—within the limits offered by funds, engineering skills, techniques of handling materials such as stone, iron, wood, concrete, and glass—to make a construction that will satisfy the social needs and functions of the users. Perhaps more than other art, architecture is the embodiment and expression of the general feeling and orientation, the style of life of the period.

The living quarters reveal much of the life pattern. It has been pointed out that the Baroque house expressed the idea of the stately life of oligarchs, living in beauty and convenience. The Englishman, on the damp island, has for centuries built his house around the expensive stone fireplace; this is also true of early colonial American houses. The medieval castle was built to be the focalizing center of a given community. In the United States the tradition still is that a man's home, even on a twenty-foot lot, is his inviolable walled castle. Many modern architects seek to build homes where inside and outside are hardly distinguishable, and there is a continuity from the inner recesses of the house out into a garden, or even into a stream. Contemporary housing experts and sociologists have studied the amount and kind of usage of the various rooms and their accessories; and have suggested spatial allocation and organization to permit maximum efficiency and convenience. The private builder, however, is interested in mass production at low cost, and a quick sale.

Public buildings likewise reflect the quality of a society. Gothic architecture was typified in cathedrals which emphasized spires, flying buttresses, stained glass windows, and individual creative work in wood and masonry. It expressed the unity and social-religious activities of the community just as the classic temples in marble of Periclean Athens displayed the communal spirit of that free city.

With modern engineering and materials new possibilities for construction emerge. The structure may convey the impression and feeling of handling cubes, using great blocks and flat blank walls; or may seek the open feeling of space; may emphasize horizontal or vertical lines; may be concerned with light and color as the day proceeds and seek to catch the light and shade; or may close out the sky and rely on controlled artificial illumination. American cities reflect the helter-skelter, confused, and individualistic quality of its society. Among the major buildings the only unity in architectural style is probably to be found in structures designed by the same architectural firm during the time when the designer was still thinking in terms of one of his "periods."

Within the United States very few cities have been planned. Washington, D.C. is a major exception, and an interesting point is made regarding its plan as related to the techniques of war. The medieval castle was built for protection against assault by armored knights and foot soldiers by being piled up behind a moat and drawbridge, or being perched upon some crag. The walled city, with its narrow streets and doors that could be closed at night, was the general pattern at least from the days of Troy till the development of the cannon. Artillery doomed the walled city. The open grillwork design of Washington, D.C., looks to the defense of the city with cannon commanding the broad radiating streets. Industrialization has brought the great increases in the sizes of urban communities and factories, with men and women to work in them, as well as persons to serve those working. The major problem of transportation resulted in a concentration of workers in the business and industrial sections of the city, and high rents pushed construction up into space. With elevators and steel came skyscrapers. Developments in transportation continued, but also developments in capacity for destruction. Modern warfare with its capacity for concentrated bombing makes the industrial concentration of the big city a major danger, and requires for military purposes what the city planner and architect has advocated futilely and plaintively for years—the decentralization of industry. With the bomber, the skyscraper is out of date.

Planners have been able to do something, but still a relatively small amount with public housing projects in this country. Little thought is applied to the problem of the housing and living accommodations, the shopping and health needs, the recreation and education of the great mass of people.

The values of a society are written into its architecture.

Literature

The novel and the story are only tenuously related to direct stimulation of sense organs. One can read a book or a magazine under considerable variations in conditions, without affecting the quality of the writing, the situations and events, the plot, the climax and the resolution of the story. These events are conveyed by signs and symbols. Some writers are concerned with the verbal tonality of the sounds, the mood quality and rhythm. This is a move in the direction of poetry, which employs primarily the pattern and quality of the sound as part of the technique of conveying the associations, similes, and figurative images.

The debate about "propaganda and art" comes up more frequently in painting and literature than most any other area. A few comments are necessary on the point. A writer is trying to say something; he seeks to communicate some feeling or notion. (If not, he can be ignored.) Furthermore, whatever the writer may say, he has taken some stand, for he has moved off the only completely neutral spot—artistic nonexistence. The writer who professes a complete distinterest and claims objectivity is deluding himself or attempting to delude his audience. He selects certain materials and this very selection is of course the result of a value judgment. The novel arose with modern society, and the writings of Fielding, Dickens, Tolstoy, Balzac, and Hardy were certainly concerned with the profundities of life. The theory that art and literature should not be "partisan" is really an attempt to discourage writing unapproved by certain classes in our society.

Writers are phrase makers, those skilled in articulation, who can catch the essence and meaning of events, and can crystallize the thinking of people by putting the phrases into words and images that express their mute intuitive feelings. As it has been said in discussing the interpretative process, the artist's function is centered around the need for meaning, for understanding on the part of an audience. Individuals are engaged in this changing world with the continuous attempt to adjust, to order themselves to the intruding events. People build up for themselves a set of beliefs and prejudices which is their picture of the world: more or less orderly, coherent, and interrelated. New events are meaningful as one interprets them into the framework of his past. When confronted by a difficult new situation, one has alternatives: he may explore it and if necessary develop new attitudes that may modify the old framework of beliefs; or he may attempt evasion and escape; or he may borrow an answer from someone else.

The social function of the creative artist is to help satisfy the imperative needs for orderliness and meaning in the world. The job of the writer is to present problems in terms of the underlying dynamic causal factors and to show the facets of the problem; to provide a basis for deeper insight and emotional understanding of the problem. His job is to reveal the underlying relationships, to expose the fallacies of existing stereotypes, to suggest interpretations which will enable a group to proceed on a basis of reality.

This quick glance at a number of the arts stresses different things with each, but many things said with regard to one are applicable with slight translation to most of the others. By looking at these arts from the point of view of psychology it appears that the subject matter has both relations and meanings. With this in mind the discussion will now proceed from the art object around the corners of Figure 13.1 with greater emphasis on the people involved in the arts, as audience and as creator.

ART APPRECIATION—THE AUDIENCE

The members of the audience must first perceive the art object, but even the simplest perception is only roughly determined by the physical nature of the stimulating object. In a complicated activity like seeing a play or hearing an orchestra, much more is involved from the perceiving organism than the reception of the stimulation on the sense organs.

It is a misleading fiction that people are blank tablets, upon which "experience" writes. One must learn the language, whether of music, pictures or words. The song may be in a foreign language or idiom, or it may be familiar; and it may elicit feelings, moods, meanings within you that are quite stirring. They are moving, however, largely because of the background of experience, the previous living, the evaluative system that makes up so much of everyone.

The perceiver is not inert, unstructured. Perceiving involves activity on the part of the perceiver. A situation which is perceived communicates to the perceiver, who readjusts, and who prepares for reacting as a consequence of his appraisal. But how one reacts is certainly a function of the kind of organism he is, and of the skills and habits of reacting that he has established. This is the meaning back of the old saying that what you get out of an art object is what you bring to it. The newborn babe has little to bring and gets little out of exposure to an art object.

One learns how and what to appreciate. Such learning is unique to every individual. It is general enough so that one can distinguish, say, different nationality cultures. Since one is brought up usually in only a single culture one has a limited appreciation of the specifics of some other culture. But this is a question to be discussed in the last section. First examine some of the findings concerning the development of appreciative skills within our own culture.

Learning to Appreciate

To "appreciate" anything requires a considerable amount of experience. This is of course true in the arts as in every other area of human understanding. A person whose building experience has been limited to frame buildings or thatched huts can hardly be expected to design and construct a steel and concrete skyscraper. A person who can only count on his fingers cannot be expected to operate a slide rule. So, too, a person whose background in music has only been folk songs and hymns can hardly be expected to appreciate—much less construct—a symphony.

A full perception—and appreciation—comes not simply with outside knowledge of the objects or situations. It is possible to learn, say, the appearance and structural characteristics of different kinds of wood by reading about them and seeing pictures and mounted specimens. But how much greater is the appreciation of the person who has worked the wood with an ax, chisel, plane, and knife; and has seasoned, stained, and weathered it. The old phrase "We learn by doing" holds true not only for skills but for the rich perceptions of materials, objects, and values by which one initiates and guides his activities.

A most significant finding of modern psychology is that the best way to encourage the growth and maturity of the individual toward becoming a lively, adjusted, sociable member of society is in the direction of creative arts; that is, the encouragement of the growth and maturation of the child through his own active and emotional experiences, and not by didactic instruction using models to imitate and patterns to follow. The problems of learning to appreciate are similar in all the arts, and considerable work has been done on how to develop the skills and perceptions that make participation and enjoyment possible.

Children and the Visual Arts

Within the last twenty-five years tremendous developments have been made in the knowledge of how to develop skills and mental growth in the visual arts. This has been accomplished more by educationally oriented painters and genetic psychologists than by academic psychologists studying aesthetic problems. The psychological studies in aesthetics, as we have seen, bogged down in the futile measurement of the child's emotional reactions to such things as specific colors or color pairs. Those persons concerned with the development of the child, with his growing perceptions and his handling of new values and horizons, have made the major contributions. Outstanding are the studies at the Cleveland Museum of Art, the work of Viktor Lowenfeld, and that of Herbert Read.

Drawing and painting, like many other activities, can be a significant aid in the growth and development of the child. In the earliest phases with youngsters up to several years of age, their predominant concern is in sampling experiences, both sensory and motor. Their activities center about the establishment of coördination and control. Thus the first movements with crayon or pencil are simply scribbling with the emphasis upon the motor activities of arm and hand. This is parallel to the earliest random movements or the earliest babbling sounds, practice with which leads to eye-hand coördination, and to learning to produce words and phrases. The sequence in drawing shifts from the scribble to more geometric drawing, such as a back-and-forth movement and circular movements. The repetition in drawing is parallel to the repetition in speech, and in the demands to tell the story again; it extends the boundaries of the child's world, within which it has skill, security, and knowledge, and hence control. It gets assimilated and provides the basis for new, more complex adventures. For the next step in drawing the child may tell a story.

The child's perception and drawing of his world tends to be uniquely different from that of adults; and the turning point in our society comes at the preadolescent age, around 11 to 15. Prior to that time the child not only has his own qualitatively different perception of the world, but has an approach to perceiving and drawing it which should be allowed to develop. In fact, to try to impose adult patterns of perceiving and of drawing seems to have serious inhibiting effects not only on all drawing the child may do, but upon his basic personality as well.

The characteristics of this childish period are indicated by the fact that he draws representative schemata. The drawing is "geometrical" in the sense that it is made up of the skills he has recently developed, out of learning to coördinate well enough to draw lines and circles. Now when he draws and tells a story, he is representing on paper his subjective emotional experiences. The child is not interested or able to draw "how they look." Any attempt to tell him how to draw, to view his product as an inadequate effort to copy how the objects appear visually to an adult, stultifies the child. It is inhibiting, frustrating, destructive of what his real aims and goals are. If such training persists, it may result in a child who is withdrawn and rigid in his own standards, though perhaps indirectly rebellious, and totally dependent upon instructions from the adult as to what to do.

The encouraged child uses his schema of a man, or other objects, made up of ovals and lines, out of his active knowledge of what they do. Lowenfeld describes a group of young children that drew pictures of people with only a line for the mouth. He brought in some hard candies, passed them around, experienced and discussed with the children the chewing and crunching of the candy. They then drew schemata of children with teeth and jaws working, with a new appreciation of the mouth. Pictures of playing tag showed a great exaggeration of the length of the reaching arm and hand which are the functionally and emotionally important objects. A picture, "Helping little sister through the snow," left off the little sister's legs, and why not?

The child's drawings and paintings, then, are representational; they employ a schema and out of their active knowledge draw the essential emotionally significant items. Their drawings tend to be geometric; they are flat with no depth or shading; a line may show the ground; the objects tend all to be about the same size, whether houses, trees, or people. Objects are usually independent of each other and often arranged on a line, with equal emphasis, with no overlap, no perspective; they may show inside and outside, or succession, at once.

Around the ages of 11 to 15 an important shift occurs. As the child approaches maturity, he turns toward his own imaginative activity with a critical eye. A major problem is how to prepare the child for this change so that his self-criticism and inevitable social criticisms do not overwhelm him with a sense of inferiority and inhibit his creative productions. Rigid methods by the teacher who attempts to impose a style or who criticizes, however nicely, will kill any creative work. The solution seems to be to provide the child with enough skills and satisfactions while he draws at the representational level so that he keeps his self-confidence and does not become too stereotyped with his own schema, but remains growing and fluid. With encouraging teachers, he can then more easily approach the new perceptions of naturalistic drawing, and the new standards of a work that is to be looked at by someone else. If he continues to draw, the youngster tends to move in the direction of naturalistic representation; with an emphasis upon spatial presentation, with use of the principles of perspective. Organizational trends, then, shift from the overall scatter of earlier years to compositional arrangements, with related groups of units. The style of drawing also changes from the simple outlines (filled or unfilled) to more impressionistic forms and sketches, with modeling, and emphasis and other new features.

If the child's drawings express his feelings, his subjective experiences, then it is possible to employ the drawings as a kind of image or a projection of the child's inner life. In fact, finger painting (as well as other kinds) has been widely used both for personality diagnosis and as a kind of therapy. It is employed as therapy in the puddling with the paints and the emotional working out of disturbing situations that are too difficult to talk about or perhaps even consciously to admit. The use of painting with disturbed children and with disturbed and psychotic adults is now quite common. But this vast program is beyond the scope of aesthetics.

Dance and Drama

At every age, young and old, man acts. In many cultures that do not have a written language the structure of the culture is carried in ceremonial song, dance, and legend. Even in our society the child and the adult dramatize. Without its being institutionalized as part of culture or of training, the adolescent child's life includes a large amount of dramatized play. He plays at "house," and assigns the roles of parents and children, of disciplinarian and punished, of G man and gangster, princess and servant. An adolescent may identify more seriously with some person in society and he selects ideals which symbolize his values and the pattern of life he would like to follow. It guides his adjustment to his fellows. Religious leaders recognize the importance of role playing in charatcer formation, and often suggest to young people that they take the life and character of some heroic figure as their mode. "What would So-and-so do in this situation?" In our society the hero who is popularly taken up, however, may be some actress, ball player, or crooner.

Every child, every adult, wants to be somebody. An easy way to feel important is dramatically to identify oneself with a famous person. The stage thus utilizes our capacity to read ourselves into the role of someone else. Drama is effective because it provides the concrete portrayal of character and situations; it provides the actual working out of relationships in exciting and concrete detail. Drama can be convincing, profound, clear.

Everyone's movements are expressive, in gesture and facial expression, in posture as well as in speech and action. Expressive movements constitute, it would seem, the most direct, simple, natural manner of expressing feelings and desires. Modern dance as an art form attempts to return to the intuitive communication of feelings and values through body movement. A number of exploratory studies with small children have shown the possibility of dance play as a learning situation. Dance play has the advantages of being fun, of not stopping the child's actions by forcing him to grope for words, and by providing an easy way of establishing pleasant coöperative relationships with other children. Some workers have restricted the situations to "nondirective" patterns, and others have utilized the group situation in a more controlled, but democratically oriented, fashion. In such situations, animal games make it easy for the children to project parental and sibling figures and work out emotional relations to them in symbolic (safe) form. Artistically they provide many clues to the portrayal and identification of the essential movements and actions that communicate their ideas. By improvising, by constructive evaluation of their own and others' work, and by learning to be an audience, the youngsters develop standards and taste. They also develop respect for others as persons, and a self-assurance and internal strength of their own.

ART AND SOCIETY—THE ARTIST

A clue to the understanding of the relations of art and society is gained when one keeps in the background of thinking two different and complex principles. One concerns the structural background of society out of which the artist comes; and the other concerns the functional relationships of the parts to the social structure.

Function—A Principle of Social Interaction

It will be an advantage in understanding if something of the functional relationships is discussed first. The motions of history result from the alliance and opposition of forces. Persons are allied with some, and arraigned against others. In the struggle to survive, for instance, against some force of nature, one may master it or be overwhelmed, one may adapt to it, or adapt it for other uses. People have been swept away by floods; have built dams to contain the waters; have employed the flood itself to float logs to the sea. Likewise are there various relations of alliance and antagonism between people. What emerges out of this is that there are forces both human and natural; that human beings work to control nature; and that many human beings also work to control other human beings, or to avoid being controlled. The major groupings of human forces we call nations, or alliances of nations. But within a nation there are also many subclasses, occupational and regional groupings, political and other associations, which are concerned with the power relations within the community.

Not only does history move from the interplay of such forces; so does art. There is one thing we can be sure of despite all the rival theories of arts: an essential factor in every dramatic situation is a conflict of forces. Some say a conflict of wills. This is most obvious in drama and literature. Even in painting the primary formal factor is referred to as balance, which of course means the achievement of spatial arrangement of eye-pulling forms and colors whose rival strengths are integrated into a unity, but with a tension level from their competing powers which lifts the picture out of the ordinary. A fundamental factor in every artistic product—painting, sculpture, architecture, dance, music, theater, literature and poetry, and as far beyond as one wants to go—is the opposition of forces, is conflict and tension, and suggestions toward balance and resolution.

Structure—A Principle of Social Interaction

The structural background of the artist, determining his life and work, may be considered in terms of four concentric circles, which are the cultural tradition, the class tradition, the specific art tradition, and the unique nature and history of the individual person, emerging out of this context.

THE CULTURAL TRADITION

It is easy to see the cultural differences, say between Egypt, India, China, and Europe. But within the stream of European culture there are sharply significant differences. The roots of these differences cannot detain us here more than to point out the origin of two rival hypotheses. There is the view that a dominating idea permeates any culture. Thus Sorokin the great sociologist marches down the ages to prove that the "major premise" of every civilization defines all the phases of its social organization, including art, and discovers in consequence only four types of society: first, an *ideational,* which looks to a Kingdom of God or its equivalent, looks out of this world to some spiritual arena, and uses (as in art) the appropriate symbols. Second, there is the *sensate* type which is purely worldly, sensory-minded, and often sensuous; it is naturalistic in style and employs no symbols. The third he calls the *idealistic,* which is a fusion of the best of the preceding two, in that it is naturalistic with a selective vision, being blind to the "debasing and vulgar" phases of its life. The fourth, *eclectic,* is the reverse of the third, being low-grade, an unintegrated mechanical mixture, a sign of a disintegrating culture.

The materialistic approach of Marx denies the priority of the various ideas, and points to the fundamental means of production and its control as the basic determiner for any culture. The culture, the style of life of primitive groups, thus, would be determined by whether they were a fishing, hunting, gathering, nomadic, or agricultural people. A Marxian would say that the invention of the steam engine or of atomic energy, or the shift of ownership of land or of capital goods from private to public control, would be the root of vast cultural differences.

Whatever theory, and there are many, may eventually develop to account for the quality and unity—the "nest odor"—of a culture, it is important to know that such a pervading characteristic does exist. It is important to identify it for whatever period is at hand, for it contributes to an understanding of the art of the period. America was discovered out of the adventurous and enterprising search for new kinds of wealth. The growth of the U.S. is all confined to that new phase in world history, the period of commercial and industrial enterprise. The only culture pattern the United States ever had similar to medieval society built upon agriculture and the ownership of the land was the slave-supported aristocracy of the South. Prior to the American revolution was the gestation period which culminated in the birth of a culture whose ideals can be expressed as the gospel of work and the doctrine of thriftiness: "Work for the night is coming"; "Early to bed and early to rise"; "Penny wise and pound foolish"; "A stitch in time saves nine." Success meant financial independence, and was achieved by hard work and sober thrift. Around the turn of the nineteenth century, a group of men formed trade unions, and were promptly declared to be lawbreakers and conspirators against their enterprising employer. There was also invented and put to work the steam engine and machine operations in various industries, especially textiles. While daring souls moved westward, the Eastern seaboard was converted into a factory economy, into a system where hand skills in the use and operation of tools began to disappear in some industries, the skilled workers being replaced by unskilled machine tenders. The owners of the tools of production were the new class of capitalists. By the first part of the twentieth century the fundamental orientation had shifted toward a period of advertising and selling, of promotion and propaganda, of "Get-Rich-Quick Wallingford." It's no longer save, but spend; no longer work, but get by, wait for the break, the Big Chance.

The consequence of all this for art has been important and devastating. For one thing, the social structure has been in such rapid tumultuous change that there has been no opportunity for any "unitary" culture to develop, no time to be appreciative, no time to learn the attitudes of receptive contemplation. Every institution and every type of social relationship—family, church, industry, transportation, communication—has been in constant flux. Attitudes in America today are generally directed toward power and control; toward the technology of gadgets, as in movies, radio, television, atomic energy, and war machines.

Skills are compartmentalized through assembly line production and machine operation in factory, mine, and farm, and standardizations within large stores. People working in such places have no opportunity to develop well-rounded skills, handicrafts, or personal competences. The materials used in daily life are no longer constructed; they are stamped out, factory made. Kitchen furnishings, furniture, toys, bathroom equipment, foods, and even houses are prefabricated and packaged. The style and manner of their construction is determined by the interests of the manufacturer, the limitations of the machine, and access to the market.

The educational system is geared to this adult but immature society. It may be that painting, music, and dramatic play are introduced in some "progressive" schools, but these tendencies are frequently attacked as wasteful frills, as pampering and mollycoddling, as a waste from the essentials of the three R's and discipline (or military training). Such attacks are often successful in clearing the schools in even urban communities of such training programs. Persons with artistic talents, say in literature, painting, or music, as they mature are guided into practical occupations. The literary talents are directed to occupations such as copy writing for a newspaper or a promotional concern. The painter's talents are employed for layouts for department store sales, window displays, or patterns for the textile industry.

It is clear that most of modern American society, including the general educational system, does not encourage the development of creative sensibilities and potential artistic judgment, but on the contrary tends to have it mutilated beyond recognition by the time the child is 12 or 14 years old, or even younger. People have consequently little basis for the establishment of "taste" or artistic standards, and look to the professional stylists, the Parisians, the manufacturers and their salesmen to tell them what to buy. Persons without taste but with money can employ someone who is a "decorator" but even then the bareness of our own culture is reflected in the practice of outfitting the house, room by room, after the manner of some historical period, with antiques. Some persons with enough money have actually bought and transported, stone by stone, some ancient baronial castle built for another civilization, and erected it in Florida or Connecticut as an outlandish abode for all to envy.

This present inner poverty in much of American life is not something necessarily to praise or blame; it is simply a matter of historical and cultural fact, the causes for which are easily identified. It is the nature of American culture at this time, and it is in process of change.

The direction of this change, of course, is subject to some control.

THE CLASS TRADITION

Within American and European cultural history the social organization has certain general divisions or classes that are readily distinguished. One division that is not very useful is in terms of city and country, another is in terms of possessions: wealthy, average, and poor. A much more significant grouping relates to functional classes that operate as groups, that tend to coöperate or ally with each other on certain basic issues, and tend to oppose other groups.

Some of the classes in society are the culturally ruling groups. Other classes are subordinated. But in times of major cultural change, subordinated classes have been able to increase their power and threaten the control of the dominant group in the society. Such a change occurred with the death of feudalism; with the establishment of constitutional governments, the abolition of monarchies, with the civil war, and the depression. In the world today, the colonial peoples of Asia and Africa and elsewhere are fighting off the domination of foreign ownership and military occupation.

From where does the artist come? It should make a great deal of difference whether he is brought up in a longshoreman family in San Francisco, in the wealthy set of Long Island, or in the academic circles of Harvard. The art of the times is shaped up in part by the nature and intensity of the conflicts between rival classes. Where the conflict is relatively intense, the artists are inevitably embroiled in the issues at stake.

The artists and writers coming out of the middle and upper classes may be strongly aligned with and identified with the people and philosophies of the challenged dominant class, or they may be critical of it. Some of the most significant literary and artistic work of the centuries comes from the social critics, the satirists, whose breadth and vision, whose understanding encompasses the limitations of their own social order (e.g., Goya, Daumier, Cervantes, Swift, Shaw, Gorky, France, Tolstoy, Ibsen, and Mann). Those other writers and artists who accept the general cultural traditions of their dominant class may roughly be classified into three subgroups, depending upon their audience and their implicit goal effect. One group proclaims the virtues and glories of the conventional myths of the society. Their products are enjoyed by the middle-class groups who aspire to success in the conventional pattern of our industrial, financial, and entertainment heroes, and who follow these artistic products as ideals and guides to their own wished-for successes. The other two subgroups of middle-class writers are varieties of escapists. One provides escape for the poverty-stricken and dispossessed, and the other, for the bored leisure groups. There are many people who seek distraction and escape from the dullness of their empty lives, and are aided in this retreat into a fantasy world by adventure, mystery, or occultism. For the unoccupied upper-class persons of education and intelligence, a completely different kind of escapism seems to thrive. The supersophisticated cults of the arts are both exclusive and expensive, and become an exciting indulgence for many "patrons."

The arts which come out of the lower classes can be divided into two rough divisions. First are the folk arts which rarely have an individual artist as the creator but grow and mature by reproduction through generations. They embody the style of life and work of people as part of their expression of feelings in their work. Songs of work, as the sea chanties, the hauling, chopping, hammering songs, the peddlers' cries; the chain gang songs and stories, songs of protest, of longing and blues, the arts of the fisherman, cowboy, lumberman, miner, the folklore of Paul Bunyan and John Henry, come from many walks. This is the great cultural river, or better, the root and branch of a society which eventually flowers into its own artistic forms. The other style of art from the lower classes is the self-conscious proletarian art. Unions and museums have sponsored exhibits by workers of paintings and sculpture on working subjects; the great Mexican muralists and other artists are thinking from the point of view of the working classes and farm workers; plays and novels are written with workers, with union men, with oppressed

Negroes as central figures. These are of course sharply critical of the existing social order, by implication if not by direct statement.

THE ART TRADITION

The third and next of the concentric circles bounding the artist involves the specialized skills of his craft and the rival schools that develop around aims of personages and locations. In each of the arts as in many occupations a specialized language develops which reflects the belongingness of the members, and reveals the course of the trends and conventions that have developed.

The art tradition certainly is not independent of class and cultural influences. The Elizabethan drama ground to a halt with the closing of the theaters (1642) by the moralistic Puritans who later with Cromwell ruled the country for a decade; but the theaters were reopened with the restoration of the monarchy (1660) and with a drama that modified the Shakespearean traditions. In painting the reaction against the vagueness of the Impressionists and their emphasis upon painting the atmosphere of intervening space came with Cubists who were trying to get at a more solid representation of space and hoped to reach the underlying elementary forms (e.g., similar to the atomism current in science). Much of the surrealistic and subjective painting of current decades reflects not only the reaction against Cubism but also a reaction against the wild complexities and chaotic qualities of modern life, and a retreat from it.

The art movements in critical times in history, such as the twentieth century, will be found to center around the main interests of the groups and classes that are locked in struggle. But in addition there will be schools of artists whose program would restore some earlier historic period; they are regressive in their conservatism. Other movements will be essentially escapist in another direction. For instance the proponents of "significant form" were advocating "art for art's sake." This movement started in the decade of the First World War, and its function obviously was to abandon reality, and to rule content out of art—during the anguishing, devastating period of a world war.

THE UNIQUE INDIVIDUAL

Any artist, any person, is only generally located when his dates, his culture, his art and its tradition, and his class and family relations are known. Where the artist himself goes is his own personal history. It will suffice to mention two factors concerning the artist: how he makes his living, and how he does creative work. Art is communication, although a great deal of communication contains no art. The artist has something to say; he wants to move, to satisfy, to affect some audience. But who is his audience and what do they demand of him? It has been said that he who pays the piper calls the tune. The time when everyone is part artist is past; the time of a ruling class calling themselves kings and nobles who can indulge themselves by being patrons of artists is past. How, then, does the professional artist survive?

There are some artists who take the position that this is a businessman's society, and therefore they set out to be businesslike. Business and art are usually incompatible, so the person who works at being an artist during the day may work at his own "creative" products at night. The artist is not noted as a salesman for his own products. Most private artists take one of three other alternatives, none of which is very satisfactory. The artist may turn the business end over to a manager, a producer, a booking agent. What happens then, however, is that the control is in other hands. A second compromise may be that the artistically inclined person seeks employment in some business enterprise which can employ his skills. Advertising, newspapers, radio, the commercial entertainment field, or industrial design do not provide the atmosphere most conducive to on-the-job or off-hours creative work. Third, the person may seek a job as a teacher. The pressures here are more indirect.

There are other ways of being able to live as an artist in this century. Some countries provide a state subsidy for great artists. Finland is noted for having granted Sibelius an annual sum, with no reservations. The award of poet laureate in England keeps one artist from poverty. In the Soviet Union a number of cash awards are dispensed as prizes for work that meets the artistic standards of a committee.

In this country a number of cities support symphony orchestras. A more general type of subsidy on a nation-wide basis was carried out under the WPA in the depression thirties. The federal relief was designed not to sponsor and encourage arts, but to keep people from starving and to encourage them to keep up their skills so that they might more readily be "absorbed" back into private business enterprise. The venture, however, caused a cultural revolution in America. It brought artists and wider audiences together for the first time. The artists were encouraged to produce, and the people had a chance to develop an interest and knowledge of what artists could do. Not too strange was the finding that the art teachers in many schools had never seen an original painting. Art centers were started, students were instructed, regional guides were prepared, music was written and played, theaters with plays and dance groups went into production, and millions of persons were affected by a resurgent cultural life, despite the fact that the project was later cut—for support of art and art appreciation was deemed only an emergency measure for a trying economic period.

CREATIVE ACTIVITY

Psychologists have made many attempts to develop tests of various artistic aptitudes as for music, painting, and poetry. These have had some success primarily of a negative sort. It takes a certain minimum of auditory acuity, time discrimination, and intelligence, for instance, to be a musician. It requires some minimal measurable talents with colors and design to be able to draw. Doing well on these tests may indicate only an agreement with existing standards, which are frequently the standards of only a small group in our society. The tests can serve to eliminate a lot of people from professional schools who could not possibly achieve even average success. But it is another kind of a task to pick out those who will be successful. Being "successful" is not a simple thing, easy to measure. Apart from measuring creative capacities, many things are important for success, accidental happenstance of meetings, who knows whom, and circumstance. These are not subject to much prediction.

Creativity in the artist is probably no different than the productivity and creative work in the scientist. In both there is required a high level of skill attained after considerable motivation and a capacity to work devotedly and single-mindedly. There is also required a certain awareness and understanding, in our society, of the significance and function of our folkways. Most of all artists and scientists are actually prying and questioning, seeking to discover and to understand why things operate, what their meaning is. These are still limiting conditions, not the central fact of creativity.

Theories of creativity tend to get caught up in the suggestion that genius and insanity are twins, and that the artist is usually abnormal. This is encouraged by the depressing idea that all art is a circus to distract and amuse, and that artists are nothing but sublimating escapists.

It is true that some people in insane asylums paint, sing, and write. Inhabitants of these institutions are also known to formulate religious ideas and suggest theories for science, and programs for state and world government, and no one seems ready to come forward with the theory that scientists, religious leaders, and politicians are also creative insofar as they are insane. The products of the insane are not very useful in any of these fields because the productions are not very closely tied up with reality. So, too, the "art work" may be unique but it has no function as art because it is unable to communicate any significant artistic idea to any audience.

Creative thinking and creative imagination are the complicated factors involved in problem solving. The creative artist no more than the productive scientist waits to be struck by the lightning of inspiration. What difference there may be between artist and scientist is probably in the terms with which they define and handle their problems. Compare for instance the difference in treatment by the scientist and the artist of such problems as anti-Semitism; war and peace; crime and social order; democratic rights and civil liberties. The situations are the same, but the approach is different. The scientist aims at descriptive accuracy, in the direction of the formulation of causal laws, toward prediction and control. The artist handles the feeling side, the images and moods, as a value-guide to personal action. Knowledge and value are two sides of the same coin.

This completes the circle from art product through audience, to artist and back again to his product. At every turn there are exciting and significant psychological research problems which await solution.

SUGGESTED READINGS

1. Alschuler, Rose H., and Hattwick, La Berta Weiss, *Painting and Personality: A Study of Young Children*. Chicago: University of Chicago, 1947, 2 vols. 120 plates. An analysis of the finger paintings and other creative work of a group of children over a two-year period.

2. Chandler, A. R., *Beauty and Human Nature: Elements of Psychological Esthetics*. New York: Appleton-Century-Crofts, 1934. A summary and evaluation of experimental work in aesthetics.

3. Diserens, Charles M., and Fine, M., *A Psychology of Music*. Cincinnati: The Authors, 1939. Contains an excellent survey of the studies on the effects of music on mood-attitude, physiological changes, and health.

4. Flanagan, Hallie Davie, *Arena*. New York: Duell, Sloan & Pearce, 1940. An exciting survey of the WPA Theatre Project by its director. This book describes some of its social, political, and artistic impacts.

5. Graves, Maitland, *The Art of Color and Design*. New York: McGraw-Hill, 1941. A systematic and clear presentation with many useful illustrations, based on substantial principles of the psychology of perception.

6. Hudnut, Joseph, *Architecture and the Spirit of Man*. Cambridge, Mass.: Harvard, 1949. A survey by an architect and teacher of many fine architects.

7. Larkin, Oliver W., *Art and Life in America*. New York: Rinehart, 1950. A beautiful, fully illustrated account of American painting in relation to its schools and its history.

8. Lawson, John H., *Theory and Technique of Playwriting and Screen-*

writing. New York: Putnam, rev. ed., 1949. A much broader book than its title indicates, bearing with deep penetration on literature and life.

9. Lowenfeld, Viktor, *Creative and Mental Growth.* New York: Macmillan, rev. ed., 1952. The principles and practice of helping children to grow creatively through drawing and painting; lively illustrations.

10. Martin, John, *The Dance.* The story of dance told in picture and text. New York: Tudor, 1946. Ballet and modern dance, their history, development, and interrelations as seen by a most eminent dance critic.

11. Meier, Norman C., *Art in Human Affairs.* An introduction to the psychology of art. New York: McGraw-Hill, 1942. This book is primarily about painting by the author of an art judgment test.

12. Monro, Thomas, *The Arts and Their Interrelations.* A survey of the arts and an outline of comparative aesthetics. New York: Liberal Arts, 1949. A comprehensive survey by one of the most qualified scholars.

13. Parrington, Vernon L., *Main Currents in American Thought: An Interpretation of American Literature from the Beginning to 1920.* New York: Harcourt, 1927–1930, 3 vols. One of the most important and delightfully sharp studies of American life and literature.

Index

Abbott, C., 461
Ablation, 368–369
Abnormal psychology, 333–371
  case history (M.R.), 334, 339–340;
    dynamics, 340–341, 346–347
  conflict, 341–342; childhood, 354;
    old age, 354
  coping mechanisms, 342–344, 347
  experimentation, 364–369
  frustration, 342
  history of, 335–337
  methods of investigation, 337–358
  projective tests, 359–364
  syndromes, 347–354; neuroses, 348–
    351; psychoses, 351–354
  therapy, 355–358
    See also Clinical psychology;
      Projective tests; Therapy
Absolute refractory period, 429, 431
Accidents, 112–113
Acetylcholine, 425, 430
Achievement, see Measurement
Adaptation, see General adaptation
  syndrome
Adorno, T. W., 268
Adrenocorticotrophic hormone
  (ACTH), 443–444
Aesthetics, see Psychology and aesthe-
  tics
All-or-none law, 429
American Council on Teacher Educa-
  tion, 272
American Psychological Association
  (APA), 378, 388, 402, 403, 405
American Psychologist, 402, 403
Amino acids, 423–424
Anecdotalism, 450–453
Animal neurosis, 336, 367–369, 474–
  476
Animal psychology, see Comparative
  psychology
Animism, 207
Anthropomorphism, 208, 450
Aptitudes, and vocational guidance, 15

Aptitudes (cont'd)
  definition, 15–16
  in prison, 161
  special abilities, 316
  tests, 58, 62–66
    See also Vocational guidance
Architecture, 502–504
Aristotle, 281, 413
Army Alpha Intelligence Test, 61–62,
  223
    See also Tests
Aryan, 221
Atomistic approach, 482
Attitude, 209
  definition, 199
  in aesthetics, 487–488
  in industry, 58, 66–67
Aussage experiments, 126–131
Aviation Psychology Program Army Air
  Forces, 52–53, 62

Ballet, 495–496
Barnes, R. M., 105
Beach, F. A., 459
Beccaria, C., 150
Beer, C., 376
Behaviorism, 156, 284
Bentham, J., 175
Benussi, V., 121
Bernheim, H., 335, 336
Binet, A., 6, 120, 375
Birch, H. G., 446–477
Blacky Test, The, 396, 397
Bleuler, E., 335
Blum, G., 396, 397
Boredom, see Monotony
Brewer, J. M., 4
Bronner, Augusta, 151
Burt, C., 303

Carpenter, C. R., 471, 473
Case studies, abnormal psychology
  (M.R.), 334, 339–340, 346–347
  child psychology (Sam), 272

Case studies (cont'd)
  criminal psychology (Elton), 166–170
Cattell, McKeen J., 6, 375
Caucasian, 221, 224, 312
Cell-assembly theory, 437–440
Cephalic index, 222
Child psychology, 241–279
  aggression, 262–265
  authority, 266–269
  competition, 265
  cooperation, 264–265
  cultural influences, 257–258
  healthy personality, 276, 277, 315
  language development, 260–261
  level of questions, 248–249
  maladjustment, 271–274, 291
    See also Psychoses
  maturation and learning, 249–253
  normalcy, 271–274, 276, 277
  observation, cross sectional, 245–246, 303; diary records, 246–247;
    longitudinal, 246, 304
  physique, 275, 315
  religion, 270–271
  simple relationships, 256–257, 276
  toilet training, 271, 273, 274
  uniqueness, 259–260
Childhood and Society (Erikson), 276
Choosing a Vocation (Parsons), 4
Clever Hans, 452
Clinical psychology, 372–408
  definition, 8–9
  historical sources, 373–378
  in vocational guidance, 8–9
  legal recognition, 403–405
  personality, of the clinician, 401–402; normal, 398; unique, 392–394
  self evaluation, 380–382
  service and research, 389–392, 395
  training, 378–382
  types of therapy, 398–401
  values and ethics, 394, 405
    See also Therapy
Coghill, G. E., 459
Comparative psychology, 446–477
  anecdotalism and parsimony in, 450–453
  animal neurosis, 474–476
  communication in, 470

Comparative psychology (cont'd)
  definition, 447–448
  instincts, 455–459
  learning theory, 459–467
  social life, 467–474
  world of animals, 453–455
Conditioning, 321, 437, 460–463
Conflict, see Abnormal psychology
Convulsive seizures in rats, 442, 475
    See also Animal neurosis
Coping mechanisms, 342–344, 347
Cornell Selectee Index, 358–359
Corsini, R., 148–179
Creative activity, 521–523
Criminal and correctional psychology, 148–179
  cases, 166–170
  crime, and alcohol, 175; and sex, 174–175, 177; and theory of free will, 158–159; definition, 151; statistics, 152–153; theories, 155–159
  criminal, classification, 154–155; intelligence, 171–172; personality, 172; physique, 157–158
  evaluation, 159–160
  experimental prisons, 175–176
  fingerprints, 150
  institutional duties, 160–171
  parole, 176
  recidivism, 174, 176
  research, 171–177
  therapy, 162–170
Criminal Psychology (Gross), 120
Cubism, 519
Cultural analysis, 188
Curriculum, 285, 293–294, 319
Cybernetics, 433

Dance, 493–496
Darrow, C., 162
Darwin, C., 189, 242, 374, 447, 467
Davis, A., 258
De Memoria et Reminiscentia (Aristotle), 281
Deception tests, 121, 138–139
Delusions, 351
Dementia praecox, 335, 353
Dennis, W., 256
Descartes, R., 414
Diagnosis, 382–384

Distribution and Relations of Educational Abilities (Burt), 303
Dominance-submission, 204, 235, 471
Drugs, 366–367
Dualism, 413–415
Duncan, Isadora, 496

Ebbinghaus, H., 129
Eclecticism, 24
Educational psychology, 280–332
  and learning, 321–328
  counseling in, 292–293
  curriculum, 285, 293–294, 319
  definition, 284–286
  foster homes, 309–311
  history, 281–284
  nursery school, 310
  performance and ability, 295–296
  problems in, 325–328
  special abilities and disabilities, 316–318
    See also Individual differences
  the adult learner, 294–296
  the teacher, 289–292
    See also Vocational guidance
Educational Psychology (Thorndike), 283
Educational Psychology (Starch), 300
Efficiency, 81–118
  absenteeism, 99
  accident control, 112–113
  and learning, 114–116
  definition, 82–84
  fatigue, 92, 93
  in vision, 96–97
  lighting, 110–111
  measurement, 85–99; effort, 86–90; energy, 90–92; fatigue, 94, 98
  mechanical, 85
  methods of work, 104–109
  monotony, 103–104
  motivation, 99–104
  muscle tension, 86–87
  psychogalvanic response (PGR), 88–89
  physiological changes in, 88–90, 95
  rate, of performance, 94–95; of turnover, 99; of work, 84
  rest periods, 101
  rules for, 107
  specific factors in, 109–111

Efficiency (*cont'd*)
  time and motion study, 106–109
Electric convulsive treatment (ECT), 357–358
Emotional detachment, 343
Enzymes, 425
Erikson, E. H., 276
Escapism, 518
Essay on Crime and Punishment (Beccaria), 150
Essential hypertension, 350
Etiology, 348
Evolution theory, 477–478
Exceptional children, 319–320
Experimental neurosis, *see* Animal neurosis

Face validity, 44, 69
Fatigue, 92–98
Fechner, G., 480, 481, 482
Feeblemindedness, 425
Feedback, 433, 439
Fenichel, O., 397
Fenton, N., 151
Fiedler, F. E., 401
Free will, 158–159
Freeman, F. S., 280–332
Frenkel-Brunswik, Else, 267
Freud, S., 156, 190, 242, 335, 344, 377, 397
Frisch, von, K., 455, 470
Frustration, 342
Functional autonomy, 200–201

Galton, Sir Francis, 6, 150, 296, 305, 307, 375
General adaptation syndrome (GAS), 368, 441–444
Genes, 306–308, 425
Genetic Psychology for Teachers (Judd), 283
Gesell, A., 249, 250, 252, 254, 265
Gestalt psychology, 157, 336, 346, 414–415, 483
Giardini, G. I., 151
Gilbreth, F., 106, 108
Gill, H. B., 175
Glueck, Eleanor, 173, 174
Glueck, S., 173, 174
Golden section, 481
Goring, C., 173

Gross, H., 120, 121
Group mind, 189–190
Guidance examination, 30 n.
Gundlach, R. H., 478–524

Handwriting, 134–135
   See also Legal psychology
Hauptmann, B. R., 135
Hebb, D. O., 437–439
Hebrew, see Jewish
Helping Teachers to Understand Children (Prescott), 272
Herbart, J. F., 281–282
Hereditary Genius (Galton), 307
Hitler, A., 212, 218, 225, 226, 233, 237
Hollingworth, C. S., 304
Homeostasis, 193–195
Hooton, E., 173
Hormones, 425–426
Hypnoanalysis, 163
Hypnosis, 336, 338–339, 355–356, 365
Hysteria, 348, 440
   See also Neuroses

Incomplete sentences, 66
Individual differences, 296–321
   and resemblance in IQ, 307–309
   exceptional children, 319–320
   extent, 297–311
   nature and nurture, 305–311
   normal curve, 298
   profiles, 303, 304
Individual Differences in the Intelligence of School Children (Wentworth), 299
Industrial Fatigue and Efficiency (Vernon), 113
Industrial psychology, 36–118
   aims, 38
   and personnel management, 38
   criteria, 46
   data for evaluation, 40–44
   interviews, 41, 50–56
   intuition, 50–51
   quacks, 37
   references, 57
   reliability, 42–43, 50, 52, 56
   selection procedures, 44–77; items in, 48–70; standardization, 43, 49, 53, 56

Industrial psychology (cont'd)
   selection versus placement, 39–40
   suitability, 43–44, 49, 56, 63
   tests, 58–70
   validity, 41–42, 51, 52, 54, 70–77; face, 44, 69
      See also Tests; Vocational guidance
Inquiries into Human Faculty and Its Development (Galton), 375
Insect, 467–470
Insight, and past experience, 464–467
   in criminal acts, 169, 170
   in education, 324
   in therapy, 355
Instinct, 190–192, 419, 455–459
Insulin coma, 357–358
Integrative levels, 417–420
Interviews, in industry, 41, 50–56
   in psychopathology, 337
   in vocational guidance, 10–12, 17–18, 21
Intuition, 50–51
Invertebrate social life, 467–470
Involutional melancholia, see Psychoses
Isaacs, Susan, 262
Isomorphism, 414–415

Janet, P., 335
Jewish, 217, 219, 225
Judd, C. H., 283
Jung, C. G., 121, 336

Kirby, T. K., 88–89
Kohler, W., 414, 415, 464, 472
Kraepelin, E., 335
Kretschmer, E., 316

Leadership, 234–237
Learning, 191–192, 459–467
   and cell assembly, 437–440
   and memory, 128–129, 322
   in child development, 249–253
   in education, 284, 321–328
   in industry, 114–116
   in psychophysiology, 436
   selective, 463
   transfer of training, 327
Legal psychology, 119–179
   and law of forgetting, 129

Legal psychology (cont'd)
and perception, 122–146
Aussage experiments, 126–131
deception tests, 121, 138–139
effects of age, 129; attestation, 129;
sex, 130; testimony, 140–146
identification, 121, 131–139
memory, incidental, 128; intentional, 128
report, fidelity of, 128–131; immediate, 120, 121–126; method of, 127–128; subsequent, 120, 126–131
set in, 123
studies, 124–126
suggestion in, 133
types of witnesses, 130–131
word association, 121, 137
Lewin, K., 157, 263, 267
"l–i" test, 96–97
Libido theory, 344–345, 396
Liddell, H. S., 336
Lie detector, 121, 138–139
Liebault, A. A., 335, 336
Lightning calculator, 317
Likert, R., 65
Literature, 504–506
Lobotomy, 357–358, 476
Lombroso, C., 158, 172, 173
Lowenfeld, V., 508, 509
Luborsky, L., 401, 402

MacLeod, R. B., 180–240
Maier, N. R. F., 465
Malkenson, Laura, 333–371
Mandell, M., 67
Manic-depressive psychosis, see Psychoses
Marquis, Dorothy, 251–252
Marston, W. M., 151
Marx, K., 514
Materialism, 413, 416
Mayer, E., 448
McDougall, W., 190
McMurry, R. N., 55
Measurement, in education, 288–289, 329–330
in prison, 161
in psychopathology, 358–364, 384–386
of achievement, 58–59, 68, 223

Medicine, 22–23
Memory, 128–129, 322
Mesmer, A., 336
Mesoforms, 418
Meyer, A., 335
Migration, 435–436, 449
Mind-body, 411–413
Minnesota Paper Form Board Test, 65–66
Minnesota Rate of Manipulation Test, 63
Minnesota Vocational Test for Clerical Workers, 63–64
Mittelmann, B., 333–371
Monogamy, 204, 472
Monotony, 103–104
Moreno, J. L., 151, 164
Mores, 151, 184
Morgan, C. L., 451
Morgan's Canon, 451
Motion and Time Study (Barnes), 105
Motivation, 100–104, 190–191
Munsterberg, H., 7–8, 150–151
Murphy, Lois B., 241–279
Murray, H. A., 336
Muscle tension, 86–87
Music, 490–493

National Vocational Guidance Association, 2, 32
Nationality, 216, 220, 313
Needs, 193
Negro, 211–212, 221, 223–225, 312
Nelson, A. G., 1–35
Neural circuits, 431–433
Neuron, 428–430
Neuroses, 348–351
hysterical, 348, 440
neurotic depression, 349
obsessive-compulsive, 349
psychosomatic disorder, 350–351
See also Animal neurosis; Psychoses
Normal curve, 298

Observation, 245–247, 303, 304
Occupational Outlook Handbook (Bureau of Labor Statistics), 20
Osborn, A. D., 135
Osborne, T., 175
Otis, A. S., 61

Painting, 496–502
Paranoia, *see* Psychoses
Parsimony, 450–453
Parsons, F., 4
Pavlov, I. P., 284, 336, 437, 462
Peptic ulcers, 351
Perception, 122–146, 201
Personality, 359
  changes, 385
  definition, 16
  development, 282–288
  of clinicians, 401–402
  tests, 16–17, 58, 167, 336
    See also Projective tests
  uniqueness, 392–394
Persuasion, 234–237
Pestalozzi, J. H., 281, 282
Pfungst, O., 452
Phenomenology, 187
Phobia, 348
  See also Neuroses
Phrenology, 172–173
Physical factors, 13–14, 135
Physiological changes, 88–90, 95, 138–
  139, 346, 368, 369, 438–440, 475–
  476
Physiological psychology, 409–445
  abnormal behavior, 440–444
  biochemical concepts, 423–427
  integrative levels, 417–420
  methodology, 417, 420–423
  mind-body relationships, 411–413
  molar and molecular positions, 415
  neurological concepts, 427–435
  recent trends, 433–434
  reductionism, 413
Piaget, J., 265
Pinel, P., 335
Plant, J. S., 271, 277
Pointillists, 498, 499
Prejudice, 212
Projective tests, 248–249, 336, 359–
  364
Propaganda, 231, 233, 504
Proteins, 424
Psychoanalysis, 197, 198, 248, 337–338
Psychodrama, 163–165
Psychogalvanic response (PGR), 88–
  89, 138
Psychology and aesthetics, 478–524
  attitudes to, 487–488

Psychology and aesthetics (*cont'd*)
  children, 508–512
  classification of the arts, 489–506
  creative activity, 521–523
  experimental aesthetics, 481–482
  product of the artist, 485
  schools of painting, 499–501
  social interaction in, 512–521
Psychology of Early Childhood
  (Stern), 242
Psychology of Musical Talent (Seashore), 300, 301
Psychopathology, *see* Abnormal psychology
Psychoses, 351–354
  involutional melancholia, 352
  manic-depression, 351–352
  paranoia, 220, 352–353
  schizophrenia, 335, 353
  organic reaction patterns, 353–354
Psychomatic medicine, 337, 350–351,
  422
Punishment-reward, 327
Pursuit test (Koerth), 62

Quasha, W., 65

Rabban, M., 241–279
Race, 216–218, 221–226, 312
Raynaud's Syndrome, 334, 356–357,
  361, 363, 365
Reaction formation, 343
Reductionism, 413, 417
References, 57
Reflective thinking, 324
Regression, 344, 365
Reiss, B. F., 409–445
Religion, 270–271
Repression, 340, 343
Reverberatory neural circuits, 432, 439
Rogers, C., 163, 399, 400
Rorschach, H., 336, 375
Rorschach test, 336, 360–363, 375, 385
Rotter, J. B., 66
Rowan, W., 457
Ryan, T. A., 81–118

Sakel, M., 337
Scapegoats, 220
Schaeffer, A., 462
Schizophrenia, *see* Psychoses

Schneirla, T. C., 459, 471, 473
Seashore, C. E., 300, 301
Selection versus placement, 39–40
Sellers, C., 135
Selye, H., 441–443
Semitic, 281
Servomechanisms, 433
Sex differences in intelligence, 313–314
Sheldon, W. H., 259
Smith, Patricia, 36–80
Social psychology, 180–240
    and sociology, 186
    and UNESCO, 181
    applications, 238–239
    customs, 184
    defense mechanisms, 202–203
    definition, 182
    functional autonomy, 200–201
    goals, 196–198, 202
    group mind, 189–190
    groupings, 210–226
    heredity and environment, 191–192
    homeostasis, 193–195
    human nature, 191
    instinct, 190–192
    methodology, 186–188
    mores, 151, 184
    national ideal, 218, 219
    nationality, 216, 220
    needs, 193, 202
    prejudice, 212
    propaganda and education, 231
    race, 216–218, 221–226
    scapegoats, 220
    stereotypes, 211–212
    teleology, 197
    theories of, 188–192
    types of environment, 183–185
    values, 184
    war, 181–182
Sociometry, 187, 269
S-O-R, 434–435
Sorokin, P., 514
Special Talents and Defects (Hollingworth), 304
Stalin, J., 236
Starch, D., 300
Steinzor, B., 372–408
Stereotypes, 211–212
    See also Race

Stern, W., 120
Stuit, D. B., 22–23
Substitution, 343
Suggestion, 133
Suicide, 351
Survey methods, 187–188
Sympathin, 425
Synapse, 430–431, 439
Syndromes, 347–354
    See also Neuroses; Psychoses

Tantrum behavior, see Animal neurosis
Teleology, 197, 453
Terman, L. M., 283
Tests, Army Alpha, 61–62, 223
    group, 6
    in children, 254–255, 318
    in industry, 58–70
    in prison, 160–161
    in vocational guidance, 5–7, 19–23
    See also Blacky Test; Deception tests; "l–i" test; Minnesota Paper Form Board Test; Minnesota Rate of Manipulation Test; Minnesota Vocational Test for Clerical Workers; Personality Tests; Projective tests; Pursuit test (Koerth); Rorschach Test; Thematic Apperception Test (TAT)
The Authoritarian Personality (Adorno, et al), 267–268
The Envelope (Plant), 271
The Measurement of Intelligence (Terman), 283
The Mind That Found Itself (Beer), 376–377
The Physiology and Pathology of Exposure to Stress (Selye), 443
Thematic Apperception Test (TAT), 336, 362–364, 385, 400
Therapy, 163–165, 168–170, 355–358
    group, 151, 163–165, 168
    in clinical psychology, 386–389
    in prison, 162–170
    type of, 398–401, 510
Thompson, L. A., 68
Thorndike, E. L., 283, 463
Transfer of training, 327

Trophalaxis, 468
Twins, 308
Typology, 315–316

Unique personality, 259–260, 392–394
United Nations Educational, Scientific,
    and Cultural Organization
    (UNESCO), 181, 312
United States Employment Service
    (USES), 8
United States Public Health Service,
    378

Vernon, H. M., 113
Vertebrate, social life, 470–474
Vitamins, 426–427
Vocational guidance, 1–35, 40, 292–
    293
    analysis of, the individual, 12–23;
        the occupation, 7–8, 47–48
    and psychology, 5–9
    and tests, 5–7, 19, 22–23
    clinical method in, 8–9
    criteria success, 25
    data required, 12–17
    definition, 2–3
    eclecticism, 24
    evaluation, problems, 25–28; studies,
        28–32
    history, 4–5

Vocational guidance (cont'd)
    interpretation, 20–21
    interviews, counseling, 21; initial,
        10–12, 17–18
    nondirective, 24
    process, 9–24
    questionnaires, 18
    reasons for, 3
    sources of data, 17–20
    standards, 32–33
Vocational psychology, 8, 77–78
Vocational rehabilitation, 13–14
Vocational selection, 3–4

War, 181–182, 190, 504
    World War I, 6, 223, 377–378
    World War II, 97, 115, 232, 233,
        377–378, 411, 433, 519
Watson, J. B., 156, 415–417
Webster, E. C., 29, 30
Weld, H. P., 119–147
Wentworth, M. M., 299
Western Electric Company, 103
Wheeler, R. H., 468, 469
Witmer, L., 9, 376
Word association, 121, 137, 338, 385
Work Project Administration (WPA),
    521

Yerkes, R. M., 460